The

. . . . . .

Politics of

. . . . . .

Vibration

The

Politics of

Vibration

Music as a

Cosmopolitical

Practice

Marcus Boon

Duke University Press *Durham and London* 2022

© 2022 DUKE UNIVERSITY PRESS All rights reserved
Printed in the United States of America on acid-free paper ∞
Designed by Courtney Leigh Richardson
Typeset in Garamond Premier Pro and Avenir
by Westchester Publishing Services

Library of Congress Cataloging-in-Publication Data
Names: Boon, Marcus, author.
Title: The politics of vibration : music as a cosmopolitical
practice / Marcus Boon.
Description: Durham : Duke University Press, 2022. |
Includes bibliographical references and index.
Identifiers: LCCN 2021044993 (print)
LCCN 2021044994 (ebook)
ISBN 9781478015765 (hardcover)
ISBN 9781478018391 (paperback)
ISBN 9781478023012 (ebook)
Subjects: LCSH: Music—Philosophy and aesthetics. | Pran Nath,
1918–1996—Criticism and interpretation. | Hennix, Catherine Christer,
1948–—Criticism and interpretation. | DJ Screw, 1971–2000—Criticism
and interpretation. | Metaphysics. | BISAC: MUSIC / Essays |
MUSIC / History & Criticism
Classification: LCC ML3800 .B76 2022 (print) | LCC ML3800 (ebook) |
DDC 780.1—dc23
LC record available at https://lccn.loc.gov/2021044993
LC ebook record available at https://lccn.loc.gov/2021044994

Cover art: *Friction*, 2016. 11 × 16″. Acrylic on paper.
© Paula Overbay. Courtesy of the artist.

For Christie and Christer

Contents

INTRODUCTION
Music as a Cosmopolitical Practice
1

ONE
Lord's House, Nobody's House:
Pandit Pran Nath and Music as Sadhana
29

TWO
The Drone of the Real:
The Sound-Works of Catherine Christer Hennix
75

THREE
Music and the Continuum
125

FOUR
Slowed and Throwed:
DJ Screw and the Decolonization of Time
179

CODA
July 2, 2020
227

Acknowledgments 231
Notes 235
Bibliography 255
Index 269

Introduction

Music as a Cosmopolitical Practice

I

Yesterday evening we went to a free show in Scarborough, one of the annual Feast in the East events—this time in a park on Prairie Drive, against the train tracks, with high-rises looming in most directions, mostly Bangladeshi families playing in the park, dense, exuberant green vegetation everywhere almost growing visibly in the short steamy Canadian summer. A free dinner for everyone was served—a bowl of curried vegetables, a bitter melon salad, and a slice of grilled rice. Kids played on the swings, little groups of people sat on the grass and ate together.

There were three acts billed—Sandro Perri, Bernice, and New Chance—but in the end only Sandro Perri played. We spread a towel out on the grass and ate and Sandro's band started playing. For their second song, they played "Double Suicide," this song that I'd last heard Sandro sing with Ryan Driver at Cinecycle in maybe 2005 or 2006. They'd projected the Japanese movie of that name over their performance—in fact, I think that was the name of the duo too.

After they finished the song, they started another and it began to rain torrentially. I ran to the car and brought back four umbrellas, throwing them on the blanket. It really started to rain hard so we all clustered under the mass of umbrellas as the ground slowly flooded. We juggled the umbrellas around to stop the rain coming in between the cracks. The kids laughed. There wasn't much more we could do and our backs got wet. We ran under a tree nearby and when even that didn't stop the rain we ran back to the car and sheltered in it.

The rain waterlogged the ground and the rest of the show was cancelled. But the rain finally stopped and the art installations in the park were still there, including one that consisted of thousands of sponges, now soggy with the rainwater, which we threw at each other for a while. The trains went by.

We drove back to the city with the sun shining, surrounded by clouds and an incredible golden light looming out of the darkness of the clouds, with mist rising out of the river valleys and run-down shopping malls lining the roads back to Toronto. We looked for a rainbow but we didn't see one.

Sandro and Ryan must have written "Double Suicide" a long time ago, little imagining that one day they would be singing it in a park after two of their friends had killed themselves. They had been boys playing with ideas and images, and now time had passed, and things had happened, some life had happened, more than any of us expected, and yet they were still musicians despite everything and all that you could do was sing the song. My friend Adam, one of the two suicides, drowned in the lake. I felt angry at the lake for letting him drown, especially after having participated in these Tibetan Buddhist rituals for the naga that lives in the lake. Like, how could you let that happen to Adam?

When it poured down after Sandro and Ryan sang the song, it was like one of those rainy season ragas that call down the water. Except no one had really asked for anything to happen, or for it to rain. And none of us exactly believed in nagas either. But it was as if the lake burst into tears after hearing the song, and what could you do except feel the incredible sadness of their deaths, in the landscape, the landscape in its harsh historical violation by mountains of settler colonial trash and Victoriana in which Adam and Justin had lived. The lake burst into tears, and we huddled under umbrellas, and there was nothing you could do but accept it, feel the sadness of it. And then the rain stopped, would stop. And everything would carry on anyway. For a while. And then it would change again. Ragas for the times of day, for the seasons. None of us knew how to make that connection anymore, but it was almost better when it happened by accident, or through nothing more than the force of feeling, of loss, of love, of projection even, with no causality greater than the fact of its happening.

2

This book sets out a model for thinking about music as emerging out of a politics of vibration. It focuses on the work of three contemporary musicians—Pandit Pran Nath, Catherine Christer Hennix, and DJ Screw—each emerging from a different but entangled set of musical traditions or scenes, whose work is ontologically instructive. From these particular cases, the book expands in the direction of considering the vibrational nature of music more generally. Vibration is understood in multiple ways, as a mathematical and a physical concept, as a religious or ontological force, and as a psychological/psychoanalytic determinant of subjectivity. The organization of sonic vibration that is determinant of subjectivity, aka music, is understood to be pluralistic and modal—and topological rather than phenomenological or time-based. I argue that understanding how/why this is the case is of ontological and political significance. And that the difficulty or obscurity of such an argument is due to the cosmopolitical nature of debates as to what music is.

In opening up the topic of vibration, I turn to the Brazilian writer Clarice Lispector's 1973 text, *Agua Viva*, often translated as "Living Water" but also colloquially understood in Brazilian Portuguese to mean "jellyfish"—thus invoking a transparent entity that is engaged and articulated within a wavefield. In this book, Lispector explores what it means to write and be in the instant of writing and thinking, and more broadly what it means to fully BE in the NOW. She does this through an informal improvisation, which she likens to jazz and the way that jazz inhabits the NOW modally. And what she finds as she immerses herself in the now are vibrations:

> I see that I've never told you how I listen to music—I gently rest my hand on the record player and my hand vibrates, sending waves through my whole body; and I listen to the electricity of the vibrations, the last substratum of reality's realm, and the world trembles inside my hands.[1]

Sound-system style, what Lispector feels are vibrations, not simply sound, "the last substratum of reality's realm." What is that substratum then?

> To tell you of my substratum I make a sentence of words made only from instants-now. Read therefore, my invention as pure vibration with no meaning beyond each whistling syllable, read this: "with the passing of the centuries I lost the secret of Egypt, when I moved in longitudes, latitudes, and altitudes with the energetic action of electrons, protons, and neutrons, under the spell of the word and its shadow." What I wrote you here is an electronic drawing without past or future: it is simply now.[2]

In the first passage, Lispector receives or transduces vibration through her body—in the second, a transduced vibration emerges as words. I will have much to say about vibration as substratum, but the phrase *my substratum* displaces any conventional physical notion of substratum. What are we talking about here? A material, realist, mechanical, idealist, unconscious, or panpsychic substratum? Note that this is also the problem of the foundations of mathematics, which precisely concerns where periodicity emerges from—out of emptiness, mind, a formalism, or the continuum?—and it is in the midst of such questions that it becomes possible to think about a vibrational ontology. Already we are in the realm of cosmopolitics—Lispector assembles, with breathtaking succinctness and elegance a world or cosmos that is revealed in the simple act of listening to her record player.

The particular use of the term *cosmopolitics* that interests me was developed by the French philosopher of science Isabelle Stengers in the 1990s.[3] Stengers's concern, emerging out of the anthropology of science, was initially to situate scientific knowledge within the broad matrix of human practices of the production of knowledge; conversely, to understand the ways in which different kinds of being in, and knowledge of, the world can negotiate their coexistence—for example, modern practices such as particle physics and nonmodern practices such as the reciting of a spell. Although the term has historically been used, for example by Kant in *Perpetual Peace*, to indicate a "universal state of humankind (ius cosmopoliticum)" that is associated with cosmopolitanism,[4] Stengers's use of the term specifically concerns a politics that engages both human and nonhuman actors. Stengers raises the question of how nonhuman actors might be rendered visible as political actors in situations where politics, defined according to a horizon of human dissensus, denies them such visibility.

The idea has been adopted in many fields—notably in the ontological turn in anthropology as practiced by Eduardo Vivieros de Castro and others. In her book *Earth Beings*, the anthropologist Marisol de la Cadena gives a particularly striking and clear example of this: the disputes between the Indigenous Quechua people in the Andes, who view the mountains they inhabit as "earth beings," deities with particular kinds of agency, and the Peruvian nation-state and businesses, who see the mountains as the source of materials subject to extractive technologies.[5] The dispute between these actors is cosmopolitical because it concerns radically different ontologies and ways of constellating the world around particular but disputed objects, including these entities known to us as mountains. The political struggle, of course, usually involves the radical asymmetry of the parties involved—with those who hold power getting to define not only "what happens to the land" but the ontology through which actors, human and nonhuman, and their relations are articulated.

It is striking that, so far, music has not been thought of in cosmopolitical terms. Lispector's text can be understood as a deceptively modest but also radical cosmopolitical gesture—synthesizing spells and particle physics in fact—in the direction of an ontology of music. I argue that music always involves a similar act of constellation, a worlding, yet this is not appreciated in the existing scholarship on music because the modern, reified form of music—as sounds arranged for aesthetic pleasure and entertainment—is accepted as being objective and universal, despite the incredible proliferation of hybrid musical forms that anyone attentive to the diversity of global musical practices is aware of. This worlding is cosmopolitical because it is sanctioned or not sanctioned by power, in its various geopolitical and historical forms, and as such, is a place of gathering and of dissensus. It is also cosmopolitical because it involves nonhumans and their articulation—or not. It is uncontroversial today to consider acoustics, or a broader physics that is necessarily part of the understanding of music. Yet, nonhumans, whether spirits or vibrational forces, or the various materials that musical instruments are made from, or for that matter animals such as birds or whales, more generally tend to be crossed out or rendered mutely available to the almost exclusively human horizon of a secularized musical aesthetics. Even when the plurality of musical practices is acknowledged, it is their ontological dimension that is ignored or bracketed—as such, our understanding of the diversity of global and historical cosmopolitical practices of music is mutilated, fragmented, a distorted shadow—one might say that we do not (yet) know what a musical body can do.

Consider the triad: music—sound—vibration. Music is a particular organization of sound, and sound is a particular kind of vibration. Music, as jazz musician and composer William Parker put it, can be defined informally as "just sound and rhythm."[6] Patterned sound. What is a vibration? A vibration is a wave—and this is already where we seem to have to make a choice or decision as to what kind of language, discourse, cosmopolitical framework we're going to use. As per Alain Badiou, I work in this book in a philosophical language, with the understanding that philosophy's work is to clarify concepts such as they appear in various kinds of truth procedures: for Badiou, there are four such truth procedures—science, art, love, politics, to which I will add, without apology, religion or spirituality.[7] Can music be a kind of truth procedure then? If so, *where does it belong*? Again, that is a cosmopolitical question.

With this in mind, we ask again: What is a wave? In scientific terms, waves are geometric forms that can also be rendered algebraically (this is the basis of the Fourier series), which is to say that they are essentially mathematical objects that are abstractable from the particular phenomenological or physical forms or instances that they take. Vibrations make/articulate patterns—musical events (a composition, a performance, a track, etc.) take the form of a pattern, often a very complex one. The possibility of abstracting and formalizing such patterns is also the basis of musical notation, of the digital recording and representation of a performance, and more—one can code the sonic relationships that make up the pattern, whether as sequences of pitches and their combinations, or as waves occurring at certain frequencies (i.e., Hz). In this sense, vibration is mathematical first of all, since mathematics takes up the challenge of articulating what pattern is, and the Newtonian acoustics of sound are in that sense but one aspect of vibration. And this matters because it suggests that understanding what music is does not entirely depend on understanding acoustic phenomena, or even the physics of sound—it concerns patterns (and waves) at a more fundamental level.

In arguing that a mathematical sense of vibration matters here, it should be emphasized that this does not mean a reduction of music to a vulgarized high school version of mathematics—or the mathematical music of various historical periods. Contemporary mathematical attempts to account for music, such as those of Guerino Mazzola and Catherine Christer Hennix, do so via creative acts of synthesis that recognize the complexity of the space of music, including its more radical and challenging contemporary forms, such as free improvisation.[8] The version of mathematics involved is open and evolving, a field of continued contestation and debate where significant problems in the foundations of mathematics remain unresolved. Indeed, mathematics has its own rich cosmopolitical shadow, ignored for the most part by the practicing mathematician who works in a particular milieu where a set of norms as to the parameters of mathematics prevail. Hennix argues that a consideration of music can contribute to thinking more deeply about such mathematical problems. I am not a trained mathematician and the presentation of mathematical ideas here is of necessity informal. This book is, to extend a trope of Fred Moten's, an "anamathematical" work—and the essential points can be understood by anyone.[9]

I am also not a musicologist, but again, following the work of scholars like Julian Henriques and Moten, I believe that certain musicians, composers, and participants in various music scenes have an understanding of music that is cosmopolitical in its framing of the powers of vibration.[10] The wager of this book is that musical vibration stands as an example of and analogy for periodicity at the ontological level—and that this analogy or exemplarity forms the basis of music's power.

To generalize again, in this book, *vibration is understood as formally concerning periodicity and the patterns that emerge out of it*. According to the *Encyclopedia Britannica*, vibration concerns "periodic back-and-forth motion of the particles of an elastic body or medium, commonly resulting when almost any physical system is displaced from its equilibrium condition and allowed to respond to the forces that tend to restore equilibrium."[11] Vibration takes many forms—sound is a kind of mechanical vibration, as are ocean waves or the shaking of a tree in the wind; light is a kind of electromagnetic vibration; there are also gravitation waves. As to what periodicity really is—and where it can be located in terms of scholarly discipline—we will explore the ways different musics and musicians approach this problem. The decision made within a particular musical milieu as to the nature and value of periodicity is a cosmopolitical one—encompassing, for example, the Vedic/Tantric idea of Nada Brahma, the Afrodiasporic mythos of Ishmael Reed's Jes Grew in his 1972 novel *Mumbo Jumbo*, or various versions of string theory in contemporary quantum physics. Sound, of course, can be periodic or aperiodic—as the drummer and vibrational philosopher Milford Graves notes in the documentary *Milford Graves: Full Mantis*, a heartbeat is never mechanically consistent such that we could speak of it as an absolutely periodic phenomenon. Every beat of the heart is its own adventure in difference and repetition, the uncertainty of cyclic processes in living beings. This tension between the periodic and the aperiodic is also part of what music is, even at its most perfectly executed. It is part of the pathos of music, the way it leans into the now, the moment, being.

Vibrations happen in a field—they constitute a field, or more generally, a space. This, therefore, is a book about fields and spaces. What kinds of spaces? We will make use of the concept of a topos from mathematics, whose simplest definition is "a generalization of space"—rather than, say, Euclidian space. In his wonderful book *Sonic Bodies*, Julian Henriques gives an exemplary cosmopolitical account of the density and complexity of this vibrational space and the collective project of constructing it in the context of the Jamaican dancehall scene.[12] For Henriques, the sound system session can be thought of as the coming together of different kinds of vibrational bandwidths that encompass everything from the actual wavelengths of sound passing through an acoustic medium, to the cognitive psychoacoustic assimilation of these wavelengths as music, to the sociocultural organization of "vibes" as interpersonal experience in the dancehall session. In this book, we will examine what it means to think of music as an emergent property of a field—and the complexity and challenges of defining what kind of field might be involved and how to model it.

Waves constitute one of the basic structural principles of physics, whether mechanical, electromagnetic, or otherwise. Musical sound, for example, is mechanically produced by the vibration of an object, for example the string of a guitar, which sets the air or other medium vibrating, causing the vibration of the human eardrum, which in turn is transduced by the nervous system. The famous electron diffraction experiments conducted circa 1927 by George

Thomson, Clinton Davisson, and Lester Germer showing that electrons passing through slits in a screen displayed wavelike properties such as diffraction and interference, and vice versa, form part of the experimental basis of the wave-particle duality that is canonical for quantum physics, meaning that wave and particle are the two models for describing subatomic actors and events. Louis de Broglie, who in 1924 formalized the wave-particle duality and the idea of "matter waves," that is, that matter in general consists of waves, evidently came to the idea from his interest in music—the quantization of the orbits of electrons around the nucleus of a hydrogen atom being restricted in the same way that overtones of any pitch played on a string or wind instrument are restricted to integer multiples of whole wave cycles. From Erwin Schrodinger's wave equation (and the concept of "probability waves"), to Richard Feynman's quantum electrodynamics, to the various iterations of string theory, waves have played a key role in quantum physicists' attempts to build complete and successful models of the structure of reality.[13]

Quantum field theory offers a model for thinking about a universe of wave/particles and the ways in which the phenomenal world we inhabit condenses out of the interactions of these waves and their field. Indeed, it is quantum field theory that provides the crucial link or transition between the notoriously strange behavior of subatomic particles/waves and the more recognizable ordering of larger than atomic worlds. One of Hennix's preferred ways of speaking about music is to compare it to the way certain objects behave in condensed matter theory, for example the Bose-Einstein condensation that she claims occurs when one makes Bearnaise sauce, a subtle but decisive shift in the form of things caused by a shift in energy levels (the stirring of the sauce produces a viscosity that was not there before). The Bearnaise sauce, here, is us, when we are listening to music, and (speculatively) undergo a decisive psychic shift that is the result of quantum level restructuring of psychoneurophysiological systems exposed to music's vibrational force. How much more complex then are the musical scenes and events that Henriques describes with their vast but also local gatherings of actors and practices. Yet, for a successful sound system session to occur, a "condensation," call it "vibes" if you like, needs to happen, which is familiar to anyone who's attended a successful party, club night, or sound system session. This condensation can be considered, via Mazzola, Hennix, and others, a gesture—a complex, multifactorial act of field shaping in which the object called music emerges or is invited to appear. Not that physics necessarily takes precedence here—instead, we seek to open up the cosmopolitical problem of what music is, the ways different musics and musicians gather their own ontological tools in making the object called music appear, and to include within that cosmopolitical opening, scientific frameworks, as and when they arise. Stengers, it should be noted, developed the idea of cosmopolitics in thinking through the discordances that are found in the field of modern physics itself. Cosmopolitics is not an anti-scientific endeavor, or a naive celebration of relativism, but it seeks to hold a space where scientific and other kinds of explanations and narratives can coexist.

Another basic definition of vibration is "an energy transfer through a medium." This works at the level of acoustics but also at the quantum level. So would we be better off talking about energy rather than vibration here? I don't think it's an either/or issue, and as a participant in current debates about energy and the arts, stimulated by the work of Douglas Kahn and others, I am very interested in understanding the ways in which various framings of energy occur in different music scenes or musical works.[14] And I am well aware that the politics of vibration and the politics of energy are profoundly interrelated. A vibration constitutes the transmission of a quantum of energy, a unit of force, through a medium.

But what if one of those media that energy passes through is the subject? In bringing this up, we bring up another cosmopolitical matter, that of our understanding of subjectivity. Psychoanalytically, vibration is the often obscured or forgotten energetic space of subjectivity, of the unconscious in its movements (traversed by drives, by libido, by desire), and the topological arrangement of this nonspace that is contained by or situated within (or not, depending on the model) the limits of the body.[15] This may be harder to accept than references to quantum field theory because of the necessarily speculative nature of psychoanalytic theory. But in trying to understand the impact of music on the psyche, let alone the collective organization of subjects in assemblages of humans and nonhumans in music scenes, events, and so on, we need a speculative language that allows us to track and account for what happens to us when we make or hear music. And that means we need a persuasive account of interiority, or subjectivity, such as it is. Again, we could try to track this neurobiologically (although how one could practically do this in the collective unfolding of the moment of a Jamaican dancehall session is hard to say), but it would remain the case that what Vladimir Jankélévitch calls the "Charm" of music (linked to its ineffability), not to mention the many, many variations by which this "Charm" is organized in different situations, would be described or represented yet remain itself unthought.[16] In listening to Pandit Pran Nath, in reflecting on the long history of Indian aesthetics and the evolving multiplicity of musical practices in India, which Pran Nath was connected to, we inevitably confront the question of subjectivity as a cosmopolitical one, whose dimensions, most obviously those related to religion and spirituality, can only come into view at the point where we actually listen carefully to how such figures understood and practiced music.

This is also a book about music and time, and, challenged by Hennix's assertion that "Being = Space × Action," it explores the wager that music is not, as most musicologists or philosophers of music tell us, the quintessential art of or in time.[17] The linear model of time that dominated Western metaphysics (and musicology) for most of its history was displaced by Einstein's theory of general relativity in 1915. Music is an action in a space(time)(continuum). Furthermore, while music may occur phenomenologically "in time," which is to say it may be provisionally captured by our concept of time, what if music were fundamentally an art of sequence or ordering, and every piece of music, every performance, every moment of musicking were actually the manifesting of a musical object in the form of a sequence and ordering of sonic vibration and relationality? This book explores that "what if . . ." from a number of perspectives and situations and argues that many of those deeply involved with music are aware of this possibility, even as they inhabit the ideology or, if you like, lived reality of physical time under the sway of the second law of thermodynamics (the arrow, irreversibility). In that wavering between ideology and lived reality of physical time is where a cosmopolitics of vibration is to be found. Conversely, what is mysterious about music, what Jankélévitch calls its "Charm," lies in this disjuncture between the vibratory power of music and the time regime that we are subject to, that is, what we don't understand about music relates to a cosmopolitical and categorical mistake as to where its intelligibility and being is to be found.

This brings up the difficult topic of the relation between music and technics (i.e., technological systems or structures)—especially in the light of Yuk Hui's recent work on *cosmotechnics*, a term that overlaps with *cosmopolitics*, but focuses more specifically on the ways in which the articulation of technics in a particular community or society is related to the cosmology or worlding of that society.[18] The topic is especially significant for an understanding of music, given Bernard Stiegler's provocative thesis concerning the relation of technics to time—time being produced by a kind of originary supplement or prosthesis that would "always already" be technical and "relative" in the sense that it correlates different entities in their movement.[19] While musical examples and metaphors appear throughout Stiegler's work, music is not itself considered as a form of technics. And while musical instruments are obviously prosthetic technologies, it is not clear that the human voice, or harmonics and other aspects of the physics of sound, or the entity of the raga can be considered prosthetically. Perhaps they refer to a broader history of techniques (vocal training, awareness of pitch) that is covered by Hui's cosmotechnics, in the sense of a different configuration of the technical in relation to the world and being. I will argue over the course of this book, however, that music's ambiguous status in terms of technics tells us something more specific about time.

In elaborating on what it means to think of music as an action on/in a space, I explore what it means to think about "a life" (Deleuze) as a topological entity, or, in Fred Moten's words, what it would mean to embrace a "topological existence" through music.[20] If vibrational praxis and culture inevitably concern actions on or in a field, and a modal view of ontology, then the specificity of different kinds of music, music scenes, and musical practices may be found in what Giovanni Maddalena calls a philosophy of gesture—where gesture is no longer just a kind of nonverbal signaling but a morphing of a space, be it a social space or a corporeal/psychic space.[21] The world of dance, of course, takes precedence here, but so do the various forms of multidisciplinary/in-between/intermedial cultural praxis such as the dance/ritual/music/theater of Balinese gamelan, or voguing practices at the ballrooms in Harlem and elsewhere—such practices are not peripheral to music, not add-ons or ornaments, but the unfolding and flourishing of music's topological basis.[22] Improvisation takes on a particular importance in this model, in rendering and exploring the topological possibilities of a space. In writing this book, I also engage in the practice of improvisation in response to the life and work of particular musicians. It takes me to some strange places, including "myself"—and my stories—there is no (valid) way around this.

As to why there should even be such a thing as a politics of vibration, which is to say a cosmopolitical negotiation of the possibilities of organizing and ordering vibration as the collective practice of resituating ourselves where being is to be found—well, that strikes me as strange too. Jacques Attali wrote of the fear of noise engendered by power, and the need to organize, even "sacrifice" sound to a particular political order.[23] I was struck, attending a (beautiful) classical music concert in Toronto recently, by the strangeness of the formality of the string quartet's performance—their entrance and exit after each piece, the bowing, the ritual of audience applause—how rigid it felt, and how much the ritual betrayed an incredible fear of music as something too hot to be handled otherwise. Conversely, in the lives of the musicians I write about, I have often experienced a kind of bewilderment or innocence, a noble determination or willful self-destructiveness in situations where the demands of music and the demands of the world went in different directions. DJ Screw, Catherine Christer Hennix, and Pandit Pran Nath were/are all fugitive in their own and different ways, all backed into a corner by a world "of strange and brutal design," to quote the South African poet Keorapetse Kgositsile—but all also insistent on valuing music differently, otherwise, and thus cosmopolitically.[24]

The phrase *politics of vibration* clearly encompasses many things, from the negotiation of decibel levels that some DJs include in the written contracts for their festival performances, to the funding of competing models of string theory in physics. There is also, of course, a significant body of work that considers the politics of music from various viewpoints and frameworks.[25] Here, my main focus will be on the cosmopolitical aspect of the politics of vibration because it is a key in many cases to rendering explicit the political nature of questions and disputes concerning vibration, and in particular music's status as a vibrational form or practice. Music, it turns out, is cosmopolitical: it participates, actively or passively, in a worlding—the constellation or construction of a cosmos or an ontology—in precisely the way that Stengers set out the cosmopolitical "question" or "proposal." And this worlding involves a set of ideological restrictions that in turn shapes and orders the object that we call music, and our implication in it.

We usually understand the plurality or diversity of musical practices via ethnomusicology and/or the anthropology of music. But that is not exactly what is at stake here. The missing or obscured question as to the ontology of music—despite or maybe because of the vast archive of musicological treatises—can only be raised when music's ontological significance or power is actually asserted—and denied. If there is a general agreement today that this ontological power does not exist because music is nothing more than the set of examples of what a particular group of people call music (as a sociologist colleague recently suggested to me), or must be left as "ineffable" as per Jankélévitch,[26] this general agreement only attests to the success of a particular political-aesthetic enframing of music within modern societies that appears, but is not in fact, unquestionable. To recall that music in medieval Europe was part of the "quadrivium" and taught alongside arithmetic, geometry, and astronomy is just one way to remind ourselves that things were (and are still!) not always so. It suffices to start to listen to other voices who understand music otherwise, and to take those voices seriously—which is what we will do in this book—for the cosmopolitical nature of music to become apparent. The question of what music *is* depends on, in Hennix's words, what practices and ontologies are permitted within any particular society, for example what duration of a performance is allowed. It suffices to ask for more, to want more, to want otherwise, to listen to those who are already doing more, doing otherwise for music's cosmopolitical power to emerge. And this emergence should be a matter of great joy to anyone who loves the music, the game.

I came to my current understanding of these things through my association with Catherine Christer Hennix, a brilliant but still relatively unknown Swedish-born musician, mathematician, and composer. This book recounts some of the stages of that association, my attempts to unpack the remarkable assemblage of ideas and fields that Hennix synthesizes in her work, to document my own response to that work, and to show how, despite its initial difficulty, it opens up new ways of thinking about music in general. I first began talking to Hennix about twenty years ago, while researching an article on the great but also unheralded Indian classical vocalist, Pandit Pran Nath of the Kirana gharana, who is the subject of the first chapter of this book. Pran Nath, trained within the gharana system in India in the early decades of the twentieth century, moved to America in 1970 and became the teacher and muse of generations of European and American composers and musicians, most famously Terry Riley, La Monte Young, and Marian Zazeela. I had learned about Pran Nath in the late 1990s when I went on an internet date with someone in the East Village in New York City, and, feeling little attraction to each other but sharing a mutual interest in "world music," we ended up in a music store, where I discovered an advertisement offering classes in Indian classical vocal. At that time, I was practicing yoga quite intensely, and, as a soft-spoken, fairly introverted dude, I came to enjoy kirtan, the collective singing of religious songs, at the end of yoga classes. Despite playing in punk bands, it had never occurred to me that I could sing, and that singing was not only a disciplinary ritual enacted in school assemblies and churches or the work of professionals known as singers but also a social practice and a collective offering of joy (and pain). I took Indian classical vocal classes with the composer and tuning expert Michael Harrison at his piano store on West Fifty-Eighth Street, and when he told me that a group of students of Pran Nath would be traveling to India to study together, I jumped at the opportunity to go along. We visited some of the sites where Pran Nath had lived before he moved to America, took basic singing lessons, and on the last night of the workshop, for lack of any better idea, I sang a version of Donna Summer's "I Feel Love," arranged as a raga, accompanied by a tambura drone. In a sense, the continuity between Pran Nath, DJ Screw, and Catherine Christer Hennix—the three main focuses of this book—already existed for me in that act. But I didn't know that at the time!

I spent the summer working on the Pran Nath article, and La Monte Young and Marian Zazeela generously put me in touch with many of the musicians who had studied with him. My article was published in the *Wire*, but I stayed in touch with some of the people I'd interviewed for the piece—including Hennix, whom I likely first heard about from her long-term collaborator and friend, the philosopher, musical, and visual artist Henry Flynt, another student of Pran Nath's and a generous interlocutor with me throughout the 2000s. Hennix at that time was living in Amsterdam and would send me mesmerizing CD-RS of her newly composed Soliton computer drone pieces, urging me to do my singing practice along with them. I nearly crashed my car several times, driving around Toronto listening to the intensely psychotropic recordings, which would make the car's interior throb and pulse with resonances. In 2011 I began visiting Hennix at her studio in Berlin, and I immersed myself in her work— whose depth and power only expanded, the further I went into it. There were some challenges—just intonation and Lacan I was already familiar with, but despite a background in science studies, my grasp of debates in the foundations of mathematics or condensed matter physics was very limited. And Hennix not only referred to the work of key figures in this history (Brouwer, Hilbert, Grothendieck, and Lawvere, for starters) but also made her own playful and creative synthesis of this work—as it applied to music and other things too. So the bar of entry was set quite high.

As I thought about Hennix's ideas, they pushed up against my own engagement with music scenes since I was a kid. I can discern at least three separate but interwoven threads there: (1) the avant-garde and experimental music scenes, especially as they emerged globally after or around punk; (2) Afrodiasporic music scenes centered around reggae, jazz, funk, house, and especially hip-hop; and (3) much more amorphously, the sense of a world of traditional musics, each with its own historicity and politics, emerging out of the ethnomusicological practices of study and documentation on record labels such as Smithsonian Folkways, Ocora, and more recently Sublime Frequencies. The interweaving of these scenes was already happening at some of the first shows I went to as a teenager, notably the Pop Group concert at The Electric Ballroom in London in November 1979 at which, dazzled, I first heard Funkadelic's "One Nation under a Groove" over a loud sound system. One of post-punk's promises was not only the constellation of different musics from around the world but also the constellation of political struggles and solidarities—whether the Campaign for Nuclear Disarmament (CND) and the Greenham Common women, or Rock Against Racism and the Anti-Nazi League—all in the UK context, but with awareness of what was going on elsewhere and of history. Of course, now things look a little different. In fact, they looked different very quickly after that Pop Group show, where the five-white-boy unit, high on Rimbaud and P-Funk, was shaken apart by Ishmael Reed's Jes Grew virus and the politics of vibration, resulting in the formation of Rip Rig and Panic with Sean Oliver and Neneh Cherry... and Mark Stewart's collaborations with Adrian Sherwood and the dub label On U sound. I started going to the funk parties at the Beat Route, and the queer disco events hosted at Heaven—both in central London. And, in January 1982, I went to New York for the first time where I attended Kool Lady Blue's hip-hop parties at Negril and other locations. And got saturated in the Paradise Garage–nurtured sounds of West End and SAM and Arthur Russell's Dinosaur L project, which I wrote about for the *New Musical Express* (!). This book formed as I synthesized my experience of the various kinds of music in my life with Hennix's philosophical ideas—into a new kind of reflection on the nature of music.

In the first chapter of this book, I describe Pran Nath's life and work, and the complex ways in which certain elements of Indian classical music, as they existed around the time of partition, were translated and rethought as Pran Nath traveled and taught in Europe and America. I look at Pran Nath's insistence on music as a practice rather than performance—"practice practice practice!" he said—as an offering to the Divine and as a matter of cultivation of the soul, and the misunderstandings and projections that this engendered, both in India and America. I consider how Pran Nath's music emerged not as the implementation of concepts or discourses but as ways of working with the primordial vibrational structure of the universe. I explore how one might think of Pran Nath's music and its meaning as something cosmopolitical—requiring a reframing of what we understand music to be.

In chapter 2, I focus on Hennix and her extraordinarily rich and dense reframing of Pran Nath's teachings via intuitionistic mathematics, postminimalist composition and jazz, quantum field theories in physics, Lacanian psychoanalysis, transfeminist readings of Islam, and more. In this chapter, I set out the full richness of Hennix's thought as it relates to music, in a way that is rigorous but accessible to the reader with minimal technical knowledge of some of the fields involved—and I show how Hennix's life and work opens up new ways of thinking about music as emergent from a politics of vibration.

In chapter 3, I synthesize some of these insights into a model of music in its vibratory emergence from the (problem of the) continuum. Building on the theoretical work of Fernando Zalamea, Guerino Mazzola, and Hennix, I explore a variety of examples from around the world, including José Maceda's writing about Philippine musical practices, Keiji Haino's noise improvisations, and—Prince. Building on ideas of the local and global, and the rich and nuanced idea of a topos as place, space, or locale, I show how music can be understood as a pragmatic construction on/in/out of the continuum. The examples are not random—they reflect my own interests, attractions, and exposures—but the point is to integrate an affirmation of the cosmopolitical potentials of global musical practices with a specific ontological model as to what music is.

In the fourth and final chapter of the book, I attempt to think through some of these ideas in relation to an ostensibly "different" music that has concerned and sustained me since my dad first played me Duke Ellington records as a little kid—the music of the Black radical tradition, and specifically the work of the much-revered originator of the chopped and screwed dirty south hip-hop style, Houston's DJ Screw, renowned for his practice of slowing sounds down. In the chapter, I locate the importance of a politics of vibration for the Black radical tradition (indeed, it was a primary force in Hennix's education as a child in Stockholm, where musicians such as Eric Dolphy and Idries Suleyman lived in her mother's house at various points). I also think about my own relation to Black music, as itself a part of the complex politics of vibration, mediated by a "sonic color line" (Stoever) that distributes depression, utopian flashes, and "otherwise possibilities" (Crawley).[27] I reflect on what separates us from continuity, and how this separation appears in musical form—as well as the possibility, guided by the Indigenous hip-hop crew A Tribe Called Red, of its reversal in a vibrational decolonization of time.

4

I encountered the phrase *vibrational ontology* through the work of Steve Goodman in his book *Sonic Warfare: Sound, Affect, and the Ecology of Fear*. Goodman has assembled a formidable set of connections in pursuing vibration, yet the displacement of vibration within the book (it doesn't appear in the index for example) actually impedes any positive articulation of vibrational ontology. Goodman's discussion of vibrational ontology emerges out of an exploration of the political ecology of fear and the use of technologies and practices of "vibrational force" both in warfare and the broader biopolitical management of populations in modern societies. As a counterpoint to this instrumental use of vibration as force, Goodman writes of the way that subaltern dancehall or bass cultures appropriate such technologies to mobilize a community, transforming fear into joy. Among other things, this explains the preference some bass cultures have for the use of police siren sounds in the middle of dancehall sessions; the focus on intensely amplified sound that is situated at the threshold of pain and pleasure, audible and inaudible, clear and distorted; and the pervasive appropriation of military discourses in the language of "sound clashes" and "DJ battles." For early twenty-first-century dwellers such as I, who have found the cultural studies discourse of popular and subculture highly inadequate in articulating what is so powerful about participating in music cultures, Goodman's bold attempt to link music cultures to fundamental ontological and political questions has opened up a number of new fields of inquiry.

There are a number of problems with Goodman's book though.

1. Because Goodman tends to focus on contemporary UK dance scenes that are generally quite smoothly integrated into the functioning of the industrial leisure complex, he reduces collective experiences of vibration to mere epiphenomena of instrumental and industrialized societies. But looked at in a broader historical and geographic framework, human societies' relationships to music are much more varied, and at times much stronger than those suggested by the contemporary club culture. Even within club culture, the devotion to sound that is documented in a book like Timothy Lawrence's *Love Saves the Day*, in describing 1970s queer disco culture in New York, is somehow absent from his book. Yet it is precisely scenes and cultures with more intense commitments to sound that have something to say to us about vibrational ontology.

2. Because Goodman's book was published before the current renaissance in Black studies, the sense of the importance of sound and music to Afrodiasporic cultures that is conveyed by Fred Moten, Ashon Crawley, Jayna Brown, or for that matter Achile Mbembe is absent from the book. But again, close attention to the reality of Black lives in modernity shows us the importance and power of sound in its various dimensions.

3. In his 1929 book *Civilization and Its Discontents*, Sigmund Freud set out a broad and powerful model for thinking about culture as a struggle between two fundamental human, and arguably nonhuman, and also arguably cosmic forces, those of Eros and Thanatos, life and death, love and violence. Freud's model has a clear application to recent work on sonic subcultures. In *Sonic Warfare*, Goodman argues that contemporary sound cultures such as hip-hop and dancehall are built out of a reappropriation of military and industrial technological colonizations of the sound spectrum, putting them at the service of the people, who satisfy their own aggressive drives via this appropriation and sublimation of a pervasive violence. While Goodman's argument is very compelling in describing a long lineage of subcultural musics—from Throbbing Gristle and the Stooges, through Public

Enemy and gangsta rap, dancehall reggae and grime, dubstep, and so on—the absence of any discussion of Eros or sexuality in his book is also rather striking. There is a strong fear of the body, of intimacy, of the erotics of vibration in Goodman's book. He overemphasizes the real but only partial significance of military metaphors and violence in, say, gangsta rap or dubstep, at the expense of the powerful discourse and practice of love that is operative in the history of queer dance scenes such as Deep House.

4 Related to this, Goodman gives no real explanation of how specific music scenes emerge from a mobilization of sound that is at the same time a mobilization of vibration—beyond an observation as to the importance of deep bass and subsonic frequencies, which constitute a new frontier of music since they exist at the edge or limit of audition, and are explicitly vibrational since they are felt as a movement or pulsation enveloping the body rather than just as something heard. The specific music that is heard in particular music scenes remains a black box or just music. Music presents an interesting problem for sound studies when it is presented in this neutral or descriptive way. Edgar Varèse famously defined music as "organized sound,"[28] but some forms of organization have more significance than others, both from a social sciences point of view (particular communities express preferences for certain organizations of sound), and from an aesthetic-political point of view (certain organizations of sound may be said to have specific aesthetico-political consequences or possibilities attached). Music matters for a vibrational ontology, because music reveals matters of ontological significance through the particular ways in which it reveals the potential/available forces within sound and vibration.

Some of these problems can be worked through by developing the idea of a vibrational ontology in other ways. What if the "ontologies of vibrational force" that Goodman focuses on, with their obvious masculinist bias (which he points out himself), characterized by control, instrumentalization, and so on, were actually secondary or at least reactive attempts to prevent the full opening up of a different, more fundamental vibrational ontology that is variously queer, feminist, decolonial, cosmopolitical, and "of the people" in yet unprecedented ways? Furthermore, given that the opening up of vibration at the ontological level is in Goodman's work coextensive with the military and political economic appropriation of the newly enlarged spectrum of available vibratory frequencies, one wonders how it is possible today for any ontological wager, vibratory or not, to avoid becoming part of an instrumentalized political project?

Such a project, which I attempt here, is echoed and explored in a series of recent works about vibration, notably Elizabeth Grosz's *Chaos, Territory, Art*, Julian Henriques's *Sonic Bodies*, Ashon Crawley's *Blackpentecostal Breath*, and Nina Sun Eidsheim's *Sensing Sound*. Grosz's work on vibration, like that of Goodman and others, is indebted to Deleuze and Guattari's work on vibratory assemblages, notably in the "Of the Refrain" chapter of *A Thousand Plateaus*, and in scattered places throughout both thinkers' works.[29] Grosz develops a theory of music as part of a practice of sexual selection running parallel to but separately from natural selection. Music is an assemblage, an ordering of a primordial vibratory chaos that is exuberant and joyful, bringing pleasure. Grosz argues that "what science and art share is precisely the vibratory structure of the universe, the emanating vibratory force of chaos itself."[30] Art and science, then, are particular modes of ordering the primordial force of vibration. "Vibrations are oscillations, differences, movements of back and forth, contraction and dilation: they are a becoming-temporal of spatial movements and spatial processes, the promise of a future modeled in some ways on the rhythm and regularity of the present. Vibrations are vectors of movement, radiating outward, vibrating through and around all objects or being dampened by them. Music is the result of the movements of territorialization, deterritorialization, and reterritorialization of vibratory force in its articulation of (the division or difference between) the body and the earth."[31]

The difficulty with this model, as is the case with most vibrational models derived from Deleuze and Guattari, is that there is no real account given of why any particular vibrational assemblage matters to any particular community—an assemblage is anything that works, and while the free improvisation of the assemblage may feel liberating, in practice assemblages are intentional entities that can be and are repeatable and varied. Musical vibration may serve a Darwinian purpose in terms of sexual selection, it may be an abstraction or deterritorialization of refrains that serve a primordially territorial purpose, both in terms of geography and environment on the one hand (the model of bird song), and the parameters of subjectivity on the other (the model of the small child who sings to himself or herself in the dark), but the actual ordering of vibration itself as music remains unexplained or unexamined.

In *Sonic Bodies*, Julian Henriques's book, the real complexity of actually existing sonic assemblages is elaborated, perhaps for the first time. Henriques emphasizes the importance of thinking through sound, of a sonic praxis that concerns "sound qua sound, that is, auditory vibrations" (xvii). These vibrations come together in a "sonic body" or bodies. In describing what the sonic praxis of a Stone Love Movement sound system event in Jamaica entails, Henriques describes the various kinds of specific know-how, materiality, and so on, that are assembled in the session. He identifies three different media or bandwidths of vibration: (1) the material waveband of sound moving through air via equipment and audio engineers working with the physics of sound; (2) the corporeal waveband of a particular crew and crowd responding to each other with the particular choices of tracks and mixing but also the dancing of the crowd; and (3) the sociocultural waveband or the broader sociocultural context in which equipment, crew, crowd, and sound come together and are intelligible as an event. That Henriques is able to write over three hundred pages on the particular factors and frameworks that go into a particular sound system session speaks to the density of the assemblage involved—and the importance of a notion of vibrational praxis, at so many levels, as indicating the care, specificity, and intentionality that are involved. In other words, a musical, sonic, or vibrational assemblage is not simply an experiment—it constitutes an evolving, forever contingently improvised but also repeatable, specific, and noncontingent set of practices that are collectively cultivated in a scene, subculture, or community which gathers around the sound. Environment, history, ideology, and capacity all come into play. And the larger point that Henriques is making is that any musical event or performance—whether an opera performance at Bayreuth, a Balinese ritual procession involving gamelan instruments, or a YouTube video of the newest K-Pop sensation—involves a similarly dense although nonidentical condensation of different kinds of praxis, materiality, and so on, whose goal is the generation of the object that is music. It is with this expansive and cosmopolitical idea of vibrational praxis that I think about contemporary music in this book.

One of the problems that looms over Deleuzian models of vibration is the absence of a theorization of the subject's imbrication in the world of vibration. This matters because music's power is clearly connected to affect and a transformation of the conditions of subjectivity, whether these are modeled as ecstatic, transpersonal, or otherwise. While Brian Massumi's Deleuzian version of affect theory speaks of vibrational transduction across media—for example, from instrument, to air, to ear, to mind—there is little sense of the way in which music specifically produces particular kinds of affects that are integrated into the intentional structure of the subject. Ashon Crawley's *Blackpentecostal Breath* develops its own particular notion of vibrational praxis in the history of the Black Pentecostal church in the United States. While Crawley's work broadly coheres with Henriques's in describing the way a music scene emerges out of the total social, historical, political, and material conditions in which a community finds itself, it also differs by focusing not on a music scene per se, but on a scene of religious (but "atheological, aphilosophical") ritual and practice in which music and sound play crucial rather than supplementary or supporting roles. Crawley's nuanced reading of the particular ways in which vibration is mobilized as a socioreligious force brings out an ontological level of vibration that is inherently religious or spiritual in the sense that it is ecstatic with relation to the subject (in Heideggerian terms) but at the same time social, ecstatically social, or, in his word, "choreosonic"—that is, a collectively established choreography in relation to sound, that produces a sound, and is produced by a sound. Of the "noise" of Blackpentecostalism, Crawley writes: "That noise can be joyful and joy can be unspeakable produces another way to analyze and interrogate categorical distinction. And that because the unspeakable is vibrated and sounded out, and such vibration and sound is produced from, and emerges from within while producing, joy. Joyful noise, the noise of Blackpentecostal aesthetics, operates from a different epistemological decentering, a centrifugitive refusal of centeredness."[32]

As such the vibrational praxis of the Black Pentecostal church cannot be understood or framed in terms of Euro-American categories of religion and music, or of subject and object, but instead works and plays to generate a space in which an "aesthetics of possibility" in which the "otherwise" than racist, settler colonial, capitalist America can manifest. In Crawley's work, the political nature of vibration is made clear—and Crawley challenges us to think about what our own relationship to this politics, coming from different subject positions, might be. Thinking through Crawley's work via Bruno Latour's observation of the religious or spiritual impulse as being omnipresent but "crossed out" in modernity, I explore Crawley's ideas across contemporary musical scenes and genres.[33]

Nina Sun Eidsheim's *Sensing Sound: Singing and Listening as Vibrational Practice* also shifts the framework in which music and vibration are understood—the key for her is the shift from musical performance to vibrational practice. Reflecting on twenty-first-century contemporary music forms, including works by Meredith Monk and Juliana Snapper, Eidsheim argues that music is most accurately understood as an intermaterial practice of vibration, in which the body of the person making music, the person listening, and the environment all experience transductions of energy in the form of vibratory movement. Different bodies transduce vibration and energy differently at different points, and the frequencies of the vibrations involved extend beyond the limits of human audition. Thus, the emphasis on "sensing sound" as encompassing listening but also on other modes of sensing, notably touch.

Singing and listening are particular expressions of the processes of vibration. What we understand as sound ultimately reverberates throughout the material body that produces and senses it; it is precisely because sound—undulating energy—is transduced through the listener's body that it is sensed. On the one hand, by projecting music out into the air, we have an impact on the world around us. We do not engage with music at a distance but, by definition, we do so by entering into a relationship that changes us. The most extreme definition of music possible, then, is vibrational energy—and, at times, transformation through that vibrational energy, which is an always already unfolding relational process.[34]

Furthermore, even the relational model of vibratory transduction is itself a simplification of what Eidsheim calls the "thick event" of music that is entangled and beyond disciplinary and conceptual labels. What we label as music or vibrational practice is nonetheless truly a practice in the sense of an action in a space that changes the configuration of entities and/or actants in the space. Although Eidsheim does not further specify what this thick event involves beyond being a distribution within and perturbation of an energy field, I argue here that Hennix's ideas concerning continuity and vibratory condensation offer promising ways to explore the situation further.

5

As already noted, this book concerns the relationship of music to ontology—a much overused word these days. By "ontology of music" standard scholarly sources today usually mean "what music is." The metaphysical assumptions contained in this phrase are dismally predictable. For example, a recent study that proposes an "ontology of musical works" sets out the criteria as follows: "The ontology of music is its metaphysics, its identity conditions and metaphysical categorizations."[35] Similarly, the *Stanford Encyclopedia of Philosophy* begins its article on "the philosophy of music" by observing that "musical ontology is the study of the kinds of musical things there are and the relations that hold between them."[36] Both articles note that their "ontologies" are derived solely from "Western musical traditions" or to "works . . . after Beethoven." The ontological inquiry that follows, then, usually proceeds via a focus on the dilemmas created by notation and contested theories of the emotions—or, in more contemporary works, wave analysis plus some neuroscience. From this perspective, as Roger Scruton indicates at the end of his chapter on ontology in his *Aesthetics of Music*, aside from the musical object and the psychology of the listener, "there is no third possibility, which means that there is nothing further to be said."[37]

This claim needs to be understood as a cosmopolitical barring of the ontological question as it concerns music. The anthropology and history of music in all their variety suggest that there is much to be said. Where to begin? First, framing the ontological question in terms of "what music is" is not in fact a genuinely ontological way of proceeding—it merely reiterates the metaphysical stance of Western philosophy, which Heidegger already and eloquently dismissed in the opening sections of *Being and Time*. It is in the nature of music and its vibrational field to dissolve the syntax of the sentence "what music is": "is" and "music," not to mention subject and object, are co-emergent in the field of the "what" that occupies the "now." The "what" being "always already" vibratory, always already a field. In this book, I will use the word *topos* to explore the richness and particularity of the concept of "field." The field is in fact that "third possibility" that Scruton's otherwise plausible subject/object model has failed to give an account of. Recognizing the historicity of, for example, the design of the acoustic space in which music occurs is one of the simplest ways to affirm the importance and variability of the concept of the field to understanding music's ontology—but that is just one aspect of the diamondlike lattice of the topos of music.

Then there is the question of "onto-logy" itself—and what the relation between "being qua being," "being itself," or "mere being" (Stevens) and "what can be said about being" is.[38] This issue underlies the major shift of focus in recent decades away from the linguistic turn in philosophy and theory, both Continental and analytic and the (vulgarized) version of that turn which claims we can know nothing outside of language—to a speculative philosophy that takes into account the descriptive power of the sciences and is willing to engage with reality's recalcitrant nondiscursivity and insistence.

The issue here, then, is not an "ontology of music," where music serves as a specimen or example to which a general theory can be applied, but what music tells us about ontology in the sense of "being qua being" and the general theory itself. A musical ontology does not consist in describing "what" a "musical object" "is" with all the problems involved in assembling those words together in the grammar of a sentence. If, as Heidegger says, questioning opens a path, then music also opens a path, as does mathematics.[39] Here, we follow that path and see where music leads us. It already leads us, when we listen to it and/or play it—"explain by singing," as Pandit Pran Nath sang in his composition "Nadam

Brahmam (Sound Is God)." Here, we attempt to put that vibratory explanation into words, aware of the inevitably secondary or provisional status of such work. We do so in gratitude to those who have opened up vibrational paths—John Coltrane, Pauline Oliveros, Abdul Karim Khan, Claude Debussy, Betty Carter, Fela Kuti, Wayang Lotring... their names standing here as metonyms for the richness of the sonic paths they took.

Of course, not all music has ontological significance in this sense. While all music must by definition be an iteration of sound ontological principles, only some music actually and explicitly targets and reveals that ontology—and, in doing so, the cosmopolitical stakes involved in such a revealing. It is this latter kind of music that we are concerned with here. Why, then, Pandit Pran Nath, Catherine Christer Hennix, and DJ Screw? Each of these musicians pushes at the limits of what our understanding of music is in ways that open up the question of music as a cosmopolitical practice. They do so from three different situations/genres/milieus—Pran Nath from the tradition of Hindustani classical vocal music as it manifested in the middle of the twentieth century, rendered stereotypically via ethnomusicology; Catherine Christer Hennix from the space of European/North American avant-garde/experimental music in the second half of the twentieth century, rendered stereotypically via discourses of the historical European avant-gardes; DJ Screw from hip-hop and the Black radical tradition as he found it in Houston, Texas, in the 1990s, stereotypically absent from any scholarly discourse about music. *Stereotypical* here marking the particular way that their work has been obscured or undervalued. Each of these figures is also errant or uncontainable in the traditions within which they are usually located—they stray in surprising and moving ways, they all seek within music something far beyond the normative expectations of the tradition at the historical moment that they are or were working, and, in their own way, each found in music a way of opening up another world than the one they found themselves in. Is it only a coincidence that each of these musicians' sound is slow—and long? Probably not. Because it turns out that slow and long are both very helpful in terms of a tactics of attention that sustains an ontological inquiry into the nature of music.

Nonetheless, I recognize that it may seem strange to write an ontological essay built on an analysis of contemporary hip-hop, drone music, and a relatively unknown figure in the history of Indian classical music—in fact, a noted musicologist in Berlin railed against ontologies of music based on hip-hop after I gave a paper related to that topic. My choices are perhaps far away from the concerns of traditional musicology and especially the philosophy of music that still, astonishingly or not, defines music within the terms set by the Western classical tradition ca. 1800–1950.[40] And, at the same time, my analysis remains also far away from where discussion of hip-hop or experimental rock is usually bracketed in cultural studies or the study of popular music or, for that matter, sound studies. It is this sense of dislocation or feeling of trespass in raising the ontological question in relation to "inappropriate" genres, disciplines, or fields that often indicates a cosmopolitical matter. No less so, then, in music. Here, I am guided by the music itself. One of the many important lessons that contemporary Black studies scholars have given us is that there is more at stake in popular Black music than a musicological analysis, or a sociological one, can articulate. "As serious as your life," as Val Wilmer recorded in her book on free jazz.[41] Or, as Hennix told me, about her childhood exposure to jazz with the trumpeter Idrees Suleiman in Stockholm in the early 1960s, "He taught me that jazz was a serious matter." I learned it, without really understanding it, at early hip-hop shows, dub sound systems in London but also through free jazz, punk, techno, Dhrupad, Afrobeat, and ... Stockhausen. Thinking about this brings me back to my friends' deaths—Adam and Justin were both musicians, and music held them up, the way it has also held me up, in many moments of destitution. As I have suggested, their deaths, and the possibility of mourning them musically also strikes me as a cosmopolitical matter: it is cosmopolitical in the sense that we, my friends and I, seem to be almost totally lost, and have little other than our attraction to music by which to orient ourselves in the world. And I am writing this in order to understand that better, to understand what music's possibilities are, for me, for others.

I write from a position of destitution, despite my various privileges and material advantages. I see the wreckage all around me (and in me too), despite the layer of neoliberal consumer gloss and wokeness that occupies our surfaces, on social media and in the streets of the gentrified cities. It is a fucked-up moment and time, with not much light available, but some good vibrations, still. And despite the darkness, which I am not trying to avoid or escape, there is good news, and "the great game" continues. But what is my own relationship to that? It's a challenging and necessary question today, in the moment of liberal-left discourses of white male privilege, cultural appropriation, and so on, looking back on my history and identity as a white British guy exposed to and transformed by Black and other musics. I have tried to write this accordingly, understanding my structural separation from the material realities and history of Blackness (and brownness) but also recognizing my indebtedness to and transformation by the Black radical tradition, the Chisti Sabri Sufis, as well as the postwar European experimentalists and their desire to confront and transform the brutal histories that they and I are entangled in. Destitution, a lifeline, that maybe was not even intended for me, but which has nonetheless held me (and others) up. That's something worth thinking about. "Be humble. Sit down" (Kendrick Lamar). So I sit and I try to write it out.

This is a book about improvising, and is the product of my own improvisation too—in other words, by starting where I actually was/am and working with that. Thus, the choice of particular topics is not arbitrary—it represents what I was attracted to, what I love(d), and what I wanted to understand. Or to put it in Heidegger's or Cornel West's terms . . . if my existential condition is one of thrownness, if the moment that I woke up and discovered myself thrown, was that day, aged sixteen, when I put the needle to the record of a used copy of John Coltrane's *Selflessness Featuring My Favourite Things*, in my bedroom in my parents' house in the suburbs of London, England, and was immersed in that sonic glory which, despite my dad's love of jazz, I had not yet even imagined—hearing Coltrane's call and having at that moment no way of integrating it into my life, but suddenly a sense of care, purpose, and orientation in the world, then I should write about music in a way that is true to the contingency of that moment. So my own improvisation here is an offering.

More pragmatically, some of the essays in this book began as music journalism, and gradually evolved into something else. Greil Marcus once said that to understand Lester Bangs, you'd have to be able to believe that the most important literature being produced in America could take the form of nothing more than record reviews.[42] In those terms, popular music criticism of the kind practiced by Lester Bangs, Jessica Hopper, or Greg Tate but also a much broader history of informal writing about music that would include Zora Neale Hurston's descriptions of Black southern folk musics, or the German Romantic E. T. A. Hoffmann's ecstatic rants about music, or Nathaniel Mackey's profound letters to the "Angel of Dust," generated out of immediate and passionate concern for something happening around them, often brings us much closer to what music is than an academic analysis. Improvisation is a method and an ethics, both in music and in opening up a path philosophically—improvisation in the terms of the Black radical tradition rather than that of the European avant-gardes: as a matter of informality. Informality is not a failure to be formal, but a decision as to how to talk, think, and be, how to relate and offer and accept relation.

What I offer here, then, is a kind of ontology of music—one that trembles, in the sense that Édouard Glissant proposed "trembling thought" ("la pensée du tremblement") as the true horizon of a shared world.[43] Trembling—a vibrational mode. The argument is not entirely my own—I came to it over years of conversations with Hennix and other musicians, slowly trying to understand their work and how they heard the world, trembling with them too. I like to think of it as my own way of playing with them, for better or for worse. I am particularly grateful beyond all words to Hennix for her patience and generosity with me—and the generosity of her own lifelong commitment to a rigorous and emancipatory thought and practice. An ontology of music is just one part of an elaborated philosophical approach to vibration and, outside of music and sound, there is much work to be done on the ways in which vibration itself has been understood as a medium or material, central to various forms of life, practices, "lieux communs" (Glissant).

There is an important question that needs to be asked about the relation between cosmopolitical disputes and ontology. How can cosmopolitical positions and dissensus be resolved into the consensus of an ontology? Isn't it precisely because there are cosmopolitical disputes that there can be no single ontology of music? It is a problem that haunts Stengers's and Latour's network/field models—as well as the more recent work of Yuk Hui who sees "cosmotechnics" as embodying a pluralist ontological position. Consider this a wager rather than an axiom, but I believe music does tell us something about being. It points to something universal, from all the places across the globe, across history, across the sonic spectrum in which human beings and others have undertaken to make or practice it. "Music exists," to quote the wonderful title of a record by the Japanese alt pop group Tenniscoats. Philosophically and politically the word *universal* is a somewhat disreputable one today, in the wake of the long human struggle for emancipation from the despotism of ideologies of the universal.[44] Is it possible to formulate a universal that does not calcify into an ideology of the universal? What can music offer us in terms of paths of access to a real universality? We will approach these questions in new ways here in dialogue with contemporary music scenes across the globe, some of which I have encountered, others not. The cosmopolitical practice of music is a work in progress, as are we. In the words of John Coltrane, from the liner notes to *A Love Supreme* (1964):

> Words—sounds—speech—men—memory
> Thoughts—Fears—Emotions & time—all
> Related—ALL made from one ALL made in one.
> Blessed Be His Name.
> Thought waves—Heat waves—ALL
> Vibrations—ALL Paths Lead to God.
> His way—it is Lovely—it is Gracious
> It is merciful,

Thank you God.
One thought can produce millions of vibrations and they ALL go back to God—Everything Does—
Thank you God.[45]

Thank you John Coltrane.

ONE

· · · · · ·

Lord's House, Nobody's House
Pandit Pran Nath and Music as Sadhana

> Sound is God
> Explain by singing...
> —PANDIT PRAN NATH

I

The sun was going down outside the magenta-tinted windows of La Monte Young and Marian Zazeela's Dream House space in Tribeca, New York. It was a summer evening in June 2001 (or 01 VI 10 7: 01: 00 PM NYC, to use Young's calendrical system). The synthesized just intonation tuned pitch frequencies of the dronework that usually saturates this space by day were silent, giving way to the annual memorial raga cycle in honor of Pandit Pran Nath. The minimal decor of this room, in which Young and Zazeela's musical and spiritual teacher lived from 1977–79, had been transformed by a small shrine, with a picture of Pran Nath, flowers, and burning incense. Young and Zazeela sit behind a mixing desk in the center of the room, wearing space-age biker sadhu gear, and introducing a selection of raga recordings from their MELA Foundation archives, as the small crowd—a mixture of devoted former Pran Nath students and Young's current protégés—lounge on the floor or against the wall. Unless you were lucky enough to own one of the long-unavailable recordings made by Pran Nath, this once-a-year event was at that moment currently the only way that you could hear what his performances sounded like.

No Indian music sounds like Young's 1970s recordings of Pran Nath. The droning tamburas are located high up in the mix, as loud, rich, and powerful as vintage Theater of Eternal Music (the experimental group Young and Zazeela belonged to in the mid-60s with John Cale, Tony Conrad, and Angus Maclise). The tabla playing is simple but tough. The midnight raga Malkauns is traditionally said to describe a yogi beset by tempting demons while meditating. Recorded in 1976 in a SoHo studio in New York, Pran Nath's version is unspeakably moving as he slowly chants the composition Hare Krishna Govinda Ram over and over, his voice winding in stretched-out, subtly nuanced glissandos that leave you begging for the next note. The 62-minute recording sounds completely traditional in its adherence to the slow, minimal style of the Kirana School of Indian Classical Music,[1] which Pran Nath belonged to, while containing in the sound itself everything that was happening in New York City that year, the same year that Scorsese's *Taxi Driver* hit the movie houses. Pran Nath's voice and Young's production turn the city into a sacred modern hyperspace, full of tension and beauty, in which anything, from Krishna to Son of Sam, can manifest.

As the music sent me into one of Young's "drone states of mind," I recalled another sunset, a few months before, on the other side of the world. I was standing with a group of raga students at the gate of Tapkeshwar, a 5,000-year-old cave temple devoted to Siva, located about ten miles north of Dehra Dun in the foothills of the Indian Himalaya when the aged temple keeper turned to us and asked "Where is Terry Riley?" Around us a steady flow of pilgrims, old and young, climbed down the steps to the entrance of the cave, to pour water over the Siva lingam in the heart of the temple. Not a place one would necessarily expect to find one of America's most prolific composers of the postwar era. But over the last thirty years, Terry Riley had been a frequent visitor to this cave, where Pran Nath, his guru and instructor in the North Indian classical tradition, the man he called "the greatest musician I have ever heard," lived for a number of years in the 1940s.

If Riley's presence in Tapkeshwar comes as a surprise, it seems equally unlikely that Pran Nath—a reclusive, classically trained Indian singer who spent his time at Tapkeshwar living as a naked, ash-covered ascetic, singing only for God—should end his days in the former New York Mercantile Exchange Building that housed Young and Zazeela's Dream House, teaching Indian classical music to a broad spectrum of America's avant-garde musicians, including Jon Hassell, Charlemagne Palestine, Arnold Dreyblatt, Rhys Chatham, Henry

Flynt, Simone Forti, Yoshi Wada, and Don Cherry. Although virtually unknown in India, Pran Nath's devotion to purity of tone resonates through key minimalist works like Young's *The Well-Tuned Piano*, Riley's keyboard piece *Descending Moonshine Dervishes*, Henry Flynt's raga fiddling, Charlemagne Palestine's droneworks, and Jon Hassell's entire "fourth world" output.

Of the many great Hindustani (i.e., North Indian) raga musicians in the twentieth century, the master sarod player Ali Akbar Khan and the sitar master Ravi Shankar are generally considered to be the ones who brought a knowledge of their music to the West.[2] There are antecedents: the Sufi master and musician Hazrat Inayat Khan had come to New York in 1910, and subsequently taught and performed in America and Europe for more than a decade.[3] Shankar himself had first visited the West in the 1930s, traveling with his brother Uday Shankar's dance troupe, and, like Ali Akbar Khan, he later started a music school in America, transforming an exotic but foreign spectacle into a practice that westerners could participate in. The Dagar brothers, masters of the Dhrupad tradition, and sublime vocalists, toured Europe in 1964. But it was Pran Nath—an outsider, little known in India outside of musicians' circles, and most strongly connected to Western avant-garde musicians on the fringe of the culture—who brought to America a knowledge of Indian classical vocal when he arrived from India for the first time in December 1969. Singing is acknowledged in India to be the primary musical form, which all music students must learn, and musical instruments, whether sitar or shenai, are designed to imitate the capabilities of the human voice.

But more than the music itself, Pran Nath brought with him an attitude toward music as the highest form of spiritual devotion—not in the same way that a bhajan or Qawwali singer does, by sweeping the listener and performer up in a mood of ecstatic devotion through rhythm and repetition (although Pran Nath could certainly do this), but by uncovering, exploring, and mastering the most profound knowledge of music, Nada Brahma ("the God of sound"), as it manifests itself in Indian raga music. This made Pran Nath, both inside India and elsewhere, a controversial figure. "He was not a great singer," a well-known Indian musician confided to me one day, "but he was a great teacher." I never saw Pran Nath perform live, though I am extremely moved by his recordings (Pran Nath himself was skeptical that recordings had any value)—but as much as any particular musical performance style or virtuosity, it was an attitude toward music, and a method, a practice, a sadhana, that Pran Nath communicated, one that resituated music and our understanding of what its possibilities are cosmopolitically.

2

Pran Nath was born on November 3, 1918, into a wealthy family in Lahore, in what is now Pakistan. His father was in business, selling cloth.[4] In the early twentieth century, the city was known as the flower of the Punjab, with its own rich musical tradition. Pran Nath painted an idyllic picture of the musical culture of Lahore during this period, in which Hindu and Muslim musicians would practice outdoors in different parts of the city, congregating to perform and exchange compositions and to hang out with their friends, the wrestlers, with whom they formed a fraternity. Many great musical masters, including Bade Ghulam Ali Khan and Pran Nath's own guru Abdul Wahid Khan, lived in Lahore. "No friction, no religious fighting," he recalled. "They were sharing each other's festivals, like five fingers when they're together at eating time."[5] He also recalled accompanying his mother to the Golden Temple in Amritsar, the holiest site of the Sikhs, when he was three years old, and said that the first song he learned to sing was Guru Ravidas's shabad, which is included in the Sikh holy book, the Guru Granth Sahib.[6]

Indian musicology is a vast topic, with a complex history dating back to at least Bharata's *Natyashastra*, a treatise on the performing arts written approximately two thousand years ago, and to the *Sangita-Ratnakara*, a thirteenth-century treatise on music written by Sarangadeva. It should be said from the outset that in speaking of a vibrational ontology, it is standard practice in Indian musicological treatises, including modern ones, to begin by observing that in the Tantric worldview, the world begins as a condensation of the primordial sound AUM.[7] Thus, the cosmopolitics of sound and vibration are almost explicit in such treatises since they stand in uneasy proximity to similar Western treatises that begin with a summary of acoustics or the physics of pitch frequencies. The cosmopolitics consists in the radically different meanings, practices, and social structures that gather around what is ostensibly the same object—music—in each case.

The practice of making music in the Indian tradition however was generally transmitted directly, from guru to disciple. The lineages or schools through which this knowledge is passed are known as gharanas (Hindi: "family" or "lineage")—which often guard particular techniques or compositions with great zeal. The history of the evolution of gharanas is itself a complex topic, but gharanas appear to have emerged as important in the nineteenth century with the decline in power of the royal courts.

Pran Nath knew from an early age that his vocation was to be a musician, and his grandfather invited musicians into the home to perform in the evenings.

But while many eminent Indian classical musicians come from families of musicians and speak of parents whispering ragas or tal cycles to them as they slept, Pran Nath's mother wanted her son to pursue a law career, and, at the age of thirteen, gave him the choice of abandoning music or leaving home. So he left immediately and wandered, looking for a teacher, until he came upon Abdul Wahid Khan at a music conference. Pran Nath claimed that he was able to copy every musician he heard until he encountered Wahid Khan, and on this basis decided to become his student. Although Pran Nath's family initially refused to accept his decision to become a musician, he did return to visit his mother on her deathbed and sang for her, and, moved by his singing, she accepted his decision.[8]

Abdul Wahid Khan, along with his relative Abdul Karim Khan, was one of the two major figures of the Kirana gharana, named after the town north of Delhi where some of its practitioners lived, and one of North India's most important families of vocal music. Although the word *gharana* only came into use in the nineteenth century, the gharana itself is said to date back to the late sixteenth century and the Mughal emperor Humayun's court in Delhi, or, further, to the thirteenth-century musician/saint Gopal Nayak, who was a contemporary of the great poet and musician Amir Khusrau.[9] The two Khans were of very different temperaments. Abdul Karim Khan was an enormously popular and feted musician, who sang at the Baroda court in 1894, where he famously eloped with Tarabai, the daughter of a nobleman of the court. Subsequently, Khan founded a music school, gave public ticketed performances, produced celebrated gramophone recordings, and engaged with the great Indian musicologist and modernizer of Indian classical music, Pandit Vishnu Narayan Bhatkhande. His voice is like a nightingale's—an ocean of melodiousness and delicacy, light but exquisitely soulful.[10] If you have never heard him sing, please put down this book right now and google "Karim Khan Bhimpalasi" and listen to him sing "Prem Seva Sharan." The tearing of your heart that you will feel will be our concern here: it is humbling, revealing something about human subjectivity, the entanglement of sound and feeling, surprising and specific.

By contrast, Abdul Wahid Khan was a somewhat reclusive, fierce man, with a powerful voice and an encyclopedic knowledge of raga; he was famous for his methodical elaboration of the alap, the slow improvisatory section of the raga. He was also an extremely devoted Sufi, with a pir whose approval he would seek before all performances. He taught at Abdul Karim Khan's school in Pune circa 1913, and moved with him to Bombay (as Mumbai was then known) in 1917. He moved to Lahore in 1939, and to Kirana in 1945—he died of heart failure in 1948 while visiting Saharanpur.[11] He was an equally devoted guardian of the deepest knowledge of raga—and apparently known to be a committed opium smoker too. The singer Salamat Ali Khan said of him that "he would begin to improvise in Lahore, and you could travel to Delhi and back, and he would still be improvising."[12] According to the master sarod-player Ali Akbar Khan, when most singers went to the radio station, they would sing their ragas and go home. Abdul Wahid Khan would continue for another twenty hours or so.[13] Once, a disciple asked Abdul Wahid Khan why he only sang two ragas, Todi, a morning raga, and Darbari, an evening raga. Abdul Wahid Khan responded that he would have dropped the latter, if the morning would last forever.[14]

Becoming a student of Wahid Khan was no easy matter—although he did have illustrious students, including Abdul Karim Khan's daughter Hirabai Barodekar, Begum Akhtar, Suresh Babu Mane, Saraswati Rane, and Feroz Nizami. Pran Nath had no family connections or money and was a Hindu, while Wahid Khan was a devout Muslim. So, he worked for eight years as Wahid Khan's household servant before he was finally taken on as a disciple at the urging of Wahid Khan's cook. The details are murky. Some have questioned whether Pran Nath ever received music lessons in the traditional sense. It has been said that, in a typically orthodox fashion, he was not often allowed to practice in front of his teacher, and, after spending his days in devoted service of his guru, would go out into the jungle at night to practice, learning in this way to survive with hardly any sleep. Abdul Wahid Khan was a very stern teacher. According to the ethnomusicologist Bonnie Wade, "Once when Abdul Wahid was sitting on a charpai preparing his hookah, moving the coals with iron tongs, Pran Nath was at his feet playing tambura and singing. When the disciple made a mistake, the ustad pulled his earlobe with the hot tongs."[15] Pran Nath himself said that the hearing in his left ear had been damaged from all the beatings. Nevertheless, when he would speak about his guru in later years, Pran Nath remembered him with love and respect, tears in his eyes.

It was during his years of study with Abdul Wahid Khan that Pran Nath began his association with Tapkeshwar cave. The cave contains a natural lingam, formed where water drips down onto the rock, which is visited at Shivaratri every year by devotees from around India and Nepal. When he was not serving his guru, Pran Nath lived at this cave, as a naga baba, naked except for a smearing of white ashes, singing to Siva. There was no tambura at Tapkeshwar, and Pran Nath said that he used the sound of the water, flowing through the gorge there, as his drone. It was at Tapkeshwar too, that Pran Nath met Swami Narayan Giriji, at that time the master of the temple complex there. When his health failed later in life, Swamiji moved to the Jangam Sivayam temple in Dehra Dun, where Pran Nath was the temple musician when he visited India.

Throughout his life, Pran Nath enjoyed practicing in or with the aid of nature. Speaking in praise of the raga-like qualities of birdsong, he said "According to season they change their tone ... another bird ... this is a nightingale, this is crow, he's changing his tone ... so this is natural change, natural place ... Lord's house, nobody's house ... practicing open places. Walls have a stuck feeling. Open place have a ... how much can fly ideas!"[16]

Pran Nath's time at Tapkeshwar and his love of practicing in "open places" is a good example of music as a cosmopolitical practice. It is hardly a unique example—at any moment and any time, the world is alive with both humans and nonhumans, engaged in such practices. I draw attention to the matter here because of the clarity of what Pran Nath was doing—singing for God rather than performing for other humans; tuning and attuning himself to the elements of nature, whether the river at Tapkeshwar or the sounds of birdsong as they change with the changing seasons; the emphasis on practice, of music as the cultivation of an ability, even of a kind of metaphysical object (a particular raga, a tonal matrix, a sound) that has to be crafted through repetition, learning, and skill. And the sense that all of this happens "naturally," which is to say in accordance with certain cosmological principles, in this case tantric ones, in a nonetheless concrete and specific historical landscape that pressurizes this act of cultivation and devotion. Music as a home ("Lord's house") and music as homeless wandering ("nobody's house") or perhaps the uncanny (Freud's "unheimlich" or literally not-at-home) tension between the two, where music itself is home in its alliance with natural/cosmological principles, but still forced to make its way through history and all of its displacements, the waves of colonialism and empire, of political-economic forces, such that one never quite knows whether one is lost or found. And the existential decision as to what to do in such circumstances—the decision out of which a life forms.

3

It is likely that Pran Nath would have remained at Tapkeshwar, had Wahid Khan not ordered his student, in his gurudakshina (last request), to get married, become a householder and take his music out into the world. This Pran Nath did, moving to Delhi in 1949 and marrying Rani Budhiraja, with whom he subsequently had three daughters and a son. That same year, Wahid Khan died.

By all accounts, hearing Pran Nath in full flow at this time was an extraordinary experience. At the All India Music Conference in Delhi in 1953, attended by many of the giants of the classical music scene, Pran Nath's performance of the rainy season raga Mian Ki Malhar stunned the crowd of five thousand. The singer and early disciple Karunamayee recalled that when he hit the "sa" note, "he held the breath of us all, collected our breath through his own breath, held it at one pitch and then let go. When he let go, we also let go, all five thousand people in the audience. It was a shock to me. All this can be done with music! And when he ended, there was torrential rain! Suddenly he got up, he was very sad and frustrated and angry and said, 'I'm not a musician, I'm only a teacher,' and walked off."[17]

This ability to bring on the rain through singing may be considered one of the yogi's miraculous powers, or siddhis. In its divine aspect, the power of music is connected to the power of nature. It is for this reason that each raga is associated with a particular time of day or a particular season. For one who has truly mastered Nada Brahma, music may be used to manipulate nature, causing rain, and charming animals and humans. In fact, the word *raga* may be translated as "that which charms." These siddhis could also become perilous. Alain Daniélou speaks of a musician who, "compelled by the Emperor Akbar to sing in the mode of fire (Dipak raga), made the water of the river Jumna boil, and died burnt by the flames which came out from every part of his body."[18] Of course, it is hard to know what to make of stories like this. In her excellent historical book, *Two Men and Music: Nationalism and the Making of an Indian Classical Tradition*, which includes a detailed account of the life of Abdul Karim Khan, Janaki Bakhle is caustic about the myths and legends that surround Indian musicians or the music they make, bracketing such claims as "bhakti nationalism" or "religious," or at other moments as "ontological" or "anthropological." The power of music, whether figured as magic or blessings is for Bakhle in the end ideological—the construction of an often-toxic myth whose actual roots lie in historical struggle and the politics of everyday life. Something similar happens in sound studies, where the field is framed by historicist documentation of materials relevant to the field and a social constructionist or assemblage theory based doctrine, materialist or not, prevails. From this point of view, sound and music, as per the modern dogma that Latour recognized as such in *We Have Never Been Modern*, have no particular ontological meaning, and (tellingly) there is no particular spiritual significance to sound or music, aside from an anthropological one that most are disinclined to take too seriously.

But, even in Bakhle's account, what remains is that both musicians and those who listen to music do construct claims as to the meaning and value of the particular sounds and musics that they engage with—including the miraculous or magical. They seem to crowd around or haunt attempts at historical/

materialist analyses of music. Indeed, there would be no music scenes of any kind, were people not in the end attracted to situations, practices, events in which something special occurred. In terms of Latourian assemblage theory, this exceptionality, described in spiritual terms, would constitute the "crossed out" transcendental or religious aspect of modernity. Indeed, Latour's point is that the negated spiritual dimension of an assemblage is what allows a modern or materialist assemblage to appear as such—and that the negated spiritual dimension remains essential to the functioning of such an assemblage.[19] The negation itself is asserted as being ontological, that is, an indisputable and foundational fact, but is precisely what we have referred to in the introduction as cosmopolitical, that is, a position in a dispute whose goal is the marginalization or eradication of other modes of being, other practices.

While there is unquestionably also an ideological dimension to the religious or ontological formulations that are applied to music, the practice of music consists in the ways (modes) that different music scenes construct particular musical and social and spiritual frameworks built around particular sonic and vibrational practices. If I say practice, it is because this construction actually has to happen. It is not an idea, but something that occurs in practice. It is also a practice because that which occurs, which is made to occur, is repeatable and shareable, under certain conditions. Music articulates certain modes of being (more on this later)—what Ashon Crawley has called "the aesthetics of possibility" and the production of "otherwise possibilities."[20] Thus, music, in its engagement with the possible, is a cosmopolitical practice.

Of course, there is no guarantee that this will happen—or that any particular cosmopolitical framing of music is to be affirmed. This is the place of Bruno Latour and Isabelle Stengers's "parliament of things" with its delegates speaking for nonhumans and others. Who speaks for music? Therein lies what I call the politics of vibration, which is negotiated in all music scenes from that of the ceremonial music performed in church at the death of a sovereign, to a Saturday night dance held in a parking lot in rural Jamaica. Musicians and lovers of music understand this contingency and/or are able to speak about it—or perhaps endure it. More to the point, as lovers of music, we experience the ontological dimensions of music as a particular local physical, social, and political articulation of sound and vibration. It is a matter of practice in the expanded sense that Julian Henriques has given us when speaking of "ways of knowing" in relation to the "sonic bodies" of the sound system session.

To repeat, music is a cosmopolitical practice—indeed, it is impossible to understand Pran Nath, the way he thought about music, and the swirl of hagiographic tales that circulate around his name or around the history of Hindustani music without understanding their cosmopolitical nature. The ecology of Pran Nath's musical practice—of any musical practice—is fragile as soon as it is not guaranteed by a dominant social-political structure. Can a raga really cause it to rain? Can a particular sequence and combination of pitches really cause a deity to appear? Where does the "really" come from?—that is a cosmopolitical question. And the idea of a cosmopolitics allows us to at least suspend judgment about what music is such that we pay attention to what the ecology of practices that Pran Nath's music was embedded in actually consisted of. And that, in the transit from Lahore circa 1900 to New York City circa 1976 or Berlin in 2019, the status of what is included, permitted, manifested as musical experience remains open, subject to negotiation—a negotiation that certainly includes an awareness of the risk of reifying the "otherwise possibilities" in ways that Bakhle is all too aware of.

In this book, I adopt a Jamesian position on the religious/spiritual experience of music—I'm open to it, and to the accounts of those who have something to say about it.[21] Not only that... I've experienced it myself, in many situations, at many times. I recall, for example, going and hearing the sarangi player Hafizullah Khan, Abdul Wahid Khan's son, play at the Dream House in New York City in the early 2000s and falling into this deep, drowsy state, in which the music exerted a kind of strange gravitational pull—ecstatic in the sense that "I" became "it," somehow pulled outside of myself... or "possessed" in the sense that where "I" was supposed to be, now something else was, something that glowed with/as affect, juice, "rasa." And I was guided toward it by feeling, mood, desire even. The raga appeared in the room in the form of the vibrations of the sarangi player, resonating with the tambura, the tabla, the room itself, and all of us in it. "That's what it's supposed to do!" said Henry Flynt, who attended the performance. Afterward, I felt a strange hole inside myself, a yearning or loss, regret that I was no longer in that state—a kind of slow whiplash, as if something about me, myself, had been temporarily stretched, shape altered, and then had returned to its former shape. I don't say that this counts as definitive evidence of anything, but it also does not strike me as arbitrary or simply a projection or placebo effect.

If the issue is proof, Pran Nath himself clearly believed that the meaning or value of music could only be found in its performance or practice. The visual artist and long-term student Marian Zazeela recalls that "there was a story that Pran Nath was performing at a Sufi camp, and somebody asked him a question, 'What is this about music having an effect?' He then started to sing a raga and the whole audience became soporific, they almost fell asleep. When he finished he said, 'Well, this is what we mean by having an effect.'"[22]

4

Shattered by his guru's death and contemptuous of modern Indian society, Pran Nath was a moody, imposing figure during his Delhi days. Many people have commented that Pran Nath's music is a sad music. If this is the case, it may be because his music is a music of exile, searching to find its place in the twentieth century. Although Pran Nath admired Gandhi, and strongly supported Indian independence, the Lahore of Pran Nath's youth was gone after partition. Pran Nath himself helped some Hindus flee, as the nation of Pakistan was born in violence and trauma. Pran Nath's guru was dead, and with him, a link to the world that had nourished raga for several hundred years, the world in which great singers received the patronage of maharajahs and their courts, or of temples far away from twentieth-century life, a world in which an apprenticeship of fifty years was not uncommon. When asked about the fate of the tradition, Pran Nath commented: "Time is changing. Everything is changing. The living of the people in society is changing. People have to run for the bread. [Kirana style] needs half a century's time to develop. According to that, you can feel how the standard can be maintained."[23] At another time, he observed that "three lifetimes are very little for doing this work. It is necessary to remain one hundred years with the guru, then practice for one hundred years, and then you can sing for one hundred years."[24] And where could you find such time in the modern world? Pran Nath complained that he spent all day on Delhi's overcrowded bus system, going from one teaching appointment to the other.

Nonetheless, it is hard not to think that, in actual fact, Indian classical music at the time of decolonization in India and Pakistan was going through a golden age—the moment of the elder Dagar brothers, Bade Ghulam Ali Khan, Hirabai Barodekar, and so many others. In the breakdown and dissolution of the Mughal royal courts, and British colonialism, new frameworks for the production and dissemination of music were coming into being: while the gharanas were able to set themselves up as music schools, such as the one Abdul Karim Khan ran, raga was broadcast across India via All India Radio, and disseminated via gramophone records, reaching the ears of many new listeners and exposing people to styles and sounds they had not heard before; large-scale festivals, such as the one Pran Nath sang at in Delhi in 1953, used amplification to bring music to a group of five thousand people—far beyond what the privileged experienced at a house concert; and music was taught in the university system. There was a democratization of tradition going on, not dissimilar to that described by Fanon in his famous "On National Culture" chapter of *The Wretched of the Earth*—in which, at the moment of decolonization, the frozen aspects of tradition come to life in new and unexpectedly vital ways. "The storytellers who recited inert episodes revive them and introduce increasingly fundamental changes. There are attempts to update battles and modernize the types of struggle, the heroes' names, and the weapons used. The method of allusion is increasingly used. Instead of 'a long time ago,' they substitute the more ambiguous expression 'What I am going to tell you happened somewhere but it could happen here today or perhaps tomorrow.'"[25]

And that is true for music too. Pran Nath stands at a curious angle to that moment—since he was by no means a simple advocate of modernizing tradition. He was clearly nostalgic for an idealized version of music's status during his childhood in Lahore—yet he also believed in the living reality of the tradition he saw himself being faithful to, rather than considering it a mere formality. Here, it is important to clarify that we are not necessarily referring to conceptual innovations but to the actual practice of music making, the existential moment of vibratory appearance or manifestation, physical or otherwise. That power of music which "could happen here today" too.

Music, perhaps more than other fields of human activity, is subject to a chronopolitics—morphing according to the temporal horizon that a particular historical society establishes. A basic theme of this book will be the control of what Ashon Crawley calls the "aesthetics of possibility" in different human societies, possibilities emergent in music's ordering of vibratory power. Music does not inertly occupy a span of time, particularly that "vulgar" concept of linear time that Heidegger dismissed in his work (specifically, *Being and Time*, section 81). He dismissed it because it was mistaken, an intellectual error with serious consequences. Pran Nath's musical practice was facilitated by a particular organization of time, both that practical time devoted to intensively focusing on a particular activity, and musical time, in which temporality itself is probed and stretched in particular ways through rhythm and tone. In fact, those two aspects of time come together in Pran Nath's story. Pran Nath was untimely—out of touch with an emerging regime of time in India, even as (we shall see) his practice and view of tradition resonated with countercultural views of temporality in America that were coming from a radically different place. "Lord's house, nobody's house": there's the split that the musician committed to a life of music has to endure.

Was there something particular about the Kirana gharana that related to this? Although Abdul Karim was a very popular singer, he was also a controversial, errant figure. While a court musician at Baroda, he eloped in the night with the daughter of a member of the court and proceeded to set up his own music school. In Bakhle's account, Khan was an important figure in the transition from the forms that music took in nineteenth-century colonial India, principally around the courts, to the democratization of music, attempts to standardize the music via notation and education systems, and the career of making music as a reputable middle-class one. For Bakhle, the gharanas stand in ambiguous relation to this—their family-based networks with their secret knowledges of musical practice potentially threatened or eroded by public musical education and performance. In the case of Abdul Wahid Khan, the religious centering of his music was perhaps undermined or sidelined by these developments, later to return, as Bakhle notes, in reified form as "bhakti nationalism"—or its Muslim equivalent.

Although he had the respect of many musicians, such as Bhimsen Joshi and Salamat and Nazkat Ali Khan ("They spoiled my lessons!" he claimed in 1972),[26] who came to him to work on their knowledge of specific ragas, Pran Nath never received popular acclaim in India. "Those who know music know his place," said the *Hindustan Times* music critic Shanta Serbjeet Singh. "He was not a musician with a performer personality: he was too intense, too withdrawn."[27] Some say that Pran Nath, an uncompromising and blunt man, especially in his younger years, made no attempt to cultivate the necessary connections. He would interrupt famous performers as they began to sing, telling them that their tamburas were out of tune. Sheila Dhar said that he appeared to have no interest whatsoever in fame and fortune, repeatedly telling her "This music is only for the contentment of your soul."[28] Pran Nath's style of singing was also considered unorthodox by some, and his innovations and exuberant explorations of raga were criticized as erroneous breaks with tradition—Pran Nath began performing for All India Radio in 1937 but was apparently graded as a "C" class artist until late in his life, according to his student Karunamayee.[29] He valued a spontaneity, born out of discipline, which could only manifest in performance itself. When asked whether he knew which ragas he was going to perform before a show, he replied: "No certain, no thinking. How possible man going to hunting thinking, 'Tiger will come out, I will shoot this way and he will jump and I will jump this way'? This is the time when only spirits help to do performance."[30]

The Kirana style, according to various accounts, emphasizes the slow development of the alap section of a raga—the tabla-less gradual exploration and exposition of the tones (swara) of the raga.[31] In La Monte Young's account, Kirana style emphasized the importance of pitch over rhythm, and Pran Nath's music was at the extreme pitch-oriented end of the Kirana style. It's hard to say how accurate this is: all gharanas are concerned with pitch since it is one of the core principles of the system of Indian raga music—but Pran Nath was disdainful of the crowd-pleasing duels with tabla players that are the bread and butter of most classical music performers. Pran Nath's style was intense and meditative. He said repeatedly that it was a mistake to sing for other people, but that one should always sing only for God.

After moving to Delhi, Pran Nath began teaching, quickly gathering students, who were mostly reduced to silence by his skills. The singer and long-time student Sheila Dhar recalled in her memoirs: "His lessons consisted mainly in demonstrations of heavy, serious ragas in his own voice. Most of the time we listened in hypnotised states of awe. He had a way of exploring a single note in such detail that it turned from a single point or tone into a vast area that glowed like a mirage. Each of us encountered this magic at different times. Whenever it happened, it overwhelmed us like a religious experience. There was no question of our even trying to repeat this sort of thing. All we could do was to drink it all in and wait for a chance to participate in some undefined way in the distant future."[32]

The study of Indian classical music had undergone a rapid transformation in the twentieth century. As previously noted, after independence in 1947, the teaching of music was increasingly transferred to the universities. Pran Nath himself taught advanced classes in Hindustani classical vocal at Delhi University between 1960 and 1970—a prestigious position, but one he took little pleasure in, believing that only daily, one-on-one study with a knowledgeable master over a sustained period could properly train a musician. Terry Riley, who visited one of these classes recalls:

> I went out there to visit a class he was teaching. The students really loved him. It was quite a night, more like a club than a class, students were sitting on the floor . . . a lot of socializing and talk. He'd have one of the students sing a raga for me. It didn't have the feeling of any university I've ever been in. But his life was hard in those days, travelling on the bus, because he didn't have any money . . . he did that for years and years . . . and walked for miles and miles. His life was very hard in those days.[33]

Each raga is defined by a precise set of pitches, and of acceptable ways of moving between these pitches and embellishing them. Thus, when a raga is performed, there are many possible melodic shapes within each raga—and the musician's skill consists in articulating and varying these shapes—both in compositions and improvisation. This focus on purity of swara, or tone, was one of the trademarks of Kirana-style singing, and can be seen as a part of Pran Nath's celebrated claim that the essence of raga occurs "between the notes." In fact, while other teachers would quickly teach their students many ragas, Pran Nath would often insist that, for the first six months or longer, a new student would sing only the sa (or tonic) note over and over, until they had perfected it, as a way of learning what it means to be in tune. "A tone is not a point, but a melodic area to be explored," he told Dhar. "The more extensive this area becomes in the mind of a musician, the more evolved he is. You must learn to listen before you learn to sing. And you have first to listen to your own breath and then to the self it embodies."[34]

The tambura, the gourd-based drone instrument that can be heard in most raga performances, played an important role in Pran Nath's music since the raga performer tunes his or her performance to the rich overlay of tones and overtones produced by the strumming of this instrument. To say this is, of course, Hindustani Classical Music 101, but Pran Nath would spend an hour or more tuning an instrument before singing, so that this itself became an act of meditation, and he was himself responsible for a number of innovations in tambura design. It is said among musicians that "to be between two tambouras is heaven!" because in-tune tamburas produce that ocean of sound which is Nada Brahma. For this reason, the tamburas are the only musical instrument that is actually worshipped or given offerings in India. Pran Nath himself contributed a number of innovations in the design of the tamburas that were built for him and his students by the great instrument maker B. D. Sharma of Rikhi Ram and Sons in Delhi, starting in 1969. Pran Nath was also involved in the design of the Prana Nada, an electronically driven tuning fork that sustains its vibration via magnets, which was built by Terry Riley's technician Chester Wood, with contributions from Bob Bielecki, in three prototypes, circa 1977–82. The tuning fork functioned in a way similar to a sine wave generator, and Pran Nath thought it could be used as a reference tone for tambura tuning, although it is not clear how often this instrument was actually used.[35] I don't want to overemphasize the importance of these innovations for Pran Nath—rather, their importance may lie in the way in which they signal the gradual recognition of the cosmopolitical importance of the tambura by non-Indian musicians and composers such as Young and Riley. Innovations and changes in the design and production and nature of musical instruments in a culture are often important markers of cosmopolitical shifts in the way in which music is understood and valued—the birth of the piano in early modern Europe being one such example.[36]

Reverence for the tambura is not merely symbolic—the instrument is implicated in an ontology of sound that requires us to rethink the exact status of human agency in music. In the summer of 2019, I took a class with the remarkable young Dhrupad vocalist and teacher Chintan Upadhyay. The class followed a traditional call-and-response format in which the teacher sings a phrase and the student tries to repeat it. Further notes and words are added incrementally until, ideally, a whole composition is memorized. Upadhyay would sing with the tamburas, and as a lover of Dhrupad, it was incredibly moving to hear him open up the pathways of a Dhrupad singing practice and then try to follow them. But so precise was Upadhyay's mastery of pitch that there were many times when his voice would actually disappear into the matrix of the tambura's tones and overtones, becoming indistinguishable from it. It was impossible to follow because . . . suddenly he was gone! He was not singing "over" or "accompanied" by the tambura but in/with/of/to it—and his performance/practice consisted of a complicated movement in and out of the tonal matrix, almost like a game of hide-and-seek, modulated by his volume, by the most delicate nuance.

If raga singing may be said to be a vibrational practice in the way that Nina Sun Eidsheim has proposed in her recent book *Sensing Sound*, its essence is contained in the act of being in tune. To become tuneful, in tune, to concentrate in such a way as to get into tune, means to align oneself with the universal physical/mathematical structure that we call harmony. Pran Nath's student W. A. Mathieu, whose treatise *Harmonic Experience: Tonal Harmony from Its Natural Origins to Its Modern Expression* (1997) was dedicated to Pran Nath, expresses this in a wonderfully clear way:

> When you hear a perfect fifth in tune, it is pleasing enough. But when you sing it in tune it glows, and you glow along with it. Sing a perfect fifth over a drone as in example 4.5. Sing the syllable pa, with the vowel wide open, and with the steadiness of the sun at midday. Drop your jaw, relaxing its hinge muscles: relax the back of your tongue as well. (Might as well straighten your spine while you're at it.)
>
> What is this shining in the tonal world? The exercise is to experience the harmonic feeling—howsoever it may be described or thought about—consciously, so that you not only have it but also know that you are having it. The singing part isn't so very difficult. Understanding the harmonic ratio 3:2 isn't so very difficult. The difficulty lies in putting both of these in the same breath, a sung breath of harmonic experience and understanding combined.[37]

This is what Pran Nath did and what he taught. This alignment constitutes a kind of topological vibrational practice, in which the object undergoing transformation is our own body/mind, understood as a multidimensional and thus only partly visible but immanent topological structure. Or, to use a word favored by Pran Nath's student Hennix, the musician and the listeners become toposes—sites of transformation, where the modes of the raga can manifest. Such transformations, which are by definition "cosmological" (since they involve an alignment with principles posited as being universal) and thus also "cosmopolitical" (since the universality is disputed, or rendered in different terms by different communities), have traditionally taken on a spiritual or religious meaning. Saraswati, goddess of knowledge, arts, and music, carries a veena, another gourded string instrument, with her.

"The keeping of the pitches of the raga is perfect concentration of the body," Pran Nath explained. "In this life, this is the example: notes in between the pitches of the raga [shrutis] are like the soul in the body. You can't touch them, can't hold them. So this is a concentration which is a perfect approach to the path to reach that power which is the Lord."[38]

5

In December 1969, to the shock and surprise of his Indian students, Pran Nath moved to America, where he lived, on and off, for the rest of his life. One of his Delhi students, the yoga and sound therapist Shyam Bhatnagar, had moved to America in 1960, where he taught sound therapy at the Satyam Shivam Sundaram ashram in Princeton, New Jersey.[39] Bhatnagar invited Pran Nath to America to teach private students and also to give a course at the New School in New York entitled "Ragas Mantras and Contentment." He gave his first public performance in New York at the Universalist Church on March 7, 1970—and gave subsequent performances at the House of Musical Tradition on St. Mark's Place.

Bhatnagar made the acquaintance of the American minimalist composer La Monte Young at a Bismillah Khan concert at the Lincoln Center in New York on July 14, 1967.[40] Young had an interest in Indian music dating back to the mid-1950s, when he'd heard Ali Akbar Khan's recordings of the ragas Sindh Bhairavi and Pilu, the first full LP-length performances of raga to be released in the West. Young's own music had already displayed a profound interest in subtleties of tone, and the power of the drone, and he had begun singing as a way to explore tone relationships in the mid-1960s with the trailblazing group the Theater of Eternal Music (which included at various times, John Cale, later of the Velvet Underground; the minimalist composers Terry Riley and Tony Conrad; and the "fourth world" trumpeter Jon Hassell). When he heard a tape recording of Pran Nath, courtesy of Bhatnagar in 1967, Young was amazed at his purity of tone and his slow majestic alaps and extraordinarily precise intonation, both important parts of the Kirana style, were at once new but also uncannily similar to Young's own music. "If you take all the gharanas and place them on a line with pitch at one end and rhythm at the other, the Kirana gharana would be at the extreme of the pitch end of the line, and Pandit Pran Nath would be at the extreme pitch end of the Kirana gharana. So the fact that I was so interested in pitch relationships, the fact that I was interested in sustenance and drones, drew me toward Pandit Pran Nath," he states.[41]

The track that fills one side of *The Black Record* (1969), *Map of 49's Dream the Two Systems of Eleven Sets of Galactic Intervals Ornamental Lightyears Tracery*, on which Young sings shifting, raga-like phrases, backed only by a drone produced by a sinewave generator and Marian Zazeela's voice, was "heavily influenced by Pandit Pran Nath," according to Young. "It included drones, and pitch relationships, some of which also exist in Indian classical music. It does not proceed according to the way a raga proceeds. It has very static sections. . . . Raga is very directional, even though it has static elements, whereas a great deal of my music really is static."[42] *Map of 49's Dream* . . . reintroduced melody to the potent, austere sustained tones favored in *The Tortoise, His Dreams and Journeys*, the major work of the early 1960s Theater of Eternal Music ensemble.

In a piece written for the *Village Voice* in April 1970, headlined "The Sound Is God," a euphoric Young expressed his enthusiasm for Pran Nath's intonation: "His singing was the most beautiful I had ever heard."[43] But although Young emphasized Pran Nath's rock-solid foundations in the Kirana vocal style, his interpretation of his teacher was hardly a traditional one. Young had become interested in the tuning system known as just intonation in the early 1960s. The details of this system are very complicated, but the basics are quite easy to grasp. When something sounds "in tune," when there is a feeling of harmony (which is to say, pleasing, even blissful interrelationship), it is because the sounds are connected in a way that obeys the physical laws of sound. As it happens, the pitch relationships can be described mathematically as involving ratios of integers. Most traditional music forms are "in tune" in this sense, and there are many different tuning systems or scales that "sound right." Western music, around the time of the development of the keyboard (in the time of Bach), abandoned such tuning systems in favor of a simplified system. This system is known as Equal Temperament since, rather than obeying the natural harmonies when designing a scale of notes, which have an irregular though discernible order via the above-mentioned ratios of integers, the Western system equalizes them, so that each pitch is the same distance from the next one up or down the scale. This makes it easier to tune a whole group of instruments quickly (making orchestras possible), but means that most classical music since Bach is slightly out of tune.

All of these apparent technicalities have a spiritual meaning, if you consider Pran Nath's belief that to be in tune is to be one with God. The joy that many of us feel when we hear blues, folk, or ethnic music may be connected to the fact that these musics have avoided the fate of classical music and are still in tune. During his studies of Indian music during the 1960s, Young had encountered the work of the ethnomusicologist and scholar of Hinduism Alain Daniélou, who, as early as 1943, had compared Eastern and Western tuning systems and their scientific bases and argued that the West had made a wrong turn, musically.[44] Young sought in his music to find ways to make a Western music that was in tune again. He had worked a great deal on the mathematical bases of harmony and saw, in Pran Nath's mastery of pitches, proof that the spiritual power of raga could be connected to laws of harmony, which were in accordance with the physics of sound as well as the biology of the human body. Just as the precise details of the physiology of the human body underlie and make both possible and potent the practice of asana, so the whole science of sound, from the way sound waves pass through the air to the way the nervous system interprets vibrations caught in the ear, makes music a possible path to ecstasy.

Thus, after praising Pran Nath's perfect intonation and melodic abilities, Young's *Village Voice* article launched into a discussion of the physics of sound and the effect of different sound frequencies, measured in hertz, on neurons in the basilar membranes in the ear. "When a specific set of harmonically related frequencies is continuous or repeated," Young concluded, "as is often the case in my music and Indian music, it could more definitively produce (or simulate) a psychological state that may be reported by the listener since the set of harmonically related frequencies will continuously trigger a specific set of the auditory neurons which in turn will continuously perform the same operation of transmitting a periodic pattern of impulses to the corresponding set of fixed points in the cerebral cortex."[45]

In the early 1970s, Young demonstrated Pran Nath's ability to produce and sustain very precise sound frequencies using an oscilloscope, and to this day, he is as likely to introduce a raga by expressing the tonic in hertz rather than more traditional means. The notion that all aesthetic experience, be it music, film, or drug induced, is a form of programming of the nervous system, was a common one in the 1960s. Inspired by Daniélou, Young applied this idea to raga and its concern for evoking specific moods by use of specific pitch relationships.

Music makes transits. It is a modulation of the local and the global, in the way described by Fernando Zalamea in his *Synthetic Philosophy of Mathematics* (2012). Setting aside, until the next chapter, the profound relationship of music to mathematics, let's keep in mind the way that music, in its remarkable plasticity (meaning that while holding to certain structural principles it can change shape and form), moves between places. Young's interest in Pran Nath, his rearticulation of what he found compelling in Pran Nath's music, both in his words and his musical practice, shows us a transit in the moment of its occurrence. Certain elements are retained, preserved, others disappear, while new elements, here a mathematico-physical description of the principles of raga, emerge. Thus, Pran Nath's music was subject to a cosmopolitical reframing. Nor was this necessarily an unwelcome thing—in fact, it involved reciprocity in that Young's music was also reframed. Pran Nath had a perhaps surprising confidence in the integrity of his sound. In a short article published in the Indian newspaper the *Statesman* on January 8, 1970, he said, concerning his travels to America, "I feel that music is for the soul, and no matter in what country or clime it is presented, a truthful from-the-soul, as it were, rendition is bound to influence totally alien peoples, even in their first confrontation with it."[46]

6

In May 1970, Pran Nath made his first trip to the West Coast, where he met Young's longtime associate Terry Riley. Young, Zazeela, Riley, Catherine Christer Hennix, and others all became formal disciples of Pran Nath, committing themselves to extensive study with him and to providing his material needs in return for lessons. For many years, Pran Nath lived in Young and Zazeela's loft while in New York, and in Riley's loft in San Francisco, while maintaining a house in Delhi, until in the mid-1980s, he moved into his own house in Berkeley, where he remained, for the most part, until his death on June 13, 1996. On both East and West Coasts, members of Sufi communities studied with Pran Nath, but in New York there was also Young and Zazeela's gharana-like circle of downtown musicians, hosted from 1979 to 1985 at the sumptuous Dia Art Foundation–funded Dream House at 6 Harrison Street.

Like many raga singers, he was against the recording of music and placed little emphasis on issuing recordings. Nevertheless, from his time in Delhi in the 1960s onward, students did make recordings of his performances, and in return for large sums of money from foundations approached by Young and Zazeela, Pran Nath finally agreed to make recordings in the 1970s and 1980s. Pran Nath's first release, *Earth Groove*, on Douglas in 1968, was culled from home recordings made in Delhi, without Pran Nath's knowledge. The sound quality is much better on *Ragas Yaman Kalyan and Punjabi Berva* (1972), issued by the French label Shandar, which also issued Young's work during this period. Young's label in the 1980s, Gramavision, put out *Ragas of Morning and Night*, 1968 recordings by Alan Douglas of Ragas Todi and Darbari. In 2003 the Cortical Foundation published *Midnight*, two-hour-long versions of Raga Malkauns recorded in 1971 and 1976, and Riley's Sri Moonshine label has since issued two volumes of *The Raga Cycle*, recorded at the Palace Theater in Paris in 1972.

Similarly, he was against book knowledge of music, insisting that the only way for a student to learn properly was in the traditional call-and-response manner, where the teacher sings and the student attempts to imitate or repeat. "Everything is written fast," he commented. "But raga is slow, deep like ocean and waves coming out, that is music. How many waves can you write, this is a deep thing."[47]

He founded several schools for the study of Indian classical music, including the Kirana School of Indian Classical Music in New York in 1972, where La Monte Young and Marian Zazeela still offer lessons; Surlaya Sangam in Berkeley, California, directed by Joan Allekotte; and the Chisti-Sabri School of Music in Sebastopol, California, where Shabda Kahn, now the pir of the Sufi Ruhaniat International, teaches. "He ordered us to make his own school," Young recalls, "the Kirana School for Indian Classical Music; and then he ordered us to teach. And when I said, 'No, Guruji, I'm not ready,' he said, 'You have to do as I say, it's not up to you.'"[48] Pran Nath made a similar demand of Riley, and Riley, Young, and Zazeela have continued teaching Kirana-style Indian classical vocal to this day. Conversely, Pran Nath was artist in residence at the University of California at San Diego in 1973, and a visiting professor of music at Mills College in Oakland from 1973 to 1984.

Pran Nath told his disciples that music was the best form of spiritual practice, since it was such a delightful practice and gave so much pleasure. Nevertheless, his own sadhana was an exacting one. According to Terry Riley,

> Pran Nath always rose very early, between four and five in the morning, to begin his practice. He was around 51 years old when I met him, but he still practiced for 4 or 5 hours every morning, always the same ragas. Just like someone who was polishing their pots, he went over and over again the details of these fine ragas. As a student, I would sit with him and observe his practice—how he approached the ragas and how he took care of his voice. He always said, "I take care of my voice like a mother takes care of her baby."[49]

In his prime years as a musician in Delhi in the 1950s, Pran Nath could be found late at night practicing a midnight raga against a favored wall of one of the mosques. At other times, he would practice, immersed up to his waist in a river, building up the strength of his breath. He would tie a string to the top of his head late at night while practicing, so that if his head dropped and he began to fall into sleep, the string would jerk him back into full consciousness. According to La Monte Young and Marian Zazeela, he even had a repertoire of dishes (nonvegetarian, lots of butter) that he felt supported his voice. He was fully devoted to music and sought to give his students a taste at least of what such devotion meant.

During this period, Young, Zazeela, and Riley, and later the trumpeter Jon Hassell, accompanied Pran Nath on his return trips to India, often staying for extended periods of time to study music at a temple in Dehra Dun, where Pran Nath was temple musician to Swami Narayan Giriji, the former temple keeper at Tapkeshwar. "We'd come to the temple early in the morning," recalls Hassell, "and Swamiji would be there. I remember playing on the roof for him. He came up and sat and listened to me, with these brilliant eyes shining and smiling, seeing what I was doing on the trumpet. We would go to the market, buy two ladu [balls of hashish and almond paste] and listen to the children sing, the arti bells clapping, the swallows overhead, the muezzin singing from the minaret nearby. I mean, it was total ecstasy!"[50]

These trips gradually evolved into a yearly ritual, which has continued under the guidance of Riley and the West Coast Sufi teacher Shabda Kahn, who still take groups each year to visit Pran Nath's sacred places. There, they would study with Kirana masters like Mashkor Ali Khan, a blood relative of Abdul Wahid Khan, who commands a vast knowledge of ragas and a fiery vocal technique.

Young, Zazeela, and Riley's commitment to Pran Nath involved more than a superficial absorption of a few Indian mannerisms. When Pran Nath lived in Young and Zazeela's loft, the New York night owls were typically required to rise at 3 a.m. each day to prepare tea for their teacher, who slept at the other end of the loft. He would then perform his riaz (practice) and give them a lesson—if he chose to.

"He was the head of the household," recalls Young. "We were not allowed to have friends. We had to give up everything—rarely did we even get to visit our parents. He was very protective of us and extremely possessive of us. But we got the reward. The reward is, if you make the guru happy, then you get the lessons."[51]

Much of the rest of the day would be spent taking care of his financial affairs, booking students and concerts, and raising money for dowries so that his three daughters in India could get married. Riley, Young, and Zazeela all sacrificed their own careers while serving Guruji (as he was affectionately known), alienating patrons who thought they should be focusing on their own work. In a 1976 interview, Riley noted that "actually, I've had a lot of criticism because of my studies with him. People seem to be afraid of a cultural invasion, afraid their artists are going to lose their integrity and go scampering off after some charlatan.... Whereas, what studying with Pandit Pran Nath has done is made me go deeper into the thing I was already doing to try to make it more and more profound."[52]

The effect of study with Pran Nath on Young's and Riley's work is difficult to measure since, when they first met their teacher, both were already in their thirties with major works behind them. Young speaks of Pran Nath's use of badhat, "a magical formula for the organic unfolding of the alap improvisations,"[53] as a crucial influence on post-1970 versions of *The Well-Tuned Piano*, generally understood as Young's masterwork. It's easy to say "influence," but it should be understood that *The Well-Tuned Piano* is a five-and-a-half-hour piece featuring a just intonation–tuned piano and densely composed but also improvised clouds of harmonics that open up anew with every performance of the remarkable work. For some people, it's the most remarkable piece of music created in the last sixty years. I have felt that way at times. I once listened to the whole piece twice on an overnight bus journey from Toronto to New York in the middle of one of the most intense snowstorms the region had seen in many years. I remember emerging from the bus in New York, knee deep in snow, sparkling inside and out, filled with awe and gratitude.

After meeting Pran Nath in 1970, Riley had his keyboards retuned to just intonation pitches, which, along with gorgeous badhat-like melodic unfoldings, were used in works such as *Shri Camel*. Raga-like modal structures also feature prominently in several keyboard works from that period, notably *Persian Surgery Dervishes* and *Descending Moonshine Dervishes*. Indeed, both Young and Riley's keyboard/piano works from the 1970s surf on a seemingly infinite ocean of melodic variation that is sustained by badhat.

Pran Nath's emphasis on precision of tone, viewed through the prism of Young's own passion for just intonation made possible a new synthesis of Eastern and Western musical systems. This synthesis can be heard to great effect on *The Tamburas of Pandit Pran Nath* (2001): a single 77-minute recording of a drone created by Young and Zazeela on two of the tamburas that Pran Nath himself designed, static but sparkling with the natural overtones that correctly tuned tamburas produce. The tuning and playing of the tamburas is traditional, but where in Indian music the tamburas usually accompany a vocal or instrumental recital, here their hypnotic sound becomes the sole object of focus, which can be heard simultaneously as a sustained-tone minimalist artifact, as a high-resolution homage to one of the fundamental building blocks of Hindustani music—and as a tool for musical practice, a cousin to the electronic "shruti boxes" that are sometimes used by Indian singers to simulate the tambura sound.

Both Young and Riley have performed vocal pieces that emerge out of the Hindustani vocal tradition. Riley's most clearly Pran Nath–inspired piece is *Songs for the Ten Voices of the Two Prophets* (1983), an impressive song cycle, with Riley displaying his raga moves over two Prophet synthesizers. With Young, there is the Just Alap Raga Ensemble, formed in 2002, featuring Young, Zazeela, and Jung Hee Choi on vocals, over the tamburas recording, and with tabla accompaniment.

7

While a number of high-profile students of Pran Nath became his formal disciples, there were others who avoided becoming so closely entangled with his circle. "I never became a disciple," recalls Henry Flynt, the reclusive composer and violinist whose sound became an important influence on the contemporary experimental folk scene, "because the culture of the apprentice and the master, that kind of authority . . . I have a problem with that. I am culturally extremely American. It was all I could do to take private lessons and behave myself—that already tested my ability to submit to somebody else's regimen."[54] This distance may have given Flynt the freedom to produce the track "You Are My Everlovin,'" an explosive fiddle rendering of Raga Tilang, performed over a tape of Christer Hennix on tambura. Several tracks on the collection *Graduation* also reflect his raga studies, including the title track, "a hillbilly response to the low-and-slow vocals of Pran Nath."

Although he formulated his notion of "new American Ethnic Music" in the early 1960s after abandoning a Harvard education for John Coltrane and country blues, Flynt's cosmically inclusive ethnic music (he describes his "Lonesome Train Dreams" as "contemporary cowboy raga over tonic pedal-point harmony and a polymetric rhythm riff") clearly integrated his studies with Pran Nath. Flynt wrote a poignant essay "On Pandit Pran Nath," circa 1996–2002, in which he reflects on the surprise of encountering Pran Nath and his mastery of music. For Flynt, who in his philosophical work of the 1960s had called for an end to art, at least in the form practiced by Eurocentric modernism, Pran Nath embodied a different path that aesthetic practice could have taken—one that Flynt compared and connected to a related practice that he saw emerging from the Black radical tradition. He writes:

Pandit Pran Nath was more fully realized than blues musicians—no less honor to them—but he had an advantage of context. He did not have to practice an "illicit" music while situated socially below a hostile majority. (Although his parents threw him out at 13 for wanting to be a musician.) He was "at home," in his own country, his own tradition, and the musical vocation entailed a comprehensive "yogic" discipline which is not expected in the West. The European modernist project of annulling tradition was not an issue in his landscape.

All the same, he departed the expected Hindustani practice to the point where he was alone (and not universally beloved) in his originality.

Guruji went to strange emotional places, already familiar in his native culture, which the West would call surrealistic or like an inexplicable dream. But instead of being odd in an estranging way, it involved you; he forcibly confronted you with your own appreciation of emotion, poignancy, and exaltation. It took you into yourself and showed you that you have sensibilities, and nobility, you did not know about.

A sensibility of poignancy and exaltation. Other Hindustani singers are great entertainers. Guruji's job description was: to awaken your true self. The most remarkable thing is that he chose the path of probing people emotionally, reaching them in an earthy and basic way and yet with an underlying strategy of the highest intelligence. He channeled his incredible technique into emotional confrontation, into involving us emotionally.[55]

Flynt's essay is intriguing because in it he seeks an existential and secular understanding of the power of Pran Nath's singing, both in performance and as a teacher. He rejects or at least brackets the religious framing of this power that he (rightly) believes Pran Nath would have given—locating the power in a kind of "affective athleticism" similar to that described by Antonin Artaud in his work on the theater of cruelty. Perhaps unlike Artaud however, Flynt saw in Pran Nath's practice an education in sensibilities, nobility, and dignity—valuable human potentials that were mostly lost within the milieu of the (white) American avant-garde but also within the much broader arc of European civilization and culture and its configurations of the category of aesthetics, including in it the category of music. Pran Nath's singing of a raga revealed this loss in a direct way, and, through negating and refuting the universality of European values, indicated the possibility of new kinds of valuation and praxis—post-art modalities that Flynt called "brend" or "veramusement" at different points.

Musically speaking, there are some similarities between Flynt's ideas and fellow Pran Nath nondisciple Jon Hassell's fourth world music. Flynt speaks of the importance of the meend, a sliding movement between the notes that Pran Nath specialized in. Flynt describes this form of glissando as "that dying cow sound," and he acknowledges it as a key component in much of the music he loves, from US country pedal steel and Robert Johnson's bottleneck guitar blues, to Coltrane's shenai-like runs on the soprano saxophone.

This in turn became one of Jon Hassell's trumpet signatures. "I had to find a way to make the meend," Hassell recalls, "by using my lips as a secondary voice, transferring the vibration point from the vocal fold to the lips and thinking of it as a conch sound, blowing primitively into it and making the pitches with just the lips and the resonating chamber."[56] Hassell had joined Young's Theater of Eternal Music in the late 1960s, after studying with Karlheinz Stockhausen at Darmstadt and playing on Riley's original recording of *In C*. He remembers a significant moment prior to a performance in Rome in the early 1970s: "I was warming up in the space one day, playing some pattern, and Guruji picked it up and started singing it and running rings around it and I thought, why am I not studying with this man?"[57]

The notion of fourth world music coalesced as Hassell discovered the depth and breadth of Pran Nath's approach to music, one that could incorporate many different musical forms within the vast harmonic matrix of the well-tuned tambura, and the melodic line that the individual raga weaves through the matrix. Study with Pran Nath opened Hassell to "a microworld of connections. It allowed me to see African and African American music, every music through the lens of that shape making ability."[58] The sequence of records Hassell issued in the late 1970s and early 1980s—beginning with *Vernal Equinox* (1977), and passing through *Fourth World Music*, volume 1, *Possible Musics* (1980, recorded with Brian Eno), *Fourth World Music*, volume 2, *Dream Theory in Malaya* (1981), and *Aka/Darbari/Java: Magic Realism* (1983)—all explore the common melodic and rhythmic ground between different global musical traditions, with Hassell's trumpet usually playing over a synthesized drone or repeated motif. Of these records, *Vernal Equinox* remains the closest to Pran Nath in its leisurely alap-like trumpet improvisations over warm electronic drones and field recordings, and to me the most compelling of all Hassell's work, foregrounding the music's emergence from a kind of tonal glow in a way that is similar to Riley's *Shri Camel*, released the same year.

Looked at retrospectively, fourth world music clearly owes a huge debt to Miles Davis's work from his late-1960s *Bitches Brew* through to his temporary retirement in 1976. Not only is the sound trumpet-led and improvisatory, but the synthesis of musics from across the world, incorporating a framework of electronics and collage previously set out by Stockhausen in works such as *Hymnen*, had been achieved by Miles already in the early 1970s—indeed, Miles had employed a sitar player as well as the percussionist/tabla player Badal Roy, who later also worked with Hassell. The question and/or problem of musical tropism on a planetary scale was an important one in the 1970s, and one that generated many responses across the world as musicians sought to reconcile tradition with modern electronics and nonlocal musical techniques, forms, and practices to local situations. In recent years, critics have accused Hassell of cultural appropriation in his working with non-Western musics and musicians.[59] While Hassell variably emphasized the imaginary nature of the local site in which fourth world music occurred ("I wanted the mental and geographical landscapes to be more indeterminate—not Indonesia, not Africa, not this or that. I thought I was more successful in trying to create something that *could have* existed if things were in an imaginary culture, growing up in an imaginary place with this imaginary music"),[60] what I find still compelling in Hassell's music is the strong sense of a responsive and relational musical path created in the act of wandering and wondering. Pran Nath himself clearly had no time for fusion or synthesizers or transcultural collaboration in the music itself. The invocation of nature and cosmopolitical principles (also there in fact in Hassell's work, such as the ocean sound on *Vernal Equinox*'s "Toucan Ocean" or the insect sounds of "Caracas Night September 11, 1975" on the same record) suggests a different kind of rapprochement of the global and the local from that of what we now know as "world music"—a speculative interest in first principles, which could be emergent anywhere on the planet, and what might happen if one stayed true to them, honored them. It is not necessary that one needs to be ethnically or racially connected to the geographical or cultural origin of such first principles, in order that one might learn them, value them, or use them in one's work. Though, of course, that origin needs to be acknowledged. Pran Nath understood this—it was the basis of his work as a teacher. The beauty of *Vernal Equinox*, now nearly fifty years old, speaks to the success of his method.

Many of these issues were also explored by the trumpet player Don Cherry—another pioneering figure who developed a multicultural approach to musical improvisation rooted in jazz, contemporaneously with Miles Davis. Cherry is said to have taken a few lessons with Pran Nath, probably in New York, during one of Pran Nath's residencies there in the mid-1970s. Cherry met Pran Nath in Sweden, which Pran Nath visited for a week in February 1971, en route between America and India, and where he gave concerts at the Moderna Museet and Uppsala University. Terry Riley recalls Cherry driving him and Pran Nath from Stockholm to Uppsala and back—but no lessons.[61] At this time Cherry, together with his partner, the artist Moki Cherry, were engaged in their communal experiment in art/music/living in a schoolhouse in Tagarp in rural Sweden.[62] However, Cherry's interest in and practice of "collage music" and improvisation occuring between different global musical traditions, including Indian classical music, dates back to at least 1968, when Cherry gave a series of workshops to the ABF ("Workers Educational Association") in Stockholm, which included Indian musicians and musical principles.[63] Cherry is said to have taken lessons with Pandit Ram Narayan, the great sarangi player, whom he likely met through Narayan's Swedish student Hans Isgren, and in Mumbai in 1976, with Ustad Zia Moinuddin Dagar, the master of the rudra vina, whom he was introduced to by the tabla player Bengt Berger, a student of the Dagars.[64]

Virtually all of Pran Nath's musician students made contact with their teacher through association with Young, Zazeela, or Riley. An exception is Charlemagne Palestine, who met Pran Nath in New York when he was twenty, almost immediately after Pran Nath's arrival in America. "i arrived one late morningg,, , and met with him,, and i told him that i had begun in childhood as a singer in synagogue and he asked me to sing a little for him from that tradition,, ,and he was veryyy movedd by myy Chazan (sacred jewish singer) timbres and then proposed that I sing immediatelyyy then the SA with him, which i did and we began our first sa, re, ga, ma, pa session togetherrrr!! and i think he was a bit amazed at how quickly I was able to sounddddd in the righttt wayyy!!"[65] It turns out that even email can vibrate when it's Palestine who's writing it.

Palestine studied with Pran Nath briefly, without becoming a disciple. For Palestine, who had begun his life in music singing in New York synagogues as a child, Pran Nath provided a link between the explosive world of the avant-garde and a lost sense of tradition. "I was brought up with that notion of genius: that you do something that nobody else did and you try not even to do what you did after awhile otherwise you're already finished. Which is the contrary of the Oriental tradition where you make more and more perfect the tradition which goes from generation to generation."[66]

Palestine points out that Pran Nath succeeded in bringing together Young's Mormon roots, Riley's Irish Catholic roots, and his own Jewish background. "At that time we were all searching for a kind of identity. Our own born tribal units had disintegrated into an American pablum, and so it was hard to say who you were if you were American. What his being there helped me to feel was that I was continuing the chant of the synagogue, and that we were all part of some larger force that was coming of age, that would then create a new kind of world. His being there and attracting so many people and his coming from such an ancient culture was a very powerful social force."[67]

Although known mostly for his instrumental works, Palestine's vocal pieces like *Karenina* (1997) and *Hommage à Faquir Pandit Pran Nath* (1997) feature a kind of free alap modal improvisation that recalls both Pran Nath and Abdul Wahid Khan's heart-tearing gravitas and that curving meend sound. Palestine's search for what he calls "the golden sound" was stimulated by Pran Nath's emphasis on teaching the sa, the tonic note in a raga scale. Palestine connects works like the stunning 1988 church organ drone piece *Schlingen-Blangen* to Pran Nath's sa: "It's not sung, it's sung by an enormous instrument, but it's a way of humming in space." Having started out as a singer, the singing of Pran Nath, along with the synagogue singers of his youth, provided the model for a perfect sound: "The pure voice without anything else is the most intimate and expressive sound that a being can make. If it's an animal, it's their screech, or the bark of a dog. For me there's nothing more intimate, and the essence of the animal or the being is the voice. Even though I did many things that were not the voice. But I started with the voice. And he was the voice."[68]

Palestine also collaborated in the early 1970s with another of Pran Nath's students, the dancer, choreographer, and visual artist Simone Forti—indeed, Palestine and Forti met in California while trying to arrange a concert for Pran Nath. Forti was/is one of the most important figures in contemporary dance. She studied with Anna Halprin in California from 1955 to 1959 (La Monte Young and Terry Riley provided the music for Halprin's workshop in 1959), and after moving to New York, presented an evening of seminal dance pieces as part of the now famous nights curated by Young and Yoko Ono at Ono's loft on Chambers Street in 1960–61. Her works of the 1960s include a number of pieces in which a musical or vocal performance is presented as a dance, and Forti also provided drone-based sounds for performances of other dancer/choreographers such as Trisha Brown. Forti took several singing classes with Pran Nath in 1970 in New York via La Monte Young, but she was not comfortable with the guru/disciple relationship and did not pursue further studies. However, the impact of Pran Nath was evident in a series of improvisations she undertook with Palestine. The improvisations that unfolded in a large raw studio space (dubbed "the temple" by them) at the then new California Institute for the Arts in 1970–71 were named "Illuminations."

In her essential text *Handbook in Motion* (1974), Forti defines dance in relation to music in the following terms. Dance is "a state of polarization into harmonic channels along which motor energy pleasurably flows. When I'm dancing I am moved by that mysterious response to the music."[69] In the improvisations that constitute *Illuminations*, Palestine would play various musical instruments and sing, while Forti would meditate and move in circles, exploring centrifugal and centripetal forces while on occasion also singing.

> An important element that Charlemagne and I had in common was that we had both worked for a short time with Pran Nath. This gave us a clear, common point of reference—an approach that begins with perfecting a pitch until it is a pure and constantly coherent vibration. In order to arrive at a pure vibration one must develop the ability to sustain the necessary balance of the physical elements involved. And in order to do this, a centering, a state of calm receptivity, is necessary. Once a pure pitch is established as a fine point of dynamic balance, its harmonics become clearly manifest.
>
> Pran Nath has compared the state of mind at the time of singing to the flame of a candle. If there is any disturbance in the mind or in the environment, the flame will flicker. I imagine he is speaking in terms of protecting the flame from disturbance. But the image helps me understand something else which I feel must be related. When I achieve precisely regular intonation of balance shifts, any kind of freeze passing through my field of consciousness will touch off my center of balance, and variations of form will reverberate as shadows of that breeze. When Charlemagne and I work together he centers through pitch and I center through balance. And his sound and my movement form part of each other's effective environment, which gives motion to our equilibriums.
>
> ... Sometimes, having achieved a state of balance, I would lift my eyes up and to the right as if saying hello. The sudden asymmetry would take me by surprise and the resultant internal careening of my center seemed to radiate into an outburst of a kind of song whose melody was made of movement. And I would find myself weaving movement melodies charged with stories the body holds.[70]

The analogy or relationship between musical harmony and the balance of the dancer is a striking one—with Forti's circular movements through space articulating the vibratory repetition of the sonic drone. Unlike the stasis of much of Young's music, Forti, who was also beginning her studies of tai chi at that time in California, focuses not on the consistency of tone that Pran Nath emphasized but on the tension between that consistency (and repetition) and the fluctuations that throw both dancer and sound off balance, setting in motion a countermovement that restores balance via a creative line of flight—whether in tone or in the movement of the body. In what follows in this book concerning tuning systems and mathematico-musical structure, no matter how teleological or targeted the music is, this losing and regaining of balance seems essential to me as part of the pathos and practice of music.

Forti's response to Pran Nath constitutes a wonderful critique of a static concept of pure or perfect tone, which risks becoming a rigid or lifeless tone, and presumably a kind of parody of the One or of a monistic philosophy. The yogi sits lifeless, completely calm in a state of samadhi, as the story goes, until he (it usually is he) feels a rat gnawing at his hair or clothes and is forced to leave the state of samadhi to swat the mischievous rodent. Perfect tone is rather a state of balance or equilibrium that includes within it all the contingent shades and distortions of finitude, which it incorporates and absorbs into its own shapes, geometries, and movements. The raga singer does not sing one note forever; the performance is contingent, and in leaning in the direction of that which is "not yet in tune," the performance and composition unfold, full of drama and small surprises. Even the tambura—which is played only on four open strings, three pitches—is in fact subject to the drama and contingency of the musician who uses his or her fingers to pluck the strings of the instrument, rhythmically yet still subject to a certain contingency that results in a shifting constellation of partials and overtones. La Monte Young's Dream House compositions of recent years—composed and performed on a synthesizer such that a sustained combination of tones saturates the room, producing standing waves of overtones and pitch combinations—actually obtain much of their interest from the contingency that the listener in the room introduces by raising or lowering their head so that a slightly different space in the tonal grid is occupied by the ears. More remarkably, when I've visited the Dream House with my kids, their joy in the piece consists in running around the room. As they do so, their movement perturbs the tonal grid in the room in intriguing ways, almost as if one could sense their bodies and movements in the movement of the sound and air in the room.

Another figure who made his own way was Yoshi Wada—a Japanese-born artist and musician who moved to New York in the 1960s and became involved with the Fluxus group—through which he met La Monte Young and later Pandit Pran Nath. "La Monte was taking care of Pandit Pran Nath," recalled Wada when I met him in January 2019.

> He came to New York to teach and I got to know him in the early 1970s. He did concerts. Whenever he came to New York, I saw him and started taking private lessons which I felt that was the only way I could get into singing: one to one, oral, traditional teaching. It was great. I would get up very early, 5 a.m., and practice singing for at least one hour... of

course I was working and I had to go to work. But I was a much stronger disciplined younger guy so I was able to do it. It was a great time."[71]

Wada remains a relatively uncelebrated figure in part because his life in music was built around a practice, music as an action, a mode of living, rather than practice as preparation for performances or recordings. In fact, he has issued very few recordings—and those that do exist are often recordings of installation pieces. Wada's practice was multivalent, including the building of pipe-based instruments such as his amazing "earth horns"; his male choir from the 1970s, Modal Improvisation; and his own vocal improvisations. His first issued recording, *Lament for the Rise and Fall of the Elephantine Crocodile* (1982), emerged out of a three-day session that Wada spent in an empty swimming pool in Buffalo, New York, sounding out the space with his voice and pipe organs. The echoes and reverberations the pool walls create turn Wada's actions into a vibrational funhouse—a practice of freedom that remains "modal" and rooted in Pran Nath's ideas about raga, but new, unprecedented even, as if we are listening in to someone practicing, testing the walls of reality itself.

Although musicians who encountered him continue to sing his praises, opinions vary as to what Pran Nath thought of his students' nonraga musical activities. A man of few words, with no time for politeness or other formalities, Pran Nath generally supported his students' activities, without actually commenting on them. Catherine Christer Hennix, whose work with Pran Nath I will discuss in the next chapter, says, "In the sense that he didn't have anything to say about it, that was his way of talking about it. I think he was quite distressed that we tried to do what we did. I remember La Monte playing him John Coltrane and he was very taken with him, he could feel the enormous soul behind Coltrane's music. But I don't think he felt we were up to Coltrane's level. He thought probably we should have practiced tuning the tambura and singing our scales instead of doing our own adventures."[72] Although he was full of encouragement for Riley, who had contemplated giving up his own composition in order to practice raga full-time, most of his words of praise were fleeting. At the premiere of *The Well-Tuned Piano* in Italy in 1974, he commented that Young had taken the traditional instrument of Europe and transformed it before their eyes. When Jon Hassell played him "Charm"—his take on Raga Tilang, from *Possible Musics*, volume 1—he simply said, "It was good." "That was a big moment for me," says Hassell. "That he could actually see how something could be taken and how his art could be absorbed and translated in another way. He was certainly expansive enough to understand how things grow and don't stay static. For him, forward and backward were the same. There was no avant-garde."[73]

8

It's difficult to talk about Pran Nath today without considering his involvement in the Dream House, a Dia Art Foundation–funded installation/performance space in the spectacular Mercantile Exchange building at 6 Harrison Street in Tribeca, New York, created by La Monte Young and Marian Zazeela, that was operative from 1979 to 1985. As Alexander Keefe has observed, the Dream House was much more than a venue—it was intended as an artwork in its own right on the scale of other Dia Art Foundation–funded locational works such as "Donald Judd's Marfa Project, James Turrell's Roden Crater and Walter De Maria's Lightning Field."[74] A multilevel space with state of the art sound for Young's drone works and piano performances, and featuring Zazeela's psychedelic light/space sculptures, the venue also hosted performances and singing classes by Pran Nath, during the two-month periods he visited most years.[75] When Pran Nath would sing on the former trading floor, large Persian carpets were rented for the occasion. The Dream House was many things, and one of those things was a realization of the dream of a sonic shrine that Young had written about in his 1970 *Village Voice* piece about Pran Nath. The Dream House served as a modernist materialization of Pran Nath's devotion to "sound as God," and conversely Pran Nath also served as a court musician in the neo-Orientalist fantasia of the Dream House, funded by Heiner Friedrich and Philippa de Menil and the Dia Art Foundation's oil money. Along with the "Raga Cycle" performances that Pran Nath gave, usually in May and June, at the Dream House, he also performed at least twice at the Rothko Chapel in Houston, Texas.[76] Likely, this caused some resentment among other New York musicians and composers who had no access to the space for their own performances or this extraordinary level of funding and support. Temporary autonomous zone or a hallucination of capital? Perhaps both.

Pran Nath was not without his detractors, even in the milieu of the downtown New York art scene. According to Henry Flynt, John Cale quipped that it was Pran Nath who should be studying with Young, so that he could learn his "hard sound"—in other words, the power of the amplified drone.[77] When I first began researching Pran Nath, several musicians and composers who wished to remain anonymous cautioned me about not buying into the (to them) hyperbolic accounts of Pran Nath that Young and others offered, including the repeated and likely pointless claim that Pran Nath was the "world's greatest musician." There were stories about his love of Johnnie Walker Black Label and meat—which clashed with other accounts in which he was described as (nearly) vegetarian and abstaining from alcohol.

And it was repeatedly pointed out that Pran Nath was not in fact a well-known figure in India. The stories were intended to dissipate the discourse of the holy man/guru that sometimes seemed to form an Orientalist fog around the singer—especially in the opulent surroundings of the Dream House, and in the years after Pran Nath's heart attack (1978) when his singing abilities were clearly diminished.

This Orientalist fog surrounded a number of Asian men and women who traveled to America from the 1960s on, to be received as holy men or gurus or spiritual teachers by middle-class, often white seekers who turned religion into a kind of consumer item. Pran Nath was evidently very aware of this when asked, in a 1989 interview, what he had found in America, he responded "The people of this country are great Customers!"[78] This fog in the end always serves as a legitimation of disciplinary power. There was also some settling of scores going on. This is what Jeremy Grimshaw, in his recent book on Young, refers to as "the ideology of the drone."[79] Grimshaw summarizes the now well-known dispute between Young and Conrad and Cale as to the ownership of the recordings of their 1960s ensemble, the Theater of Eternal Music. I will discuss this dispute in detail in the next chapter in relation to Catherine Christer Hennix. Its relevance here is that some have argued or implied that Pran Nath served chiefly as a kind of fetish object (and thus ideologeme) to legitimate Young's desire to be received as a master or guru—and, by implication, that Pran Nath's music had little value in itself, especially given that his work was little known or respected by Indian musicians with an international profile. While I think that critique is worth thinking about (it more or less corresponds to a Saidian analysis of Pran Nath as an Orientalist figure who is put at the service of imperialist musicological fantasies), it also feels inadequate to me, in that it fails to give an account of what it was that Pran Nath actually believed about music, and what in his attitude toward music those he encountered, wherever they were geographically located, found valuable—and how the dissemination of his work and ideas transformed those people. While the response of his Indian musical peers is significant, it does not constitute a definitive assessment of Pran Nath—and it ignores the fractured nature of the Indian classical music scene, and the divergent goals and practices that one might find even within the Kirana gharana. Indeed, the breach is already there in the trajectories of the enormously popular Abdul Karim Khan and the hermetic praxis of Abdul Wahid Khan—not to mention the paradoxes that surround Karim Khan's celebrated daughter, the singer Hirabai Barodekar, a true star of stage and screen who was also a devoted student of Wahid Khan's. Not to mention that Pran Nath's "errancy"—what if we called it "agency" instead?—might itself be valuable in ways that would be unlikely to be authenticated by musicians who stayed within a normative or even commercialized version of Indian classical music. Nor does it address what actually concerns me the most: what we might still learn from him today and in the future, what remains unlearned, unrecognized, untimely, and perhaps true to the errancy, the line of flight, happening somewhere between India, Europe, and America, that he made happen. I maintain that if there is a mysticism in Pran Nath it was that "mysticism of music, word and sound" that Hazrat Inayat Khan had talked of—and this mysticism was immanent to the vibrational practice of making music, and singing, as Pran Nath understood it.

Still, anyone hearing Pran Nath perform after 1978 would have experienced only a shadow of his former powers since he suffered a heart attack in that year and developed Parkinson's disease during the following decade. Even in his prime, Pran Nath was an unorthodox performer, often dwelling on the first three notes of a raga for fifteen minutes or more. "Sometimes," recalls Riley, "in the middle of the raga he would suddenly stop and start singing another raga in a performance and it would feel fine. He would maybe sing one tone that would remind him of that other raga and he'd get so inspired he'd just go off into that."[80]

Pran Nath himself cared little about building a public reputation: in India, he snubbed critics and patrons, insulted master musicians during their performances, and had an aversion to recording and radio work. Even in America, throwing in his lot with Young and the New York avant-garde or the California Sufis was hardly a guaranteed road to fame and fortune. Aside from one track recorded with the Kronos Quartet in 1993 ("Aba Kee Tayk Hamaree"/"It Is My Turn, Oh Lord," from *Short Stories*), there were no collaborations with Western artists, no "fusion" experiments, no compromises. He didn't care.

According to Charlemagne Palestine, Pran Nath was attracted to the American avant-garde because "he also was out of his culture, he rarely went home, he preferred to be in the West. As we were tormented by being a lost culture looking for our roots, he was tormented, being from a culture with enormous roots that he could no longer live in socially, as a normal member."[81] But despite Pran Nath's reported fondness for Chivas Regal, watching television, and (to the chagrin of his minimalist students) classical symphonic music, he was not unduly impressed with the West either. Hennix recalls, "The only time I remember he was enthusiastic, we were in San Francisco. He liked to watch TV, and we were watching a program about whales. He heard the whales sing and he started to cry. That was his most profound spiritual experience of the Western world."[82]

Pran Nath's relationship with the minimalists can be seen as part of a broader history of cultural exchange between East and West that blossomed in the twentieth century. Debussy began the century taking inspiration from Balinese gamelan; while in America a variety of composers, including Charles Ives, Henry Cowell, and Harry Partch, explored and appropriated different elements of Indian and other Asian musics. As performers like Ali Akbar Khan and Ravi Shankar made their first tours of the United States and Europe in the mid-1950s, it became possible for westerners to study with them: Shankar, for example, performed at one of Stockhausen's 1957 Darmstadt seminars. The most famous (and yet often dismissed) figure for such cross-cultural musical explorations, Yehudi Menuhin, the American classical violinist, began his association with Shankar in Delhi in 1952.[83]

For the post-Cage generation—who had already taken the leap beyond notated composition into the uncharted worlds of improvisation, ambient sound, chance operations, and systems—Asian classical music offered a way of reconciling the structural concerns of the Western classical tradition with the freedom of improvisation. Nearly all of the minimalists actually studied with major figures in Asian music traditions in the late 1960s and early 1970s: Young, Riley, and Palestine with Pran Nath; Philip Glass with Ravi Shankar and the tabla maestro Alla Rakha; Steve Reich, Palestine, and Ingram Marshall with Indonesian gamelan ensembles.

This is the context in which Pran Nath performed internationally in the 1970s—often accompanied by Young and Zazeela on tamburas, and often at events where Young was performing. These events included the Nuits des Fondation Maeght (1970), the 20th Olympic Games (Munich, 1972), documenta 5 (Kassel, 1972), Colloquium on Traditional Modes of Contemplation and Action (Houston, 1973), Contemporanea Festival (Rome, 1973), East-West Music Festival (Rome-Macerata, 1974), the 8th Iran Festival of the Arts (Shiraz, 1974), the Metamusik Festival (Bonn, 1976), and so on.[84] The organizers of many of these often interdisciplinary events consciously worked toward presenting Asian music (and other) traditions alongside European and American avant-garde experimentation, and music emerging from the Black radical tradition—as a kind of countercultural synthesis of global "ways of knowing" that extended beyond music (or art) in the direction of an embodied, universal spirituality or "general intellect" (Marx). Similar movements were happening in literature and in visual arts and film—part of an emerging institutional critique of Eurocentricity in the curation of culture, even while that curation was still usually dominated by people of European descent. While such gestures were of course often self-serving (the world of music offered up via festivals as an easily consumed smorgasbord for a still mostly white European and American countercultural middle class) and ripe for misunderstanding (the audience applauding the musicians' tuning up, mistaking it for a performance; the decontextualization of musical practices whose meaning is contained in the ways in which they are embedded in the life of a particular community, not in performances made on a stage for a paying audience)—they also performed necessary and complex work in opening up (or amplifying) a discussion concerning musical, aesthetic, and political value that continues today. And while cosmopolitanism, musical or otherwise, is often associated with empire, the meetings and events it engenders have on occasion had real significance in the history of music—and a fugitive status in which many things may be passed on or shared, outside of the dominant frameworks of imperial culture in which such events occur.[85]

In these terms, Pran Nath's performances at the 8th Iran Festival of the Arts in Shiraz, in 1974, are of particular interest. The festival itself, which ran from 1967 to 1977, is generally understood today as a showcase for the Pahlavi regime (which came to an end with the Islamic Revolution of 1978) and its Occidentalism—a presentation of European and American avant-garde artists, including John Cage and Merce Cunningham, Karlheinz Stockhausen, and Robert Wilson, along with Persian artists, and also pan-Asian and African perspectives, emphasizing Islamic performing artists. The festival events often occurred at spectacular cultural sites around Shiraz, such as the ruins of Persepolis, the capital of the Achaemenid Empire, where Iannis Xenakis famously presented his *Polytope de Persépolis* during the 1971 festival.[86] Indian musicians, including Vilayat Khan (1967), Bismillah Khan (1968), Shiv Kumar Sharma (1969), Ravi Shankar (1970, 1976), and Ram Narayan (1975) performed.[87] Pran Nath gave two performances in 1974, accompanied by Young and Zazeela on tamburas, in a garden at the tomb of the Sufi saint and poet Hafez (1315–1390). Apparently Pran Nath sang a Persian ghazal by Hafez at one of the events, impressing the largely Iranian audience, who generally did not take kindly to the attempts of Indian performers to play Persian music.[88] Despite the complex geopolitics of the festival—the Occidentalism; the support by and for the Shah's regime; the belated attempts at convening a group of nonaligned countries, including Iran, Indonesia, India, and so on—the question remains as to what it meant to Pran Nath himself to perform at this festival. In a short article written by Peter L. Wilson for the festival's "Daily Bulletin," we read: "Afterward, in answer to questions about the difficulties he has faced here, he pointed to the tomb of Hafez and said, 'It is because of the presence of that holy man that I have felt so inspired here, and because of the spirituality of Shiraz, which you can smell even in its earth.'"[89]

It's a beautiful statement of Pran Nath's values: his transnational connections with and devotion to Sufi lineages and saints as an important source of his music, and conversely, these saints understood as addressees of his music, his music a gift offered to these saints, such that a triangle of singer-music-saint is established in which it becomes finally impossible to distinguish or separate out the elements—but in which the singer's agency or responsibility is also crucial. And this not as a generic or bland internationalism of spiritual faith, but a real and concrete appreciation of Hafez's greatness, his visit undertaken as pilgrimage, an act of Sufi cosmopolitanism connecting with a long history extending into the present, where (some) Sufis visit the shrines (dargas) of great saints to seek their blessings.[90] And then there is the "spirituality of Shiraz" emanating even from the smell of its earth—a clear statement of Pran Nath's geomantic and cosmopolitical sympathies, of his music's relation to earth, the specific quality of the vibration of the land in the place where he is singing, and which then emerges in his singing too.

According to Riley, Pran Nath "strongly believed that music should be an offering to God. In that sense it should have the purest intentions, always have the musician's deepest concentration, and the musician should make this offering as beautiful and pure as he can. And in this way, he never thought of himself as singing for people. He used to say many times that, if a musician is saying to himself as he's singing, 'I am singing for other people,' then this would be a second-rate kind of music. But if it's an offering for God, then it's done with the deepest emotional, mental, spiritual, and physical perfection."[91]

But although Pran Nath spent much of his life around both Muslim and Hindu holy men, it was music itself that formed his spiritual practice. In 1977 he declared: "Music is the language of God; it is a holy thing! Music and spirit are the same, like two hands. Music is not religion. It is the same in the temples of India, at the Himalayas, in a village in Africa."[92]

10

In an interview at the end of his life, Pran Nath observed: "Without spiritual help, music don't give effect, music will just be some special effect. Spiritual help is necessary to the musician." He went on to quote the words of Lord Krishna from the Gita: "I don't reside in the hearts of yogis but those who sing with devotion to me."[93] Throughout his life, he sought for and found this help. Terry Riley recalls that "he often told me when we were touring together in Europe,

'First we must go pay our respects to God.' So we would go to a cathedral, if there was one in the town, before we performed. In India it would be the temple, or the mosque. But always going to get blessings before you performed was very important to him. He often said to us that this music was impossible to do without the blessing of saints."[94] As Shabda Kahn says, the background of these saints wasn't so important: "As a musician and as a spiritual devotee, Guruji spent his time looking for wisdom. He would sit at the feet of wisdom. He didn't care whether someone was a Sikh, or Muslim, Hindu, Christian, Cave-dweller. Wherever there was wisdom, he was willing to sit."[95]

Although he was born a Hindu, Pran Nath gave up his given name (Budhraja) when he became a singer, so as not to identify himself with the caste system. Pran Nath's guru was a devoted Muslim and Sufi, and Pran Nath's connections with Indian Sufism were strong. This movement between Islam and Hinduism was not so uncommon in the history of the Kirana gharana. Gopal Nayak was a Krishna devotee who converted to Islam at Allaudin Khilji's court in Delhi, after encountering the great Chishti Sufi saint Nizamuddin Aulia. Pran Nath had a special devotion for the founder of the Sabiri Sufi lineage, Hazrat Allaudin Sabiri, whose shrine is at Kalyar Sharif, near Dehra Dun, as well as the village of Kirana. In fact, at the end of his life, Pran Nath requested that his grave read "Faquir Pran Nath: Slave of Chishti Sabiri." Pran Nath said that Sabiri had appeared to him one day at the bus stop outside of Kalyar Sharif, and, according to La Monte Young and Marian Zazeela, "gave him prasad of gular fruit, the only food Sabiri was known to eat. When Pran Nath turned to thank him, he had disappeared, and it was only then that Pran Nath realized that it had been Sabir himself."[96] Music played a very strong part in Chishti and Sabiri Sufism (as it continues to do today—the Pakistani singer Nusrat Fateh Ali Khan was a Chishti Sufi, as was Hazrat Inayat Khan). It was said that the reclusive, awe-inspiring Sabiri's aura was so overwhelming that at the end of his life, no man could come near him, except for a musician, who sat fifty feet away, and would play for the saint, with his back turned to him.[97] To this day, Sabir's shrine remains a place of great spiritual intensity, with intoxicated devotees pacing the marble steps of the shrine while Qawwali singers perform, and others, in tears, pray inside the saint's darga—as I saw on the two occasions that I visited, in the early 2000s.

Pran Nath also participated in and supported Sufi communities in America. These communities have a complex history that dates back (at least) to Hazrat Inayat Khan's visits to America in the 1920s. One part of the lineage of the Sufis was passed down through Hazrat Inayat Khan's son Pir Vilayat Khan, who in 1974 organized a Sufi community called The Abode in New Lebanon,

New York, where his son, Zia, currently teaches—and where Pran Nath performed, on occasion. Another lineage passes through an American student of Inayat Khan's, Samuel Lewis (aka "Sufi Sam"), who taught a syncretic Zen-inflected version in San Francisco until he died in 1971. These Sufi orders present a universalist version of Sufi teachings whose relation to orthodox Islam is ambiguous and variable. While some consider them to be "not Islamic," Hazrat Inayat Khan's darga (shrine) is a short walk from Nizamuddin Aulia and Amir Khusrau's darga in the Muslim neighborhood of Nizamuddin in Delhi—and various members of the American communities have links to the Chisti Sufis in India, as well as the Turkish Naqshbandhi Sufi organizations.

According to Terry Riley, Pran Nath was also a devotee of Shirdi Sai Baba, a North Indian saint who died three weeks before Pran Nath was born.

> I often wondered if Pran Nath was an incarnation of Sai Baba. He seemed to resemble him so much, and his ideals were exactly the same as Baba's. He was neither Hindu nor Muslim. Sai Baba had turned up mysteriously in the village of Shirdi as a youth, and started meditating on a garbage heap, attracting the attention of the villagers because of his serene and peaceful nature. He later set up in an old abandoned mosque in Shirdi and kept a constant fire as a vigil. His deeds and teachings became legendary. He was a Christ-like figure for the Indians. . . . To the end of his life, Pran Nath was extremely devoted to Sai Baba. He had claimed that when he had his severe heart attack in 1978, he fell into the arms of Sai Baba who had held him until he was revived after being dead for 13 minutes.[98]

If music itself is a vibrational practice, then it is one that can allow people to join together, regardless of their religion (or lack of it). This was not always the case in twentieth-century India though. Marian Zazeela recalls Pran Nath telling her that "there was a law passed that Hindus and Muslims couldn't perform together and so Abdul Karim Khan taught a dog to sing sa and pa, and a monkey to play tambura, and he sang onstage with them. And Guruji saw them, so we asked: 'How were they?' and he said they were pretty good in their monkey and dog way."[99] As Shabda Kahn says,

> Music is a universal language. The musical community is used to being together. Hindus and Muslims are already together, and used to harmonizing together through music. The best musicians love to play with the best musicians—they don't care. Guruji gave a concert near Haridwar and afterwards a very big swami came up to him and said "I loved your

music and if you like I'll give you this great mantra which will make you an even greater musician." Guruji thought for a minute and then he said "I already have my mantra: sa re ga ma pa da ni sa." And that was it.[100]

Pran Nath always returned to the primacy of the music itself as a spiritual fact. "How can one affix labels of Hindu, Muslim or Christian to any music?" he asked. "It's the same octave in every system of music. Gaana tho Khuda ki jubaan hai (singing is the voice of God)—same all over the world. By means of his metaphysical make-up, the singer can actually delve deep onto the realm of abstract definition and come up with the methodology of 'swara,' tonal purity, such as can instantly influence the thought-stream of the listener."[101]

As I understand it, Pran Nath is asserting the ontological significance of music, whether it emerges from a particular religious tradition or not. And the ontology in question here is not that of the logos or discourse but "the methodology of 'swara'"—the word *swara* meaning pitch, perfect pitch, or tonal purity. Which is to say that it is a question of a practice of vibration that is capable of revealing and articulating the structure of reality. In this sense, music is located before religion and religious structures—even though it has historically and normatively appeared as their ornament or adornment. It also has priority over language—even when the voice is implicated in it. In his charming memoir *Travels with Pran Nath*, Pran Nath's student Nataraj recalled a composition "Nada Brahma" that Pran Nath would sing in the raga Yaman Kalyan—also the raga that Pran Nath would use to teach many students as their initiation into raga. The song begins:

Sound is God
Explain by singing[102]

II

After his heart attack in 1978 and the development of Parkinson's disease in the mid-1980s, Pran Nath's health declined, even as the number of his students increased. His vocal range declined, if not his spirit. Pran Nath, by all accounts, mellowed in his later years. Many of his students, while speaking with awe about his musical skills, talk with great affection of him as a man and a friend. When he died on June 13, 1996, his body was laid out in his room in Berkeley, and well-wishers and students came from around the world to say goodbye. Terry Riley recalled that "there was a radiant luster that emanated from his body and his face, the kind of thing that I had only read about in books. But here was a living example of it. People felt that he was still with them. Until the moment of his cremation, his face became more and more ecstatic, and at the very end his smile became quite radiant, happy, and childlike."[103]

What, at the deepest level, was raga, according to Pran Nath? On occasion, he would reply that "raga means living souls."[104] One of the main ways that one can measure the quality of a performer of Indian classical music is whether or not he or she is capable of offering a living experience of the ragas to listeners, who should feel a change of atmosphere in the room, and a change in their own consciousness, that is quite tangible and not in the least metaphorical. It should be an experience that is shared by others in the room without consultation with each other. In other words, the performer should really be able to invoke the spirit of the raga in and as sound, in the concert room. Shabda Kahn explains: "Music gets life from humans. Each raga has a living atmosphere, vibration and when you invoke it, it's like rubbing the lamp . . . and the genie comes out. When you invoke the raga by calling on its shape, then this very powerful blessing or feeling comes into the room, much more than you could imagine. Just as the Tibetans have deities that aren't embodied, in the same way, ragas are energetic forms."[105]

Pran Nath had the ability to invoke ragas in this way, even on the recordings that are left to us. Sri Karunamayee observes:

> When the singer invokes the spirit of a particular raga, his own spirit gets attuned to a pitch of the raga, and through those sounds, he says to the spirits please come down and manifest. He offers himself completely. When he is singing a raga he is not thinking of anything else, every drop of him is taken possession of, there is no individuality left. Unless that surrender is there, we have not invoked the spirit of the raga. Pandit Pran Nathji was a Siddha-Nada-Yogi of the highest realization. With his natural gift, and his sadhana of the purity of sound, he was able to offer a living experience of Ragas as divine entities coming and manifesting in their celestial true forms. Every note and nuance had the power and potency to bless the singer and the listener alike with felicity and Ananda.[106]

Throughout this chapter, I have referred to Pran Nath's insistence on the effect of music—that music is a practice whose aim is to produce a certain effect, bringing to life the "living soul" of the raga for the singer, for the audience, for the space in which the sonic matrix of the raga vibrates. I have noted that such an insistence is in itself cosmopolitical since the normative ontology of music offered by Western musicologists is that there is no such effect, just subjective and diverse claims as to what music "is," usually bracketed either by a Eurocentric musicology or a general account of acoustics. My own understanding of this has grown in conversation with Catherine Christer Hennix, who speaks of music in an almost teleological way—that when you play music, you play it until an intended effect is produced. And to stop or perform a different piece of music before that effect is achieved would be a puzzling thing to do in the same way that someone who sets out to bake a cake and then leaves the cake mix on the countertop and forgets about it and gets involved in doing something else is puzzling—and even wasting their time. There is a fascinating kind of patience in Pandit Pran Nath's singing... a slowness that his teacher Abdul Wahid Khan clearly had and taught him too. It is not performative, but contingent and probing, working with the moment, with the vibrational matrix as it exists in its psychoacoustic cosmopolitical totality in a particular time and place, such that an emergent possibility whose exact nature (which raga, which composition, which shaping of the alap?) is only known in the moment of singing.

There is a historical drama unfolding in all of this—the insistence on a specific effect usually refers to a particular tradition, but that insistence turns too easily to coded and cliched reifications of something now dead or reduced to an ideological motif—Bakhle's "bhakti nationalism," for example. Conversely, the lost or impossible or crossed-out status of such an insistence, rehearsed again and again in experimental music, which is predicated on the belief that all such teleological goals and traditions are dead, and that one can only begin again from ground zero—that is what Bruno Latour calls the ideology of modernity. The cosmopolitical wager of music unfolds today somewhere in between the lost or reified status of tradition and the learned helplessness of the moderns in their belief that music can only be a desacralized, aleatory, or entertaining creature. In Henry Flynt's terms, it consists in the possibility of discovering a potential that you have, that you ignored or neglected or did not know about.

Given Pran Nath's views on what was needed for the proper study of raga, it is perhaps hard to imagine what he thought would happen to his music after he died. His students were aware of this fact. Shabda Khan recalls saying to Pran Nath, "'Guruji, when you die, the encyclopedia will go from six inches thick to two inches.' He said 'Gold is gold, whether it's a small piece or a big piece.' He tried to keep us thinking about gold, pure and rich. He wasn't looking for quantity so much."[107] The fact that Pran Nath committed himself to work with the American avant-garde in itself indicates that he knew that his music would undergo some kind of transformation, and accepted it. Terry Riley agrees.

> He felt strongly that a good seed had been planted by his work here. And that a lot of people understood very well the basic meaning behind his tradition, enough to continue their own practice. In terms of what it

means for America, what I gleaned was that he felt that each place has its own big influence on the musical life of that place. And the vibration of the land, what's going on in the land will create a big effect on what kind of music it is. So by his saying that, I know that he couldn't expect Indian music to exist over here only as it does in India. That something would happen to it. I imagine that he would hope that some of the purity of the approach toward pitches and frequency would continue on, and also, just the general spiritual quality of his music would be transmitted.[108]

12

There is a politics of vibration that is operative in what is called Indian classical music. What did it mean for Wahid Khan and for other Indian classical musicians to devote themselves to the practice of music in early twentieth-century India at the moment of decolonization? Throughout the colonial period, many great Indian musicians worked as court singers (for example, Ustad Nasiruddin Khan, father of the Dagar lineage of dhrupad singers, was court singer for the Maharaja of Indore), and performed at "house concerts." Satyajit Ray captured the pathos of the end of this era in his 1958 film *The Music Room*, which featured the voices of Salamat and Nazakat Ali Khan, who had taken singing lessons with Pran Nath at one point. The "music room" is the prize possession and fantasy object of a zamindar in 1930s Bengal, whose estate is slowly crumbling as the winds of political change reach him. The music room is a shrine to a vibrational ontology, the place of the purest aesthetic enjoyment, and, as Ray makes clear, the most sublime site of the ideology of the landowning class in Bengal, whose enjoyment is propped up by hierarchies of caste and coloniality, encroached upon by entrepreneurs with vulgar taste in music (the zamindar stages his final concert in the music room in defiance of the crass tastes of his arriviste neighbor) and movements of decolonization.

In moments of doubt I ask myself whether, following Slavoj Žižek, all talk of "the sound itself" is in the end sublime in the sense of reaching toward a supposed transcendental beyond whose nothingness (i.e., nonexistence) crystalizes instead as a pure and purified ideological figure.[109] The more talk there is of "pure sound," the more one looks around for patrons that can bankroll the purity. Certainly, Young's story is cautionary in that regard—the Dream House funded by the Dia Foundation's oil money and the vicissitudes of the stock market.[110] Pran Nath himself seems to have passed through nearly every possible social structure that has a place for music in it: the church, the feudal court, the university, the patronage of wealthy American donors, the neoliberal New Age spirituality workshop. Did it really work out? Does it ever? "My music is a sad music," Pran Nath said to Terry Riley, who noted that Pran Nath's life was a difficult one.[111] A musical life is a fugitive one, in the sense given by Fred Moten and other Black studies scholars—the environment is hostile, unlivable even, and nevertheless, out of that, music happens. Yet the desire that it be possible to live in the sound, to be at home in the sound—shared by Pran Nath and his American students, and many others too—returns again and again. And contra Žižek, it is not just a desire, or for that matter an ideological figure, since musicians and musical practice realizes this desire in many fugitive but nonetheless decisive instances. So far music, at least as far as Jacques Attali is concerned, has been an ornament to political economy—at best an ambiguous force to be controlled and put at the service of power. But that necessarily implies an outside too—in which music has some degree of autonomy. The forgotten core of Attali's work is that music is not just prophetic of shifts in the political economic order, but that a liberation of music is possible such that it becomes the unalienated practice of free people in their collective engagement and motion.

La Monte Young tells an (apocryphal?) Sufi story in which it is music that lures the soul (back) into the realm of matter. Sometimes I imagine that I am floating for a long but perhaps not infinite period of time on a small planet moving through space. The pleasures of love and work, of philosophy even, gradually exhaust themselves as time extends. Only music remains of value in this time span. Could we imagine a revolution in political economy one of whose goals is to reconfigure the place of music in the world and to finally make possible a life spent making, playing, thinking about, listening to music? Or is it only ruin that will make this possible, in the sense that it leaves only the vibratory ground of being explicit and exposed?

TWO

. . . . . .

The Drone of the Real

The Sound-Works of Catherine Christer Hennix

I

"The whole universe is vibrating," the Swedish-born composer, mathematician, writer, and musician Catherine Christer Hennix said to me when I interviewed her in 2009 for the *Wire*. She continued:

> The whole universe can be understood as just one single vibration. All atoms are continuously vibrating, the vacuum is vibrating, the whole cosmos is vibrating. When things vibrate they generate these harmonics. Each harmonic is a state of nature. The higher the harmonic the higher the energy state. The lowest energy state is the lowest fundamental. If you supply more energy you get an octave, more and you get a fifth and so on. In physics harmonics correspond to different states of matter. It's empirical. As humans we are reconfigurations of cosmic matter, all the atoms come from outer space. We are simply reconfiguring them via the DNA molecule or whatever. When we hear these vibrations our system of molecules vibrate with them. It's a completely natural phenomenon—in other words it would be strange if it were otherwise. You can think of sound as a medicinal tonic. You are exposed to sound as you are exposed to a liquid and it may change your ground state and you go from one state to another because you are exposed to this radiation of sound.[1]

I find Hennix's work remarkable in its single-minded focus on vibration at the ontological level and in the way her profound and unusual ideas about vibration resonate with her musical performances and recordings. Listening to Hennix's celebrated 1976 performance *The Electric Harpsichord*—a 25-minute keyboard piece originally performed at the Moderna Museet in Stockholm in March 1976—at sufficient volume remains an uncanny, unique experience in which the floor and walls around me appear to melt. Her friend and collaborator Henry Flynt has described it as "life-changing."[2] But from Flynt and Hennix's point of view, the recording is important because it's proof of a method, a way of making something happen, that points beyond the framing of music as product, or even art, to an entirely new way of philosophically understanding and inhabiting the universe. As for what that method is, Hennix—a sometime math professor; philosopher; visual artist with works in major national European, American, and Asian collections; and disciple of the raga master Pandit Pran Nath and the minimalist composer La Monte Young—weaves a dizzying range of disciplines and histories, from the latest developments in quantum physics, to Asian religious mystical traditions, to her own deep background in jazz, in order to make a highly original argument about the power of sound.

What would it mean to fully recognize the implications of our own and everything else's ontological status as vibration? Although the way I am phrasing the question may be new, the first thing to note is that many thinkers in the twentieth century were profoundly concerned with this issue because of the discoveries of quantum physics, which affirmed the importance of vibration within the most prestigious knowledge systems. The atom bomb is an immediate indicator of an associated politics of vibration and the intense drive to instrumentalize any insight into vibration at the ontological level. Today, that instrumentalization continues with nanotechnology as a model of future capitalist production; with the use of sonic and other wave-based policing technologies, many of them described in Steve Goodman's *Sonic Warfare*; and with the incorporation of various vibration-based modalities of Foucauldian "care of the self" into the economy.[3]

There have been a number of moments when counterpractices and politics of vibration have been proposed and enacted in the last century. We might mention Wilhelm Reich's work, which began as a psychoanalytic practice of revolutionary liberation through orgasm in the 1920s,[4] morphing over time into a more general interest in "bio-energetics" and cosmic radiation as political forces that enable and disable bodies and environments. Reich's work was continued and refracted in the 1960s by various radical psychotherapeutic communities; the emergence of countercultures built around practices of music and sound making from jazz and the blues, through Cage and Stockhausen, along with their various subcultural echoes, all focused on the event of a certain sound as the highest point in human life; and the spread of a variety of meditational and bodily practices such as yoga, Buddhism, and the martial arts, in which alignment with a deep awareness of mental and physical vibration is emphasized. Most of these counterpractices have been neutralized in large part through their commodification, although that hardly makes them less important to individuals concerned with establishing their own autonomy and health. It may be that such a focus amounts to a depoliticization: Reich becomes interested in vibration after he gives up leftist politics; so does Bataille. On the other hand, Reich died in jail in the United States in the 1950s because his claims regarding vibration were disputed by the FDA. In other words, vibration remained political, even in the absence of a conventional political discourse.

Hennix's work is important because, to put it in the language of Flynt, she proposes a practice of vibration that is not a counterpractice in the sense of a Romantic retreat into aesthetics in the face of the encroaching power of science and technology, but an appropriation and radicalization of scientific knowledge in its most prestigious and valorized forms, in the cause of a different way of living, a different civilization. Her argument concerning and practice of vibration is situated within some of the core scientific debates of the last one hundred years, including the quest for the foundation of mathematics; the relation between quantum-level events and phenomenological experience in physics; and neuroscience and the debate over whether psychoanalysis can (or should) be considered a science or not. At the same time, these scientific arguments are interwoven with a religious and devotional aspect, emergent from her studies with Pandit Pran Nath, a musical practice that has been engaged over decades with maqam and raga and their complex histories and geographies, a profound reading of the philosophical fragments left to us by Parmenides, which stand at the beginning of the Western philosophical tradition—and much more. Thus, we will consider Hennix's work here as a cosmopolitical practice—a bold attempt at a novel synthesis of "ways of knowing" through music, sound, and vibration, that constitutes a "worlding" in a challenging contemporary way.

2

Hennix is known as a composer of drones (she currently detests the term, preferring "modal music," but I will use the former to describe a subset of her work). A drone, in musical terms, is a sustained set of composite sound wave forms, in other words, a vibratory field. The word *field* conveys the way that the repetition of a set of waveforms opens up the possibility of exploring a tone cluster as a space that retains its form over time. While drones can be located in the history of music everywhere, from the tambura-led sound of Indian classical music to the prelude to Wagner's *Das Rheingold*, drones became important cultural artifacts in their own right in the early 1960s, through the work of La Monte Young and a group of people collaborating with him conceptually and musically including Marian Zazeela, Tony Conrad, Terry Riley, John Cale—and in 1970, Hennix.[5]

While the history of Young's work—from his early Fluxus-related text scores circa 1960, to the collaborations with Conrad, Zazeela, Cale, Angus MacLise, and others as the Theater of the Eternal Music in the early 1960s, through the various iterations of his just intonation–tuned piano masterpiece *The Well-Tuned Piano*—is well known at this stage, the philosophical meaning of that work is still relatively unexplored, and part of Hennix's contribution has been to draw out and expand the meaning.[6] Young contrasted his work to that of John Cage, which can be said to be truly phenomenological, in the sense that it is concerned with the way that sound appears to a particular subject in space and time. In contrast to the "silence" of compositions such as *4′ 33″*, Young's drones fill space and time. They are intensely repetitive; they emphasize a quality of sameness that bifurcates temporally into an experience of difference as the repetition of the same. In Young's formula "tuning is a function of time," meaning that as one tunes into particular groups of frequencies within a particular drone sound, further levels of harmonic structure become audible as does a sameness that in some sense is "always there" whether the drone is being played or not.[7] In this sense, one could argue that drones represent a structural response to the Cagean phenomenology of sound. And perhaps it is this structural dimension that gives the vibratory field of a drone ontological implications. At least according to Young and some of his colleagues, this is particularly true when the production of drones is formulated from within a mathematical paradigm of just intonation. Just intonation refers descriptively to tuning systems that use tones or frequencies that can be written down as ratios of integers. Such frequencies are in accordance with the natural harmonics of sound, that is, they will occur naturally as overtones of a fundamental frequency, as the German physicist/acoustician Hermann Helmholtz observed in his book *On the Sensations of Tone as a Physiological Basis for the Theory of Music* (1862).[8] A drone produced according to the principles of just intonation is a mathematical structure enacted within a particular space by a particular sound-making apparatus, whether musician or machine.

Aside from Helmholtz's work, the French musicologist Alain Daniélou's work on tuning systems in traditional cultures, notably his *Tableau comparatif des intervalles musicaux*, published in 1958, made a major impact on Young, Conrad, and others.[9] In this work, Daniélou compiled in a single list or catalog, many of the intervals that he knew of in the just intonation scales that are the basis of many traditional musics around the world (he makes reference to ancient Greek, Arabic, Indian, and Persian sources). Daniélou catalogs these intervals (interval here meaning a note or pitch expressed in its relationship to the tonic of the scale) as a series of fractions or ratios of integers. After 1/1, labeled "Shruti Chandravati, Unisson") comes 1025/1024, and so on. The effect is like a menu or cookbook of intervals, necessarily incomplete but highly suggestive as to the multiplicity of possible intervals; over fifteen hundred are listed. In this sense, the Cagean argument that any sound could be considered music could be modified via just intonation so that the expanded universe of human musical practices is not completely aleatory, but iterative in the sense of allowing any scale that employs notes which can be expressed as a ratio of integers. Rather than utilizing an arbitrary rule (as with the equal-tempered scale, which simply sets an equal tonal distance between notes in a scale), Daniélou argued that particular permutations of particular just intonation scales are associated with particular kinds of affects or feelings. In his essay "The Influence of Sound Phenomena on Human Consciousness," Daniélou argued that there were really two musical systems in the world, "those which start from the psychological effect of intervals and of rhythms, according to the sentiment which it provokes in us; and those which start from their purely physical relation, their numerical relation and their harmony phenomena."[10] Thus, Hindustani raga music associates each raga, which is a composition of a particular scale, with a particular set of rules for movement around the scale, with a particular mood or feeling. A great raga performance evokes this feeling, which has been described as a "living spirit" that possesses those who listen to it. This adds important dimensions to the structural nature of just intonation–based musics since it effectively makes the argument that particular kinds of affects or feelings can be described as particular sound forms that can also be mathematically formalized. In other words, there is a mathematical structure to feeling. In performance, a raga pulls you into its sound world. It evokes a yearning that could be described as the sense that the sound and the feeling it elicits are more real than the apparently real world that exists outside of the performance.

But to claim that "there is a mathematical structure to feeling" could also be a very trivial claim—either in terms of instrumentalizing feeling as a kind of behaviorist banality that is becoming increasingly present today in the world of algorithmic marketing of mood musics, or as yet another ontological substrate that can be said to appear universally without allowing for any further or deeper understanding of anything. Young, Conrad, and others, including Hennix, proposed that if traditional musics can be defined in terms of a mathematics of affect, and if the basis of that mathematics is the extrapolation of musical scales based on ratios of whole numbers, then the implication of this knowledge is not only a description of traditional musics but the possibility of an experimental music based on hitherto unheard-of scales built around hitherto unarticulated ratios of whole numbers, which have yet unknown affective powers. Hennix's *The Electric Harpsichord*, which is based on the scale of Raga Multani, one of the more popular Hindustani ragas, clearly involves a reconfiguration of the rules and practices involved in using the scale.

As is well known now, there has been a "politics of vibration" around Young, Conrad, and other members of the ensemble known as the Theater of Eternal Music. The core of the argument—which has been documented in Jeremy Grimshaw's "Ideology of the Drone" chapter in his monograph on Young—is about intellectual property and who holds the rights to the recordings that Young possesses of the Theater of Eternal Music ensemble in the 1960s, which included Conrad and Cale.[11] While Young claims the rights of the composer, and therefore exclusive ownership of the recordings and decisions as to their circulation, Conrad and Cale have argued that their work together was collaborative and that they share ownership of the material. Conrad's critique of Young also involves an attack on the mathematical bases of his project and the notion of an eternal music based on mathematical principles, which Conrad sees as antidemocratic.[12] It's striking that it was the shift from the notated score and the demands of the composer to group improvisation focused on inhabiting "the sound itself" that precipitated these battles—almost as if the structures or discipline that could sustain such openness did not yet exist. The argument is riven with paradoxes: first, that it was Conrad who introduced Young to the mathematical principles of just intonation in the 1960s; and second, that given that we are talking about mathematical principles, they hardly seem copyrightable, in the same way that attempts to copyright yoga poses also seem suspect. While Young may try to copyright scales using novel combinations or absences of prime-number ratios claiming that they constitute an original composition, all the intervals documented in Daniélou's work would appear to be in the public domain—or perhaps the property of the musical communities that originally used them.

Nonetheless, Conrad's politics of vibration actually obscures a deeper politics of vibration that is key not only to the Theater of Eternal Music and its members but also to Conrad's oeuvre as a whole, spanning cinema, video, and sound works.[13] This deeper politics has to do with the actual possibilities inherent in a mathematical and physics-based music, the dangers of the instrumentalization of such possibilities (more or less Goodman's argument concerning the weaponization of subsonic frequencies in *Sonic Warfare*), and the possibility of liberatory counterinstrumentalizations that are nonetheless grounded in the real order of the universe. By *real order*, I refer to an order not dictated by tradition or by any particular ideology of science, but rather an order to be discovered in and through practice and experimentation. Such sonic practices would constitute new forms of life and gather humans and nonhumans around them in new ways.

Daniélou's arguments regarding the politics of musical scales are relevant here. He appears to have been an adherent of the conservative European mid-twentieth-century milieu around the Eranos conferences and a group of thinkers that includes Carl Jung, Mircea Eliade, René Guénon, Ernst Junger, and Aldous Huxley. All of these thinkers had variously right-wing views and believed in a hierarchical, rather than an egalitarian ethos, often backed up by an interest in mythology as the secret password/handshake shared by a political-aesthetic elite who saw themselves as rulers of the masses. In his key musicological works such as *Introduction to the Study of Musical Scales* (1943) (later republished as *Music and the Power of Sound* (1995) and *Sémantique musicale* (1967), Daniélou applies such ideas to the study of music and musical scales. Daniélou argues that there are two kinds of music: one that is built around intervals and scales that can be notated as ratios of integers, which Daniélou argues have a very strong psychophysiological impact on listeners, rooted in a mathematically based microcosmic relationship of interior to exterior; and another kind, modern music, which Daniélou argues is aleatory, ungrounded, and egalitarian (in the sense of equal temperament as a scale constructed out of equally sized intervals between the notes of the scale) and, therefore, lacks any strong power of affect on the listener.

The reactionary aspect of this argument has to be acknowledged. Daniélou's examples are traditional Indian and Chinese music, and ancient Greek music, all of which are associated with conservative political ideologies, from Confucianism and its notion of obedience to the state as a principle of nature, to the relation of Indian classical music to the royal courts and the hierarchies of caste and deities, to Pythagoras's antidemocratic politics. Daniélou explains: "For the world to be in a state of equilibrium, it is necessary that its different elements be harmonized. Music being the expression of the relations between human and cosmic order, it is essential that it should respect the data on which these relations are based, that is to say, the exact intervals of notes as determined by the traditional data which define these relations. The disregard of such an obvious law leads necessarily to a rupture of equilibrium, that is to say, to social disorder."[14]

By claiming an "eternal music" built around a specific set of mathematical principles that exerts a hierarchical power over all other sounds, it could be argued (and Conrad does argue) that a kind of antidemocratic music is being proposed. And that Young's treatment of ownership issues is symptomatic of this. However, Daniélou's argument is not simply one that is nostalgic for a set of given musical forms that were handed down by the Greeks, Indians, or Chinese. Daniélou also argues that great art requires an expansive vocabulary, and that modern music has essentially limited itself to one particular tuning and, therefore, a highly limited affective repertoire. Although Young and Hennix both immersed themselves in the Indian classical musical tradition, particularly in their studies with the Hindustani vocalist Pandit Pran Nath, both also understood Daniélou's work as proposing not merely a scientific/mathematical rationalization of the superiority of various traditional musics, but a set of formal but open-ended principles for the construction of affectively powerful sonic works that was democratic in the sense of being constructable by anyone who understands the principles.

If both Young and Hennix understood this possibility of an almost infinite new music that could be constructed from the principles noted by Daniélou, it must be said that Young's work occurs within the understanding of this possibility as a set of iterations, decisions. Hennix, however, develops the thought of a new mathematical music in ways that go considerably further—in part because of her much deeper involvement in contemporary mathematics.

3

Hennix was born in 1948 in Stockholm. Her mother, Margit Sundin-Hennix, was a jazz composer, and Hennix grew up in a household saturated with the sounds of modern jazz. Hennix's mother owned an apartment building in Stockholm, which she gave to the trumpeter Idrees Sulieman and his wife Jamila (who lived there for most of the 1960s). Eric Dolphy and Dexter Gordon were among those who passed through the apartment. Hennix began playing drums at the age of five and started taking lessons from Sulieman when she was thirteen, the same year (1961) she first heard John Coltrane play live. Hennix played around town, sitting in on occasion with Albert Ayler.

Despite this early exposure to it, Hennix is dubious about the Swedish jazz scene: "We thought we were extremely hip playing 'modern jazz' but it didn't have the punch that jazz played by black people had. It was sort of a hallucination."[15] At the same time, Hennix was exposed to the sounds of John Cage, Stockhausen, and David Tudor who all visited Stockholm repeatedly during the 1960s. Hennix began making avant-garde compositions and working with the computers at the Electronic Music Studio in Stockholm. A track from this period, six minutes of voice synthesis, can be found on *Text-Sound Compositions 5*, part of a series of compilations of concrete poetry and computer-based compositions put out by the Swedish label Fylkingen, and recently reissued as a CD boxed set. Working with the computer led to a fascination with mathematics and mathematical logic, which Hennix pursued in graduate-level studies in Sweden and the United States, as well as later in a period of teaching in the math department at SUNY New Paltz. The connection of music and mathematics came early. Hennix recalls an epiphany when she first discovered the French mathematician Jean-Baptiste Fourier's theorem:

> Fourier analysis is for example what you use when you do analog to digital conversion. It analyzes sound in terms of sine waves. The theory says that any continuous sound can be analysed as a certain set of sine waves. Sine wave components are like the atoms of the sound. And like in nature you have in the spectrum of sound infinitely many sine waves. I was blown away by this.

The epiphany for Hennix evolves, in a surprising way. She continues:

> As it turns out, this was just the rediscovery of something that has been done already a thousand years ago. There was an Arabic Sufi mathematician named Al-Farabi who came from Baghdad to Spain. He's the first person to be credited with the discovery of the 49th harmonic. But that's not all he did. He brought the concept of a drone, sustained notes to Europe. He introduced Europe to what is known as the Quadrivium, which consists of mathematics, geometry, astronomy and music. That was one part of the school. So, music was already integrated with math, astronomy and physics. It was an Islamic tradition which became a Catholic tradition. It was taught this from way until the Renaissance, when Islam was thrown out of Europe. Music was separated from science, it became entertainment. Music was artificially separated from mathematics, it became part of liberal arts, what is known as trivium: rhetoric, grammar, logic.[16]

This resituation of music is at the core of Hennix's work. It also accounts for Hennix's obscurity. She has released few recordings, seldom performs, and her writing is rarely shared with others—not out of a lack of interest, but certainly out of a different sense of priority. Music is a way of living: it is meditation, thought, daily practice, and research before it is something to be shared with others.

Hennix visited America twice in 1968—the first time for a family gathering; but while visiting New York, she met an assortment of key figures in the American avant-garde, including Dick Higgins, John Cage, Merce Cunningham, Jasper Johns, and James Tenney. The Swedish artist Öyvind Fahlström had an apartment on Second Avenue. On her second visit that year she experienced Jefferson Airplane and MC5, amplified rock music at the Fillmore East in New York, and was impressed by the sound levels of the bands playing there. On a follow-up trip in 1969, Hennix had two decisive experiences related to sound. The first occurred through her brother, who invited her to attend the launch of *Apollo* 11 at Cape Canaveral in Florida:

> The strongest bass I ever heard was when they sent the people to the moon. It was amazing because the bass notes were absolutely out of this world. The rocket is like 1 km away from you and there is water separating the audience who is sitting watching the whole thing, television cameras and the whole thing. First you see the flames under the rocket, but it doesn't move one inch it just sits there, with just more and more flames. Then very slowly it goes up, and you're looking at that slow movement but you don't hear anything. Then all of a sudden you hear this rumble, then you start to feel it in the ground, as the rocket is about to go up from the ground from this scaffolding that it sits inside, this cage. The whole earth is shaking and you think it cannot be louder than this and it only gets louder and louder and louder until the rocket starts to disappear out into the sky (laughs). It was an incredible sound experience. But it was a very bad sound, a really evil sound I would say.[17]

Hennix is interested in sounds that make material reality shake, and in the psychotropic potential of loudness—she speaks with approval of the show her group played in Krems in 2016 where the building itself began to vibrate, and a show at the Kraftwerk space in Berlin where the sound was so loud that there was a palpable although subtle change in the ambient temperature of the room which she describes as heating up attendees' body temperature from the bones. While the *Apollo* rocket's vibration was an evil one, a condensation of all kinds of Cold War–era fantasies of human omnipotence, Hennix is interested in an immersive sound that produces jouissance (ecstatic enjoyment), healing, and emancipation. If the *Apollo* launch stands as a model, it is a model that suggests the power of scientific praxis, and the extraordinary events or possibilities that it is capable of revealing, for better or worse (one thinks of the atomic bomb, for example) and the possibility of reconfiguring and extending that model toward other, better goals. The idea resonates with her friend Henry Flynt's concept of "metatechnology," in which a broadly technical organization of human praxis is reframed toward emancipatory goals.[18] It also resonates with George Bataille's claim that the most significant human dilemma is that of how to consume or expend a constitutive planetary and cosmic excess—and that human societies are defined by their decisions, conscious or not, as to how to consume this excess (warfare, capitalism, the splendor of the medieval Christian church are examples).[19] Art, in both of these framings, is also a decision as to how to frame human possibility. The question is: How to do that?

An answer to that question began to emerge for Hennix that same year when she visited La Monte Young and Marian Zazeela's loft where she heard a drone playing:[20] "It's the sine wave composition that he has on all the time in his loft. It took me about sixty seconds to decide that this was the definitive new sound. It was completely related to Fourier's theorem and here I found someone who knew how to deal with this, deal with sine waves. His was the first successful application in terms of sound experience. I didn't leave his place for three or four days. I was just listening and from time to time he and Marian would sing with the drone which was even more fantastic."[21]

Young visited Stockholm the following year and Hennix worked with him at the Electronic Music Studio, realizing his *Drift Study 15 X 70 2:00–3:00 PM Stockholm*, which she considers to be one of his most spectacular works. At this time, Young had already been working with sine wave generators for a number of years, producing the *Drift Studies* series, which consists of unadorned, very slowly shifting tones, and major works such as *Map of 49's Dream*, which also features Young and Zazeela's voices. Recordings of these pieces can be found on 1969's *The Black Record* and the Shandar disk of 1974.

Young's major theoretical work, *The Two Systems of Eleven Categories*, which also dates from this period, sets out the basis for these works—the text, about twelve pages long, was written in collaboration with Dennis Johnson. Young lent her the text and she went back to her loft where she rewrote it (a version that became known as the "Blue Paper," unfortunately now lost) according to a complexity measure that she introduced.[22]

Hennix speaks with approval of Young's practice during this period:

It makes no sense to have a composition that has a beginning and an end. You can cut the before and after out, you just have the composition going all the time. The problem with the way you consume sound today is that you come to a performance, you're ushered in and when the musicians are tired of playing you are ushered out. But that doesn't work for the type of experience I'm talking about. You have to dedicate the space to the sound and the sound has to be there all the time, and you come to it when you can but it's on your conditions, not the ushers. That's why electronic music is so fantastic. The equipment doesn't get tired. I have a drone in my house that's on 24 hours a day every day, every week, every year. If you do this eventually the sound settles in your bones. It's like drinking sound, you just suck it up and as you do that it will reconfigure your mind. It's a totally psychedelic experience. A mind altering drug if you wish.[23]

Of all the various figures that have been associated with Young over the years—from Terry Riley, Jon Hassell, and Rhys Chatham to Tony Conrad and Yoshi Wada—Hennix's music and ideas are perhaps the closest to Young's. Hennix's work in the 1970s largely reflects the interests of Young. For example, the Deontic Miracle was a Gagaku-inspired trio (whose musical style she gave the name Chagaku—a reference to the Japanese tea ceremony) that Hennix assembled after returning to Sweden from America in 1973. It was originally proposed as a kind of big band, but in the end consisted of her brother Peter Hennix playing amplified Renaissance oboe, Hans Isgren on amplified sheng and sarangi, and Hennix on oboe, sine wave generators, and keyboards—the group meeting several times a week at Hennix's loft in Stockholm between 1973 and 1976. Their sound was inspired by Young and Terry Jennings's duos in which they play combination tones together. Nonetheless, Hennix says that she didn't want to imitate Young or the intervals he used, so she used a Japanese model in contrast to the Indian aesthetics that Young generally favored.[24] Hennix explains, "In Gagaku you have the same effect when the hichirikis [a type of oboe] are playing. It's quite eerie, when they play you have sound flying through the air. Like bats. It's incredible. The combination tones have this emergent structure that is almost indefinable."[25]

In 1970 Hennix traveled to Saint-Paul-de-Vence at the urging of Young, to meet the Hindustani classical vocalist Pandit Pran Nath, whose life and work was the subject of the first chapter of this book. She recalls:

> I was completely blown away by his sound. What I was focused on was the sound of the tambura. I told him I wanted to study the tambura and its tuning and he told me the only way to do that was to learn to sing

ragas. But I'd never sung in my life. In jazz the singer isn't that important, and I thought singing was for the stupid people. I thought playing instruments was the cool thing to do so it took me a long time to get adjusted to the singing he asked me to do. I do voice exercises but I prefer to listen to the tamburas without my voice. My idea was to use the tambura as a way of making solo compositions. The tambura is a treasure trove of harmonics and my idea was simply to make compositions that had parts of those harmonics in them and work them out as much as possible within a context of precision tuning.[26]

Hennix became a disciple of Pran Nath at a ceremony in Terry Riley's studio in San Francisco in 1971, and she later assisted along with Riley when Pran Nath taught a course at Mills College in 1973.

At the same time, Hennix continued her mathematical studies as an exchange student in 1971 and 1973 at the University of California, Berkeley, where Alfred Tarski taught. Berkeley (and the broader academic community of the Bay Area) was an important center of innovative work in logic, set theory, category theory, and related fields—and Hennix was able to absorb a state-of-the-art education, particularly in questions related to the foundations of mathematics. Through a chance meeting with the composer Maryanne Amacher in 1973, Hennix met the Russian mathematician and dissident Alexander Yessenin-Volpin with whom she has collaborated over the years. Yessenin-Volpin, the founder of the school of ultra-intuitionism, stands in about the same relationship to mainstream mathematics as just intonation does to mainstream classical music. Somehow, Pran Nath recognized that there was no contradiction between Hennix's various interests. She recounts: "He realized I was not keen to be a performer that I was just doing this for my spiritual development. He thought my contribution to Indian music might be more as a mathematician than as a performing artist. And he may be correct in this. I have a complete mathematical theory of the sound of the tambura. I'd like to simulate the sound of the tambura by means of computer, I have the equations for it. If I succeed with this I can do new electronic music that no one has ever heard before."[27]

4

If speculative philosophy's origins can be found in the limits of the linguistic or discursive turn, sound and music obviously arise as one explores the phenomenal zone of those things that are poorly rendered in and as language. Furthermore, in the shift from musicology to sound studies, and from the musical to the sonic, one quickly reaches the limit of correlationism: a world of sounds, frequencies, vibrations that are there but not necessarily there for us (Hennix coined the term *ananthropic sound* to describe this). Having said that, and being wary of glib claims of being able to leave the correlationist circle, I wonder whether the charm and power of music doesn't already and in general consist in the fact that it is simultaneously inside and outside the correlationist circle, making it possible to answer the question "What is the specific power of music?" with the statement that music opens us up to a vibrational exteriority, a great outdoors, an excess or nonknowledge, that nonetheless constitutes us and our interiority too.

Indeed, Bataille's term *nonknowledge* is helpful here.[28] It is that aspect of the world that cannot be correlated with our knowledge of the world, but which nonetheless is decisive for us. Nonknowledge can be the object of a practice that plays with, realizes that object without discursively knowing it. Music, in this sense, accesses, or allows us to access the great outdoors.

How does it do that? Perhaps here one should speak of Badiou's hypothesis of a mathematical ontology, and then, noting the relationship of mathematics and music stretching back to Pythagoras and beyond, observe the connections between a mathematical ontology, a vibrational ontology, and a sonic or even musical ontology. This is in fact the claim that La Monte Young made for his own music, which he called "meta music" in the 1960s.[29] Grounded in the notion of the syllable *Om* as the sound of the universe, the universe as a wave or vibration, which, in Hennix's recent work, takes the form of the Hubble frequency, defined as "the lowest possible frequency the universe can sustain at any future time."[30] Long-duration works bring up the question of ancestry. Hennix wrote of her own pieces that they should not be understood as having a beginning and end corresponding to the moment of performance, but that their performance is without end and is merely suspended or becomes inaudible at certain moments.

If one is to make the claim that ontology is mathematical, the next thing to observe is that there are important debates when it comes to the foundations of mathematics, which is more or less where mathematical ontology would have to be found. Hennix found these debates intriguing, and the results that mid-twentieth-century mathematicians arrived at were "far out," to use a favorite phrase of hers. Furthermore, Hennix believed that there was a strongly aesthetic aspect to mathematical creativity, particularly in the work of the figures she was most drawn to, such as David Hilbert, who founded metamathematics; the Dutch intuitionist mathematician L. E. J. Brouwer, founder of "intuitionistic mathematics"; William Lawvere, who did important work in category and topos theory; Alexander Grothendieck, author of numerous important mathematical results including the original idea of a topos as a "generalized space"; and the Russian dissident mathematician and "ultra-intuitionist" Alexander Yessenin-Volpin, with whom she collaborated from the late 1970s until his death in 2016. Interestingly, many of these mathematicians also had significant political or spiritual commitments that shaped their lives and work: Grothendieck more or less withdrew from professional mathematics after realizing that his work was being sponsored and used by the military-industrial complex; Lawvere was a Marxist interested in dialectical approaches to questions of mathematical foundations (as well as being an antiwar activist); Yessenin-Volpin was imprisoned in Russia because of his criticisms of the Russian state; Brouwer was deeply religious and saw his work as part of a withdrawal from and transformation of "the sad world."[31] Hennix's own life trajectory similarly has involved a fidelity to certain intellectual principles at the cost of institutional success and sanction.

Even those with a mathematical training may struggle with Hennix's work, which synthesizes mathematical and nonmathematical approaches in original and noncanonical ways. Hennix observed an aesthetic quality to the work of Grothendieck et al.—and the creativity of these mathematicians had implications for Hennix for artistic practice as well, providing tools, theories, ideas, and frameworks that offered new artistic possibilities. In other words, mathematical logic, formulae, diagrams, and so on could become artistic materials—and part of what she called an "algebraic aesthetics." This also amounts to a serious challenge to the nonmathematically literate listener, who needs to both understand quite advanced and often controversial or nonstandard mathematical ideas in order to be able to follow Hennix, and then also understand the ways that she is creatively absorbing and playing with those ideas as the basis of sonic and visual works, as well as in theory.[32]

Hennix's interests are already evident in the course she proposed (but did not teach) for Mills College in 1973, in which she suggests "investigating so-called infinitary compositions, a radically new approach initiated by La Monte Young and subsequently formalized by myself. An infinitary composition is based on an abstract (formal) pattern that allows for it to be indefinitely expanded in a non-trivial sense. These expansions are provided for by means of a process of iterative procedures called algorithms which incidentally play a key role in the processing of information in digital computers." In terms of music's leaving the correlationist circle, Hennix notes that "the sounds thus created have never before been heard, but in addition, and this is the most important part, the sounds will follow in a coherent pattern."[33]

In "Fixed Points," one of the "Infinitary Compositions," composed in February 1973, the composition consists of a set "w," which includes all fractions, that is, ratios of integers whose value falls between 1 and 2—"in a natural way these can be made to correspond to the corresponding rational intervals within the octave," that is, all the intervals that are defined as just intonation intervals.[34] Hennix then proposes operations on a segment of these intervals—without specifying which precise intervals they will be—since there are in fact (infinitely?) many. This lack of local (though not global) specification, or conversely the highly abstract and general nature of the composition is characteristic of Hennix's mathematical interventions in music. There are few if any traditional scores in Hennix's oeuvre, even though the selection of a matrix of pitches is key to the (almost entirely) modal music that Hennix plays, and she takes great care with teaching her musicians accuracy of pitch (mostly by ear).

By the mid-1970s, Hennix spoke explicitly of her music as an "intuitionistic modal music" in a response to Stockhausen's concept of "intuitiv musik." By modal music, we can understand the world of tuning systems and scales that they engender, as elaborated above. Intuitionism in mathematics is a school of thought founded by Brouwer in the early twentieth century. Although it is frequently marginalized within the history of mathematics, intuitionism is still acknowledged as being one of the three core modern schools of mathematical thought: the others being formalism (in which a number, formalized as a numeral notation, does not represent anything, it is merely a syntactic element within a system or structure, cf. Hilbert) and Platonism (numbers are real because they are forms that the mind perceives as real as perceivable realities in everyday life—cf. Kurt Gödel).[35]

The core of intuitionism, according to Brouwer, is that mathematical entities, such as numbers, emerge out of the self-contemplation of the mathematical thinker, who Brouwer calls a *Creative Subject*, a term that Hennix also adopts in her own work. A Creative Subject has the (foundational) experience of the splitting of time in that self-contemplation into what Brouwer called the "twoity": the present moment and its passing into the past as memory.[36] All of mathematics can be constructed out of this "twoity," which is an active construction of thought one form of which is what Brouwer calls "choice sequences" that are determined by a kind of logic, known as intuitionistic logic. Interestingly, for Brouwer, it was the act of thinking these choice sequences that mattered, not the writing down of the sequences as completed constructions (although Brouwer did, of course, write down many of his results). Hennix's notion of "infinitary compositions" is built around the Brouwerian idea of infinite sequences of integers of which only a finite initial segment is mentally available at any one time—these being the choice sequences in question. In intuitionistic mathematics, these choice sequences unfold in the form of Heyting algebras—similar to Boolean, that is, conventional algebra, but without the requirement of the law of the excluded middle, one of the classic laws of logic. It is in this (logical) space opened up where the law of the excluded middle is suspended that something of ontological—and musical—significance emerges.

For example, Hennix's drone can be thought of as the articulation of a constant choice sequence, in which the same choice is repeated potentially ad infinitum. In her brief essay "Notes on Intuitionistic Modal Music," which was published in a booklet that accompanied Hennix's multimedia show *Brouwer's Lattice*, of which the recorded performance of *The Electric Harpsichord* was one part, Hennix writes:

> Maybe the most vivid of the Modalities of Modal Music is the Modality of Infinity. The idea of the infinite refers to an unending process, that is, a process without any conceivable end, reaching out toward the Future, while constantly leaving the Past pulsing behind. Here, one can find the basic substance of the intuition of Time as it reveals itself in its most undisturbed form. But although Time might be the most requisite part of music, there are nonetheless equally vivid and important vertical tactics of attention, each requiring its specific spectra of Modalities, all of which unfold with the directed spreads of time. It is the liberation of the latter Modalities that the Creative Subject constructs when he is subject to an activity involving the 2 Basic Acts of Intuitionism. . . . Here, the mind is cleaned from its excess garbage by controlled acts of intuitions and the vertical Modalities crystallize out to abstract configurations of intensions and arrow diagrams.[37]

Note the way that the phenomenological core of intuitionism, the awareness of time, becomes the basis of both mathematical and musical entities. Note also the importance of "tactics of attention," implying practices by which the subject comes into being in relation to a nonlinguistic nonknowledge. And note that, in contrast to the apparent orientation of speculative philosophy toward a pervasive exteriority, the orientation here is toward an interiority that is noncorrelationist. Because awareness is evolving or crystallizing, there is the sense in which a knowledge beyond correlation is being constructed iteratively. "The whole inner self can be mapped onto modal structures," says Hennix in an interview accompanying *Brouwer's Lattice*, "What you get aware of by exposure to our music is awareness of general patterns, it's a purely abstract and private imprint, not a factual thing. . . . And that is why I insist on claiming that music should open up new tactics of attention, in which terms the audience can redevelop their ambiguously acquired modalities."[38] In her more recent writings, Hennix talks about this emergent property in terms of neuroplasticity and practices of attention that retune neurocognitive structures, allowing for new kinds of attention and affect to occur.[39]

It's worth dwelling on the word *awareness*, and on practices or modalities of awareness, because part of what is at stake in debates about correlationism is what is meant by a subject of awareness. What intrigues me about Hennix's commitment to intuitionism is the possibility of an interior exteriority, or put another way, a breaching of the limit of correlationism in inner rather than exterior space. At first, it sounds very solipsistic. But if intuitionist practices are to be presented, and not just thought, then what they refuse is not external reality, but merely a discursively conceived public space. Hennix's "intuitionistic modal music" offers a startling model for improvisation: a logic of improvisation, if you will, built around the construction of sonic choice sequences. And a different way of being in, if not of the world.

5

It is this thought of "intuitionist" art that forms the focus of what remains, to date, Hennix's most important public presentation of her work: an installation piece/space entitled *Brouwer's Lattice*, in which the Deontic Miracle performed a ten-day program of music and soundworks (March 20–30, 1976) at the Moderna Museet in Stockholm, built around a composite waveform that saturated the space.[40] The installation consisted of lightboxes (presenting an illuminated print made by Alison Knowles) showing the waveforms that were part of the drone, as well as a laser projection of the composite sound wave form picked up from vibrating mirrors. This installation was to be presented in conjunction with a visual art/installation exhibition entitled *Toposes and Adjoints*, which used the same drone sound as *Brouwer's Lattice*.[41] The presentation of *Toposes and Adjoints* was in fact delayed and then presented at the Moderna Museet from September 4 to October 13, 1976.

The phrase *deontic miracle* indexes the word deontic, referring to deontic logic, which sets out the logical structure of an ethics, involving modal notions such as obligation, permission, and so on. Therefore, a "deontic miracle" would be a miracle achieved or produced through a necessary and sufficient set of logical premises and/or structures in an otherwise merely "possible" situation. In other words, a miracle that (paradoxically) is achieved through logical application. In 2019 Hennix described it as "an impossible event in a possible situation" and then quipped that since the group had never been allowed to play in Sweden, getting to play at the Museet was itself "an impossible permission" and a kind of miracle.

The group performed a number of "chagaku" compositions at the March festival, including "Choshi, Netori, Music of Auspicious Clouds, Waves of the Blue Sea, Five Times Repeated Music, Butterfly Music, Central Palace Music"; the compositions were defined via a mixture of Japanese notations, rational intervals, and verbal instructions. "It's a massive sound that's deployed," Hennix recalls, "and it's rather unpredictable where it's going, so you have to be there and guide it in one direction or another but you never know where you end up so you have to be prepared for any possibility when you play."[42]

Hennix also performed solo on keyboards (a three-manual tunable Yamaha synthesizer and a Fender Rhodes) during the festival. Hennix's most well-known recording, *The Electric Harpsichord*, was made during one of these performances: the piece is partially an improvisation on the scale of Raga Multani (one of the basic teaching ragas that Pran Nath would have used with students) made on the just intonation–tuned Yamaha and put through a tape recorder–based time lag system that introduces a variable delay over a sine wave oscillator drone. It was performed over a sound system that outputs 100DB so that the full range of harmonics can be heard. At least two performances were made, one using a harpsichord setting, the other using a marimba setting.[43] Although the audience who heard the piece was apparently enthusiastic, there was no follow-up and there were no further invitations to perform the piece, which became a kind of samizdat recording heard by only a few over the following decades.

The premises of intuitionism suggest, however, that the creation of public works may not be the most important function of a vibrational practice, aesthetic or otherwise. Having visited Hennix over a period of a number of years, and listened to the drone that is always on in her living space, I think that her sonic practice serves a primarily meditative purpose, of constant phenomenological alignment with a truth, that makes public performance epiphenomenal. What matters most is to remain attuned: and given the improvisatory nature of intuitionist acts of attunement, the construction of states of heightened awareness is active and dynamic, rather than consisting of stale acts of repetition. Which is not to say that there are no paths or logics that are worthy of being retraced, or that the mental states that are attained in these practices are not worth sharing. Furthermore, in terms of the uncanny way Hennix's drones seem to exert surprising and specific effects on listeners relative to other musical works that superficially resemble them (i.e., drone music), one has to take seriously the notion that Hennix's improvisations do involve a logic that unfolds within the space of improvisation as a series of informed intuitive discernments. Still, the notion that there might be an inner work of transformation of the subject without which all exterior communications of a vibrational practice, all politics is pointless, is worth taking seriously. It is a spiritual idea. It goes profoundly against the politics of communication, mediation, and collective engagement within which most of us live today.

In an essay on *The Electric Harpsichord*, Henry Flynt wrote:

> These projects had a common feature which traces back to the culture of tuning championed by La Monte Young. The thrust of modern technology was to transfer the human act to the machine, to eliminate the human in favor of the machine, to study phenomena contrived to be independent of how humans perceived them. In contrast, the culture of tuning which Young transmitted by example to his acolytes let conscious discernment of an external process define the phenomenon. The next step is to seek the laws of conscious discernment or recognition of the process. And the next step is to invent a system driven by improvisation monitored by conscious apperception of the process.[44]

Charles Stein once said to me that the core of Hennix's work was ethical. At the same time, this ethics is mathematical, it takes the form of a logic, and music is one of the creative products of such a logic. This notion of ethics is an important part of the work of one of Hennix's key mentors/collaborators, Yessenin-Volpin, founder of ultra-intuitionism. An introduction to how Yessenin-Volpin thinks may be found in his essay "On the Logic of the Moral Sciences," which forms a key part of *Being = Space × Action*, the 1988 volume devoted to Hennix's work and edited by Stein.[45] The core idea in this essay is that it suffices that freedom is defined negatively (as freedom from coercion, fraud, and deprivation of means) and requires that one should be able to fully account for the actions one takes, in order that any coercion or denial of means may be detected. In mathematics, the result is indeed an "ultra" "intuitionism" in which a claim must be fully proven or demonstrated: thus, the question of whether or not there is such a thing as a countable/denumerable infinity would mean actually producing that number sequence. In her 1976 essay "Notes on Toposes and Adjoints," Hennix transposed this argument to aesthetic practice:

> One of the basic tenets of our (eleutheric) relevance theory is its commitment to just and purposeful acts of communication. Id est acts freed from obstacles, fraud and coercion. Obviously, this principle is clearly related to ideas in ethics as well as epistemology (of certainty) and it

constitutes a cornerstone of our general theory of modalities, which will be developed in a subsequent paper. Purposefulness means, above all, that the means associated with the aims are sufficient for achieving the aims.... The justness of an act is simply its admissibility in the context of its appearance.[46]

This observation relates to one of Hennix's core claims—that ethics and aesthetics are inextricably linked in that what is aesthetically permissible in a society is a consequence of the ethics of that society. Concerning long-duration works, Hennix observed: "Length has to do with space in society, how much space can be taken up by musical performance?... Our long performance styles are very good pedagogic examples of overcoming the obstacles existing for Freedom in our society. This is how musical performance connects with ethics. There are obstructions for these long style performances and our music documents the overcoming of those obstacles."[47]

If the kinds of long-durational works that Hennix favors—with the intense demands they make on musicians in terms of practice, research on the acoustical environment they are playing in, and so on—are pragmatically impossible, this is because of that society's refusal to step up ethically. And, as a result, music becomes a dumbed-down, commodified, abbreviation of what it might otherwise be—an observation strikingly similar to what Pandit Pran Nath might have said about the situation of Indian classical music in the mid-twentieth century. The point in the end is a cosmopolitical one: where the limits of society's definition of what music can be are pushed against, in the name of a different audition and framework.

But the logic here also involves a strange twist: in both her writing and in conversation, Hennix is interested in producing "languages" that are beyond interpretation, that are definitive in terms of the ways in which inputs result in a reliable way in outputs. This appears then to be a kind of programming language with a semiotics to be distinguished from that which is operative in everyday life—a seemingly impossible one, in the same way that the foundational intuitionist moment of the "twoity" could arguably never exist without the subject who experiences it bringing some kind of preexisting mathematical understanding to the supposedly originary event of the "twoity." In "Modalities and Languages for Algorithms," Henry Flynt's 1983 parsing of "Toposes and Adjoints," the term *epistemic modality* is used to describe such a language—an epistemic art if you will.[48] The point of such a modality is to reliably lead the person who engages with the procedures to an elevated epistemic state or illumination. "Reliably" in this sense means that the protocols are elaborated in sufficient detail or depth that they can be carried out without going astray. Interestingly though, in "Modalities," Flynt "editing" Hennix observes:

> In order to reach a highly articulated result, you have to have an algorithm.... If a highly articulated result could happen spontaneously without guarantees that its prerequisites had been met, I would call that a miracle.... My personality is not especially consistent. For example, I claim that my intuitionistic modal music, exemplified by "Electric Harpsichord No. 1," is one of these "miracles" by the norms of rule-logic (deontic logic). This music is a borderline case between a theoretical activity and a dream activity: because it is grounded in the law of sufficient reason (in this case, the requirement to be rational and not arbitrary); yet a miracle relative to rule-logic is present in it (a highly articulated result comes without an algorithm).[49]

This tension between an increasingly rigorous algorithmic proposal aimed at a state of illumination and a principle of improvisatory activity whose closest correlate is "dream activity" is characteristic of Hennix's work. When I met with her in February 2016, she complained about how difficult it was to get her band to play intuitively within the pulsating spaces of the modal compositions that she constructs. We had been sitting in her studio listening to a new version of "Solo for Two Tamburas and One Player" and I had drifted off into a state of dream-like unconsciousness triggered by the deeply psychotropic qualities of the music.[50] When she spoke to me, there was an uncanny sense of a bubble popping, or a taut piece of elastic being loosened up, or being snapped out of a trance. What she requested of her musicians was that they in some way play from the unconscious, while paradoxically retaining the performative discipline required to stay precisely within the pitch structure of the piece. What Hennix was arguing for was something like a raga, in the sense of a "living soul" or a negentropic principle of self-organization taking the form of a pitch structure. The elevated state that interested her would arise immanently as a result of the algorithmic prescriptions she was making, and when it did, this "miracle" or principle of self-organization would somehow play the band, who would become the vehicles or instruments of an increasingly deep elaboration of this vibrational matrix—a matrix that would guide the musicians, whose job was to stay open and attuned to it.

There is a very interesting politics implied within this approach to making music: against the risk of the instrumentalization of a set of algorithmic principles, Hennix's music requires an act of noncoercive engagement that she sometimes calls a "freedom," which would be that of acting from the site of the unconscious. Indeed, in 2017 she spoke of her interest in "the practice of the unconscious" that Italian feminist groups such as the Via Cherubini collective had explored in the 1970s.[51] Hennix approached such a practice via music. Such a practice was not arbitrary, nor exactly irrational—it was "a concerted human action . . . which places man in a position to treat the real by the symbolic" as mid-career Lacan noted.[52] It owed much to the mathemes of Lacan's later work, which he thought more efficacious than linguistic formulations in mapping and/or working with the unconscious.[53] If most of Lacan's mathemes, however, remained basically hieroglyphic, with very little actual mathematics involved, Hennix's mathemes engage the rigor of her own mathematical work—via Brouwer, Lawvere, Grothendieck, and others—while still engaging, among other things, psychoanalytic notions of the unconscious. And, as a "practice of the unconscious," they take the form of music, albeit music developed according to certain mathematical ideas and practices. This is also what distinguishes Hennix's music from, say, traditional raga or modal jazz for that matter, both of which could be trivially or nontrivially described as involving an intuitive improvisation mobilizing the unconscious while requiring disciplined articulation of pitch structure. Something opened up in Hennix's performances/compositions that was "in you more than you," to use Lacan's expression.[54]

6

The Deontic Miracle continued to practice in Stockholm in anticipation of phone calls and invitations to play that never appeared, and in 1978, Hennix moved to New York to take up a position in the math department at SUNY New Paltz, which she held until 1982 or 1983. In 1978 she also had a gallery show at Redbird Gallery in Brooklyn. She also resumed an ongoing connection with the philosopher/fiddler Henry Flynt that had begun in 1969. "I met Henry at La Monte's loft, he was doing this fantastic violin solo, he blew me away," Hennix recalls. "I asked him about concept art and that was how our friendship began. I came to New York as a visual artist but I was also known as a composer of Darmstadt type music. At the beginning we were both obsessed with physics, and Henry started a seminar on physics, which Tony Conrad was a part of too."[55]

The resonances between Flynt's work and Hennix's are complex—for example, Flynt's 1961 composition, "Each Point on This Line Is a Composition," clearly motivates some of the Infinitary Compositions. More generally, Flynt's formulations of concept art and his critique of existing art structures contribute to the sense of a radically opened-up field of activity in which

Hennix's metamathematical propositions might flourish—although Flynt's "cognitive nihilism" and Hennix's intuitionistic constructions are by no means equivalent.[56]

In terms of music, Flynt was stunned when he heard *The Electric Harpsichord* and the two began collaborating on electronic pieces, Flynt producing some of his most remarkable violin recordings, including "Celestial Power," "You are My Everlovin'," and "C Tune," over Hennix's tambura recordings.[57] They also collaborated on an important but at the time mostly unnoticed event at the Kitchen on February 7, 1979, at which they announced "a new kind of interdisciplinary genre, the hallucinatory/ecstatic sound environment (HESE)."[58] In a highly unusual press release that announced Flynt and Hennix's intentions, they describe the HESE project as follows:

> A taped synthesis of musical sounds, the HESE typically uses modal scales and sensuously appealing timbres which fill the audio spectrum. The audio programs consist of semi-regular processes, but they are multilayered and micro-irregular, producing variable diffraction effects. The listener's attention is monopolized; the physical vibration is physically felt; the uniformity of texture produces a sense that time is suspended. The "natural highs" experienced by the listener call for a new logico-mathematical structure, and Flynt and Hennix will provide expository material on a structure congruous with these ecstatic states of consciousness. The two composers collaborating on the project have differences on the state of consciousness sought and its logico-mathematical interpretation, differences reflected in their respective approaches to the work. Hennix's approach originates in a study of the relationship between modal music and states of consciousness. Flynt conceives of the HESE as a counter-attack on everyday life and consensus reality. . . . Not only are the HESEs sensually appealing, they utilize aural illusions which produce logically impossible or unnameable perceptions. The aim is a state of being with no foundation.[59]

Recordings of *The Electric Harpsichord* and two Flynt tape pieces, "Glissando #1" and "Celestial Power," were played, and a booklet was distributed containing an essay of Flynt's on *The Electric Harpsichord*, and a text of Hennix's entitled "17 Points on Intensional Logics for Intransitive Experiences." The event appears to have failed with at least some listeners: a *New York Times* review praised Flynt's work, while noting that Hennix's piece "concluded an otherwise fascinating evening on a shrill, buzzing note that rang unpleasantly in this reviewer's ears."[60]

The "natural highs" and "new logico-mathematical structure," that Hennix and Flynt called for in the press release suggest that the recordings were not to be understood as music or art but as a new kind of post-art work that, in accordance with Flynt's post-concept art philosophy, would usher in a new kind of society. The press release also notes that Flynt and Hennix had differences on this point: "Hennix's approach originates in a study of the relationship between modal music and states of consciousness. Flynt conceives of the HESE as a counter-attack on everyday life and consensus reality."[61] Despite his close association with Young, Flynt was relatively indifferent to the claims regarding the power of just intonation-based music, and the mysticism of mathematics that it implied. In his various writings on Hennix and the HESE event, he emphasizes a subversion and appropriation of prevailing forms of art and science in the name of a new project, one of whose names would be the aforementioned metatechnology (which term he first coined in 1979 too).[62] Metatechnology was to function both as a deconstruction of prevailing scientific norms and ideologies via technological propositions and artifacts (for example, a hypothetical technology that could erase or neutralize all nuclear weapons), and it was to propose new kinds of scientific/postscientific praxis that were put at the disposal of a new kind of society focused on new kinds of telos. Therefore, HESE was metatechnological because it was a technology aimed toward producing preferred or highly valued states such as ekstasis or dignity. In a conversation with me in 2017, Hennix emphasized that she had never seen herself as producing art, music, poetry, and so on—but that she was part of a movement of people in the 1960s who sought to replace art with something else (Flynt's 1960s writings on the supersession of art by "brend" are a key example). She lamented that the movement did not get very far, and that now the work that she and others had done was being reappropriated back into traditional aesthetic frameworks (the music festival, the art museum, and so on).

In the abstract, these kinds of metamusical frameworks might appear at best tautological, and at worst an irritating attempt at scoring a theoretical home run around the historicity of actually existing musical practices and the challenges that come with them. But Flynt and Hennix's argument is not merely metadescriptive. It both describes what music is normatively understood as and places this description within a cosmopolitical framework that suggests a radically expanded definition of what music can or could be, while also prescribing specific rules that define the success or failure of particular experiments at producing particular metatechnological effects. This model involved a noncorrelationist theory of the subject, driven by an evolving concept of practice and improvisation within specifically articulated frameworks (which in some cases Hennix would call "toposes"; see section 7). To quote Flynt again, from his essay on Hennix: "The state of consciousness that matters for philosophy is an exceptional state, and it has to be attained. Hennix delineates this state with a logical theory."[63]

Hennix and Flynt's project, and indeed their disagreements as to some of the details, raise a number of important questions: What is the relationship between music and technics? Is all music "technological" and therefore potentially the site of a metatechnological intervention? Indeed, is "metatechnology" an expansion of technics or a reframing that goes beyond technics? Conversely, in making the argument that music is a cosmopolitical practice, is it in fact technics or technology that determines what music can be, and should we therefore speak of a "cosmotechnics" in the sense that Yuk Hui has recently developed—cosmotechnics representing the way a technological structure or practice emerges in relation to a particular cosmology or worlding in a particular community?[64] I will address some of these questions in a more general way in the next chapter and confine myself here to Flynt and Hennix's milieu. Pandit Pran Nath's musical practice, which was a factor that stimulated both Flynt's and Hennix's work, suggests that not all music can be framed in terms of technics, even in the rigorous and radically expanded way that Bernard Stiegler and Yuk Hui have reformulated the term.[65] There is an ambiguity there: while music that involves instruments can be thought of prosthetically, the human voice is not prosthetic in the same way. But Pran Nath's singing certainly involved practice and technique—clearly framed by a radically different cosmology from that of modernist music. Are all practices therefore technical? And what then of the "inner sound," or for that matter the sound of the unconscious, which seem to exist outside of any concept of technique, other than that of listening? Flynt has argued that metatechnology is intended to open up in the direction of "cognitive nihilism"—thus it suggests an experimental or speculative cosmopolitics, rather than one rooted in tradition or an existing community. In his key 1996 essay "The Collectivity after the Abolition of the Universe and Time: Escaping from Social Science," Flynt writes:

> In this hypothetical civilization, the collective can freely change the laws of nature. That presupposes claims, made previously and elsewhere, that scientific reality can be superseded. There is a dispelling of deceit and gullibility, concomitantly with the awakening of faculties, and with emotional sensitization: yielding intellectual techniques which supersede the compartmentation of faculties characterizing the present culture. Thereby, new mental abilities are invented. The community is open to avenues of

metamorphosis of the life-world. The comprehensively assembled "metatechnology" would be self-conscious about the inherited view of factual reality, going beyond it in an operative way. Again, my perspective is that of a novel arena which outruns what was formerly considered factual reality.

Metatechnology reaches out toward a "community that is to come," although so far, as Flynt has repeatedly observed, there have been few takers.[66]

Hennix's perspective is cosmopolitical in a more synthetic sense—her work opens up the complex relationship and divergence of science and technology, where disputes in the foundations of science, mathematics, logic, and philosophy and the application of novel positions within these disputes create a highly elastic version of "technics" that makes situational use of existing musical instruments and technologies while also generating new ones. As with Flynt, the pathos of these ambitious and rigorous propositions consists in the indifference with which they were received—a praxis that only unfolded in a limited way, within an alternative music scene.

The HESEs, or "illuminatory sound environments" as Hennix later preferred to name them clearly, had a precedent in the sound and light installations known as "dream houses" made by La Monte Young and Marian Zazeela in the 1960s. In a text dating back to 1964, Young wrote:

> In the life of the Tortoise the drone is the first sound. It lasts forever and cannot have begun but is taken up again from time to time until it lasts forever as continuous sound in Dream Houses where many musicians and students will live and execute a musical work. Dream Houses will allow music which, after a year, ten years, a hundred years or more of a constant sound, would not only be a real living organism with a life and tradition all its own but one with a capacity to propel itself by its own momentum. Thus, music may play without stopping for thousands of years, just as the Tortoise has continued for millions of years past, and perhaps only after the Tortoise has again continued for as many million years as all of the tortoises in the past will it be able to sleep and dream of the next order of tortoises to come and of ancient tigers with black fur omens the 189/98 whirlwind in the Ancestral Lake Region only now that our species has had this much time to hear music that has lasted so long because we have just come out of a long quiet period and we are just remembering how long sounds can last and only now becoming civilized enough again that we want to hear sounds continuously. It will become easier as we move further into this period of sound. We will become more

attached to sound. We will be able to have precisely the right sound in every dreamroom playroom and workroom, further reinforcing the integral proportions resonating through structure (re. earlier Architectural Music), Dream House (shrines, etc.) at which performers, students, and listeners may visit even from long distances away or at which they may spend long periods of Dreamtime weaving the ageless quotients of the Tortoise in the tapestry of Eternal Music.[67]

The roots of the Dream House are themselves to be found in the evolution of the visual arts toward installation art and the configuration of space and/or duration as an aesthetic act or project. It was a project explored by many people in many ways in the United States after Cage, after Fluxus (which of course Young and Flynt were part of) and others, yet the Dream House has its own specificity as a vibrational space composed through the selection and modulation of highly specific sound and light frequencies. While much of the text above is a complex allegory concerning the members of the Theater of Eternal Music (advanced research question: What in fact is a theater of eternal music?), the vision of sonic spaces as shrines devoted to sustained sounds remains a powerful, and for the most part still unrealized vision, outside of the Dream House space on the top floor of Young and Zazeela's loft in Tribeca, New York. Hennix elaborated on her version of the HESE in a text written with Flynt to accompany the "illuminatory sound environment" created at ZKM in Karlruhe in 2013:

> By an Illuminatory Sound Environment (ISE) is meant a psychotropically working sonic agency which transports the listener to an alternate state of mind the portals to which are closed without the sound as guide and input. ISE works on more than one level of mind and the priming of all these levels increases the listening subject's receptivity to the ramified lamina of 'sheets of sounds' which build up the integral sound defining the sonic space engaged.
>
> An ISE needs a dedicated acoustic space which provides the listener unlimited access to its sound which is often continuous and frequently cyclic and all pitches are fixed in accordance with standards of just intonation. The repeated exposure to this sound environment exerts a priming of the attentive listening subject consisting in an activation of neural plasticity dynamics which lays down new signal paths connected with neural sound processing sites. As a function of this neural priming activity, the listening subject acquires a heightening sensibility to present threshold acoustical events by cultivating new neural tissue—the innervation of

which provides the portals to hitherto unvisited and unmapped sonically mediated sites and regions of mind.[68]

This text reiterates the argument of earlier texts, while providing a neurobiological mechanism by which the immersive "dedicated acoustic space" can produce particular desired effects on a listener. In the final paragraph of the text, the authors focus on "tactics of attention" again as the key to shifting the mind in the direction of ekstasis and dignity via a languageless activity. There is a coalescence of inner and outer. The tactics of attention would not work with an arbitrary set of tones. The structure of the tones involves a logic (an intensional logic), not simply in the fact of designing a certain sound, but because iterative exposure to the sound works "logically" on the subject in moving her toward a particular exposure to the vibrational/mathematico-physical-spiritual structures of being, or, conversely involves the subject's elaboration of a wordless sequence of logical transformations and propositions that take affective and sonic form.

7

To think of Hennix's sound environments as merely the installation of a sound in a space, as opposed to, say, a concert or a performance fails to capture Hennix's thought however. The framing of the events of the HESE evening as "sound environments" involved a much deeper sense of sonic space. This brings me to the second of Hennix's innovations in terms of an ontology of sound—which is connected to the word *topos*. While the mathematical ideas here are challenging, and difficult to give a nontechnical introduction to, we can start with a philosophical idea of a topos as a site or place in which abstractions, generalizations, or modelings of the concept of space can occur, beyond the intuitive ideas of Euclidian three-dimensional space that we have. Space is a mystery, space is a question mark, and space can be mathematically modeled in different ways. Or, to put in Lawvere's terms, "The core of mathematical theories is in the variation of quantity in space and in the emergence of quality within that."[69] Everything will follow from this.

There are two separate but interrelated versions of the idea of a topos, one emerging out of Alexander Grothendieck's work in algebraic geometry circa 1958–70, associated with what are now called "Grothendieck toposes"; the other by William Lawvere, emerging out of category theory, as a formalization of notions from mathematical logic, with the idea of an "elementary topos." It is Lawvere's ideas that were most significant to Hennix in the 1970s—but since Grothendieck was an important source of Lawvere's ideas, and because (I will argue) Hennix draws out certain consequences from Lawvere's ideas that are closer to Grothendieck's expansive vision, it is hard to entirely separate the two.[70]

What is the relationship among different mathematical fields such as algebra, geometry, topology, set theory, which are each capable of describing universes of mathematical objects? Mathematicians such as Grothendieck, working after World War II, demonstrated the possibility of the transformation/commutability of these different mathematical fields, along with their objects and functions, into each other, such that a problem in geometry or topology could be rendered and worked on in algebraic terms, and vice versa. Lawvere and others did something similar with set theory, which for most of the twentieth century was considered the primary mathematical language for defining mathematical entities. Building on the earlier work of Saunders Mac Lane and Samuel Eilenberg, Lawvere and others developed a powerful and flexible language which was abstract and general enough that it was capable of encompassing and articulating diverse mathematical fields. In Alain Badiou's words:

> Mathematicians and logicians have been able to propose (this is the formal substance of the most contemporary logic) a *general theory of possible universes*. In essence, we start with letters ("objects") whose signification remains indeterminate, with relations ("arrows") which are just as empty, and we define the operations in an entirely abstract way, through diagrams and algebraic calculations. In this way we produce absolutely general concepts of what the product or sum of two entities is, of what the exponentiation of one entity by another is, of what the fibred product of two relations is, etc. These minimal operations on letters and arrows provide an initial framework, which we call a category. The more operations a category admits, the richer and vaster for thought the universe it formalizes is.
>
> Schematically, a category which admits every operation that can be performed within the basic ontological situation (set theory) will be considered a 'complete' universe, that is, a universe wherein thought moves without encountering its impossible limit. Such a category is called a *Topos*.[71]

Category theory has ontological or foundational significance since, aside from providing a general language of objects and arrows that describe the logical operations that are possible within a particular universe, it also explores the general logical operations that allow one to connect or correlate or establish equivalence between elements of different categories via the idea of a functor (an arrow or morphism, if you like, between categories). Intriguingly, as Hennix points out, a "site" can be occupied not only by objects, but by arrows, that is, not only the variety of objects that could be instantiated as x at a site but also the arrow or morphism by which generic object x can be translated into generic object y. Also, intriguingly, the internal logic that is operative in a topos is intuitionistic logic (i.e., Heyting algebras), meaning that the law of the excluded middle is not (necessarily) applied. I will stop there—for me, understanding these points as a mostly nonmathematician has been like learning to ride a particularly wild horse, leaving me ontologically bruised but occasionally exhilarated by a particular vista. Hennix's invitation to the "non-alien reader" is that there is something worth understanding here, and that the reader should apply herself accordingly and patiently, assuming the dignity of a challenging but very possible activity, modestly but seriously.[72]

Hennix has used the ideas of topos and category, and their associated machineries, in a variety of ways throughout her career, often in playful or paradoxical ways. In order to appreciate how the idea of a topos can be used to think about music (something we will explore further in the next chapter), it is helpful to understand some of the more general ways in which Hennix understands toposes in her work.

1. The idea of composing (art, poetry, music) via diagrams—that a painting, a poem, a piece of music can all be understood as occurring in a "logical space" that can be rendered explicit in the work itself. Conversely, an appreciation of the poetic composition of rigorous mathematic theories such as those found in Grothendieck's algebraic geometry seminars. While the idea of constructing by diagrams, particularly those framed as input/outputs as in category theory, is obviously attractive in fields such a computer science, the idea is more unfamiliar in the arts. What it raises, in Hennix's work, is the idea of composing in relation to target states, that is, starting with a desired output, and developing a flowchart whose machinery results in the desired output. In Hennix's case, the target states have been variously labeled "sustained states of awareness," eleutheria (i.e., freedom), ekstasis, jouissance, and a feeling of being united with an undifferentiated cosmic whole or totality (figured as the continuum, Buddhist sunyata, the Beloved in Sufi monism, the Parmenidean One, etc.). Hennix's program, then, is to (logically) propose a series of musical events in relation to these target states. Needless to say, these are not standard mathematical goals or practices. Category theory offers a very abstract

but also very flexible method of notation for arranging sounds. Perhaps equally importantly, it opens the possibility of thinking music from the perspective of abstract diagrams that can include but are in no way limited to the modern Western staff-based system.

2 From the beginning, Hennix applied ideas of category and topos to different scholarly and artistic fields of art. Influenced by Richard Montague's set theoretical framings of natural language semantics and Joachim Lambek's algorithmic approach to linguistics, both of which attempt to set out a logical structure for natural languages, Hennix incorporated these ideas into a theory of mind.[73] Reframing Husserl's "noemas" as initial pure or stainless mental objects or acts, which are then captured by normative language structures, Hennix proposed to generate "just and purposeful" languages, including musical ones. The idea clearly resonates with practices of computation too, from the 1973 Mills College prospectus, and its emphasis on sonic algorithms, to her work in the early 1980s at Marvin Minsky's AI laboratory at MIT, during which period she wrote the brilliant "Pre-History of Cybernetics" paper.[74] It should be noted, however, that Hennix distinguishes between analog and digital computation processes and wryly proposed, in line with intuitionist ethics, a computer that would be assembled for a single task and then abandoned. Conversely, one might say that practices of composition must emerge from the composer's local and specific creative acts of construction, not from a preset program, but from an interactive one, in the sense that this phrase is used in computer science. "Notes on Toposes and Adjoints" was originally written for an exhibition of paintings, sculptures, and installation works, with the idea of a canvas as a logical space, and "4-color algebras" computing in that logical space. Hennix's later work "La Séminaire," which also references the idea of the topos was written for an exhibition of paintings, including the *Tryptique Lacanienne*, which also consists of diagrams emerging from abstract color-space. The "Abstract Noh" plays and MA theater approach the "theater of eternal mind," that is, the space of theater as one of ontological questioning by which Noh becomes a topos that exposes the conditions of its own logical space. More recently, Hennix has been interested in the ways in which ideas of topos and category have been applied in physics—notably, in quantum cosmology but also in the basic idea that the question of ontology at the subatomic level, with its stacks of particles and waves, can be framed in terms of modalities, or categories and toposes, that

is, as to the problem of what in fact occupies the site at which wave and/or particle, and so on are found—or whether indeed the problem can be stated in those terms (What exactly is a site, considered from the perspective of a quantum field, or entanglement, and action at a distance, or Grothendieck topoi, or the Parmenidean One? How do we escape the subtly pervasive "metaphysics of presence" still operative in the idea of site as a spatial location with something installed in it, whether matter or points, etc.?).

3 The idea of a topos as model of a state of awareness—of subjectivity as a topos. This was already implied in Brouwer's idea of the Creative Subject who creates mathematical constructions out of an experience of the "twoity" as a mental act. In "Notes on Toposes and Adjoints," this idea is developed so that these mental acts can be said to occur in a logical space, that is, a topos, which is that of subjectivity worthy of the name, that is, subjectivity removed from the mundane and normative aspects of the "sad world" and the poorly articulated languages and algorithms that sustain them. Thus, "modalities correspond to integrated forms of consciousness and form the substance of the awareness of the universe of all logically possible worlds" (69)—in particular, "sustained feelings of awareness" (70) generated via a "tactics of attention" (Brouwer and Young's methods are sutured here) are valued.

These modalities can take the form of mathematical propositions but also acts of musical improvisation, images, or poetry that can be understood as iterations of logical space. "Being = Space × Action" is a statement about the topos of the subject. Actions in/on a space are arrows. But, after 1990, this relatively naive philosophical framework of the topos of the subject, with its lingering existential decisionism, is reconfigured via Hennix's exposure to Lacan's ideas. In Freudian and Lacanian psychoanalysis, the psyche is already rendered topographically or topologically—particularly in terms of understanding the relation of the conscious self to the unconscious, and many of Lacan's mathemes are used to gain mathematico-logical access to this topological structure.[75] For Hennix however, subjectivity is indeed a topos rather than a rigid topological structure, and arrows and morphisms indicate the possibility of states of psychic transformation and illumination, which may themselves be rendered as other toposes.[76] At the same time, the adoption of Lacan's frameworks seems to acknowledge a basic problem: What is the relationship between the mandate for explicit and consciously articulated goals and methods, and the unconscious, which resists such explication? From this, we may extract the basic idea of music as an arrow or morphism—a morphism whose action is effective at the level of the unconscious. This idea is developed in "17 Points on Intensional Logics," the text handed out at the HESE performance at the Kitchen. Intensional logics, meaning in this case the HESE sound environments, offer an experiential decoupling of subjectivity from normative frameworks of space-time—"the intensionality of (for example) a perception can dissolve its timely dimensions into a span of loosely connected time-lines some of which even curve back onto themselves.[77] Hence one has the feeling . . . that Euclidian geometry ceases to determine the perception of space. . . . These aspects may also provide for a revelatory reinterpretation of the experience of subjective reality . . . enforced by a new radiance and space with intensional weight."[78] Discussing the "Composite Sounds Wave Environment E-H-1," Hennix noted the synesthetic experience that the work produced, describing it at once as embodying "an overflowing sense of well-being or state of ecstasy" or alternatively a "quasi-psychotic state of consciousness." Again, the transformation of the subject is stressed: "It is here (Topos) that the authenticity of the self can experience its own echoes with such intensity that the world and the self coalesce in a state of mutual complete intransitivity" (4).

4   The idea of a topos in this last example is not only something lateral, that is, concerned with a chain of arrows, but vertical, with higher degrees of abstraction connecting to higher states of subjective awareness, and with spiritual and philosophical implications. This is set out in "Notes on Toposes and Adjoints" with the idea of spectra of modalities, which are set out hierarchically with "increasingly stricter and stricter condensations of acts of confidence," beginning with generic arrows and at the highest level consisting of "eleutheria," that is, freedom. In "Notes on Toposes and Adjoints," Hennix describes a series of stacked or bracketed universes, such that sheaves ("a lattice of toposes") (111) are followed by cosmoi ("collections of sets of sheaves"), the essay ending with the proposal that it would be possible "to reflect upwards beyond the cosmois towards more and more comprehensive units" (112). The goal here seems to be a series of formalizations of a relation between an initial object or noema (an elementary flash of thought or perception) and an ultimate "target state" that is framed as the category of all categories, whether expressed via infinity, or

the One, or perhaps a black hole—which nonetheless would retain the specificity of the lower-order entities and processes that are held within the higher-order formalizations—such that the lower-order processes would reveal what is to be found at the highest of the high. Once again, we are in the domain of the deontic miracle. This general process is to be found in Hennix's reading of Lacan in "La Séminaire" in the 1990s, where the supposedly structural invariant principle of sexual difference speculatively opens onto a higher-order topos via the adjoint of jouissance. It is also a feature of her abstract Noh plays, in which Hennix recognizes, within the traditional structure of the Noh play, a vertical arrow or adjoint opening onto satori, sunyata, emptiness.

5   The specifically musical applications of these ideas. In simple terms, a musical composition, defined in Hennix's terms as "intuitionistic modal music," involving the construction of a scale, rules for moving around within the scale, and the act of improvising a specific performance within the logic of that structure, can be considered a topos, in terms of a topos's outer and inner formalisms, where the latter comes with an intuitionistic logic, in particular a "continuously variable" locale. But as we have already seen with Hennix's "Notes on Intensional Logics," "the topos of music" and "the topos of the subject" are connected (i.e., "adjoint") in important ways.

In her notes to *The Electric Harpsichord*, Hennix elaborates a series of abstract musical ideas or "Soliton(E) Compositions" that she considers to be "a framework for a topos."[79] These include "The Sound of Shiva—OMSAHASRANAMA," "The N-times Repeated Constant Event [The Five Times Repeated Music, etc.]," "Short Infinitary Processes," and "Topologies for a Vertical Sound."[80] Many of these pieces involve the production of drones, or sustained tones, which are framed as moving toward and approximating a "continuous musical event" via a density of sonic repetition—the time element asymptotically approaches zero leaving a continuously variable space of sound in its place: "Finally, at the 'transfinite stages' of experiencing $\frac{1}{2\pi}^N$ [i.e., the N times Repeated Constant Event], the Creative Subject arrives at a stationary subset of the generated continuum of perceptions at which she retains complete facultative control of the continuum of time-elements which defines the transfinite time object."[81]

The mathematical concept of the continuum is usually rendered via the image of the number line, a simple line between, say, 0 and 1 that contains every possible number between 0 and 1, therefore an infinite number of numbers, although the magnitude of this infinity remains one of the great unsolved problems of mathematics. The intuitionist conception of the continuum emerges out of Brouwer's "twoity," the splitting of time into a passing, past moment and a present. As such the possibility of mathematical systems emerges simultaneously from the splitting or cutting of the intuitive continuum into discrete moments, providing the basis for counting, for example. Yet, conversely, this splitting affirms the continuum as being that which is marked or split open, and which in fact is conserved in the act of being split apart.[82] For Hennix, the "N Times Repeated Constant Event," generated sonically, "splits" time in such a way that the "split," via repetition, becomes static (since, following Zeno and his paradoxes, there is indistinction or nonseparation between the successive elements of the "split") and the "split," in a "deontic miracle," disappears or reverses, exposing (or intending) the Creative Subject to her nonseparation from the One (or continuum). To repeat, the site or space in which this happens is called by Hennix a topos—and in a striking interpretation of what a topos is, Hennix explores the way in which the "logical space" of the topos, in which intuitionistic logic is operative, is emergent from this continuum.

8

Hennix's sound work reached a hiatus in the early 1980s. Inspired by Flynt's proposal for a Genius Liberation Project, the two briefly attempted to start a salon/commune devoted to Flynt's radical ideas for a new society in Woodstock in Upstate New York. But there were few takers. The two also continued to play together with Hennix on drums, as Dharma Warriors. According to Flynt, there are also unreleased recordings from 1978 of a jazz rock trio featuring Arthur Russell on keyboards. Flynt and Hennix played their final show at Phill Niblock's Experimental Intermedia space in 1984, with Marc Johnson on bass, whereupon Flynt, disenchanted with the lack of audience response, packed up his violin. Hennix continued to play drums through the 1980s, notably with the jazz legend Arthur Rhames until his tragic early death in 1989 from AIDS.

Hennix continued her mathematical work, participating in Marvin Minsky's famous AI laboratory at MIT circa 1981–83. Her philosophical work was celebrated in the publication *Being = Space × Action*, which includes a long freeform metamathematical/philosophical text entitled *The Yellow Book* that runs to over one hundred pages. Between 1991 and 1996 she regularly visited Paris, attended Jacques-Alain Miller's seminars, participated in various Lacanian splinter groups, and talked with more broadly psychoanalytic thinkers such as Monique David-Ménard (whose work on the history of hysteria was crucial for her). Hennix produced a number of installation pieces in this period, which were exhibited first at the Fodor Museum in Amsterdam in 1992, in Paris at the Espace Tanguy in 1994, and at the Foundation Enkehuset in Stockholm in 1995. Some of these installations involved her *Tryptique Lacanienne* painting, which juxtaposes some of Lacan's mathemes with her homotopies. These pieces were accompanied by the important text "La Séminaire," subtitled "Intervention Zero," perhaps as a playful "other" seminar that would precede Lacan's Seminars I–XXIV—which Hennix obtained in Lacanian circles in the samizdat copies that were circulating of the still sometimes unpublished seminars.[83] Much of Hennix's work from this period concerns questions of sexual difference and the basis of gender and sexual norms, and is associated with her own process of transitioning, which occurred at this time. Hennix also gave an important series of talks on concept art with Henry Flynt at La Monte Young's Dream House between 1995 and 1999.

Hennix returned to making music in the early 2000s in Amsterdam. Working with computers she began to compose new sine wave drones, which were then the basis for more complex compositions and improvisations for voice and brass instruments. Moving to Berlin in 2010, she formed a band, the Chora(s)san Time-Court Mirage, whose members have included the trombonist Hilary Jeffery, the tuba player and microtonal tuba player and composer Robin Hayward, the vocalist Amelia Cuni, and, more recently, the trumpet player Amir ElSaffar. The increasingly complex computation and sound design involved was done with the assistance of Stefan Tiedje, who had previously worked with Xenakis and Stockhausen. In format, this work was similar to that of the Theater of Eternal Music of La Monte Young, Terry Riley, Tony Conrad, and others (although was there actually a drone for their performances or did they sing and play the entire pitch matrix themselves?)—or to the work of her mid-1970s Stockholm trio, the Deontic Miracle. It drew more on the sine wave and voices pieces that Young had produced, some of them with Hennix, around 1970. However, the sound that Hennix achieves—captured on the CD *Live at the Grimm Museum*—remains uncanny in its corrosion of the phenomenology of sound, as if the vibrational or mathematical substrates somehow pushed through the tones themselves in such a way that reality in its vibrating splendor might appear, and time might slow down or stop or even disappear.

I first spoke with Hennix by phone in 2001 when she was working with Yessenin-Volpin in Cambridge and I was writing about Pandit Pran Nath. We stayed in touch and I helped her distribute a handmade edition of *The Electric*

Harpsichord (the Etymon edition), which she made in an act of devotion for Pran Nath. In 2011, I was in Berlin for a conference and was able to visit Hennix for the first time in the carriage house she rented until the fall of 2019 in Neukölln, the working class/Turkish neighborhood in the south of Berlin. Given that there are very few recordings of Hennix's work available, and that she has not performed very often over the whole expanse of her career, visiting her clarified that being a musician or a composer had an entirely different meaning for her than for most people. A drone played in her house 24/7, a low, pleasant hum that at first sounds slightly off, but which you adjust to over time, as with other just intonation sounds. She regards the drone as a tonic or therapeutic sound. It hums away but then, at odd moments, the sound expands to fill inner space (and its projection, the outer space of the room we're in), as though a sudden dilation has taken place. On her bookshelves were what looked like a complete set of recent Springer Verlag publications on the foundations of mathematics, a complete set of Lacan's seminars in samizdat photocopied form, and CDs of most of John Coltrane's recordings. Upstairs was a bedroom. On the floor was a piece of colored cloth on which two tamburas were lying. Hennix says that she needs to tune the tamburas every day. For Hennix, music making radiates out from this daily practice of tuning, of immersion in sound, and of thinking about sound. While playing, and playing with others, and playing in public, and developing new work, are clearly also part of her practice, the core is a devotional one, a devotion committed to free but rigorous construction of musical universes.

Sometimes, Hennix's philosophical ideas are attempts to track what for her remains a miracle, or mirage, or singularity of sonic illumination. At other times, her actual musical work is the enactment of her philosophical ideas. And, sometimes, there is a fascinating gap between the music and the ideas. In a series of essays that remained unpublished but shared informally as pdfs or photocopies until the 2019 publication of her selected writings by Blank Forms, Hennix set out a new framework for thinking about her music, and music more generally.

An important aspect of this model was readings in quantum field and condensed matter theory and, in particular, the work of the MIT physicist Xiao-Gang Wen on the quantum ether: a pervasive quantum level vibratory field out of which greater than quantum level reality, including light and sound, condenses via bosons.[84] Of interest to Hennix in particular was the importance of "phonons," which are quantum level vibratory fields that also form sound at other levels. As always, Hennix's interest is focused on models where the One and the many are correlated, and the transition between them clearly accounted for—the most obvious example of this being Hennix's critique, with Yessenin-Volpin, of Gödel's incompleteness theorem. In terms of physics, the transit between the One (modeled via quantum cosmology) and the many (modeled as quantum level reality and its condensation in phenomenal greater-than-quantum level reality) was again the focus—but specifically the possibility of music's basis in quantum level effects on consciousness, and a quantum field traversing the unconscious—and acoustic space.

Hennix synthesized these ideas with computational mathematics and harmonics in an important essay called "Hilbert Space Shruti Box" that deploys the foundational quantum mechanical idea of a quantum harmonic oscillator—basically the wave-function of a particle, using Schrodinger's equation, revealing the quantized energy states of the particle in its orbit around the nucleus of an atom.[85] A "Hilbert Space" is the mathematical space in which this wave function is modeled—an extension of Euclidean (three dimensional) space to higher numbers of dimensions. A "shruti box" is a mechanical, usually electronic box that can be used to generate combinations of microtones (i.e., shrutis) for the purpose of providing a drone (i.e., sustained pitch combination) in Indian classical music. What Hennix proposed in this essay was a connection between musical harmonics, the harmonics of the wave function in quantum mechanics, and the formal mathematical space underlying both of these, which takes on a simultaneously ontological and spiritual aspect (which in this book we describe as cosmopolitical). Reality is a condensation of harmonic structure. Furthermore, these quantum level harmonics are constitutive of the human subject, neurocognitively and otherwise, and suggest why we are attracted to music.

These ideas were deployed in the installation *Qalam-i-Nur: The First Light, the First Sound*, which involved a drone based on the ratios of the hydrogen atom's spectral series (i.e., the quantum states of the electron that orbits the nucleus of the hydrogen atom at different energy levels and the respective distances from the nucleus at these energy levels) as part of a sound-and-light environment that provided the framework for performances by the Chora(s)san Time-Court Mirage at MaerzMusik in Berlin 2017:

> The sound is the signature ratios of the string-net vacuum's first-born element, Hydrogen, which form a tetrachord in the prime number proportions 31: 23: 17: 13 which for a long time have been known from Eastern systems of tuning in just intonation each interval of which can variously be heard in the traditions of maqām, pentatonic blues and raga. These ratios have been continuously sustained since the beginning of cosmic time (counting from the last scattering surface or the acoustic peak)—the

oldest tetrachord we know of—and tuning in to them and being attuned to them may carry a particular significance in their superposition as a signature signifier of nature's fundamental co-vibrations.[86]

The drone sound for the installation replicates the harmonic structure of the resonance frequencies of the electrons orbiting the nucleus of a hydrogen atom. Because of the prevalence of the hydrogen atom in the universe (75 percent), human beings have (arguably, or playfully) a deep unconscious familiarity with this harmonic structure, which is brought forth in the installation, and becomes an object of meditation for the listener—much as for La Monte Young, the 60 Hz vibration of the electric grid in America resulted in a strong, and again unconscious familiarity with that frequency.

The psychoanalytic concept of the unconscious, especially insofar as it complicated and also structured the Brouwerian Creative Subject's freedom, also became more significant, reflecting Hennix's studies of Lacanian thought in Paris in the early 1990s. Hennix was interested in the possibility of something like a sonic unconscious, connecting it to the notion of chora, as explored by Julia Kristeva. The chora is a figure for the vibrational body of the infant: "Discrete quantities of energy move through the body of the subject who is not yet constituted as such and, in the course of his development, they are arranged according to the various constraints imposed on this body. . . . In this way the drives, which are 'energy' charges as well as 'psychical' marks, articulate what we call a chora: a nonexpressive totality formed by the drives and their stases in a motility that is as full of movement as it is regulated."[87]

The chora, Kristeva continues, functions through "rupture and articulations (rhythm)" (26). It is nonrepresentational. It is "vocal and gestural" (26), it is subject not to law but to "ordering" (27) relating it to the history of the relations of mathematics and music. Reading a text of Mallarmé's as an exemplary articulation of the chora, Kristeva notes that "indifferent to language, enigmatic and feminine, this space underlying the written is rhythmic, unfettered, irreducible to its intelligible verbal translation; it is musical, anterior to judgment, but restrained by a single guarantee: syntax" (29). The chora is a field, a matrix of energy or pulsation that includes and exceeds the limits of "the" body.[88] To put it simply, this vibrational body is ordered and abjected with the imposition of language and the symbolic order. According to some versions, as thinking beings we have no direct relationship to the choric vibrational body. Yet, clearly, music does address this vibrational body and it could be said that we are abject precisely in our (non)relationship to that vibrational body. Or: music has a special relationship to abjection in that it brings forth that choric, vibrational body that is said to be impossible or inaccessible. In one of my earlier meetings with Hennix, perhaps in 2012, and, unfortunately unrecorded, I asked Hennix whether the chora was an important idea to her, and she responded by saying yes, of course (given that the name of her music ensemble was the "Chora(s)san Time-Court Mirage," pun intended), the trajectory of the Creative Subject was in fact to pass through the chora and arrive at a topos, a site at which free choice, in relation to sexual difference, but no doubt other things too, could be made. In this dense but powerfully clear statement, Hennix superimposes a psychoanalytic reading of the topology of the subject onto an intuitionistic mathematical idea of choice sequences as constructions of the Creative Subject, onto a topos theoretical idea of a site between ontologies in which the intuitionistic apparatus of construction might come into play, onto an idea of musical improvisation to be found in Indian classical music, post-Cagean experimentalism, and the Black radical tradition.

For Hennix, music, sound, and vibrational practice offered the possibility of a reattunement of subjectivity away from the distortions of language and socialization back to a kind of divine harmony with mathematical-physical-harmonic ordering. In conversation with me, Hennix indicated that her intentions went much further than this. If for Lacan, sexuation—that is, the production of sexual difference, our labeling as male and female—is a consequence of the law of the father, language, and so on, then a return to the chora also implies the reversal of this production of sexual difference and the possibility of a freedom in relation to gender that is beyond the father's law. Conversely, practices of deconstruction of the law of gender, such as those associated with queer and trans communities, would seem to imply exposure to or immersion in the chora. Thus, a link between the deconstruction of sexual difference and sonic play is formed. To reiterate, Hennix spoke of "passing through the chora"—in other words, she saw the chora not as a final place, say, of embodied materiality but as a zone of vibration. By passing through the chora, not "to the other side," but perhaps resting in it without attachment or without conceptualizing, the chora became a topos. The topos could be a topos of sexual difference, that is, a site in which various iterations or transformations of "male," "female," and "neither of these" can occur. But the topos itself could also shift, that is, link itself or be translatable to another topos. Sound, vibration here, is both a model for this state and a direct expression of it too. Passing through the chora meant to establish a state of true freedom, and of choice—perhaps that of the "stardust" that she observed all human bodies were ultimately composed of. Here, Hennix's thought clearly connects to her readings on intuitionism, where, rejecting the clamor of the social world, the mathematician constructs her own logical frameworks around an exposure to the schism of time—but also to the intuitionistic logic (i.e., Heyting algebras) that is formally understood as being operative in the construction of a topos.

Hennix had read Lacan's famous *Seminar XX: Encore! On Feminine Sexuality* as an aesthetico-political tract, one valorizing a feminine jouissance that Lacan linked as much to the experiences of female Christian mystics such as Teresa of Avila as to sexual pleasure. This jouissance contrasted with a normative masculine jouissance that misrecognized its own being, while articulating this misrecognition as knowledge, identity, and so on. Jouissance, here, has an at least double meaning in that it relates both to sexuality and the gendering of sexual pleasure, of how men and women (normatively are said to) come ... but also to another kind of enjoyment that operates at the level of the articulation of subjectivity itself, such that a subject can be said to "enjoy" his/her/their self-articulation as a subject. In Lacan's formula, masculine jouissance is a kind of fantasy or illusion, or enjoyment of illusion, while feminine jouissance may be said to actually consist of a subject-annihilating ecstatic occupation of the place (topos?) of the real—but one that the person occupying this site, presumptively but not definitively feminine, cannot, according to Lacan, know anything about. Music, or at least the music she wanted to make, is a trans-feminist vibrational practice of the unconscious—and going all the way back to her interest in epistemic art, Hennix was tuned in to the possibility of an epistemic feminine jouissance that decoupled from discursive (masculine) misrecognitions and phallogocentrism through mathemes, intuitionist choice sequences, devotion, and vibrational practice. Subverting gender norms, this practice offered the possibility of being both fully immersed in the real while at the same time capable of choice sequences in that state—choice sequences that bypass the pitfalls of linguistic or discursive error.[89] In that state one could both "know" and "be." And come.

For Hennix, Lacan provided a way to think about the chora as unconscious and about the paradoxes of our relation to our own unconscious, including what, for her, is most puzzling: why we generally refuse or resist the truth of the unconscious. Here, the vibration of erotic jouissance, the vibration of quantum states, sound as vibration, and the vibration of a particular kind of mathematical ontology intersect. Music is "unheimlich"—uncanny, in Freud's term, our haunting by something that we know but prefer not to think about, perhaps something fearsome or repulsive, but at the same time, something desirable too which we turn away from.[90] And, of course, the notion of "unheimlichkeit," literally "the state of not being at home," provided a potential explanation for why her own work had been ignored or not supported. Conversely (again), it might be possible to live in a world where music was "heimlich," where vibration itself felt like a home. This notion appears in the previously mentioned composition built around the spectral series of the hydrogen atom—the tonal structure of the composition using the same mathematical ratios as that of the spectral series of an atom which, as Hennix points out, occupies two-thirds of phenomenal reality. If La Monte Young tuned his pieces to 60 Hz because that is the frequency of the electrical system in the United States, Hennix was tuning her work to an equally pervasive physical structure, whose "heimlichkeit" is surely even more unconscious for most of us, while at the same time being constitutive.

9

On April 23, 2014, Hennix's work took a different turn when she presented a new piece *Blues Alif Lam Mim in the mode of Rag Infinity/Rag Cosmosis (1434 A.H.)* with an expanded version of her band Chora(s)san Time-Court Mirage and a brass ensemble, at Issue Project Room in New York City. Additionally, the group featured the remarkable Iraqi American trumpet player Amir ElSaffar, and solo vocals by Imam Ahmet Muhsin Tüzer, a young Turkish singer who is an imam in a small mosque in the southwestern Turkish seaside town of Kas, and who also plays in a rock band there with considerable success. The performance, which lasted over two hours, moved between the imam's recitation of a Koranic diary written by Hennix using modulations of various maqam scales, to complex raga-like group modal improvisations, with a recording of the digital version of "Solo for Two Tamburas and One Player" providing a tonic throughout. Hennix points out that this is the first time in centuries that tambura accompanied maqam scales as was once common in Kashmir (where ragas based on maqam scales often retained the name of the scale deployed).

Hennix had started studying the Koran at the Berlin Sufi Center after moving there, and was part of an international Sufi community in that city. She saw her spiritual devotion as a fulfillment of a promise to her guru, Pandit Pran Nath, who was born a Hindu but became part of a predominately Muslim gharana, the Kirana gharana, and who had "Fakir Pran Nath" (an honorific name for a Muslim holy man) written on his tombstone. Pran Nath had advised her to work on her mathematics as her contribution to the practice of music, and this she had done. As with Hennix's other interests, as she investigated and incorporated her research on Islam into her work, it fed into and condensed further the notion of a fully explicated and valid monistic ontology. Medieval Islamic thought and specifically mathematics was the substrate of musical innovation in both Europe (Leoninus and the Notre Dame sound) and India. Raga, while often being thought of as an eternal Indian and specifically Hindu form, had, according to her, at least some of its historical origins in Arabic maqam, of which it formed a subset. Even the blues, that itinerant form transmitted to the Americas from West Africa via the Middle Passage, had its origins in the scales brought by the Arab conquests. Hennix herself believed that her music had always had a connection to Islam since her earliest music teacher as a teenager was Idrees Sulieman, an African American trumpet player who brought Islamic jazz to Sweden in the 1960s.

I had mixed feelings about the Issue Project Room show. The juxtaposition of Koranic-style recitation by the Turkish imam with the feminine drone sounds of the ensemble appeared to stage a struggle between monotheistic discourse, thick with words, embellished melody and virtuosic masculine solo singing, and the choric world of monistic vibration in which the ensemble of feminine voices, brass, and tambura drone reigned supreme. A theater of sexual difference in the juxtaposition of masculine and feminine vibratory matrices was, therefore, also staged. The vibratory drone passages were familiar to those who know Hennix's work, especially with earlier iterations of the Time-Court Mirage that featured the wonderful Italian-born dhrupad singer Amelia Cuni. But now those passages were bookended in a jarring way by the imam's singing and discourse and words. Did the piece represent an acknowledgment of an existential or spiritual defeat, since it seemed to recognize the impossibility of the choric realm ever sustaining itself explicitly without eliciting in the end a patriarchal, phallocentric framing of some sort? And if so, was this actually a sign of maturity: a recognition of the dialectic of form and formlessness, even a submission to it? It was hard to say. Hennix spoke of moving to Istanbul, where she participated in weekly Sufi rituals and spoke of the dazzling rhythmic virtuosity and swing of the musicians there. It was a divine, devotional music, not primarily made for marketing or consumption. But an invitation to perform in Saudi Arabia went sour at some point—and it was not clear whether Hennix seriously expected to find a place for her sound in increasingly conservative Islamic places (such as Erdogan's Turkey). But somehow, her work and thought kept evolving.

In the spring of 2017, the Berlin-based experimental music festival MaerzMusik devoted itself in part to Hennix's work, offering her the use of an abandoned funerary chapel in Wedding for a two-week sound installation, as well as a new performance of *The Electric Harpsichord*. I participated in a thankless hunt for one of the original 1970s Yamaha tunable keyboards that she had used for the original. Perhaps fortuitously, no such keyboard was forthcoming and, instead, with her sound engineer and collaborator Stefan Tiedje, she put together a new keyboard system in which, using Max/MSP programming, a MIDI keyboard with a piano-like sensitivity triggered just intonation–tuned samples of a tambura. Hennix seemed genuinely surprised at the sold-out event, even though few of the people filing in even recognized the skeletal figure sitting in a wheelchair by the sound desk. People chattered. The light show projected images from Xiao-Gang Wen's work as part of the aforementioned sound-and-light installation *Qalam-i-Nur: The First Light, the First Sound*. But when she began to play a slow, gathering silence and introspection descended on the crowd, almost as though a spell had been cast on them. Eyes closed, people lay back on the Oriental rugs that covered the floor of the space. The sound was sweet, with an almost marimba-like quality (an alternative version of *The Electric Harpsichord* using marimba stops from 1976 has been made public in the recent *Selected Early Keyboard Works*), it was delightful to be around and, like a great raga performance, the sound pulled listeners affectively toward it, as though it had its own gravitational field. Waves, surges of sound that you could almost float on. And as you did, the sense of time diminished.

The high point of the festival, however, was the two-week sound installation *Qalam-i-Nur*, a sound-and-light environment featuring Hennix's hydrogen drone, with doors open from around 2 p.m. to midnight and people free to come and go as they pleased. Hennix's band would show up at different times to play along with the sound and Hennix herself would sing sustained tones into a microphone. Often the space was just about empty—even the organizers had no idea how to promote or describe what was happening. The daily practice of making music was translated inadvertently by the promoters into "a rehearsal" and the final day of the installation "a performance"—missing the point, which was to reconfigure both listening and play as devotional practices. For me, it was the first time I'd really seen Hennix's idea of a sonic shrine in operation. True, there was the model of La Monte Young's Dream House—but that sound was static although always fascinating. Here, the sound was more like a waterfall or fountain, constantly flowing, but as different musicians would come and go, constantly changing too, as a fountain does. And because of the nature of the just intonation–sustained tone matrix, when musicians played different tones into the sound, the sound as a whole would shimmer and shift, as different combinations of overtones and difference tones were triggered. In particular, there were certain trumpet improvisations that would produce an incredibly loud and aggressive bass sound that would make the building shake—returning to that initial insight of the late 1960s that sutured the vibration of the *Apollo* rocket launch to La Monte Young's drone sound. The music created certain technical problems: it required musicians to play with a degree of tonal precision mostly associated with classically trained musicians, but it also required an emotional and relational intelligence more associated with jazz or other kinds of improvisation. Because the music was specifically designed to be psychotropic, that is, it got you high, it required that the musicians were able to maintain a particular kind of discipline while being high. It felt a little like trying to deliberately sleepwalk, or dream lucidly. You could probably train yourself to do it, as with the various dream yogas in the Buddhist tradition—but this was not something they taught in a conservatory.

10

Throughout my conversations with Hennix, the figure of Parmenides loomed over nearly everything we talked about. Hennix's interest in Parmenides went back to the early 1980s, when she read his extant brief philosophical fragments in the library at SUNY/New Paltz, noting that "I could have written this myself."[91] In a recent poem written to commemorate the fiftieth anniversary of John Coltrane's *A Love Supreme*, she speaks of divine love as "the shortest path to monism."[92] The word *monism* denotes the philosophical belief that there is only one single indivisible reality. This belief has a long history that spans philosophy and religion—but for at least the last one hundred years, it has had very few adherents, compared to pluralism in its many forms. Or nihilism, for that matter. What is important in Hennix's formulation, however, is her insistence on the "shortest path." The implication is that monism cannot simply to be intellectually understood, but has to be realized through a practice. Discernment of the true form of monism can only be made through a realization of it, not from speculation. Music, sound, vibration are the objects or tools of practices that form this shortest path. In fact, the path is so short and so familiar that we scarcely think about it when we are transported by an experience of the power of music. Nor, apparently, does it seem to us that, given the self-evidence of the path, there is any need for intensification, deepening of the path or the place to which it takes us.

Heidegger famously said that he was interested in that which remained unthought in Parmenides, believing that, at the dawn of Western philosophy, a misunderstanding of Parmenides, a rejection of him, determined the consequent path of Western philosophy in toto.[93] Plato's misrepresentation of Parmenides in his dialogue of that name is part of that history. Arguably, Heidegger himself did not recognize specifically what was significant, and unthought in Parmenides. (He got hung up on the goddess Aletheia, and truth as revealing, and not *what* was revealed!) For Hennix, it was Islam that took up the challenge of articulating a rigorous monistic thought, after the forgetting of Parmenides in ancient Greece and Rome. Going back to Parmenides, even today, suggested the possibility of new paths, or other paths, whose value is not recognized as such.

The key passage from fragment 8 of Parmenides states:

There is only one path left
and that is
that   "it—is."

And on it there are many indications
that Being is unengendered
that it cannot be broken apart
        (for it is whole, without parts)
that Being does not fluctuate,
that it has no end.

It never *was*. It never *will* be. It is all NOW—
                    one—continuum.[94]

The thought of the continuum haunts Hennix's work, just as it haunts the Western philosophical tradition. Although it plays a crucial role in modern mathematics, the continuum is not simply a mathematical concept, or for that matter a set theoretical one, but a philosophical concept of a primordial, undifferentiated sameness that underlies everything, and which appears as a problem or question or hypothesis in mathematics and elsewhere too when conceptualizations of a foundation are raised. Drones offer a way of experiencing a model of the continuum since they generate a state of indifferentiated sound that persists over time. In Hennix's version, a drone is, speculatively, more than a model. True, her drones are mathematical propositions taking the form of a sound matrix. By effacing (through a kind of sonic illusion, a parsing of the "continuity of discontinuities") the experience of difference established through the movement of time (since the moment that preceded and the moment that is to come are sonically equivalent in a drone, therefore disallowing the experience of the "twoity" or rather shifting attention to the vertical aspects of sound, i.e., movement and space), a peculiar form of sameness opens up, one that is not merely predicated on the identical. The point of Hennix's work then would be that there are formal descriptive languages that can not only represent aspects of the continuum, but expose one in various ways to the continuum itself. In this sense, Hennix's work has remained true to intuitionism, which is constructed on the experience of the continuum, that is, the splitting of the continuum into a "twoity," containing the possibility of numbers and, with them, the problem of the number line. Music, for Hennix, is a construction on the continuum, just as for Brouwer, mathematics was.

In recent years, Hennix has come closer and closer to a grand synthesis of the various ideas and disciplines she's explored. In an essay in the 2014 *Blues Alif Lam Mim: Blues in Ba* booklet that accompanied the Issue Project Room performances in New York City, she proposed:

> Sound has the power to scatter the inner dust universe making the free path of light unending from its last scattering surface on. NADA BRAHMA, Sound is God, is not an empty phrase but a mirage-like moment of daseinization, a modality of self-illumination where the listener spontaneously decouples from the sense of gravity—from gravity to grace (Simone Weil) by way of sound. The concept is far from new.
>
> There is a point—not necessarily the same for all listeners—in the unfolding of BALM when the psychotropic force of the sound takes over and the listener experiences an internal transfiguration as reality turns into a single, integral sound. There is nothing incoherent about this experience. In fact, if anything, by it, reality solidifies as a fluid, single, indivisible whole with no separable parts, having neither beginning nor end, having suddenly, unanticipated, emerged out of nowhere and now ruling everyone's integral experience, a daseinization mediated by a Bose-Einstein-like condensation of neural signal paths activated by and in resonance with the incoming stream of sounds.[95]

Here, sonic and vibrational philosophy is synthetically elaborated in relation to Brouwer's intuitionism, Hindu metaphysics, Xiao-Gang Wen's version of condensed matter theory, Heideggerian ontology, Simone Weil's écriture féminine, and certain versions of Islamic monism as the foundation of a sonic practice of what she elsewhere calls "sonoilluminescence," which is a metatechnological practice whose goal, or implication is spiritual and ecstatic. Hennix goes on:

> This is the realm of the unconscious which opens itself in the dream state which is here activated by difference tones in the γ-range, $\sim$30Hz–100+Hz. In Sufi Mysticism, what happens in the dream state is accorded a higher degree of reality than any perception suffered in the state of being awake (when other brain wave frequencies are activated and screen the world of dreams). This is, indeed, also the ultimate ontology of (La-

canian) psychoanalysis. However, while psychoanalysis treats the traits of this ontology as pathological and a hindrance to Being in its social function, the "Rumi cure" accesses the dream state in order to liberate the mind from the impact of a chronic dysfunctional social order which leaves anyone caught by it disturbed. It must be noted, as Parmenides did 2500 years ago, that the laws of classical logic furnishes this dysfunctional order by bending and binding the mind to its narrow scope, being short-changed from running on, or acted by, the wrong program (cf. the recent similar view by the mathematician L. E. J. Brouwer). The path to Divine Love offers an alternative program for Being to run on which escapes the shackles of classical logic and returns it [Being] to a freedom of thought which nourishes an affect towards dignity and social independence governed by an aesthetics of the sublime. Ultimately, this path (tariqa) harbours an alternative culture where shrines are dedicated to sounds which expand the mind to its other openings.[96]

The practice that Hennix proposes is therapeutic and implies a different way of living, including the construction of shrines (Dream Houses, Illuminatory Sound Environments) that would host the practice of music conceived of at this level. The frameworks have shifted over the years, but the meaning stays the same—as appropriate to someone who claims to have refuted Gödel's Incompleteness Theorem.

In Hennix's formula "Being = Space × Action," the word *time* is conspicuously absent. In that formula, being equals awareness, full realization of the primordial nature of space as continuity, and then the possibility of dynamic action constructed in awareness of this. What others might call "time" is for Hennix a sequence of actions, an ordering of actions, a logic of actions, occurring in a topos. Composition, performance, improvisation iterate, instantiate Brouwerian intuitionist choice sequences within a logic.[97] In dispensing with time, they open a vibratory field in which everything is contained as resonance, as a pathway through the matrix. But what then of "time's arrow," which is not so easily dismissed, according to the second law of thermodynamics in physics? There were days when I walked around Neukölln with Hennix when it felt to me that the city moved around her the way cars driving at full speed on a highway move around a child who has somehow wandered out into the middle of the road in the night: a flash of headlights, a screaming of horns, a skidding of wheels, then gone. Mostly though, they didn't notice, but she did I think, and she was patient—or tried to be. She persisted or insisted in thinking a possibility that music reveals and that stands in ambiguous relation to time's arrow.

THREE

. . . . . .

Music and the Continuum

The differences between rhythm and blues and the so-called new music or art jazz, the different places, are artificial, or they are merely indicative of the different placements of spirit. (Even "purely" social, like what the musicians want, etc.)
  For instance, use of Indian music, old spirituals, even heavily rhythmic blues licks (and soon electronic devices) by new music musicians point toward the final close in the spectrum of the sound that will come. A really new, really all-inclusive music. The whole people.
  —AMIRI BARAKA, "The Changing Same: R&B and New Black Music"

$1 \to \Box$
—CATHERINE CHRISTER HENNIX

I

One afternoon in Berlin in 2016, when I was talking with the composer/mathematician Catherine Christer Hennix at her house, I saw a copy of Alain Daniélou's *Tableaux comparatif des intervalles musicaux*—the 1958 booklet in which Daniélou, a French musicologist, lists every pitch that has been calculated by human beings within the octave. The booklet was important to minimalists such as La Monte Young who work with just intonation, since the book is effectively a catalog or recipe book of tuning systems. When I asked Hennix about the book, she said, "It is you may say, the continuum of the octave."[1]

The continuum or continuity refers philosophically to the notion of a partless or undifferentiated whole—for example, the space-time continuum in physics, or nonduality in certain religious traditions such as Advaita Vedanta or Dzogchen in Tibetan Buddhism. Continuity can also be thought of more locally, as the continuum of mind, body, and world. In mathematics, the continuum generally refers to the set of real numbers on a number line, that is, all of the points on this line. This set, like the set of integers (i.e., whole numbers) on the number line, is infinite. But while the set of integers on the number line is countably infinite, that is, you can keep counting ever greater integers, the set of real numbers is uncountably infinite, due to the infinitesimal differences marked as real numbers that can be demonstrated between any points on the line. Georg Cantor determined in the late nineteenth century that the magnitude of the infinity of these real numbers was demonstrably greater than the infinity of the natural numbers. This magnitude he referred to as cardinality, and he hypothesized that there was no cardinality, that is, order of magnitude, between that of the real numbers and that of the natural numbers. This claim, which is foundational for modern mathematics, is known as the continuum hypothesis, which Hilbert listed as the first of his famous twenty-three problems in modern mathematics in 1900, and there remains no consensus as to whether the hypothesis holds.[2]

But this is not the only way of thinking mathematically about the continuum—as we noted in chapter 2. For Hennix, it is Brouwer's intuitionistic conception of the continuum that is significant. And the significance lies in the fact that, for Brouwer, mathematical constructions emerge from the mathematician's awareness of and attention to the breaking of the now into a present and a previous moment, retained in memory, which he called the "twoity." This break, cut, point, mark, however carries with it that which was broken, cut, and so on, that is, the undifferentiated whole.[3] Hennix transposed this act of awareness to music, which in sonically cutting the now, initiates the choice sequences in which music unfolds, now by now. While Hennix cautions that this model applies only to her own music, in this chapter we will explore to what degree Hennix's ideas hold for music more generally.

The relation between the mathematical, physical, religious, and philosophical meanings of the word *continuum* is complex. In his celebrated book on the continuum, Hermann Weyl noted the disjuncture between the mathematical continuum and what he called the intuitive continuum, that is, our experience of the continuity of the unbroken flow of time, and of space.[4] But given that the problems raised by the continuum as to the foundations of mathematics remain unresolved—and that these problems find an analogy in philosophy and elsewhere—an openness as to where, disciplinarily, the problem (and explanation) of the continuum is located is, I believe, permissible. Indeed, the question of what the real continuum actually is, in relation to the mathematical, musical, sonic, vibrational, and philosophical understandings of the continuum is a challenging one—and, in the terms we have already established in this book, a cosmopolitical one, in that arguably the same object is framed differently according to different practices, cosmologies, and societies.

In these terms, when Hennix speaks of "the continuum of the octave," she is speaking of a countably infinite number of pitches that exist within the octave and, via a kind of set theory, speaking of tuning systems as subsets that are emergent from this continuum. For musical systems such as South Asian raga or Arabic maqam, which use a variety of tuning systems, this is self-evident—and may offer a first perspective on the question of music and pluralism. There is a plurality of tuning systems and a plurality of ways of moving within specific tuning systems. Going beyond the specific just intonation–based systems that are used in traditional musics around the world, contemporary just intonation musics from Harry Partch onward propose a much larger possible number of pitches within the octave that accord with the mathematics of harmony, being based on ratios of integers. Even music based on equal tempered scales (which can in fact be thought of as an approximation of a particular kind of just intonation scale, i.e., the equal tempered pitches can be approximately rendered via ratios of integers) could be added to this as a particular, perhaps anomalous case. A similar kind of analysis can be made of rhythm, as in the recent work of Godfried Toussaint on the geometry of rhythm, where all possible rhythms can be presented as geometric divisions and articulations of points on the perimeter of a circle—the unit of periodicity, aka the "timeline," being subject to "cuts" in the same way that the number line of the octave is.[5]

But this raises a broader issue of the relation of music to ideas of the continuum. On the one hand, "the continuum of the octave," or of the rhythmic "timeline," suggests the possibility of musics of near infinitesimal subtlety, in which the differentiation of such musics has its roots or core in tiny but decisive decisions and events as to the ordering by which tones and tone clusters occur. In other words (and uncontroversially), by the organization of vibration, which is to say the physico-mathematical rules/laws by which waves propagate. On the other hand, according to Hennix's argument, all music emerges from and bears with it the indifferentiation of the real continuum—a super-sameness that underlies all difference and which in her work Hennix models via the Parmenidean notion of the One, or Allah, or, asymptotically, mathematical and physical formalizations of the same, such as the number line or the space-time continuum or the quantum ether.[6] Many have argued that there is a constitutive gap between the mathematico-musical elaboration of sonic patterns and the continuum they emerge from—or, indeed, that there is no real continuum from which anything emerges, just chance, void, chaos, or nothingness. Badiou's materialist ontology of being sutured to the void would be exemplary in this regard. Here, guided by Hennix but thinking about music across its cosmopolitical breadth, we will explore an alternative to this model, one which takes seriously a "continuum hypothesis," though not necessarily that of Hilbert and the mathematicians—the value of this lies not only in understanding music in a different way but also in using musical ideas to think about ontological questions more generally.

2

An initial hypothesis: Considered globally, the cosmopolitical practice of music addresses and articulates the continuum.

Mental exercise: Imagine the totality of all musical activity on the planet at this particular moment. Include the 400 million times Kanye West's *The Life of Pablo* was streamed on Tidal in the first month of its release. Include the anonymous bossa nova singer and guitarist who was playing Milton Nascimento's "Tudo que você podia ser" on a makeshift stage on the roof of a beach bar in Trindade, Brazil, last March while a group of us played or floated in the waves. Include animal sounds. Include all organic life. Include all the sounds of inorganic life. Now extend this in time. Now extend this across the cosmos. From there, you begin to approximate the continuum as we are defining it: the universe as an ultimately undifferentiated One or whole, a single object composed of a very large number of sonic cuts, marks, traces, local mappings, happening in space/time. A supermultitudinous vibration, emerging from, but also articulating with each iteration, the continuum itself.

In speaking this way, I am drawing on the work of the Colombian philosopher of mathematics Fernando Zalamea, who, in his book *Peirce's Logic of Continuity: A Conceptual and Mathematical Approach* sets out a striking rethinking of what is meant by the continuum through the work of the American philosopher and founding voice of both pragmatism and pluralism, Charles Sanders Peirce.[7] Peirce's work on the continuum is complex and evolved over the course of his career. Zalamea's presentation emphasizes that Peirce's idea of the continuum was of a continuity beyond that of Cantor's mathematics yet still able to support mathematical ideas of the continuum. In other words, points on a number line are insufficient for representing the continuum in its full reality.

He describes it as a supermultitudinousness, a multiplicity so dense that in the end all possible singularities fuse into continuity and vice versa.[8] The point is that this is not a confabulation of science fiction or fantasy, but the basis of our own reality. Zalamea describes Peirce's theorization of the continuum and how particularity emerges from it as involving a modal logic. The continuity of the true continuum, which is ultimately unrepresentable, supports the discontinuity of particular points and relationships of points. In other words, it supports modes and modalities.

> Peirce's continuum is general, plastic, homogeneous, regular, in order to allow, in a natural way, the transit of modalities, the fusion of individualities, and the overlapping of neighborhoods. The generic idea of a continuous flow is present behind those transits, fusions, and overlappings, ubiquitous osmotic processes that Peirce notices in the plasticity of protoplasm and the human mind, and that, in a bold abduction, he lifts to a universal hypothesis.[9]

From thinking about the continuum in this way, Peirce derives a pragmatic and pluralist logic: pragmatic because all existent forms and events are local arrangements of and improvisations on/in the continuum; pluralist because the local constructions that constitute cuts or workings in/of the continuum are variable types of discontinuous pragmatic constructions. In other words, there is not just a single relation of continuity to discontinuity. If we apply this way of thinking to music, we might interpret "modality" in the strict or literal sense of modes as scales. Recall that, in a 1976 interview, Hennix described her own musical work as "intuitionistic modal music," meaning that the construction of modes proceeds from the existential engagement of the mathematician with the "twoity" of time, which is the basis of Brouwer's intuitionism and his theory of the foundation of mathematics.[10] Hennix transposes this to music and sound, emphasizing that "we aim at evolving frames of musical structures, rather than trying to obtain completeness."[11]

However, we might speak of improvisation in general as a local articulation of a structure, or more generally of a musical event per se as being *modal* in some broader sense of the word. Musical genres such as the blues, musical practices such as *possession* in the sense that Gilbert Rouget uses the word, ensembles and works created for them such as the string quartet, and events such as the Jamaican sound system clash could all be thought of in this expanded sense of *modal*.[12] Modality is therefore connected to the idea of cosmopolitics—a cosmopolitical framework in which a particular form of music emerges is necessarily modal. Different modes can occupy space or incorporate different objects into their framework—disputes as to the value or permissibility of such modes and their coexistence are cosmopolitical. The attentive reader will also notice the overlap here between arguments regarding cosmopolitical frameworks for ontological questions and the idea of the topos as a generalization of space which allows us to think of that space as being occupied or shaped by different frameworks, modes, and logics, and to establish the arrows or morphisms that allow for transits between those modes as they are articulated in a particular (but necessarily bare or abstracted) space.

There has been a modal turn in a number of quite different recent philosophical texts, including Bruno Latour's *Inquiry into Modes of Existence* (2012), his formulation of actor network theory in terms of ontological pluralism; Alain Badiou's *Logics of Worlds* (2009), the second volume of *Being and Event*, and his modification, via Grothendieck's work on toposes, of the first volume of that book's claim that set theory provides a fundamental ontology; and Giorgio Agamben's *Use of Bodies* (2014) in which the problem of bare life's elaboration as social and political form is worked through via the idea of modes as "forms of life."[13] While each of these texts uses sound as an analogy at certain points (Latour reflects on tonality [375]; Agamben on originary echos [149]; Badiou on serial music [79–89]), none of them consider sound and music in any depth in their elaboration of modal ontologies. In each case, what is missed is that sound and music are not just arbitrary examples or peripheral to ontological inquiry—they are "the shortest path to monism" and offer the clearest embodiment of a modal ontology. Music is a superpositioning of waves or vibrations in a field—and modality describes the specificity of possible paths of superpositioning as well as raising the question of what a field-based ontology, that is, an ontology that understands reality as a field rather than a set of points, would really consist in. What is at stake in Zalamea's and Hennix's work is a pragmatic or practical sense of what it means to elaborate a mode—as creative mathematical endeavor for Zalamea, and as musical, aesthetic, and ontological wager for Hennix.

The entire data of ethnomusicology could be seen as evidence of the pluralism (and modalism) that inheres in music. To take but one example, José Maceda's wonderful book *Gongs and Bamboo*, in which he describes the varieties of gonged and bamboo instruments and the ways they are played in different parts of the Philippines, today, but also historically.[14] Every regional variation in the music played constitutes a kind of act of musical pragmatism, that is, the form that music takes in that time and place but also the form that musical access to the continuum takes in that time and place. As soon as an act of sound shaping occurs, it manifests with it the continuum as articulation of space produced by sound shaping. To make musical sounds is to sound shape—not any particular shape, but a shape in the sense of a geometric invocation (a few points/tones, some kind of harmonic and/or melodic organization, rhythm, timber) nonetheless. And, of course, there are more or less arbitrary shapes and more or less significant ones. Music is the pragmatic local elaboration of such shaping. Even at the level of the construction of musical instruments, Maceda notes that, in order to understand the forms of bamboo instruments played in the Philippines, you need to know the botany of bamboo varietals, just as the history of trade routes is revealed by the ways in which the resonant forms of the gong are used in different geographical regions of the Philippines. Music emerges out of a certain material set of histories and practices and potentials for the making and sharing of sounds. The important thing to understand here is that if pragmatism is considered as merely the local arrangement of things, what we would have is a fairly unremarkable sociology of music or even ethnomusicology. But there are constraints on pragmatic local elaboration that remove music from being arbitrary, though not from being diverse or pluralistic. And these constraints have to do with the relationship between music and the continuum.

To restate the hypothesis here in more detail: music in the end has to take place in the now—the score must actually be played, the play button that triggers the broadcast of the recording must be pressed, the crowd must gather for the sound system at the crossroads, even the mental exercise of thinking a scale or a tune must actually take place. In engaging the now in the particular ways that music does, music necessarily engages the problem or question of the continuum in its unbroken, Parmenidean Oneness. By *unbroken* we mean that the universe is to be understood as a vast single object, thus a "One." As "One" it is neither space, nor time, insofar as those already constitute divisions of a One. This One leans into the now—as do we! We have no choice but to do it, even if in a Heideggerian/Lacanian way, the forgetting of being is also constitutive for us. Mostly. Thanks to Hennix and her rethinking of Parmenides, Brouwer, and Grothendieck, we can appreciate how music operates via choice sequences, Brouwer's intuitionistic logic, in the generalized space, that is, the topos that appears when we rigorously explore the "point" of the now and its (non)relation to the continuum. In music, the point dissolves into a resonant field, what Grothendieck would call a locale or region, or what is labeled in quantum physics nonlocality or entanglement. This engagement of the field, pursued in all musical events, whether explicitly or not, opens in the direction of the unbroken One—sometimes (and this is where the social and political character of the practice of music becomes crucial)! These choice sequences are pragmatic in the Peircian sense—if they are not, if there is no means of implementing them in the now, then they do not exist and there is (as per Wittgenstein) nothing to say about them.

3

In giving a more precise meaning to the expanded sense of "modal music" that I introduced in section 2, we should further track Zalamea's thought in his work on Peirce and in his later book, *Synthetic Philosophy of Contemporary Mathematics*—precisely because Zalamea attempts to show the ways in which contemporary mathematics explores plural ontologies.[15] Key in this undertaking is category theory and its offshoot/relative topos theory as developed by midcentury mathematicians such as William Lawvere and Alexander Grothendieck—and which I introduced in the chapter on Catherine Christer Hennix. For Zalamea, topos and category theory point to the need for a "synthetic philosophy" in which the pragmatic elaboration of connections or "transits" between different modalities is emphasized over a concern with a singular fundamental ontology or "foundation of mathematics"—even as there is a continuous modulation of local and global perspectives. Here, *topos* will be used to explore an expanded sense of the ways in which modality works in music.

Recall that mathematically, the word *topos* refers to a generalization of space and can be understood as a particular kind of category defined by the logical objects and arrows by which it is organized, along with several other restrictions, a "complete universe" that can be connected via further arrows (functors, adjoints) to other model universes. In Olivia Caramello's gloss (2017), topos theory concerns the building of bridges between mathematical theories or models.[16] How might one think of music in relation to topos theory? I would like to present two possibilities: one is the work of Guerino Mazzola, whose book *The Topos of Music* (2002) sets out in fifteen hundred pages a detailed elaboration that among other things has received the approval of Grothendieck.[17] The other is Hennix, for whom the figure of the topos and, crucially, toposes, have been important since the mid-1970s both in her writings about music and sound and in her compositions.

Mazzola uses the notion of topos to present as thorough and deep a set of parameters as possible by which to model or categorize music via a musical semiotics. The importance of this work cannot be overstated since Mazzola makes a compelling and rigorous argument that—despite all the random, improvisatory, spontaneous, and singular aspects of a musical performance that would seem to place it beyond science or mathematical description—contemporary mathematical tools are capable of rigorously describing, at least in principle, even the most chaotic or arbitrary sounding free jazz performance. Which is simply to say that music does always involve some element of structure or pattern. Thus, Mazzola sets music out as a collection and organization of musical signs, which are organized from the local objects of tones, chords, meters, and motives in a particular musical performance, in the direction of a global "patchwork" of musical styles, compositions, and so on that are all "covered," that is, "englobed" within a logical/topological structure (i.e., a topos) capacious enough to include all of what makes these local forms and signs what they are: "Summarizing, the topos of music first centers around the concept architecture of music objects in the general denotator theory, and therein around the presheaf topos over modules, and secondly, it evolves to a universe of local-global perspectives which are readily described by Alexander Grothendieck... with his awe inspiring topologies and their functors and cohomology theories."[18]

In the second edition of the book (2017), Mazzola significantly modifies his model, via the introduction of an idea of gestures, which along with facts, that is, musical objects and processes (sequences of sounds essentially) form an expanded "topos of music." For Mazzola, who is a practicing jazz improviser, the concept of gesture is important because it helps explain musical forms, such as free improvisation where performance is more than the sonic outputting of a musical score. Mazzola gives a rich and varied review of gestures as embodied actions—pointing out via a thoughtful examination of the physically disabled pianist Horace Parlan for example, the ways in which "what music is" are constrained and shaped by the body and its gestural capabilities—in a way that's similar to the musical pragmatism in Maceda's *Gongs and Bamboos* that I described in section 2.[19] The concept of gesture introduces a "pre-semiotic" perspective into music, an idea of an action that is more than the musical sign systems captured in the first edition of the book—yet still something that can be rendered mathematically as a complex space shaping and action. As with the first edition of the book, Mazzola then presents a detailed mathematical model of performative musical gestures that uses category and topos theory to show how the transit from bodily gesture to instrument to sound occurs—showing very clearly the ways that there is a "homotopy" between the body's position in space and the sound that it makes that is itself subtle and complex, but real, in the sense that the sound and the body's movement that generates the sound are "the same," that is, "adjoint." As with the first edition also, the book then focuses on computer software (called Rubato) that offers tools for the analysis, composition, and performance of music.

Mazzola is not the first to propose such an expansive categorization and enframing of music. In the 1960s, the folk music researcher Alan Lomax developed "cantometrics" as a general system for categorizing and distinguishing different kinds of song from around the world. Initially conceived of as an informal way of developing a sociology or anthropology of song, Lomax, responding to critics of his "unscientific" method, developed a system of "37 rating scales on a data sheet . . . , each parameter had between 3–13 points, limited to the 13 punches per column on an IBM card. All the sheets for a given culture were added up and compiled to provide a master profile. 'Cantometrics' was originally defined as a 'measure of song' but the term took on a new meaning later on, positing song 'as a measure of society.'"[20] Granted the primitive nature of the hole punch computation system, there is considerable poignancy and cross-cultural astuteness in Lomax's categories, which, in making a break with formal notation, include everything from "type of vocal organization" to "words to nonsense" to "nasality." This data is then informally indexed to anthropological observations concerning the social space in which music happens. This system was applied to over 700 recordings from 250 cultural areas. Given that much of this work was built around listening to sound recordings and anthropological reports made by others, the limits to the project are painfully clear. In fact, Lomax's earlier, more informal recordings and presentations of work songs and other social musics, bearing a more humble witness to music as it appeared in the difficult lives of poor and marginalized people, probably captured the cosmopolitical breadth and political urgency of music's topos more accurately—and copiously.

While the relation between music and computation is without a doubt profound, and one that will increasingly occupy us in the age of algorithmic capitalism, the difficulties involved in using such a model for fully characterizing music become evident when one compares even the gestural version of Mazzola's model with the recent work of Julian Henriques, who in *Sonic Bodies* attempts to give a full account of the "sounding" "wavebands" that go into a single session of the Jamaican sound system Stone Love Movement at one of their weekly dances.[21] Henriques identifies the descriptive musicological qualities of the sound as just one element of a threefold structure that includes material (the physics of sound and electricity), corporeal (the way particular bodies shape both the production and reception of a specific musical event), and sociocultural (the "ways of knowing" that give particular kinds of social meaning to a musical event).[22] The corporeal bandwidth corresponds to what Mazzola means by gesture—but it also significantly expands the domain of gesture beyond the action of the performer(s), in ways that we have just explored—such that the gestural space of music would have to include not only the performers but also the instruments, the technologies of amplification, the acoustic space in which the sound event occurs, and the gestural involvement and interrelations of the listeners in relation to all of the above—as well as the complex reciprocal engagements of all of these. While the sum total of these qualities may indeed constitute a "topos of music" or maybe even *the* topos of music, it is hard to see how they could be quantified by computer software in any meaningful way. In this sense, we can raise a question of the magnitude of pluralisms (or categories, or toposes) that Mazzola's model of music is able to contain or account for—and, in this sense, we might speak of degrees of pluralism internal to a single model of what music is. Clearly, the question of which pluralisms are allowed or accounted for in such a model is a cosmopolitical one. Indeed, Mazzola recognizes this problem, acknowledging that *topos* has at least a twofold meaning in his work, one the strictly mathematical version associated with Grothendieck, the other a more general philosophical concept of place, which he associates with Kant.[23] Does the latter constitute simply the domain of the "not yet computable"—or is it in fact resistant to computation—or mathematization? Note that these last two are not necessarily identical.

In the first edition of his book, Mazzola rejects ontological inquiries into music—that is, "what music is"—as being meaningless after the Kantian bracketing of "the thing in itself." In the second edition of the book, the ontology of music opens up via the pre-semiotic theory of gestures, which would appear to happen in a place very similar to that of a "thing in itself" which would nonetheless be accessible via mathematical formalisms. Gestures then refer not only to the actions of musical performers but also to the "topos of music" as such, which might be considered a "thing in itself" that "gestures" or acts via algebraic geometric/topological parametrization. In the end, however, Mazzola still cleaves to Badiou's and perhaps Grothendieck's idea that category and topos theory are in the end ways of describing "what appears" in increasingly dense diagrams of functors moving between descriptive languages and formalisms. This would correspond to the modal ontology whose conditions we briefly set out in section 2. Even so, one wonders whether an ontology of gestures goes far enough and is actually adequate to understanding music. What is a relationship between a gesture and a field? Are they one and the same? Is nonaction, for example, a gesture, or gesture's shadow or necessary substratum? A gesture may be thought of as a shaping of vibration, but, curiously, vibration itself is not explicitly thought in Mazzola's book—even though the replacing of musical points with continuous functions (i.e., waves, curves) itself opens this up in a brilliant and original way.

If we compare Hennix's use of the topos with Mazzola's in deriving an adequate model of what music is, there are three distinctions that strike me as important: (1) Hennix's insistence, especially in her recent work, on the complex overlapping of fields—sonic, subjective, spatial—each of which could potentially be modeled via an idea of toposes and adjoints (i.e., fields, "universes," and the functors/arrows that connect them), in understanding what music is; (2) the idea of music as a cosmopolitical practice aimed at a target state that is psychotropic, altered in relation to normative subjectivity, transcendental, and valued as exceptional—which is to say, "ontological"; and (3) the idea, adapted from Xiao-Gang Wen's version of condensed matter theory, that for both physics and music, an ontology of information is required.

In a recent email, Hennix proposed that one could think of (her) music as involving chains of elementary toposes: a harmonic topos that would be defined by a set of intervals using pitches derived from ratios of integers; a "crystal lattice" topos in which these microtonal intervals would be fed into an acoustic space setting up standing wave patterns; and a wave topos that would consist of the interactions of the sound waves in space. Each of these elementary toposes can be defined with considerable precision—as can their relationships and the "arrows" by which transits can be (and are) made between them. As such, Hennix recognized in the language of category and topos theory and its emphasis on arrows and diagrams new ways of composing, and new ways of formulating experiments with sound. In other words, topos theory offers not just a way of modeling or describing music but also a way of composing new kinds of sonic events.

However, this series of toposes, while offering a diagram of significant design parameters in constructing musical works is, of course, incomplete since it gives no account of the parameters of the listener (or, intriguingly, of the performer). (Note that intuitionism gives no account of the unconscious of the Creative Subject, or what might determine the subject's selection of particular choice sequences.) Hennix has given considerable thought to this matter from the beginning of her career. The subject can also be considered as a topos—or perhaps as a series of (elementary) toposes, with morphisms connecting them (a topos of the listener and acoustic reception; a topos of neurocognitive affective response; a topos of the arrangement of body and mind and of individual bodies in relation to other bodies and to the environment?). Freud, and later Lacan, had already conceived of subjectivity in topological terms, in other words as a spatial arrangement or structure.[24] The Japanese philosopher Kitaro Nishida had also used the word topos in his own dialectical attempt to model the relation between subject and world via a "field of consciousness."[25] More recently, the philosopher Reza Negarestani has used category theory in his (re)modelling of the (Hegelian) subject's movement toward pure spirit/ geist, via a speculative functor F such that the subject I, the current, historically contingent intelligent subject, is transformed into I*, the fully realized geist, or universal/general intelligence. The use of the word *functor* at least gestures to the idea that this transformation consists of a specifiable set of logico-mathematical operations and actions. Negarestani seems primarily interested in AI and computation as operations of intelligence—but what if, like Hennix, we think about music according to this model?[26]

Let us take a step back here. Given that the "space" of subjectivity is obviously not a Euclidian space (how would you locate it? where? in the body? not in the body?), the abstraction or generalization of space proposed in mathematical terms by Grothendieck provides an opening in thinking subjectivity spatially in new ways. We begin by acknowledging that we do not know what kind of space might be involved, but that there are reasons to think about the subject spatially (for example, that thinking of subjectivity as nonspatial or not-occupying-space seems much weirder!). First, we propose that "there is a topology of the subject"—in other words, a productive way of thinking about subjectivity in spatial terms. Second, we propose that such a topology of the subject is traversed by morphisms in such a way that it is capable of deformation (still topology) or modal transformation (topology > topos theory). We might consider mood, gestalt, ekstasis, even perception in these terms—in other words, subjectivity is constituted as something shifting or variable while at the same time retaining an invariance. Third, we ask whether, in fact, there is a topology of the subject, that is, an invariant, formalizable structure, as speculated on in psychoanalysis, that undergoes temporary modifications while remaining structurally unchanged—or whether it would be more accurate to speak of a topos of the subject where, as per Negarestani, the evolution of geist or spirit involves a level of freedom and transformation, such that it becomes more challenging to speak of an invariance. Fourth, this question needs to be considered pragmatically, or at least experimentally—and music would be one of the sources of data on the topos of the subject, given the well-known though historically and geographically diverse forms that music takes, and the demonstrable impact of music on subjectivity: we listen to music, we feel, feeling is a kind of change, but when the music stops, we return, to some degree, to the more familiar shape of our psyche. Or do we? These last two points would correspond to a cosmopolitical framing of subjectivity.

In terms of the second point—eventually, we reach a limit of morphisms and sheaves and elementary toposes and even "Grothendieck toposes"—the point of ontology. And this is a key aspect of Hennix's work where the "deontic" must pass into the "miracle," where the "twoity" of Brouwer's intuitionism folds back into the continuum that it bears with it. In a recent text, she writes that, "in the passage to this topos of maqam during Sam'a (Sufi congregation for prayer), the ultimate goal is to experience fan'a, a state of annihilation carrying the subject fading into infinity, a state that comes in distinct degrees and modalities all of which are accompanied by specific inner sounds that arise in the course of arriving at the crossings of remembrance and oblivion."[27] "Maqam," here, is being used in multiple ways, including its general meaning in Arabic of "place, location, position" and the more specifically musical (and mathematical) sense of the set of just intonation–tuned scales that constitute maqamat as a musical system.

While Hennix is specifically talking about particular Sufi devotional practices, one might ask whether most or all of the musical examples that interest her, including those of Afrodiasporic musical cultures, and including of course her own work, bear some kind of "Sufi trace." In a recent conversation, Hennix illustrated this idea in relation to Moroccan Gnawa music, which she claimed has similarities to her own musical practice:

> The point is to provide for an opening to an alternative universe. Note that this Latin word ["universe"] means "one song" or something like that—to turn a single song into a cosmic event. . . . I just came across an article about Randy Weston and Pharoah Sanders working with Gnawa people. One line, which Pharoah stated, struck me: [he] said that before they move on to another stage of the lila ceremony, they have to reach a certain level in the section of the sound that they presently are at. I thought that was incredible. In other words, you're not allowed to move on until you've gotten all the way. That's my idea too—which I take to be an instance of the Principle of Sufficient Reason. That's what I feel it takes. Coltrane was the last Western improvising musician who did that in a concerted and deliberate way.[28]

While Zalamea (and Mazzola) sees in Grothendieck's use of the idea of the topos precisely a way of bypassing "meaningless" ontological or foundational debates in favor of a synthetic mathematics built around a gradual but inexorable densification of specific connections between different mathematical categories, Hennix appears to have derived the exact opposite meaning, that is, that a topos potentially represents a target or "output" foundational space/state that is sutured to a particular group of mathematical-musical methods of occupying and exploring it. Thus, there is a stacked series of ideas of space in Hennix's work, moving from an elementary topos that is mathematically well defined, toward a Grothendieck topos, perhaps compatible with Mazzola's topos of music, in which the abstraction and capaciousness of the concept of space has been considerably enlarged, toward an open and free concept of space that is asymptotic with (that is, tending toward absolute equivalence) philosophical and religious ideas of the One. This is expressed succinctly in the category theoretical formula quote from Hennix with which I open the chapter: "1 → □" "There is an adjoint or functor such that the One's transits to the category (of music) can be described."

While not all music, or even most music, has such explicit aspirations, a lot of music made around the world does involve target states, though their iteration is usually local and quite specific. In the world of Hindustani ragas where the target state is the presence of the particular deity associated with a particular raga, one might say that each individual raga is a topos, and the tambura matrix is a sheaf covering all the individual raga toposes; in the world of West African drum music, particular rhythms are associated with particular deities; in Indigenous musics, the target state might be alignment with traditional law, history, or nonhuman relatives and allies; in other traditions, certain musics are explicitly therapeutic and aimed at healing body and mind; in medieval Christian and Islamic music, the target state is the presencing of God; in secular European classical music, the apprehension of particular aesthetic states or judgment such as beauty or the sublime or "joy"; for Cornel West, the music of the Black radical tradition involves "agapic praxes of community"... and so on.[29] Clearly, we are dealing here with a profound cosmopolitics of address and teleology with no evident metalanguage that can claim authority without exposing its own preferences, biases, or values.

We, as moderns, claim not to believe in target states formulated in such explicit terms. Modern aesthetics were enframed by Kant's "purposive purposelessness." But the statement "there is no target state," only a diversity of forms, is obviously untrue when considered globally and historically. Why we do not believe in musical target states is one question, but not necessarily the one that interests us here. What happens when we do acknowledge the existence of target states in the practices of musical communities? Anthropologically, we are committed to faithfully describing how those who do believe in them frame them—that is, with raga, we are interested in the entire philosophical, historical, musicological, psychological, political, aesthetic, and practical matrix by which the idea of ragas is articulated as "living souls." Prospectively, we ask how we can think of "contemporary music" in these terms, where the target states are secularized or speculative? How does music change when these ideas are introduced? It's pretty obvious that jazz's challenge to classical music was precisely this, that is, it's a music organized around target states, particular kinds of pleasure, jouissance, and "agapic praxes of community," which are not necessarily discursively articulated or formalized, but which, for those involved, are carefully assembled, realized, and collectively shared, as Henriques notes, through "ways of knowing." One danger or risk in pursuing this logic is obviously that the idea of "target states" is used for a kind of sloppy branding where the word and the state are trivial or mere advertising or packaging or illusion. Another danger or risk is that of instrumentalization, where target states are formulated in biopolitical or other terms as tools of population management, or part of the machinery of global capitalism—or, for that matter, a violent reassertion of a particular nationalist tradition or ideology. The question of defining and realizing a target state is in fact quite a delicate one—but music is delicate in that way, or can be: a "fragile absolute" in Žižek's phrase.

Nonetheless, the question remains: can we generalize about music and the diversity of target states that have been associated with it, such that we gain a deeper understanding of what music is? What is it that the target states associated with music share? An effective musical practice can be defined via an elementary topos that sets out tonal, rhythmic, and perhaps other parameters of the sound in relation to particular target states. It is effective if these target states are reached. These target states are associated with the vibratory exposure and transformation of space in its general or in—relative to societal norms—unrestricted forms. This exposure has as its correlative a realignment of human subjectivity in relation to the space, or, in more cosmopolitical terms, of the humans and nonhumans that share the space. Freedom consists in the ability to manifest such musical frameworks as life-worlds. Understood this way, the cosmopolitical practice of music is quite specific in terms of its intentions but (radically) pluralist in the ways in which those intentions are framed and articulated. And because these intentions are implicitly or explicitly understood by those participating in music scenes, music making necessarily takes certain forms in seeking to attain these states.

4

Looking beyond Hennix, one observes that one of the main trajectories of nineteenth- and twentieth-century music emerging from the Western classical tradition is the gradual expansion of possible tonal and rhythmic elements that can be included in a composition. From Wagner's Gesamtkunstwerk; the discovery of atonality; the twelve-tone system; twelve-tone serialism; musique concrète and the recording and manipulation of field recordings as musical material; the advent of sine wave generators and composition via pitch rather than note; Stockhausen's and Xenakis's statistical composition; Cage's opening up of the entire world of sound as musical material; the gradual recognition of non-Western musical systems and alternative tuning systems, including just intonation scales; and the digital creation and manipulation of sound, including granular synthesis—all increase the number of possible articulations of music as a topos. This particular topos is to be constructed synthetically by increasing the number of possible musical points that can be included in a piece of music as well as the number of possible ways (i.e., arrows) by which such points can be connected. In doing so, and breaking with musical tradition, even the most aleatory practices of the organization of sounds act as a spanning or parametrization of the continuum since these sounds must be articulated in the now. Conversely, while the expansion of musical material or points is relatively unrestricted, the broader parameters of this musical tradition—the concert hall, expectations of performers and audience, target states defined via a secular Kantian aesthetics—have remained relatively rigid and inflexible.

Xenakis, an important influence on Hennix in his application of set theory and computation to both his musical theories and practice, argued in his book *Formalized Music* that music could be thought of as a synthesis of Pythagorean and Parmenidean ideas (scales plus the now, the continuum)—or alternatively of Heraclitean and Parmenidean thought (the flow of time and the continuum). The disjunctive doubling of the model is itself evidence of the difficulty of thinking clearly about this. In proposing a general model for what music is, Xenakis suggested a play between "outside-time," "inside-time," and "temporal aspects": outside-time referring to tonal, harmonic, and possibly rhythmic structures; inside-time referring to the ordering of movement, such as the left to right placement of notes across the musical staves in a page of notated music; and temporal aspects referring to the sequencing of performed sounds with its existential implications.

> This degradation of the outside-time structures of music since late medieval times is perhaps the most characteristic fact about the evolution of Western European music, and it has led to an unparalleled excrescence of temporal and in-time structures. In this lies its originality and its contribution to the universal culture. But herein also lies its impoverishment, its loss of vitality, and also an apparent risk of reaching an impasse. For as it has thus far developed, European music is ill-suited to providing the world with a field of expression on a planetary scale, as a universality, and risks isolating and severing itself from historical necessities.[30]

Thus, the perception—common among European American musicologists and philosophers of music—that music is essentially an "art of time" is based on a particular set of musical practices and structures that seem to affirm this position and its universality while obscuring other possibilities, which are evident to anyone with a global consciousness of the diversity of musical practices historically and geographically who thinks otherwise. Curiously, in his own work, it's not clear that Xenakis was able to develop any particular musical consequences from these observations. He introduces mathematical procedures and practices into his compositions and theory (set theory, composition via graph or diagram, the use of probability and group theory in the distribution of tones) which result in brilliant new shapes and forms but little or no sense of the "outside-time."

We might make a similar observation concerning Stockhausen and his approach to the newly expanded world of sound opened up by post–World War II sonic technologies: "What I use is the mutation process of nature; that's what music is all about. It's an intermodulation so that one being can become another. I'm not interested in collage, I'm interested in revealing how, at a special moment, a human sound is that of a duck and a duck's sound is the silver sound of shaking metal fragments. All these sounds are interrelated very subtly just by the manner in which you listen to them and in the way that they're exposed in time and space; the basic material is all the same."[31]

This is a beautiful statement regarding music as a topos, or at least something topological. Mazzola notes in his opus that the irony of the use of the arrow symbol in topos theory (indicating a morphism) is that it does not imply movement, but rather the same thing revealed two ways—as duck and as shaking metal fragments. Not that Stockhausen takes priority here: after noting that "every conceivable sound has its place in traditional African music," the Cameroonian musician and writer Francis Bebey notes dryly that "it was no doubt this extremely concrete aspect of African music that prompted Léopold Sédar Senghor to remark that recent Western experiments with 'musique concrète' are but a belated attempt to catch up with a musical form that has been practiced in Africa for many hundreds of years."[32] Nor do I claim that in itself an awareness of the interrelatedness of all sound results in better music—indeed, a pragmatic ontology of music suggests that it is always a particular local set of sounds and sonic practices out of which music develops and a "total" music is, therefore, meaningless—but it is noteworthy nonetheless. Furthermore, according to Daniélou, there are at least two kinds of musical mathematics and science—the one found in traditional musical systems with their highly specific affective mathematics of tone, whose goal is to produce an intense feeling of continuity, the other found in modern composition where this vastly expanded quantity of sounds is distributed in a way that is often affectively neutral.[33]

A number of years ago, I interviewed the post-Fluxus composer Philip Corner, who expressed this notion of an expanded musical vocabulary beautifully:

> The essential harmony is dissonant. Everything we call harmony is essentially counterpoint. Putting together single tones—the relationship between single tones. We use harmony as a kind of prejudice, against disharmony: some relationships are acceptable, some aren't; some we call harmonious, some we don't. But I see it all as essentially counterpoint: whenever you take distinct pitches and put them together in combinations, it's counterpoint.... Harmony has to do with a sonic entity that does not collapse into an accumulation of components, pitches. It's inherently dense. So the closest approach in equal temperament is a cluster. It's no surprise that the effect of a cluster is not really violent—if you want violent, dissonant sound, one does much better to have say major seventh and minor ninth chords with spaces in between, emphasizing the dissonant intervals. When you use a cluster, you can play them very subtly, very softly, and they're cool, they're very refreshing, very harmonious. You approach the limit where you can distinguish the components. If you go further, into entities where the component vibrations are much smaller, narrower than the limits of equal temperament, you start getting what I call real harmony. And the model in nature for that is a waterfall. Which is a super cluster. And the flat gong, which doesn't emphasize a single tone, also creates a wash of sound over a broad spectrum in which the individual components are not extractable. So, to me, that's harmony.[34]

A waterfall, or water more generally, is a lovely image of vibration, a time/movement image, a totality of the waterfall or the ocean. Waveforms cascading down a rock, or standing forms in the freefall of water in the waterfall itself. I recall a story that Henry Stobart, an anthropologist who works on Bolivian music, told me. When certain of the Quechua folk singers that he works with have to write new songs for a new year, they go to the waterfall nearby and receive the melodies "'as if in a dream,' whilst listening to the sound of a waterfall."[35] They attribute these melodies to sirinus, mermaid-like spirits associated with the water, with music, and with carnival. I've experienced similar things. I remember walking with a friend to Buttermilk Falls in Ithaca, New York, looking at the shards of ice in the creek, after the temperatures had skyrocketed above zero, this still in the middle of January. My friend said that this is what his mind felt like after his recent brain injury. These shards and chunks of reason all piled up on each other, not at all a smooth sheet of ice. We walked up the creek to the waterfall, crossing an icy bridge that leads up to the metal bars that prevent direct access to the waterfall. We stood and stared through the bars at the falling water. Listening. Walking back to the car we spoke of the difficulties of our lives, directly and simply, without sadness.

Thinking about the sound of a waterfall is another way of approaching the continuum—a very dense sonic cluster offers a spread of points which begin to cover the continuum without collapsing back into mere noise. Corner continues:

> I was interested in moving beyond pattern! I feel it's necessary to go to the circumference because the circumference is where any one thing equals everything. And it's just as important to go there as to the center. But, going there (to the circumference), what you get on the way is the elimination of pattern and you end up with raw material. My music has been concerned with all these elements, possibilities, whether of pulse, single tones, even spontaneity, outcry—as raw material, a totally distilled element of raw nature. As you move towards the center where human cultures have always been, you find patterned complexities of these elements. I was always interested in revealing the elements, through a process of microscopy, finding the elements, asking: what's underneath, what's the thing behind them all?[36]

Perhaps there is nothing behind them, yet they are still part of the continuum, which never or very rarely becomes fully present to us, and thus appears behind, underneath, beyond—even though it is simply, in Parmenides's terms: what *is*. Meanwhile, sonic density becomes a key strategy in seemingly covering the continuum. It's there in the drone music of Phill Niblock, who speaks appreciatively of a vibratory density created by tonal clusters in his music that you can physically feel—with relative indifference to any specific tonal or harmonic structure other than what actually emerges, dissonances included.[37] But it's also there in popular sound forms—such as the massed vuvuzelas that appeared during the 2010 World Cup in South Africa. I didn't know what I was hearing at first, a big kind of static roar, full of bass, ripples of distortion. It sounded like a drone, but where was it coming from? The TV was on in my living room in downtown Toronto, and I didn't have cable, so I was used to getting a crappy signal and at first I put it down to static or some kind of sonic distortion. Then, like everyone, I started reading about vuvuzelas, cheap plastic single tone trumpets that South African fans attending the games blew on to create a dense wall of sound. I started to listen more carefully and I came to savor that wall of sound, also getting off on the way that it was driving a lot of other people crazy, in much the same way that drone music seems to drive a lot of people crazy. What was it really that we were hearing when we listened to the vuvuzelas? I came to think of it, perhaps naively, as the sound of the global South, the buzzing hive sound of the people of the world, contaminating the otherwise clean hyperspace of the globalized spectacle of soccer, now trademarked and sold to us by FIFA. A reminder that you can't send a message without distortion entering in, and that if you listen to the messages of global capital, they will always be accompanied by their subaltern support, the global multitude. Just as I love the way that drones piss people off, I loved the appalled reaction of many commentators to the vuvuzelas, and the calls for these trumpets and the drones they created to be banned. Apparently, the mere sonic presence of the people in the curated space of the contemporary sports stadium constitutes a disturbance which must be managed through public health discourses, including not just claims that vuvuzelas can cause serious hearing loss but, more remarkably, that they can spread flu viruses and other contagious diseases. In Baraka's terms, the density of the sound was that of the people.

Today, the dichotomy Daniélou makes between potent traditional musical systems defined by restrictions of tone and order, and a stagnant aleatory or statistical modern music in which any sound might appear, is no longer entirely relevant. Much of the interesting music that has been made in the last fifty years could be called synthetic in the sense that Zalamea uses the word in describing contemporary mathematics. For Zalamea, *synthetic* refers to the propensity of mathematicians to displace questions or problems of the foundations of mathematics and therefore the ontology of mathematics, via syntheses that establish links between formerly disparate or apparently separate domains of mathematics. For him, the displacement of ontological questions does not mean their dismissal or bracketing—rather, synthesis results in a more detailed or dense description of mathematical reality, a finer covering, one might say, of the continuum, as that from which mathematical ontologies arise.

The same processes can be found at work in contemporary music and many of the great achievements of the last fifty years. Among them one might name Miles Davis's slow expansion of the vocabulary of jazz to a "fusion" that would include rock, electronic music, and elements of Indian classical music between 1960 and 1980; Stockhausen, the serialists, and Pierre Schaeffer's various attempts to reformulate musical composition and performance on the basis of the tape recorder and the manipulation of any and all recorded sounds, and of digital sound synthesis that allows for the combination of almost any pitches and pitch combinations ("music consists of order-relationships in time; this presupposes that one has a conception of such time. We hear alterations in an acoustic field"[38]); psychedelic rock and pop in its global varieties, including Brazilian Tropicalia, Bollywood music, the Sun City Girls, Sam Shalabi and many of the projects he's been involved with, and other post-punk groups; and hip-hop and the aesthetics of the sampler/sequencer, which bring together diverse sound sources in an incredibly dense weave that is affectively powerful. Where Daniélou's observations may still be important is in understanding the broader cosmopolitical milieu in which music takes place globally. Cosmopolitical diversity is threatened by global standardization and normalization of musical practices such as the use of software- or hardware-based sound synthesizers and digital recording technologies, distribution platforms such as Spotify—or for that matter the rock gig or rave—at the expense of local and traditional forms where music is part of different ways of life. Yet—as we will see in the next chapter when we consider DJ Screw's chopped and screwed DJing style and the Houston hip-hop scene in the 1990s—local scenes continue to appropriate and find their own uses for globally distributed technologies thus renewing and deepening the cosmopolitical practice of music in ways that continue to astonish and nourish us.

5

How do we understand, then, music's relationship to time if, as Hennix's arguments suggest, it is actually space that is the more generative model for understanding music? No clear understanding of music can emerge without a clear understanding of what time is—yet what is that clear understanding? Veiled by the inaccurate, metaphysical rendering of time as flow that the Western philosophical (and musicological) tradition adheres to, music's reality is obscured. Conversely, what kind of model of time (and space) emerges if we take music as our guide, using the model we have set out in sections above?

In trying to unravel the mystery of the relationship of music to time, let's consider Bernard Stiegler's highly original theses on technics (i.e., technological systems) and time, especially insofar as they inform the equally original work of Yuk Hui on "cosmotechnics," which I have mentioned at different points in this book. It's challenging to summarize Stiegler's multifaceted argument, which necessarily examines the core ideas in the Western philosophical tradition from Plato to Derrida.[39] Stiegler argues that the prosthetic nature of technology, which is well known and accepted in the idea of "Homo faber" ("man the toolmaker") or Marshall McLuhan's "extensions of man," is not an addition to an already fully developed ontology; that prosthesis needs to be understood as "always already" there in any event of ontological investigation. A student of Derrida, Stiegler argues that all writing, all memory, all inscription, whether of image, sound, or word, is technical and prosthetic and is structured by the trace and supplement. Thus, that which appears as present, that which "is there," is only there because it is supplemented by something that is "not there" or outside of itself. Thus, Stiegler argues that Kant's attempts at modeling the internal structure of consciousness, or Husserl's, a century later, inevitably involve a tertiary or external technical supplement that is necessary for the functioning of the internal structure. The past as historiality is given to us in such technical supplements as the history book or the photograph—but more generally, in tradition itself, whether taking the form of linguistic expression or the organization of space and environment in a particular society. These are themselves technical, in the sense of being inevitable and necessary prostheses by which individuals are articulated as social beings. The experience of time particular to a society is also rendered via such technical systems. Today, we live in an age of the industrialization of tertiary mnemonics—recording technologies of many kinds, computers, and so on that generates a radically altered experience of time. Stiegler argues that our sense of time is always linked to the technical systems that organize this sensing within a society.[40] Despite, the title of Stiegler's opus, *Technics and Time*, it is not clear what, beyond recognizing the entanglement of time and technics, Stiegler's understanding of "time qua time" is—and the fact that the opus, as with Heidegger's *Being and Time*, is unfinished, suggests how challenging this question is.

What is the relationship of music to Stiegler's thesis? Insofar as music is music made by musical instruments, or involves recording practices whether notation or phonography, then music is always and obviously prosthetic and always part of a technical system that would include acoustics, agreements about pitch and rhythmic structure, vocal techniques and so on as well as the above-mentioned technical objects. As we have already seen, it is also easy to understand music as involving a cosmotechnics in which the particular form that music takes in a particular society (recall Maceda's work on Philippine musical practices and the ways in which particular instruments emerge from particular kinds of bamboo and metals available in the environment) involves a set of technical operations that emerges in relation to a particular cosmology and environment. Thus, what we have called pragmatism and technics are entangled in complex ways. As such, and as per Stiegler's theses, music as technics then necessarily involves a particular rendering or presentation of time—uncontroversially, an experience of time that unfolds during musical experience according to the musico-technical system that is operative. In Stiegler's words:

> It would then be a matter of thinking aesthetic techniques from the perspective of a general organology, where the organs of the living, together with artificial organs and social organizations, constitute the total aesthetic occurrence, combining in what Gilbert Simondon refers to as transductive relations (relations that constitute their elements). Music, as restricted organology (before the machinic turn) or extended organology (after the turn), would then be a privileged field of investigation, as the relation binding technics and sensibility is seen here with particular clarity.[41]

While Stiegler wrote relatively little about music, the musical example of the melody, crucial to Husserl's description of consciousness and time in *On the Phenomenology of the Consciousness of Internal Time*, is also crucial for Stiegler's model of technics, memory, and time developed in *Technics and Time*—indeed, he returns to it again and again.[42] While the temporality of the melody may seem self-evident, as well as the exemplarity of this self-evidence for a model of time—not to mention music—it is precisely this apparent self-evidence that we are questioning here. Melody as logical rather than temporal sequence, musical forms that emphasize rhythm and rhythmical models of time, musics that are slow or even static such that melody folds back into a sustained tonal cluster, music considered as "action on/in a space." Our wager is that music built around these principles is not just one choice among others, but that it guides us in the direction of a more accurate model of space, time and consciousness—and one that allows us to honor the diversity of musical practice better than the current models we have. What is important here is to acknowledge that musical forms and events do involve a technics in the sense that Stiegler describes so well, and that our understanding of time is intimately linked with the particular organization of technics observed. Therefore, the consideration of musical forms outside that of notated Western classical music performed in a concert hall matters—since the technics involved will point to a different model and experience of time.

If a musical melody does not indicate a linear flow of time, then what might it indicate? First let us observe that if Stiegler and Husserl had used a rhythm as their example, we would immediately be confronted by a different relationship of sound and vibration to time—a cyclical one, a wave based one, rather than one of linear flow. And this is also true of modal music where tonal constraints mean that improvisation in the now does not consist of a series of events that simply recedes into the past, but again, a recursive or cyclical set of movements where primary and secondary retentions form ever increasingly intense loops—with target states attached to them (feelings, the presencing of spirits and other entities, the One). Again, note the way that it is a spatial model of the now that emerges when one relinquishes a model of music based on the linear flow of time. A rhythmically intense music for example stretches the supposed point of the now into a geometric shape that is continuously present throughout the cyclical moments of the iteration of the rhythm. It "spaces out" and we "space out" into it. However, one can say that the bare, minimal fact of music, let us say a single sound wave as it extends into and occupies acoustic space, is already irreducible to a stack of points in a linear, flowing now: the waveform itself, as object already spans the supposed point of the now and extends spatially in doing so. This is all the more so for a more complex tone cluster with its overtones, not to mention the echoes and reverberations of any particular sound in an acoustic space. Does it need to be pointed out that this is not just a model, but music as it actually exists, and the world as it actually is? This is why we are speaking about a vibrational ontology.

The spatial model of the now has the qualities of a field. Prosthesis and supplementarity are ways of talking about the (temporal) displacement of musical entities that are more easily modeled as field phenomena, generated by entanglement, as emergent properties, or by vibratory condensation. Music, as we have presented it here, is a cosmopolitical practice of engaging with the field. The field is coextensive with that which technics describes (since prosthetic relay and supplementation can be described spatially as well as temporally), but this field is already there—and either we twist the meaning of the word *technics* so that it describes vibratory phenomena such as a heartbeat, the cyclical movement of electrons around a nucleus, or the movement of the earth around the sun, all of which are vibratory and periodical without being technical in the way that Stiegler uses this word, or it is more accurate to speak, as Hui does, of a cosmotechnics. Indeed, Stiegler himself suggest something similar.[43]

The relationship of music to space has, of course, been one of the most significant and disputed topics in musicology and the philosophy of music. Consider the work of the Austrian musicologist Viktor Zuckerkandl, notably his book *Sound and Symbol* (1956)—surely one of the greatest attempts to establish an ontology of music while working mostly but not exclusively with the classical canon.[44] In trying to establish the "reality of music," Zuckerkandl argues that "tonal motion," which he considers to be the core of music, consists in the experience of "continuity." In other words, music is characterized by tonal shifts (a melody, a rhythm) that are more than just a sequence of notes happening in time, but the experience of the continuity that underlies and is also articulated by the tonal shifts (the melody as a whole, the rhythm elaborated in time). So far, so good. He then analyzes that continuity in terms of time and space, and decides that music involves the production of a "time image"—by which he means a specific melodic shape that spans or, following Bergson, articulates a duration. Zuckerkandl then goes on to consider the relation of music to space—and makes the argument that rather than being a solely time-based art, music is indeed concerned with space, but not necessarily a visually oriented Euclidian space: "Far from taking us out of space—as common opinion holds—music discloses to us a mode of being of spatiality that, except through music, is accessible only with difficulty and indirectly. It is the space which, instead of consolidating the boundaries between within and without, obliterates them; space which does not stand over against me but with which I can be one; which permits encounter to be experienced as communication, not as distance; which I must apprehend not as universal place but as universal force."[45]

Such a space is clearly to be understood as a field in which the subject is entangled via music's vibrational "force." Withdrawing from a 3D model of space, Zuckerkandl's thought gestures forward to Hennix's ideas concerning music and an ontology of information, via the work of Xiao-Gang Wen. In this work, reality is a condensation of a quantum level information field composed of bosons. Space is a space of information states "experienced as communication" across the field.

In his analysis of music's relationship to time and space, Zuckerkandl is clearly influenced by Henri Bergson's work—and its many temptations for the philosopher of music. Fundamental to this would be Bergson's concept of duration (la durée) which, in a basic way, can be understood as a block of temporal continuity, continuity of change or becoming that is the articulation of time—a time that flows, and a time, according to Bergson, that is not the same as the time of modern physics. As Deleuze observes in his brilliant parsing of Bergson, the precise nature of duration shifts over Bergson's career, from a specifically subjective experience of time in *Time and Free Will* to a radically expanded version in *Matter and Memory* and *Creative Evolution* in which all beings are definable by their particular duration within a universe that itself is the Whole as duration, containing all the other durations.[46] It is not difficult then to read every musical event as consisting in a duration with its own particular articulation of continuity that would be locally discontinuous but ultimately contained within the continuity of the whole. This continuity, according to Bergson, would be that of "Time," and it is against this idea of time's continuum that Zuckerkandl is pushing in his exploration of musical space just mentioned.

The question of whether the real continuum is one of space or time, or nondual and neither/nor, is a subtle one, and one that bears in important ways on the way we understand music, its ontology and its cosmopolitics. The specifically Bergsonian lineage of the question is of significance to the student of vibrational ontology since the first philosophical statement concerning a vibrational ontology is contained in the "Rhythmanalysis" chapter of Gaston Bachelard's *Dialectics of Duration* (1936)—a book written as a critique of Bergson's philosophy, using the now mostly lost work of the Brazilian philosopher Lúcio Alberto Pinheiro dos Santos, which was also directed in part against Bergson.[47] In this book, Bachelard asserts a fundamental discontinuity or dialectics against Bergson's version of continuity, that is, "duration."[48] At first sight, it would appear that Bachelard is denying the existence of continuity per se in favor of discontinuity—but in the aforementioned last chapter of the book, Bachelard articulates as an alternative to the Bergsonian model of time, the space of rhythmanalysis or vibration as a fundamental periodicity revealed by contemporary physics:

> Like radiation, matter must have wave and rhythmic characteristics. Matter is not spread out in space and indifferent to time; it does not remain totally constant and totally inert in a uniform duration. Nor indeed does it live there like something that wears away and is dispersed. It is not just sensitive to rhythms but it exists, in the fullest sense of the term, on the level of rhythm. The time in which matter develops some of its fragile manifestations is a time that undulates like a wave that has but one uniform way of being: the regularity of its frequency. As soon as the different substantial powers of matter are studied in their detail, these powers present themselves as frequencies. In particular, as soon as we get down to the detail of exchanges of energy between different kinds of chemical matter, these exchanges are seen to take place in a rhythmic way, through the indispensable intermediary of radiations with specific frequencies.... It is now impossible to conceive the existence of an element of matter without adding to that element a specific frequency. We can therefore say that vibratory energy is the energy of existence. Why then should we not have the right to place vibration at the heart of time in its original form? We do so without any hesitation. For us, this first form of time is time that vibrates. Matter exists in and only in a time that vibrates, and it is because it rests on this time that it has energy even in repose.[49]

While it is not clear whether Bachelard's criticism of Bergson is valid for all periods of Bergson's work, the transition that is established here from a model of linear time (albeit one of a pluralism of durations) to one of vibration and energy is striking, all the more so since it gestures forward to developments in quantum field theory and condensed matter theory.

We might wonder, following the famous debate between Bergson and Einstein, whether in the end the continuity of music is the same as that of modern physics's space-time continuum. And, here, we come back to Peirce's assertion of the real continuum's supermultitudinousness. At first, it seems absurd to argue that music's continuity, which is experienced "in" space-time, could be anything other than that of space-time. What makes Hennix's work interesting, then, is that if the basis of music is generally considered to be that of "interval," she explores what happens when there is no interval, that is, only a "continuous musical event." And what seems to happen is that as the interval dissolves into a vibratory field, time and space also disappear, and a more basic kind of continuity opens up, which presumably was there as a kind of substrate all along. But it is not clear whether it is accurate to label this kind of continuity as that of "time"—or "space." Cage's *4′ 33″* gestures toward this too—yet, in some ways, it is a misleading piece, since there is no real attempt at vibrational continuity. Every rhythm, every musical gesture is surrounded by silence, and is shaped in relation to silence—there is a miniature *4′ 33″* in the spaces by which any rhythm, or any series of musical gestures, is constituted. This is something that Miles Davis, whose work is, of course, contemporaneous with that of Cage, understood very well: "play what's not there!"[50] In a silent way. But doing this isn't playing nothing, it's playing the continuum, or better, engaging with it, in it, evoking and invoking it as immanence in its most complex and subtle shapes and shifts of tempo, glissandos, stretching time and space. In Hennix's work this "playing of silence" is explored via her interpretation of the Japanese concept of ma.[51]

In pursuing these questions, I am trying to understand what Fred Moten, in a recent talk, described as the possibility of a topological existence, in which the reality of music as sonic shape-shifting suggests another way of understanding what it means to live.[52] Black people in the Americas were exposed to a topological violence in the Middle Passage, in the period of slavery, in Jim Crow, through to the present day—a series of forced changings of shape—that, as the quote from Nathaniel Mackey in my next chapter on DJ Screw suggests, remanifests in contemporary Black music as an attempted "alchemization of lynchings." A changing of shape that never comes to pass due to the persistence of structural racism, or that only fleetingly comes to pass in impossible flashes. Dancing or moving to music gives a suggestion of such a topological existence, as we shift or stretch our bodies. There is an affective stretching that happens, too, that is equally significant—as Ashon Crawley suggests in *Blackpentecostal Breath*—indeed, the idea of the "choreosonic" that he explores is a topological one, in which interior and exterior, sound and flesh, organization of sound and relationality of bodies are gesturally immanent. Such an "alchemization" means transformation, or even healing, but mostly this does not happen because our body-minds are locked by the forces that govern our reality.

If Parmenides, fragment 8, is actually true:

It never was, It never will be. It is all NOW—one continuum.[53]

The obvious objection would be the one made of any monism: that it denies change, specificity, difference. But there is no difference in the absence of continuity; this is what Bergson was grappling with, and it is also the basis of Deleuze's core philosophy in works like *Difference and Repetition*. Hennix's formula "Being = Space × Action" offers a precise definition of a topological existence within the continuum, one based on the elaboration and deformation of shapes or number systems—an elaboration that we might call gesture, or better, mode. Indeed, as Mazzola has also recognized, gesture takes on an extraordinary importance in such a model—gesture as articulation, a form of expression, the local shape of continuity.[54] I am capable of many different gestures while retaining the same structural body. This is true too of course of a tree, or a river, or a sun. It is also true of a sound, as noted in the Stockhausen quote in section 4—and, fundamentally, it is true of any space in which "a sound" "appears." Here, we start to approach the idea of a modal ontology in which what something is can best be described by the way (mode) in which it vibrates, and this vibration as a change of shape. But, in order to recognize this possibility, we need to in some way be open to the possibility that we ourselves are modal beings, that is, not entirely fixed but subject to structural principles, that is, modes and their functorial determination of us as entities.

In these terms, music's relationship to time is best understood as a topological transformation of a space, much as Hennix—and Moten—have argued. In a conversation with Bruno Latour, Michel Serres has argued for a topological model of time—that as opposed to the linear, flow-based model of time, we can think of time as a set of folds or deformations of a space, such that things which seemed far apart are suddenly close together and vice versa as time folds or unfolds. "Time flows in a turbulent and chaotic manner: it percolates."[55] Musical time, then, would also bring things close together via a vibratory transformation of space that changes our perception of time in striking ways. In fact, this is as good a definition of what "rhythm" is as you can find: rhythm as folding, as fascinating whirlpool, interrupting linear flow.

6

In an interview conducted in Delhi in 2001, the Indian singer and philosopher Karunamayee, a long-term student of Pandit Pran Nath, explained to me how she first learned to sing:

> At the age of six, good teachers were coming and teaching my brother and sister. But I was very small and it was not considered necessary for me. But I had a gift. Whenever I heard some music it just became ingrained in me. My consciousness of silence kept my slate very clean. Most of the time I enjoyed the silence. Even when everyone was talking, I felt a kind of echo of the silence, as if I was in a tunnel, untouched by any of it. Whatever I heard was imprinted, and I found myself singing in that way. Nobody cared. I would just put my head down and start going sa-re-ga-ma. Sometimes I would hear my sound very clearly. I would think: it may be that my sound is not heard, but I can think of music! And holding that thread, not of the sound that I'm making, but of the concept of sound, with that I would go up the scales for many octaves. And then I would say, all right, let me come down, keeping the thread, and I would find my voice becoming audible, very clear, and then deep, and then less clear, more unheard, but I could go deep also. This was my favorite exercise. I would go higher and higher like the birds at noontime in the sky. Then I would imagine that somebody is taking water out of a well. You can go as deep as you want. There is no limit on either side, up or down. So I experienced infinity in height and depth through sound and silence. It gives you control over your mind. A thread of sound.[56]

There is a topological aspect to the story—of a house too small, and a person (female, not coincidentally) considered too insignificant to be granted the space in which to sing, so that she locates sound and space internally. Karunamayee's story is an important reminder that subjective issues in the ontology of music cannot be reduced to the psychology of the listener, or a behaviorism coupled to a materialist notion of vibratory sound. Vibration is both inside *and* outside of us, and music's enigma can be evoked via cognitive acts that produce no exterior sound. Put differently, if there is a continuum, it is not just the continuum of Kantian space-time, which we as subjects receive as a phenomenon. Our interiority is itself part of the continuum, and our ability to practice with inner sound (anahata nada) is (extraordinary!) evidence of this. Karunamayee's story points us again to the importance of intuitionism. In his Cambridge lectures, Brouwer argues that "intuitionistic mathematics is an essentially languageless activity of the mind having its origin in the perception of a move of time. This perception of a move of time may be described as the falling apart of a life moment into two distinct things, one of which gives way to the other, but is retained by memory. If the twoity thus born is divested of all quality, it passes into the empty form of the common substratum of all twoities. And it is this common substratum, this empty form, which is the basic intuition of mathematics."[57]

Music's relationship to the continuum is constructed in a similar way—and by a "languageless activity of the mind," as you can experience for yourself right now, if you imagine a scale and then extend the scale either up or down through the octaves. It is not clear, however, that this approach is the same as the idealism that Brouwer is regularly described as endorsing—just as it is not so clear that the yoga of "anahata nada," the unstruck sound, is a form of idealism either. The distinction made is between "struck" and "unstruck"—not between, say, mind and universe. A languageless activity of the body too. The body-mind: if there is continuity, if there is a continuum, it means that mind and body are also a part of that continuity. In Mazzola's interest in thought as a kind of gesture, perhaps we find another way of thinking about this "languageless activity of the mind." Alternatively, perhaps we reach the limit of a gestural model of music, even in the expanded sense indicated in section 3, where the entire spatialization of music in its contingent specificity is "gestural." At this limit, the question of the relation of vibration and gesture to information becomes important.

The following quote is from the Japanese noise/rock/improv musician Keiji Haino, who describes his (learned) ability to immerse those who come to his performances in a vibratory intensity that he himself becomes inseparable from:

> Before I make any sounds, first of all I breathe in all the air in the performing space. Most performers feed off the audience, but I'm conscious of entering into a relationship with the actual air in the place, even before the audience has arrived. After breathing in all the air, when I breathe out again I want to engulf the audience in that air. And then on top of that, I want to return the air to its original state again. When I breathe in all that air and engulf the audience in it, it feels like I have become god. That in itself would be blasphemy, which is why I then return the air to its original state. That's the process that I'm always aware of. This might sound like a joke, but it's not—it's easy to become god, but difficult to keep that power. People often say that my sounds are loud, and that can

be a negative thing. It's not the sounds that are loud, it's me. I actually become the sounds. People often say how opera singers should sing not from the throat but from the diaphragm, or with their whole bodies. But that just limits the sound to yourself—what I want to do is make the air *itself* vibrate. And that's why it's loud. I give my body to the air. That makes the air vibrate—that's what I'm doing with the percussion. In the past, when I didn't have that much power, I wasn't able to make people concentrate fully on the sounds. Now I can do that because, in one sense, I can control the whole space. And everyone then goes along with what I want to do. That's how I become god. But because that's blasphemy, I always return the air again to its original state. And by doing that I will be forgiven.[58]

Haino immerses his audience in the sound, which has become a part of him. The figure of immersion is an important figure in practice of vibration, sonic or otherwise. Immersion is part of an aesthetics of continuity. Yet Haino considers such a practice blasphemous—returning us once more to the taboo on a fully realized vibratory ontology.

The lore and history surrounding Indian classical music has many stories of performers' ability to somehow connect with the local environment—indeed, in the Hindustani tradition, specific ragas are themselves linked to specific times of the day, or seasons of the year, or environmental events. While it is often said that ragas are "paintings" and thus representations of what the dusk, or midnight, or monsoon feel like, a great performance of a raga goes beyond representation to actually transform or induce a particular environment—recall, for example, Karunamayee's recollection of Pran Nath's rain-inducing performance of Mian Ki Malhar in Delhi in 1953, detailed in chapter 1. From such specific local engagements to cosmological and astrological tales of music taking form and shape from the juxtaposition of the stars or in relation to a comet, or the many ways in which Indigenous musical practices around the world are formed in relation to land or nonhuman entities, music exists in continuity with the environment. Music is part of a vibrational ecology. Music is a hyperobject in the senses given by Timothy Morton.[59] It is not that music is simply a metaphor for continuity—in Indigenous Australian worldviews, "songlines" are the local vibrational articulation of the continuum, and their audible form emerges from sitting on the land, letting it vibrate through you.[60] When I met the Japanese sound artist Akio Suzuki, whose work is a profound exploration of environmental resonance, I asked him how he understood the power of sound as a form of vibration. He responded that, according to the traditions he emerges from, the power of sound relates to the form that stellar configurations take for us.

7

We struggle, as we go deeper into the modalities with which a vibrational ontology is articulated, to keep subject and object in their places. Keiji Haino's subjectivity saturates a performance space with a vibration that he claims to be indistinguishable from; in other cases, subjectivity itself is penetrated by, immersed in, and saturated with vibration—with the nontrivial but everyday consequence that our own emotional moods change as we listen to music. This is particularly the case with music's ability to induce trance or possession—as described in the French ethnomusicologist Gilbert Rouget's book *Music and Trance: A Theory of the Relations between Music and Possession*, with its conceptually outdated but empirically provocative examination of "the strange mechanism" of music's trance-inducing properties.[61] As compendious as Rouget's book is in its global cataloging of examples of the use of music to induce trance, what is strikingly absent in the book is the sense of a sonic ontology—or, put differently, a sense that musical trance arises out of the ontology of sound and vibration rather than being a psychological, physiological, or sociocultural one. Rouget argues that the ethnographic data does not support the idea of a single mechanism of musical trance—but he also makes little attempt to rethink the conventional parameters of subject and object within which trance is forced to locate itself. Is it possible that trance has a not-yet-understood mathematical structure built around the vibrational ontology of the continuum and our immersion in/extrusion from it? Should we rethink subject and object so that they align with the data from the ethnography of trance states? Trance involves a move toward the indifferentiation of the continuum—it is ekstatic. But it also reveals specifically transpersonal formulations of occupation or relocation of "the subject," the body, and so on by deities, specific spirits, and the like.

In asking these questions, we are raising much broader questions about the relationship between music and space, as they are understood outside of Western musicology. While we have already explored these questions in relation to traditional Asian musics, to the global project of contemporary experimental music, and to some degree music of the Black radical tradition (which we will return to in more detail in the next chapter). Indigenous perspectives on these questions are highly instructive also. The contemporary Indigenous Canadian scholar Dylan Robinson, for example, criticizes the lack of "theorization of the subjectivity of space in musical experience.... To acknowledge spatial subjectivity means addressing the ways by which space exerts agency, affect, and character beyond the realm of striking aesthetic impact. In certain cases, it may mean experiencing it as a partner, interlocutor, or kin."[62] In other words, space cannot just be considered a neutral or passive receptacle in which music happens—even though, as Robinson notes, experience of this spatial subjectivity is highly variable, according to positionality and many other factors.

Based on his fieldwork with Indigenous groups in the Brazilian Amazon, the Brazilian anthropologist Eduardo Viveiros de Castro argues for an Indigenous or nonhuman ontological pluralism—or, to use his word, "perspectivism"[63]— which resonates with Robinson's idea of a spatial subjectivity in musical experience. Viveiros de Castro describes an Indigenous worldview in which all entities have the same "soul" or core, but are adorned by particular forms—animal, spirit, human—that can and do transform. This worldview is sometimes described using the word "animism" or, for Robinson, "animacy." Perspectivism consists in this universal shape-shifting quality. Does music also involve a kind of cosmological perspectivism? It is striking how topological both Rouget and Viveiros de Castro's formulations are. Bodies and minds are locations, topological sites in which, under the influence of music and other factors, transformations, changes of shape, can occur. Does music itself have a perspective that is separate from or different from ours, as one might argue concerning possession by a specific deity in a Black Atlantic ritual? This would be the "spatial subjectivity" that Robinson describes. Or is music rather a vector of transformation? Are vectors themselves to be considered entities in the same way that functions are in topos or category theory? In this sense, we "are" the vectors that locally operate in the place where we find ourselves, rather than being preexisting entities on whom vectors of transformation operate. Topology not as the transformation of a preexisting shape but as operations in a topological vector space—vectoral sequencing. Given the chatter of the unconscious mind, is it even possible to present a model of "our" consciousness that is not sonically or vibrationally ecstatic, in the sense of marking a ground or space that is in-between, that is, both "us" and "not us," traversed by vibratory vectors? Are not the vectoral dynamics of music as they emerge from the continuum omnipresent, although they are anthropologically and cosmopolitically framed differently by various societies and entities (I am thinking of bird song or bat echolocation)?

Here is Davi Kopenawa's account of the Yanomani sound world:

Omama planted the amoa hi song trees at the edges of the forest, where the earth comes to an end and the sky's feet are rooted, held in place by the giant armadillo spirits and the turtle spirits. Here, these trees tirelessly distribute their chanting to the xapiri who rush to them. These are very tall, decorated with shiny down feathers of blinding white. Their trunks are covered in constantly moving lips, ranged one above the other. These innumerable mouths let out splendorous songs, which follow each other as countless as the stars in the sky's chest. Their words are never repeated. As soon as one song finishes, the next one has already started.

They are constantly proliferating. This is why the xapiri can acquire all the songs they want without ever running out, no matter how numerous they may be. They always listen to these amoa hi trees with great attention. The sound of their words penetrates them and fixes itself in their thought. They capture them like the white people's tape recorders, in which Omama also placed an image of the song trees. This is how they can learn them. Without them, they could not do their presentation dance. All the spirits' songs come from these very old trees since the beginning of time. Their fathers, the shamans, merely imitate them, in order to let ordinary people hear their beauty. Do not believe that shamans sing at their own initiative, without a reason! They reproduce the xapiri's songs, which follow each other into their ears like into microphones. It is so. Even the heri songs we strike up when the food at reahu feasts is abundant are images of the amoa hi trees' melodies. The guests who appreciate them keep them in their chests so they can sing them later, during the feasts they hold in their own homes. This is how they spread from house to house.[64]

From the Indigenous worldview that Kopenawa articulates, music is a "nonhuman" gift that is shared with humans, exchanged through mimetic processes whose function is similar to that of recording. In this model, human and nonhuman are entangled via these songs and the xapiri who disseminate them. But the blessing of this entanglement must be solicited and maintained—it is not quite a right. Speaking more generally, we might propose, then, that music does not belong to us—it is a kind of nonhuman agency to which we may affiliate ourselves in musical experience. According to Amiri Baraka, the free jazz musician Albert Ayler would ask people: "'You think it's about you?'" Or at times, talking about other musicians, usually his peers: "'He thinks it's about HIM!'"[65] Why? Baraka explains: "'The Music,' in its selfless performance and the widespread acknowledgment of its 'glory' and revelational purposes, was absolutely primary! This was the reason that the vulgar 'use' of it, as self-promotion for commerce, etc., was a violation of it and a stain on the morality of its perpetrator!"[66] Music exposes us in a profound way to the problem of appropriation, of property, and its elusiveness, even illusoriness. Pandit Pran Nath once said, "I never met the man who could put the notes in his pocket."[67] We can align ourselves with "the space of music," but we cannot own it.

Why? In his critique of Bergson's theory of time as duration, Bachelard enigmatically insists, "Duration is a synonym of a possession, a gift. The clear fact of possession helps to uphold the promise of duration."[68] For Bachelard, what seems like a continuity, that is, the "clear fact" of duration, is actually a higher-level bracketing of a particular relational time span that is discontinuous with other time spans. Duration, from this perspective, is an illusion that is sustained by the notion that the lived experience of time can be possessed by a subject who "experiences" it (the grammatical structure of the verb in the phrase "I experience" seems to hold or prop up this promise), and which therefore "is," because it has achieved the status of a thing. It is not clear that Bergson himself would have endorsed this version of duration after his earliest framings of the topic, but this illusion is still a common feature of the way that music is understood as object or event. The musical score, the object of recorded music whether digital file, CD, LP, or tape, the musical performance or event that "I experience" are all reifications of this all too human attempt to possess something that we call "time." How clear is the clear fact of possession after all? There is a particular kind of feeling that raga and just intonation–based musics produce in me—it's also there in some other musics such as the highly repetitive trance blues sound of northern Mississippi. I can only describe it as a yearning—like a hunger for deeper and deeper immersion where I feel a gravitational affective pull into the sound. But it would be just as accurate to say it's a desire to be possessed—or, liberated from the syntax of property, a desire for the event of possession to occur. It may be that, as Lacan famously says, "I am thinking where I am not, therefore I am where I am not thinking. . . . I am not, where I am the plaything of my thought; I think about what I am where I do not think I am thinking."[69] Does music happen there where I do not think? If so, does it follow that "I am" there where music draws me? There where music draws me is characterized by feeling. Feeling happens where "there is" or "it is"? But "there," other than as pure awareness, "I" "am not." Rather, that which "is" (speculatively: the One) includes "me" in the fact or act of its occurring.

8

Speaking of his relationship to the free jazz musician and composer Albert Ayler, Keiji Haino says this:

> All I'm aware of is that he took the music to a certain point, but no further. I was thinking about this earlier—and I'm old enough now to start making sweeping statements. There are all these people—The Doors, Jimi Hendrix, Ayler—people that I like. They've all possessed parts of the essence of expression. If you imagine the essence of expression as a huge object, then Jim Morrison and so on are all just a minuscule part of that. They didn't have enough—all they had was maybe one thousandth of the whole. Albeit that's a lot better than most musicians who don't even have that. I think that I can possibly become the sum of all those bits. Ten or twenty years ago, the power and effectiveness of my performances were very slight, but I have managed to really increase that through training. If the essence of expression actually exists, then I am an amalgamation of all those separate essences. Though I think that probably this essence of expression doesn't actually exist.[70]

If we "imagine the essence of expression as a huge object"—we are imagining something like the continuum. Haino thinks of the musicians he admires—or with whom he is competitive (although those he describes are all dead, but does that matter to one who is attuned to the continuum?)—as attempting to articulate "the essence of expression" and he imagines a musician who somehow has the resources to make a music that contains and articulates all possible sonic approaches to the continuum—a kind of superhero-like continuity of all musical expression. At the end of the quote, he wryly acknowledges the impossibility of this—for Peircean pragmatic reasons, there can be no one, totalizing sonic approach to the continuum.

Following Peter Sloterdijk's recent book, *You Must Change Your Life*, we are aware of models of spiritual and aesthetic practice that stress discipline, overcoming, and anthropotechnics.[71] It is tempting (as Haino is tempted) to think of the essence of music in terms of the mastery of the virtuoso, or of musical mathematics as an attempt at a reductionist model of the essence of music. Yet it is abundantly clear from musical traditions and practices around the world that virtuosity is not required for music to be powerful. Thinking about music, a little bit of method can go a long way. All kinds of people make music, which does not mean that all music is the same, or of the same power. Yet just about any kind of music could pragmatically access the continuum. Our existence as contingent beings suggests that there must be weak access to the universal—we are part of it, we emerge out of it like waves from the ocean, yet we do not realize it, even if what we do engages with it, shapes it. Universal access is weak access. Weak access means pluralist pragmatic access. The weak and the informal, in the sense that Fred Moten has recently used the word in describing the aesthetics and politics of the Black radical tradition, are related. Informality is necessarily pluralist because there is no single mode of informality—informality is necessarily local, contingent, attuned to a particular situation. It is a form of what Moten calls elsewhere "radical indistinctness."[72] And the point, then, is that this is not a lack of depth or gravitas, but a kind of method, as elaborated in jazz for example. That it has emerged out of the violence of dispossession is worth dwelling on.

Music is not just virtuoso performance. It's also practice, vibrational practice in the expanded sense of the word that Nina Sun Eidsheim has given it in her recent book *Sensing Sound*.[73] But it's not just practice. It's also humming while gardening or singing to yourself while working.[74] Or worshipping. It's vibratory action in the broadest sense—vibratory being. It does matter whether something takes specific shape: anyone who's attended an elementary school concert is aware of this. But it matters locally, according to the specific situation. Thus, music can be many things (the basic insight of the sociology of music) while at the same time always articulating continuity. There is the genuine beauty of the lumbering attempts at coordination that a third-grade elementary school ensemble makes at playing together, not quite able to control their instruments in the way they want to, or the way their teacher wants them to. Or a kindergarten concert where the very possibility of children repeating the words of a song takes on a miraculous quality. But then also the murmur of toddlers repeating lines from Kendrick Lamar's "Humble" or Justin Bieber or Nina Simone. Or the way my son starts singing quietly to himself sometimes when I hold him in my arms. He relaxes and he sings. Music is love, music is the path to a love supreme.

What to make of something like GarageBand and the delight a kid takes in being able to create an EDM track in five minutes? Here, music is truly "mathematical" and "algorithmic." But the pragmatic element is really reduced to pressing a few buttons and in some sense requires a much more subtle sense of the pragmatic and the informal—which is in fact what you find with great contemporary electronic music, like gqom producers from Durban, South Africa, or the Principe Discos people—or Footwork producers.

Informality, however, should be distinguished from the haphazardness of the school concert. Informality is not a lack of mastery, but a decision to inhabit the continuum otherwise. Informality relates to a certain kind of improvisation.

Pandit Pran Nath disdained both the notation of music and the recording of it. He argued that if you were going hunting for a tiger, what was the point of saying the night before that the tiger will appear here, then I will jump at him, then he will leap to the left and then dive back into the undergrowth. But this necessary immanence of musical improvisation is no less true of the teenager in a bedroom in Durban or Montreal, playing with a copy of Fruity Loops on a beat-up old laptop or PC.

Informality is key to what Ornette Coleman means by harmolodics. Although the roots of harmolodics in Coleman's music can be found as far back as "Free Jazz" and the classic early 1960s quartet pieces, evidently Coleman coined the term after a visit to the Master Musicians of Jajouka in Morocco in 1974, when Coleman played for a few days with the ensemble of ghaitas (a kind of reed instrument) and drums. He was confronted with the question of how to improvise or respond to a very specific local musical tradition without simply repeating it or drowning it out with his own improvisation. In other words: how to play together with Others who play otherwise—and reciprocally too. According to the journalist Robert Palmer, who accompanied Coleman on the trip (and played clarinet):

> That's when it all came together. He found a theme, a kind of riff that was a perfect bridge from his idiom to theirs, and by conducting while he played he managed to weave a whole symphony of changing textures around his riff. And he developed the piece in three movements, so it had a really rich formal symmetry. The rest of the music we recorded in Joujouka was very much a meeting of worlds. Ornette was soloing in the jazz sense, the Master Musicians were playing their traditional ritual music, and I was playing textures off their harmonics, sort of trying to link the two. But all the musicians on "Music from the Cave" were playing in one world, and I think that world was equally new to all of us.[75]

According to Philip Schuyler, who interviewed the Jajouka musicians about their time with Ornette, "they were very impressed by Coleman's musicianship but also confused by his performance practice: 'He could write down anything we played, exactly. But when he played what he had written, it didn't sound like us at all.'"[76] Did it have to? When Ornette's band plays they are invited to express themselves freely within the context of a particular melodic line, meaning that they all construct their own pragmatic sonic relationship to the melody—which, in local terms, means that they also play together and construct something together. But this happens differently from a situation out of the classical tradition or perhaps even in certain versions of the jazz tradition where the musicians are playing a score that elaborates some kind of geometrical shape, or they are playing modal music, or even chorus plus improvisation within the tonal matrix of the song. The creation of "ensemble" in harmolodics assumes that, pragmatically, each person creates their own geometry and that at the same time these geometries can be responsive to each other in such a way that a metashape is emergent out of this—which it is since Prime Time is very far from being "free improvisation" in the classical sense of the phrase. Ornette talks about what it means to play in unison—that the members of an ensemble might all be playing the same pitch, but that it means something different to each of them on their particular instrument; conversely, they might be playing the same melody, but transposed onto different interests, different pitches, different tempos.

9

If music is a path to the Parmenidean One, why do we not choose to take it immediately? Conversely, why do ideas of music's relation to the One generate either indifference or hostility so often today? If the obvious secular response to this is simply, "because there is no One," hopefully the foregoing comments on this topic have at least left the secular reader open to the idea that, as Lacan says, "Y a de l'Un" ("There is some One")[77]—at least when it comes to music. Philosophically and politically we are in the domain of the problem of universals—and the long human struggle for emancipation from the despotism of ideologies of the universal.[78] Is it possible to formulate a universal that does not calcify into an "ideology of the universal"? I have set forth in the preceding chapters some ways of thinking about music's relationship to a universal—figured as the One or the continuum. In doing so, what is instructive are the actual cosmopolitical practices found in various music scenes—to varying degrees and with varying success. Living at a moment when emancipatory possibility seems so strongly sutured to ideas of difference and hostility to that which might underlie and support such difference raises a question as to whether there is a human fear of the real universal (the universal real?) and, at least in understanding music, the question as to why such fear exists.

In Hennix's terms, this is because music concerns jouissance, the disturbing, intense "enjoyment" of the subject and the complex ways in which we are open to or barred from such jouissance. Cosmopolitically, cultures also vary considerably in their relation to jouissance, and this includes the ways in which the ontological potentials of music are developed, ignored, repressed, or "perverted." In thinking about music we find ourselves in the middle of a complex geopolitics and geohistory of enjoyment. Hennix posits this problem in explicitly Lacanian terms, without entirely agreeing with or endorsing Lacan's assessment—but recognizing and asking us to recognize that we lack an adequate theory of the subject, and need to start somewhere. So, let's begin with Bruce Fink's gloss of Lacan's concept of the real:

> So too, Lacan's real is without zones, subdivisions, localized highs and lows, or gaps and plenitudes: the real is a sort of unrent, undifferentiated fabric, woven in such a way as to be full everywhere, there being no space between the threads that are its "stuff." It is a sort of smooth, seamless surface or space which applies as much to a child's body as to the whole universe. The division of the real into separate zones, distinct features, and contrasting structures is a result of the symbolic order, which, in a manner of speaking, cuts into the smooth facade of the real, creating divisions, gaps, and distinguishable entities and laying the real to rest, that is, drawing or sucking it into the symbols used to describe it, and thereby annihilating it.[79]

Note that the language here is almost identical to that which we have used in articulating the mathematical and philosophical problem of the continuum. The real, for Lacan, constitutes a kind of underlying continuity, associated with the unconscious but also associated with a global concept of environment from which the subject extrudes even while being nonseparate from it in the same way that a wave is not separate from the ocean it occurs in. This environment—or field—is separate from language and from the symbolic order, though we exert considerable efforts to catch it thus. Insofar as this environment can nonetheless be described in vibratory terms (via the wave/particle duality in quantum physics, via the energetic pulsation of the unconscious), one could say music, as vibratory practice, has greater proximity to the real. Already we are forced to depart from most readings of Lacan here, in simply insisting that human and nonhuman relations to the real do not end with the infant's acquisition of language (or successful Lacanian analysis!), nor are they always traumatic, but rather that our relation to the real is a cosmopolitical one that is mediated through the valorization or denigration of diverse and specific kinds of practice, of a surprisingly fragile and delicate kind—in a world where delicacy and fragility are not much honored.

What is implied by this greater proximity? For Lacan, it is *jouissance*, a word with a complicated and variable definition, connoting enjoyment, orgasm, extreme pleasure, but also a kind of pleasure containing an unpleasure or even suffering attached to it, or to the subject that undergoes the experience of it.

Jouissance, according to Lacan, contains in it a remainder/reminder of the lost unity of mother and infant. This unity is necessarily broken as the infant grows into a separate being, but floats on the horizon of the subject as an imaginary or desired possibility in a variety of situations, notably those connected to eroticism, to bonds with a larger Other or One, whether religious, spiritual, political, social, or the like. Yet this desire contains ambivalence, and is experienced as pleasure-pain since it involves a dissolution of the boundaries of the subject that is ekstatic, opening up in the direction of something unbounded, undifferentiated, potentially joyful, but also as something threatening to the boundaried subject in its fragile but situationally necessary sense of separateness. In Lacan's terms, the desired object, the object of jouissance, is referred to as *objet (a)*—an object thought to contain the excitement, pleasure of that lost unity, but, at the same time, acting as a kind of shield against the intensity or threat suggested by that excitement, allowing the subject to keep a certain distance from it.

For Hennix, music often functions as a kind of objet (a). We take pleasure in continuity, and specifically we take pleasure in musical continuity. Too much pleasure, too much dissolution of the self, too much immersion in the unfolding of the Parmenidean Now, may start to turn into pain, suffering, fear—and so, as Attali documents, music is historically subject to controls, limits, rules. As Sebastian Leikert notes in his essay on music and jouissance, musical forms such as opera parcel out the exposure of the sonic remainder of the real in the wordless climax of certain arias—framing this exposure with all the paraphernalia of cheap semblance, kitsch plots and librettos, the overdetermined (and presumably reassuring) architecture and spacing of the opera house.[80] In the dance hall or party, as we see in Steve McQueen's beautiful film *Lover's Rock*, bodies are much closer together, move much more freely in relation to each other; erotic dissolution, subjectivized freak-outs, spiritual recollection, collective violence, and solidarity all pulse through the crowd and through the lovingly curated vibrational space of the sound system, which has its own rules, its own sense of "ethical know-how." This is the cosmopolitics of music and vibration.

At a more basic level, music embodies the ambivalence of objet (a) and the subject's relationship to jouissance. If music directs the subject toward an unfolding of the Parmenidean Now, that is, for a certain kind of subject, unbearable, then music, at a very basic level, also contains this unbearability by providing that wavering or circulation of desire around its object that consists in playing another note, making another sound, modulating in relation to the object of desire. If desire, according to Lacan, circulates around its object, maintaining a certain distance, music, in general, does precisely this. Musical progression, that is, from sound to sound, may be both distraction/repression/evasion . . . and the disjunction/conjunction in which the real qua continuity opens up. In an interview published in a Swedish magazine in 1971, Pran Nath commented on this distance in an instructive way: "Guruji [i.e., Pran Nath] says that if he could tune exactly he would disappear and the tanpura would disappear if it was tuned perfectly. It is necessary for a degree of tuning imperfection for the instrument and the singer to be recognizable as such."[81]

While some music wavers through an excessively rigid iteration of a predictable musical structure that is heavily and institutionally embedded (national anthems, popular music in general!), and while some music wavers through an aleatory quality that neutralizes it in relation to the now (ironically, post-Cagean improvisation), one might say that modal music and polyrhythmic music, too, seek to create a structure of dynamic repetition in which the flash of the real, that disappearance of singer and instrument in a moment of being perfectly in tune, is always a possibility. And, more than a possibility, a desired opening or unfolding, that is held to via a particular modal framework. Within such scenes, jouissance is a desired outcome. The framework in which this desired outcome is held may be called a topos.

Is there really a difference between the operatic relationship to jouissance and that of the sound system? It is a difficult question to answer since, at some level, respect for the various subject positions in relation to jouissance, a certain gentleness or appreciation of the fragility of our engagement with jouissance, is important—especially in relation to a kind of anthropology of discretion, in which the relationship between what happens and what can or cannot be said about it is crucial. Still, without a real appreciation of the ways that nonhegemonic musical cultures and forms have approached such questions, and an accompanying loosening of Eurocentric musicological and philosophical commitments, there can be no meaningful analysis of what music actually is.

To return to the theoretical core of the argument here: we are concerned with models of a field or a space—a space in which subject and object are emergent properties. This space can be described in terms of a network or a field—even in Lacan, "the chain of signifiers" has something like this function especially in its displacement of the ontological status of subject and object into the network of signification. In ontological terms, a philosopher of music such as Roger Scruton may claim that, for music, there is the sound object and the psychology of the listener, and "there is no third possibility"[82]—but music is the generation of the field, of a field, and the field is indeed a third term—the "topos of music" describes this field and its parameters. Enjoyment, pleasure, jouissance are also emergent properties of this field—of what happens to "the subject" (in quotes to indicate its provisional or normative status) immersed in the field, unraveled by the sound, body/mind adjusted or transformed in the field. This is illustrated in a lovely way in the following description by the godfather of house music, DJ Frankie Knuckles, of his first visit (with the revered New York DJ and originator Larry Levan!) to the fabled New York party space the Loft in 1973:

> I remember the room moving in such a tight rhythm that all the bodies felt like one. The front room was lined with church pews. On the floor in front of the booth was a bean-bag chair and snake pillow. At the head of the room by the front windows was a fully decorated Christmas tree.
>
> There were people standing in the pews beating tambourines, blowing whistles and playing a wide assortment of percussion instruments.
>
> I don't remember what song was playing when we got there but, all of a sudden it came to an end. The room is now dark. You can't see anything. Then, the sound of a Hammond organ is building in the room. A cool breeze is blowing now thru this room that was seconds before, a sauna. As the song builds to a fever-pitch with its percussive and Hammond crescendos it breaks to percussive toys (bells, timbales, congas etc.). The song was CITY, COUNTRY, CITY by WAR. The room is crazy now. Ev'ryone is locked in a spell.[83]

There is a relationship between pleasure and the production of continuity, in the renunciation of some amount of discontinuity, perhaps. What this pleasure is, whether pleasure is the right word for it, whether what we call pleasure is the same in the opera house, on headphones in the winter in the subway, in a dance hall or at a party, a body moving with other moving bodies, are all important questions.

All of this brings up the relationship of music to eroticism. In the Bataillean version of things, the move toward continuity is described as follows: "For us, discontinuous beings that we are, death means continuity of being. Reproduction leads to the discontinuity of beings, but brings into play their continuity; that is to say, it is intimately linked with death.... On the most fundamental level there are transitions from continuous to discontinuous or from discontinuous to continuous. We are discontinuous beings, individuals who perish in isolation in the midst of an incomprehensible adventure, but we yearn for our lost continuity."[84]

Erotism, or eroticism, or sexuality exists anthropologically when "the concern is to substitute for the individual isolated discontinuity a feeling of profound continuity."[85] Furthermore, what Freud (and then Lacan, responding to Bataille) calls the death drive is related to continuity. Indeed, for Freud, the death drive is a force "whose function is to assure that the organism shall follow its own path to death," that is, toward continuity, while, for Lacan, the circling of the death drive around its object (i.e., death, continuity), describes a simultaneous movement of fascination and deferral in relation to continuity. Law, taboo, often exists to prevent continuity from occurring: taboos on incest; taboos on killing and eating members of the same species; and laws around violence or appropriation or the disposal of the dead. Language itself, especially in Lacan's version where language bars access to the maternal vibrational body, expresses a very particular kind of discontinuity in relation to the continuum. All of human life happens in this space between discontinuity and continuity—or should I say "nearly all"?

Is music an exception to the barring of human impulses toward a realized continuity? Music's relationship to eroticism has been noted—most recently by Elizabeth Grosz.[86] What has not been noted is that this sense of an erotic impulse toward continuity can be related to the specific ways in which music engages the continuum—a politics of vibration at the limit of discourse and signification, of negation and expenditure as a passage toward an experience of continuity that by definition cancels itself out as "experience" in the act of taking place, and the proliferation of sonic and performative stratagems or practices in music that explore this limit.[87]

I remember a trip to Marrakesh in 2002, where I spent a night in the Jemaa el-Fnaa, the medieval square that is the social and cultural hub of the city, listening to a group of Gnawa musicians in the square, chanting their hypnotic songs over the darting bass sounds of the guimbri and the shuffling rhythms of the qrakesh, large iron castanets that are rubbed together. Around dawn, my partner and I went back to our hotel and made love for hours, without any sense of fatigue, and without it deteriorating into some display of athletics. It was beautiful and hot, and somehow I felt that our lovemaking was the continuation of the rhythmic, vibratory matrix of the music in the square. In both sexuality and music, there is a craving for rhythm that is similar to the craving for a certain tonal matrix in raga that, I argue, has its origins in a vibrational ontology.

Conventional wisdom would say that we enjoy rhythmic music because it is the sublimation of sexual desire and provides a memory of the rhythms of sex and erotic arousal and, beyond that, the rhythms of the maternal body and our earliest experiences of periodicity or the immersive aquatic vibratory spaces of the womb. My experience with the Gnawa made me feel that maybe this was at least in part backward—that maybe sex and its rhythms are themselves a reminder of a broader ecology of vibration and that eroticism is one of the pathways into a much wider space of the chora, not one that transcends sexuality, nor one in which sexuality serves as a gateway for a more profound experience, but simply a space in which eroticism functions, too, in which eroticism is one of the principal modes of vibratory continuity, given that we are human. In other words, an ontology of vibration in which eroticism is algorithmic and topological (i.e., concerned with geometric parametrization as an essentially queer and non-Eurocentric play with form and space). Just as the MCs of Odd Future and other contemporary hip-hop formations are capable of turning this space inside out and upside down in profound and complicated ways, this was also where the humor of the Gnawa comes in—they are well aware of the way things can turn into other things, of the omnipresence of eroticism, of playfulness, of loss, of nonsovereignty.[88]

The sense of continuity evoked by Freud, Lacan, Bataille, Irigaray, and others, and the mathematical/philosophical problem of the continuum come together in contemporary music, where negation, transgression, exposure to death—a more or less limitless exploration of eroticism—are articulated through an expanded concept of music in which all of the above appear to be at stake via particular sonic structures and events that engage the problem of the continuum. Existentially, if you like. If I say "appears," it is because there is something performative about it—note that Bataille does not say that erotism will result in actually full manifestation of the continuum or continuity, but rather "a feeling of profound continuity."[89] We are left with this ambiguity, which at times seems to make proximity to death the measure of musical authenticity (especially in the racialized sacrificial economy of contemporary hip-hop). But it is also unclear whether Bataille is correct: are living beings truly separate from continuity? Is "discontinuity" ever actually possible? Would it not rather be a "feeling of discontinuity" that we experience mentally while at every moment the broader forces of continuity, biological, physical, and otherwise, from the micro-organisms that pervade our bodies, to the operation of electromagnetism and gravity, not to say quantum entanglement, proceed inexorably? Here, in this ambiguous space, music happens. The pathos of music would not exist, would not be pathetic, were it not for this ambiguity, for this "incomprehensible adventure" that we find ourselves in.[90]

10

I stared at the ocean waves for a long time, hoping that they might hold the secrets to the continuum. Nothing much happened—just two images from two movies—the view of the ocean at the end of Jean-Luc Godard's *Contempt* (the cold, impassive backdrop revealed after the failure of erotic love), and the photograph of the ocean that fills the screen at the end of Michael Snow's *Wavelength*, a frozen picture of home that endures the electric dramas of a downtown New York loft. Still, I stared for so long that eventually I did have a thought about them. I thought about the Brazilian musician João Gilberto's guitar and the waves, especially on his 1972 self-titled record, where his acoustic bossa nova playing somehow achieves the heaviness of dark metal. The curves of iteration, of shape within the continuum. Oneness, sameness, not as always the same, but the contingency of ripples, the timing of a chord in a rhythmic sequence, the playful fatalism of it; the inescapability of the mode except through the infinitesimal precision of the rhythmic, détourned cut. Fantastic in the drama of its specificity. Complex dynamic systems . . . of harmony and rhythm. Rhythm as return of the same, the cycle, periodicity . . . a topos! And the sensuousness of that. Vibratory touch, wavesound. Complexity as a kind of touch or tenderness.

 I saw a lovely performance of bossa nova guitar in a pizzeria called Punto Divino just off the church square in Paraty, Brazil, in 2017. A sixty-year-old Afro-Brazilian guy playing a lovely beat-up old guitar, some singing, mostly just guitar. The first and last chords of each song somehow conveyed whole universes of their own—though what follows or what has led up to this particular chord matters too. But how do you think of that? How is that part of the continuum, because it clearly is? The chords in sequence in time constitute not only "the continuity of discontinuities" in the Buddhist sense but also the (apparent) discontinuities of which the continuum is composed. "It is all now." Rhythm would then in itself be more continuous since it iterates sameness as a mark or pattern in time; while harmony would be a vibrational spread vertically across a moment in time . . . though the arpeggiated chords that bossa uses at the beginning and end precisely blur that sense of time.

 There's a cliché that guitar players often say: "It's just a wooden box with some strings attached." The wonder of it. The possible ways of playing this object, this wooden box, are supermultitudinous. Not every way of playing it sounds right. Nor is there—in advance—a wrong way. You have to construct it, and there are ways that don't work. There is a matter of precision there, which allows access to the continuum—but there are many forms of precision too. The precise is also a form of the contingent—a working of the contingent. There are many ways to work it. Why is pleasure, or even ekstasis, the sign of it working? It's easy to see that one leans into the continuum, "ekstasis" therefore meaning "out of discontinuity, into or toward continuity." But we also have our own precision and our own way of relating to contingency; it does not happen simply outside of ourselves. We call this "style" and there would be no music without it. Perhaps this is where practice comes in. Something needs to happen out of the pragmatic possibilities of the moment or situation. Practice as the rehearsal of a pragmatic possibility, the mastering of a possibility so that it can be realized in the contingency of a particular musical moment. A certain looseness in it too, that can go many directions, as the moment does.

In 2016 I saw the great experimental folk guitarist Peter Walker play at the Tranzac Club in Toronto. Walker made two beautiful acoustic guitar records in the 1960s, and then mostly retired to practice, and to study Flamenco with the masters who live on the hill in Granada—a life that he describes in his excellent self-published autobiography. The room is dark, spacious, and, Toronto being Toronto, mostly empty. He plays a song/track. Then he muses that it's hard to know what people want to hear in different places. That what people play resonates with the local language, how people speak. And he says that he doesn't know what to play here in Toronto. So he starts at random. And it feels that way. It doesn't quite work. It's almost like the parts, the runs of notes and chords, don't quite fit together. He's warming up. He knows it. But it gets better. He's unusual . . . naive almost. He plays something beautiful and complex and then looks up at the audience as if to see whether they are listening and whether they get what he's just done, or maybe just to see whether they look like they're enjoying it. There's nothing accusatory about his look, no sign of resentment. In between the songs there's banter, but it's banter about Cordoba in the seventeenth century, the transit of music from Bengal in the seventh century AD to Spain via the Muslim conquest. The curse of Gregorian chant. And things like that. It's clear that he recognizes the depths of what he's doing. Or heights. And he's thought about the indifference of the audience, of a particular audience, and the delight of the audience too.

Walker too is interested in building transits. He spends a lot of time retuning his guitar in the middle of songs, marveling or surprised when a particular tuning allows certain scales or chords to come into focus in a new, satisfying way—the way that the practice of strumming a guitar, and all the endless years of practicing Flamenco scales, blues scales, many traditions, might allow something different to come alive in the moment, without it sounding like, to quote Sam Shalabi, "fucking Gypsy Kings licks." He carefully avoids certain things as much as he's attracted to others. There are musical gestures that are, for all purposes, dead. Not that it's about novelty then.

How then to think about Gilberto's voice, the low hum of it? So much of it is about affect, feeling, even in its understatement. A delicate relationship to the continuum. If the music is about "saudade," if it is about love and loss, separation, homelessness, then it is about separation from the continuum. With hands one builds a bridge to the continuum, with voice one destroys it again. And one holds these things together, if one can.

Perhaps this could be understood the other way around too? Character, personality, informality in music involves a certain rhythmic and harmonic cut, a style that is unique or utterly contingent in its breaking up of time.

Surely, music is about separation, its pragmatism always includes some acknowledgment of separateness, loss, failure, impossibility in relation to continuity as such. Yet this performance of separation happens within the context of continuity. In the astute words of Sister Sledge:

We're lost in music
Caught in a trap
No turnin' back
We're lost in music

We're lost in music
Feel so alive
I quit my nine to five
We're lost in music[91]

It is an impossible situation either way, precisely because musical and political-economic pragmatism are so completely at odds with each other, leaving music in the position of being "prophetic," to use Attali's word, since it never quite belongs to the social space in which it happens, even if the social space is ostensibly built around it. In writing this book we've moved from Goodman's "politics of subfrequency" to a politics of vibration, and now to a politics of the continuum. But while the capitalist inhabitation of subfrequencies via earworms, sonic weaponry, and the like has been compellingly documented by Goodman and others—what would a topological or "choreosonic" capitalism look like? If capitalism operates ontologically, in other words, by extracting a surplus value from an ideological configuration of the Real, can it do so from the continuum? The wager of Badiou—and equally, but differently Hennix, or even the Black radical tradition—is that another form of life is possible, in relation to the problem or promise of the continuum. The political radicalism of the mathematicians who developed category and topos theory in the 1960s, in particular Lawvere (who was a committed Marxist) and Grothendieck (who had an anarchist background), is also enigmatically related to this.

The ways in which we enter and exit the topos of music take on extraordinary poignancy when considered in this way. Leaving the space of continuity and going back to the everyday space of discontinuity, we linger on the edge or the perimeter or the space of transition in a multitude of ways. The endless rounds of applause and bowing at the end of a recital in a concert hall. The phenomenon of the encore, and the ritualized clapping and stamping of feet and shouting of demands that the musicians return found at a rock concert. The introduction of the band members by name before the last number in a jazz set. Then there is a whole category of musical composition that is performed at the end of a concert as a farewell, ritualizing but also initiating the process of departure, whether we're talking about "When the music's over/turn out the lights" by the Doors, or the song in Rag Bhairavi that Prabha Atre performed to great acclaim at the end of the Kolkata celebration of her work that I attended in 2007. There are the rituals of audience departure, the heading for the exits, lingering outside to smoke and talk, or drink. And for the musicians, the rituals of packing up instruments, the staircases, doors—the whole apparatus of disassembling the topos of music. For now.

11

When someone dies, they disappear into the continuum. This is what we find in the Tibetan tradition and the *Tibetan Book of the Dead*, aka the *Bardo Thodol*. What happens to a person at the moment of dying? Their consciousness slowly disentangles itself from the body that it has been associated with and leaves, passing through the Bardos of Becoming on the way to either reincarnation or Nirvana—which is expressed as a kind of continuity.

> Alas, now as the intermediate state of the time of death arises before me,
>
> Renouncing [all] attachment, yearning and subjective apprehension in every respect,
>
> I must undistractedly enter the path, on which the oral teachings are clearly understood,
> And eject my own awareness into the uncreated expanse of space.[92]

"Uncreated expanse of space"—primordial continuity. This continuity is described as a subjectless-objectless radiance. It flows, but the flow is not that of time or duration. It is flow itself.

> Be certain that pristine cognition, naturally originating, is primordially radiant—Just like the nucleus of the sun, which is itself naturally originating. Look at your own mind to see whether it is like that or not! Be certain that this awareness, which is pristine cognition, is uninterrupted, Like the coursing central torrent of a river which flows unceasingly. Look at your own mind to see whether it is like that or not![93]

"Uninterrupted." "Unceasing." Out of this primordial continuity emerge the Bardos of Becoming, which are characterized by booming sounds and flashing lights, which are terrifying or attractive.

> From within these lights, the natural sound of reality will resound, clear and thunderous, reverberating like a thousand simultaneous peals of thunder. This is the natural sound of your own actual reality. So, do not be afraid! Do not be terrified! Do not be awed! The body that you now have is called a 'mental body,' it is the product of [subtle] propensities and not a solid corporeal body of flesh and blood. Therefore, whatever sounds, lights or rays may arise, they cannot harm you. For you are beyond death now! It is enough that you simply recognise [the sounds and luminosities] to be manifestations of your own [actual reality]. Know that this is the intermediate state![94]

In the Tibetan tradition, when we die, we enter into a different relationship to the continuum in which, after a brief exposure of the primordial continuum as such, the vibratory spaces of sound or light appear—or perhaps sound and light, experienced as forms of vibration, are the only metaphors left for what can be perceived or known about the continuum at "the ground level."[95] All of this has been rendered sonically in the practicing Buddhist composer Éliane Radigue's dazzling drone piece, *Trilogie de la Mort* (1993), with its shimmering, sustained, interlocking harmonic fields.

I went to a Prince tribute concert at the Holy Oak in Toronto in May 2016, shortly after Prince's death. Due to some new law, the Holy Oak now has a capacity of thirty-seven so the place appeared to be half empty. There was a group of young white guys who call themselves April Snow who formed a Prince cover band in 2013. And then a half dozen or more vocalists from the Toronto indie scene. They played the Prince songs very tightly. Some of the vocalists went their own way, others imitated Prince. It was somehow extremely moving.

We danced. Everyone danced. Except for a couple on some kind of first date where the guy insisted on trying to shout snarky comments to his date over the music. But then they left after the interval. Their out of sync-ness was somehow offensive in the space, even though there's so much freedom in the space. I looked around. I couldn't see that well in the dark. I saw a middle-aged woman standing on her own looking around. Someone sitting near the bar looking at his phone. People who are drunk. Beautiful women. Crusty guys. A couple of white-haired older women who stayed for the first set. "It's just a room!" always feels like a profound insight when things are musically alive. I believe that's because, when music is alive, a topos is created in a meaningful sense of the word. You are dazzled by the transformation of the space, which is an affective geometrization—in other words, you feel the space change. This is not simply a matter of the physics of acoustics or resonance. It's an affective power in the sense of a production of astonishing shapes that are perfect, impossibly possible, actual (not virtual!), but actual in a way that stretches any conventional Euclidean sense of actual space, while at the same time remaining local and specific. The air crackles with homotopies, transits between modal systems, and we become a part of that.

I realized that I hadn't mourned Prince's death yet. Mostly what I'd seen are the flood of social media links to great songs and performances. I posted my own: just a simple link to the long version of "I Wanna Be Your Lover" and a memory of first hearing that song on Greg Edwards's radio show on Capital in London around 1980. The minimalism of Prince's funk, emerging out of P-funk and stuff like that, but really just him in a studio playing all the instruments—still a true form of minimalism at the moment of Glass and Reich. That strikes me today too—the unlikeliness of hearing a specific song on the radio at a particular time and place. How that unlikeliness has happened to so many people over time, over history. How it is what our life consists of. Everything that goes around the music of course, and everything that Henriques says goes into a specific moment of sharing music. But there were no doubt hundreds, thousands of instances of people hearing and playing music last night in Toronto. And Toronto is just one city in the world.

The music poured out of Prince. The music pours out of Ryan Driver, who melted our hearts with his version of "The Beautiful Ones," a song off of *Purple Rain* that I didn't know (that I know). These forms that we call songs poured out of Prince. You can see that in the sheer variety of tracks that people threw up on Facebook—not just the incredible number of songs, but all the performances of the songs, and all the versions of the recordings, many of which contain crucial differences, crucial specifications, as in the 12-inch single version of "I Wanna Be Your Lover" with its three minutes of minimalist instrumental funk at the end. And the pluralism by which different people love different songs, are exposed to different songs as part of their history. And the way those different histories come together at an event like the one at the Holy Oak—in the way the musicians play "The Beautiful Ones" and the crowd dances, on their own, with each other, and shouts, or sings alone, or gets quiet, or goes to the bathroom, or is bored, all the while sharing for a while a certain sameness which is the vibratory parametrization of the continuum that we call music.

The pluralism is there in Prince's repertoire of course. So many songs that you've forgotten you loved, or you've never heard, or you already know that you love. And so much of the repertoire is a meditation on Eros. Learning the value of informality, as Fred Moten says, for sure (what's more informal than replacing for with 4, and you with u), but learning to be direct, and in being direct learning the sexiness of vulnerability, the chain of statements and actions that it initiates, the risk of loss or failure, maybe even the inevitability of loss. And the unusual sense of caring, of respect that somehow emerges from all of that. Which made our first date friends seem so weird. Or am I resorting to scapegoating to channel the death drive that's always there when we talk about Eros? Maybe. I feel so happy when anger and struggle and frustration temporarily melt into the ecstasy that music and dance bring. It does not feel to me that there's anger in that state, but only in the disruption of that state. But that disruption has to be factored in then too—from the inspectors or police who come to make sure capacity is not exceeded, or that fire safety rules are being obeyed (often as a pretext for controlling or stopping a party), to the drunken people who do sometimes get violent. To the fact that it ends, that the sun comes up, Sunday afternoon arrives, at some point it ends, except perhaps in places like that music academy in Kolkata we visited where the Kirana gharana vocal master Mashkor Ali Khan teaches his students every morning and in the end the performance is subsumed to the study and practice of music as ends in themselves. Which is something that Prince might have understood too. Or felt completely indifferent to since it seems like sometimes, if he felt like it, he would go play a show in a small club after a big theater show, suggesting that practice or performance were for him both just particular places in the topos of music.

What to say about death though? We all know that Prince died. His death is a real breach in the realm of the possible, of what musics might still be made. At the same time, it is possible for a group of musicians who probably never met Prince, and now never will, to play those songs in a meaningful or even a new way. Or for the DJ to play a bunch of Prince records, mixed in with other early 1980s boogie classics, all on vinyl, and move the crowd. Recordings are a transit, just as performances are, but with their own specificities. A recording may be deeply entangled in the commodity form, the form that objecthood takes under capitalism, and yet, it is not simply a commodity either. Storage and retrieval are also possibilities within the continuum, within the mathematization of vibration and energy. They are implied somehow in the very concept of "form" and the passing down of forms from musician to musician, which is what the history of music consists of. I think of Peter Walker moving to Granada to learn from the masters on the hill, of Coltrane listening to Bismillah Khan for the first time. I think of Betty Carter and what she did with whatever melody, whatever song she was singing.

Actually it's not so clear that when someone dies, they disappear from/into the continuum. Maybe that from/into is the key. Living is indifferentiation with an arrow passing through it that leaves marks, spans locations, which draws into being a space. Indifferentiation is vibrant, not blank. Being dead is indifferentiation without a sensory mark, other than the marks of graves, coffins, shrines, ghosts, recordings.

FOUR

. . . . . .

Slowed and Throwed

DJ Screw and the Decolonization of Time

>   Time: I understand it
>   But I never choose it
>   I can't explain it with words
>   I have to do it
>   The ship I came here on vanished
>   We automatic
>   Don't try to plan it
>   But chyeah, just when it comes, handle it
>   —SHABAZZ PALACES, "Are you?... Can you?... Were you? (Felt)"

I

We live in a time regime—or more accurately in a space where several regimes or ideologies of time are operative.[1] A kind of time war is happening all the time, one that literally occupies us and exhausts us and renders possible or impossible the various forms of life that we might consent to or refuse if given the choice. Music happens in this space, variably confirming the particular mandates of the dominant time regime—or proposing, preparing, enacting a breakthrough to "otherwise possibilities," as we have seen in the cases of Pandit Pran Nath and Catherine Christer Hennix. A breakthrough in a dominant time regime, enacted through music and sound, is a cosmopolitical event that brings with it an awareness of immersive vibratory space, inside and out and beyond conceptions of either. In that emergent vibratory space, the problem or question or immanence of the continuum (indexed here as "the One") looms. It is hard to even know where to begin—although in my mind I keep returning to a quote from the rapper Kendrick Lamar in his dialogue with the recorded ghost of Tupac Shakur, the final track on *To Pimp a Butterfly*, asserting that "in my opinion, only hope that we kinda have left is music and vibrations, lotta people don't understand how important it is."[2] That's pretty much how I feel too.

It's hard to overemphasize the importance of an idea of vibration in Afrodiasporic musical cultures and the many ways in which music emerging from the Black radical tradition works with ideas of time, continuity, and the continuum that are explicitly cosmopolitical. A musical event becomes a cosmopolitical event in Afrodiasporic cultural history because there is a reaching out to the power of music as a life-sustaining or opening communal force—and the denial and suppression and repression of that force by a dominant anti-Black culture. Cosmopolitical events are everywhere in the history of Black music—and invariably involve a struggle over the right to occupy and manifest musical space.

Consider the Nigerian musician Fela Kuti and The Shrine, also known as the Kalakuta Republic, the nightclub/communal space/health clinic/recording studio but also "independent republic" that hosted his Afrobeat band between 1971 and 1977 in the suburbs of Lagos, when the compound was burned to the ground by the Nigerian military.[3] Or the complex entanglement of reggae music in Jamaica with Rastafarian communities living in the mountains of Jamaica, descendants of the Maroon communities that refused slavery. Or the various histories connected by the word *Afrofuturism*, and the cosmopolitical reappropriation of various sonic technologies but also sciences in Sun Ra's "cosmic-myth equations," in Lee Perry's Black Ark studio, in the history of the sound system in Jamaica but also ported to New York by Kool Herc as the basis of the block parties that were hip-hop's crucible.[4] Or the Sai Ananta Ashram in the mountains outside of Los Angeles where Alice Coltrane resided and pursued a spiritual community built around devotional music.[5] Or the vast topic of the Black church in America and indeed across the Black diaspora, whether we are talking about Haitian Vodou, or Bahia's Candomblé, or the Black Pentecostal church in America, as a space of musical sociality and embodied spirituality that is at least partly autonomous from the world of recordings and performance. In all of these situations, and many others, a "topos of music" is articulated under the fierce pressure of adaptation to a marketplace, to white or bourgeois tastes, to commodification, to normativity in many versions, and to the profound dislocations of time and space initiated by the Atlantic slave trade and its aftermaths, while seeking and actually/temporarily manifesting "otherwise possibilities" in conditions of near-impossibility.[6]

In understanding "the topos of music" as concerned with the emergence of particular musics from actual historically and geographically marked spaces, I ask how the topos model can be understood in relation to the racialized and colonized spaces that constitute "space" across the African diaspora (and beyond). Music is a crucial form of what Henri Lefebvre called *the production of space*: production understood in its full Marxist sense as material conditions, practice, and ideology—but also understood cosmopolitically as a mutual engagement of humans and nonhumans.[7] Black and Indigenous scholars have pointed to the racialization of space in the Americas, one that is clearly interrelated to the concept of a time regime set out above.[8] But can we go beyond understanding music as something preexisting whose discursive meaning or social structure is determined by this racialized space, to considering the production of music itself as a product of sonic, vibrational engagement of racialized space?

In his 1972 novel, *Mumbo Jumbo*, Ishmael Reed described a cosmopolitical struggle between two kinds of forces, Jes Grew, a viral and vibrational force that brings embodied joy and chaos wherever it manifests, and Atonism, meaning the disembodied force of rationality, logic, or order (the contrast with Daniélou, who also considers "atonism" the enemy, is instructive: rather than cosmic harmonic order, Reed's vibratory principle is chaotic, embodied, improvisation, the clinamen rather than the straight line). Reed playfully traces Jes Grew back through various historical "outbreaks," including those associated with the ancient Egyptian deity Osiris, as well as the birth of jazz in 1890s New Orleans. "'It belonged to nobody,' Johnson said. 'Its words were unprintable but its tune irresistible.' Jes Grew, the Something or Other that led Charlie Parker to scale the Everests of the Chord. Riff fly skid dip soar and gave his Alto Godspeed. Jes Grew that touched John Coltrane's Tenor; that tinged the voice of Otis Redding."[9]

As a viral force ("There are no isolated cases in this thing. It knows no class no race no consciousness. It is self-propagating and you can never tell when it will hit"[10]), Jes Grew is somehow immanent in the fabric of reality itself, a power and force, in my own words, emergent from the continuum. As such, a force that needs to be suppressed or repressed, in the explicitly Freudian language that Reed uses, for the historical domination of European modes of being to occur. Indeed, Papa LaBas, Jes Grew's ally and devotee, the Hoodoo priest of Mumbo Jumbo Kathedral, attempted to contact Freud during his 1909 visit to

New York, to discuss the therapeutic powers of Jes Grew, but was shut out by assorted flunkies and uptight people—a missed opportunity since "Jes Grew was an influence that sought its text," without which "it would be mistaken for entertainment."[11] Jes Grew is the cosmopolitical force of Black music—maybe even of music as a global object in all its mystery and beauty. Reed asks us: Why is there a politics of vibration in the first place? Where does the racist refusal of or resistance to vibrational truth come from, if/when vibration is a crucial part of the deep structure of reality itself? Clearly, we inhabit a particular time regime that blocks the unfolding and flourishing of other forms of life—but why?

At the moment of decolonization in various African countries and Afrodiasporic sites in the 1950s and 1960s, a number of Black writers explored ideas of vibrational power and force, with links to traditional articulations of that force such as *ase* (Yorubaland/Nigeria) and *ntu* (South Africa). In the Nigerian novelist Amos Tutuola's 1954 text *My Life in the Bush of Ghosts*, the Bush, more or less contiguous with the Yoruba mythical reality transcribed by Tutuola's illustrious predecessor Fagunwa, is characterized as a space of vibration, and where vibratory force, in the form of light beams or sound exert an extraordinary power over those who find themselves there.[12] As for continuity, the South African ANC poet Keorapetse Kgositsile, father of Odd Future MC Earl Sweatshirt, explored ideas of sonic continuity and the nature of time from a pan-African/Afrodiasporic point of view in works from the 1960s on. In "For Bra Ntemi," he writes: "Isn't sound continuity/isn't sound memory/loving care caress or rage/sticking our shattered and scattered pieces together?"[13] In "For Art Blakey and the Jazz Messengers," he begins "For the sound we revere/we dub you art as continuum/as spirit as sound of depth/here to stay."[14] In an interview, he argues: "Once you stop thinking about time in terms of hours, minutes, and days, time is always immediate, in the present, right? . . . When what you do to make your life meaningful is upset by outside forces, your life takes on a certain immediacy, so that your present, past, and future are simultaneous; they are all NOW. You reclaim and assert your past in the present, and you fashion and embark upon your future now; in the present."[15]

The point would be that the moment of the NOW, rather than simply being a place on a chronological number line, is a moment that opens in the direction of continuity, a site on the continuum, which has a vibrational structure, and which music, jazz or otherwise, serves as both model for and vehicle for exploration of. This continuity is both the local continuity of a particular tradition or community and also that deeper structure of time, space, and being that in this book we are calling a topos, which emerges when a break is made with a dominant time regime. As such, affirmation of continuity is literally a vital political practice and part of a much broader project of decolonizing a dominant time regime in which order, hierarchy, and domination are maintained through specific ways of understanding or organizing time.[16]

Amiri Baraka's famous 1966 essay "The Changing Same (R&B and New Black Music)" concerns continuity. And, although (as with Kgositsile, whom Baraka knew) the continuity concerns the continuity of Black culture ("a central body of cultural experience"[17]), Baraka articulates this through a visceral and deeper sense of the problem of the continuum, of which he writes: "The impulse, the force that pushes you to sing . . . all up in there . . . is one thing . . . what it produces is another. It can be expressive of the entire force, or make it the occasion of some special pleading. Or it is all equal . . . we simply identify the part of the world in which we are most responsive"—for/since—"we are bodies responding differently, a (total) force, like against you.[18] Baraka is working through the challenge of thinking the radical particularity of specific acts and practices of Black musicking that, on the one hand, force a rupture with a dominant and white supremacist time regime and, on the other, seek to align with/against/alongside/out of a continuum, continuity, or vibratory super-sameness that is ontological, immanent to being on this planet—and that in the end concerns "the whole people" as they make joyous sound in their various local circumstances. Thus: "the changing same."

What happens when a philosophy and praxis of vibrational continuity encounters and is appropriated by a violent praxis of discontinuity and objectification? Therein lies some of the paradoxes of Afrodiasporic musical cultures and the Black radical tradition, as they emerge from the violence of the Atlantic slave trade and European colonialism in Africa. Toni Morrison's *Beloved* (1987) graphed the situation well.[19] What leads a mother to murder her own daughter, which is to say to introduce violent discontinuity into what would normatively be the most continuous of relationships (mother and daughter)? The violence and objectification of the slave trade and settler colonialism in the Americas. The extraordinary passages in the last third of the novel, where the individual ghost of the dead daughter, Beloved, is absorbed back into the mass of bodies transported or murdered in the Middle Passage. Continuity is sought there in the very place of discontinuity—and this is a recurrent figure in Black radical thought, from the figure of the hold, and its psychic and material persistence today in the lives of Afrodiasporic peoples, in the work of Afropessimist thinkers examining "fantasy in the hold," to Paul Gilroy's *The Black Atlantic*, which is simultaneously the space of rupture and separation and historical violence, and the traces and waves from which contemporary Afrodiasporic networks are emergent.

Baraka's vacillation between the cultural sense of a continuity of Black cultural practices and an ontological/atheological (Crawley) sense of vibrational continuity whose manifestation brings collective joy/pain is significant. Ideologies and practices of racial difference produce a cut in the continuum through which (among other things) Blackness is produced as a historical or cultural racialized form. Another name for this cut in the continuum is the sonic color line, which Jenny Stoever has recently explored. "The sonic color line describes the process of racializing sound—how and why certain bodies are expected to produce, desire, and live amongst particular sounds—and its product, the hierarchical division sounded between 'whiteness' and 'blackness.'"[20] In this sense, Baraka is clearly doubling down on this racialization of sound, and inverting the hierarchical differences between "Black" and "white" sounds. Yet the music, at the same time, exists as the vibratory dissolution of that color line back into continuity itself. Baraka acknowledges this when he writes/fantasizes about playing James Brown in a bank, whereby "an energy is released in the bank, a summoning of images that take the bank, and everybody in it, on a trip."[21] It's an image of contagion and contamination of kin to Jes Grew—but it raises the question of how one reconciles the essential/historical/necessarily contingent Blackness of this vibrational energy and force when it proves its existence by its ability to affect people in the bank . . . meaning presumably that this force is also able to affect non-Black people? And this then raises, more generally, the difficult questions of how musical continuity, which can be and is produced in the most fugitive of circumstances, relates to the violent discontinuity of the world. As Frantz Fanon observed in *Black Skins, White Masks*, the NOW, the moment of ontology has been foreclosed to Black people in that brutal constraints have historically been placed on their free initiation of choice sequences.

Baraka rightly dismisses any naive idea of sonic utopianism: "The New Music (any Black Music) is cooled off when it begins to reflect blank, any place 'universal' humbug. It is this fag or that kook, and not the fire and promise and need for evolution into a higher species."[22] The inversion of the sonic color line in certain Black Arts Movement texts speaks to the difficulty of parsing whiteness as false universality while asserting continuity as real universality. Also, the gap between sonic continuity and real continuity.

This problem brings to mind a recent voiceover by queer/trans sound artist and DJ Sprinkles on his *Midtown 120 Blues* record:

House isn't so much a sound as a situation
There must be a hundred records with voice-overs asking, "What is house?"

> The answer is always some greeting card bullshit about "life, love, happiness..."
> The House Nation likes to pretend clubs are an oasis from suffering, but suffering is in here with us...
> Let's keep sight of the things you're trying to momentarily escape from
> After all, it's that larger context that created the house movement and brought you here
> House is not universal
> House is hyper-specific: East Jersey, Lower East Side, West Village, Brooklyn—places that conjure specific beats and sounds....
>
> The contexts from which the Deep House sound emerged are forgotten: sexual and gender crises, transgendered sex work, black market hormones, drug and alcohol addiction, loneliness, racism, HIV, ACT-UP, Thompkins Sq. Park, police brutality, queer-bashing, underpayment, unemployment and censorship—all at 120 beats per minute.[23]

Thus, according to Sprinkles, house emerges out of the contestation of particular kinds of racialized, gendered, intersectionally structured spaces of inequality. The paradox of this admirable statement is that it is performed over a generically accurate, classic early 1990s house groove that reintroduces all the problematic universal vibrational elements that Sprinkles's discourse disavows. True, these elements are now firmly embedded in the fake universalism of the neoliberal global leisure market and easy hedonism. But the promise of house, if not universal, is of free bodies (free from discrimination based on race, gender, class, etc.) freely moving in relation to each other and in that freedom. And various house tracks do assert this as universal, most famously Chuck Roberts's vocal on Rhythm Controll's 1987 track "My House" (which Sprinkles samples on another track on *Midtown*):

> In the beginning, there was Jack, and Jack had a groove,
> And from this groove came the groove of all grooves,
> And while one day viciously throwing down on his box, Jack boldly declared,
> "Let there be HOUSE!"
> and house music was born.
> "I am, you see,
> I am the creator, and this is my house!
> And, in my house there is ONLY house music.

But, I am not so selfish because once you enter my house it then becomes OUR house and OUR house music!"
And, you see, no one man owns house because house music is a universal language, spoken and understood by all.[24]

And the paradox, here, is that the universal is being declared by someone whose people have been historically denied participation in such universals as human rights or status. But let's be clear about what the universal is that Roberts is invoking here: it's not Hegel's famous "night in which all cows are black," by which he scornfully dismissed Schelling's too easy proclamations of the unity of subject and object and of the Absolute.[25] The universal or the path into the universal has to be constructed and, as Sprinkles says, the site of construction is hyperspecific, based on Henriques's "ways of knowing." But. It is not just hyperspecific, because when constructed, what is discovered is that "universal language, spoken and understood by all" that *is* house music according to Roberts and others. It's a fragile universal that lasts, at least for us, as long as it can be constructed and/or a community knows how to construct it. This is a matter of practice, vibrational practice—and the relationship of the local or hyperspecific, to the global, or universal, within the framework that I set out in chapter 3 via Zalamea and others. In other words, the local space needs to be actively engaged, transformed, searched for contingent possibilities that, however obscured, are nonetheless immanent or emergent properties of the space.

The pathos of music then is its ability to do affectively, or perhaps micropolitically, what can't necessarily be done in reality as a whole and so far. As such, of course, music can appear to offer the sound of a postracial world when no such world exists, and an experience of solidarity, empathy, relationality, and collectivity when the world in which this experience occurs is still structured via separation and exclusion. What Paul Gilroy has called "postcolonial melancholia" I will here explore under the name *depression*.[26] As such, the examples I focus on in this chapter—the 1990s work of Houston-based DJ Screw and his crew, the Screwed Up Click, his slowed and throwed/chopped and screwed sound, and the more recent work of the Canadian Indigenous hip-hop crew A Tribe Called Red—contemplate and explore this awareness of music's power to invoke vibratory continuity in conditions of the harshest discontinuity and abjection in the colonial, racialized spaces of Houston and Toronto, and the difficulty of holding to that vital praxis in these conditions—with depression, in Screw's case, as a symptom of this. I reflect on my own attraction as a white guy to these musics—and ask where or if my own depression is entangled with theirs, and in what way my attraction and depression is itself indicative of a politics of vibration in which a "sonic color line" and the promise of its possible dissolution are both operative. This leads to a more general questioning of "lines"—whether related to gender and sexuality, or to law more generally, drawn on the ocean of sound and the possibility and praxis of erasing such lines, or amplifying them, considered as an emancipatory politics, considered as healing. The implications for our understanding of what time is, how different bodies and minds participate in different time regimes—and the possibility of decolonizing time—will be explored.

2

Houston-based DJ Screw's mix of the Port Arthur, Texas, rappers UGK's classic elegiac rap "One Day" appears on the 1997 mixtape, *Endonesia*; it is "Chapter 70" in the chronological listing of all of the hundreds of mixtapes that Screw made. It is listed as a "Lil' Randy personal tape" meaning that Screw (born Robert Earl Davis Jr.), would make personal mixes for people who visited his house on Greenstone in the Golfcrest neighborhood on the south side of Houston, based on lists of tracks they gave him. But these mixes, personal or not, would then often be duped and sold by Screw from his house using 100-minute Maxell chrome tapes known as "gray tapes" and later "clear tapes." For a number of years in the mid-1990s, he would sell them only between 8:00 and 10:00 p.m., except Sundays, and apparently there were lines of cars outside his house, which would then draw police attention since it looked like illegal activity was going on. In 1998 Screw opened a store, Screwed Up Records and Tapes, where he sold the tapes (and CDs). After his untimely death in 2000, the store continued to sell tapes, and it is still open today.

Screw is the originator of the "chopped and screwed" style of DJing and mixing associated with Houston hip-hop. "Screwed" means slowed down. "Chopped" refers to the looping repetition of phrases and bars of a track, that is, "chopping" between two copies of a record via rapid movements of the fader on a mixer. Although the practice of slowing down tracks is said to have originated with the Houston DJ Darryl Scott, who would slow tracks down at a party, or on at least one of his popular mixtapes, Screw applied this technique to nearly every track he played and every mixtape he made. The style was developed further, after Screw's death, by DJs like OG Ron C and Michael Watts, and also formed the basis for the briefly popular style called witch house, where the slowed technique was applied to a range of dance musics outside of the R&B and hip-hop (but also reggae) that Screw played. Subsequently, the style became a part of mainstream popular music: it was a key influence on the style of Drake, whose early hit "November 18th" is basically a tribute/version of the famous 37-minute freestyle, "The Streets Ain't Right," off of Screw's *Chapter 012: June 27th* mixtape; on Houston-born Solange's remarkable 2019 album *When I Get Home*, with its expansive improvisation on some of Screw's sonic motifs; and on Frank Ocean's 2016 hit "Nikes," with its "double consciousness" suturing of slowed-down beats and sped-up vocals.

The original of UGK's classic "One Day," from their 1995 album *Ridin' Dirty*, lasts for 5:24. The song speaks of the precarity of Black life in a series of stories of those who have died or been imprisoned, and what it means to live in the middle of this. "One Day" is built musically around a reworked sample from the Isley Brothers' "Ain't I Been Good to You," taking the opening lines "one day you're here/and the next day you're gone," addressed to an AWOL lover, and shifting the focus from love's fragility to life and death in the streets. Lyrically, the song took shape in events that began around December 4, 1995, when UGK's Pimp C and Screw were arrested for marijuana possession by undercover cops in the parking lot of a Houston Stop-n-Go. Screw and C were sentenced to forty-eight hours in the county jail and a small fine. Days after, Bo-Bo Luchiano, who performed with UGK, lost his five-year-old son in a Dallas house fire that also claimed the lives of three other children. The track also includes reference to two deceased friends of UGK's MC Bun B: Charles "Chuckie" Fregia, who drowned in a ditch at the age of nineteen after passing out at the wheel of his car; and Terraine Box, who "was killed during an argument over a $5 dice game" in Orange, Texas, in April 1995.[27] Listening to the song today, it's hard not to hear in it a premonition of Chad Butler (Pimp C)'s death on December 4, 2007; or Screw's on November 16, 2000; or many of the other MCs and participants in the Houston rap game. Or the broader concerns about the precarity of Black life that we now understand via the framing of Black Lives Matter.

"One Day" is a heavy song, with its own chronopolitics, evinced in the title/chorus ("One day you're here/and the next day you're gone . . .") and in much-celebrated lines such as "tomorrow ain't promised to me/the only thing promised to a player is the penitentiary." Time is (a) privilege, a luxury for Black bodies condemned to prison or other forms of abjection. Or premature death. "The game," whether rap or another kind of hustle, opens up a fractal expansion of the now—but still no time. This fractal expansion involves the construction of a vibrational space via music in which an "otherwise possibility" is perhaps to be found. As for those of us with the privilege of "spending time," we live in a rotten but comfortable prison of delusion of our own since, for us too, "one day you're here and the next day you're gone."

There are a number of recordings of Screw's remix of "One Day" but the one on *Endonesia* goes on for 14:39.[28] The already stately tempo of the original at 73 bpm is slowed down to a dirge-like 57 bpm. The voice at the beginning of the track is Screw's, elegiacally listing the recently departed and offering shoutouts to those present or on people's minds. You can hear the way that Screw's chopping technique punctuated and interpreted the lyrics in the originals, emphasizing certain lines that interested him, but also adding to the general warping of time and continuity that is so important in his music.

Reading accounts from those hearing Screw's style for the first time, the almost universal response seems to have been disbelief, the feeling that something had gone wrong with the tape. Screw's childhood friend and collaborator Shorty Mac remembered:

> He told me to listen to this tape and tell him what I thought. So I said the first thing that everybody else said, on my way back! I'm listenin' to the tape, and I kept takin' it out, putting it back in, and I called him, and I said, "Hey, man—I think you gave me a messed up tape," and he started laughin.' He say, "Naw, it's supposed to sound like that." I said, "Okay," and I just let it play. Then I say, "Okay, yeah! Okay!" All these different songs coming in, and him mixing—yeah! So I called him back after I got to Austin, and I said, "Yeah, that motherfucker jammin'!" He say, "Yeah, appreciate it." And that's when he told me right then. . . . I don't know, he just had something in his eye, he said "Man, we got us a way out."[29]

A way out, through slowing music, sound, vibration down. At first to those who listened the time appeared out of joint—but then people got used to it, perhaps recognizing something closer to their own sense of time in Screw's untimeliness.

Born Robert Earl Davis Jr. to Ida M. Deary Davis and Robert Earl Davis Sr. on July 20, 1971, Screw grew up, after some travels, with his mother in Smithville, a rural/farming village about a two-hour drive west of Houston, Texas. He began making mixtapes with a childhood friend Shorty Mac (Trey Adkins), wiring up his mother's turntable to a tape deck, and playing with the speed of his mom's records such as Johnny Taylor and B.B. King. According to Shorty Mac, he earned the name "Screw" because he would deface records that he didn't like with a screw, scratching his way through the grooves, to his mother's frustration. At some point after the age of ten, he moved to Houston to be with his father, who drove trucks for a living and lived in an apartment near the Libby Airfield on the south side of the city. There, as a teenager, he began to make mixtapes based on song lists of requests made by his friends.[30]

Founded in 1836, during the brief moment of the Republic of Texas, Houston has grown to be the fourth-largest city in the United States.[31] People of African descent have lived in the Houston area since the 1820s, when a plantation economy emerged in south Texas.[32] After the abolition of slavery, significant numbers of African Americans moved to Houston, forming communities in a number of Houston's wards, which were shaped by the Jim Crow–era policies of racial segregation and by waves of migration from other parts of the United States. These communities expanded and were displaced by a series of political, economic, and environmental events such as the urban renewal programs that cut highways through historically Black neighborhoods from the 1950s to the 1970s. This process continues through to the present day: for example, Houston has the largest Nigerian population in the United States. It is a town with an illustrious history of Black music.[33] This history spans the Phillis Wheatley High School and Jack Yates High School marching bands that produced jazz musicians such as Illinois Jacquet; the blues sound of Lightnin' Sam Hopkins and the zydeco sound of Clifton Chenier, both residents of Houston who played together on occasion starting in the 1950s; the soul and R&B sound of the Duke and Peacock record labels; and the birth of hip-hop in Houston, usually associated with the pioneering group Geto Boys, or with the freestyle events hosted at the Rhinestone Wrangler club in the mid-1980s. As Tyina Steptoe argues in her book *Houston Bound: Culture and Color in a Jim Crow City*, all of this history occurred in a space pressurized and transformed by ideologies of race—and in which Black music offered the possibility of a countertransformation of space. So if we think about the young Screw moving to Houston—this is all part of what he entered.

The origins of "screwing" as the act of slowing down a track or a mix involve several elements. In one story, the Houston DJ Michael Price Jr. (1971–93) and friends were listening to a boombox at a regular speed, when the batteries ran out, so that the speed of the tape and the track ran down too. Given the favorable response of those assembled, Price then attempted to mechanically replicate this slowed-down sound by inserting a screw into the tape deck in such a way that it put pressure on the machine's motor and slowed it down. Price's friend and mentor DJ Darryl Scott, who opened a record store in Houston in 1984 and whose mixtapes were popular around town, also played 12-inch 45s at 33 rpm at parties and made at least two mixtapes, *8 on the Double* and *33 1/2*, the former featuring tracks that used chopping or doubling of beats, the latter featuring slowed-down tracks.

DJ Screw, who knew both Price and Scott, took these events and experiments and turned them into a sound. Screw's actual method of making his slowed-down mixtapes was more complicated than inserting a screw into a tape deck, though. He would slow down a track on his turntables using the pitch control and record his mixes onto a Tascam 4-track cassette deck. He would then slow down the speed of the recording on the tape deck, which also had pitch control, for the final mix. Everything was done without digital technologies. Within the domain of the technologies with which he developed his sound, he'd discovered the technical capability to vary speed, and to slow down (or speed up) musical time. What he extrapolated from this was something more than technical though: a different way of relating "to" time.

Screw made relatively few actual commercial recordings for record labels.[34] Apparently, he was indifferent to mainstream success and was able to make a living making and selling his mixtapes from his apartment, then in the house on Goldstone that came to be known as "Screw house," and later at his store. Screw did DJ in clubs, but it was in that house on Goldstone, especially when the mixtapes started to include local MCs/friends who would hang out and freestyle over Screw's beats, that the magic really happened—magic that was put down on tape. Screw's fame spread through the dissemination of these mixtapes, mostly as a part of Houston and Texas's car cultures, where blasting a Screw tape in your slab ("slow loud and banging"), that is, your fully customized automobile, was the thing to do. In his book *Acoustic Territories*, Brandon Labelle explores car sound systems as a mode of display—sonic, visual, and otherwise—and as a vibrational space in which life and sound can flourish, projecting out into and in part protected from the often hostile external environment.[35]

There's a long history of mixtapes and car sound systems in hip-hop that goes back at least to Afrika Bambaataa's famous "death mix" tape that taxi drivers in the Bronx rocked in the mid-1970s. In the vast sprawling metropolis of Houston, where public transit was almost nonexistent, as many have observed, Screw's music was well adapted to local car cultures. If, as Hennix argued, the measure of a society's ethics is connected to the length of a sound that is allowed, Black DIY cassette culture in the 1980s and 1990s itself expanded the duration of the sound (100-minute tapes!) and what could be listened to (mixes of tracks that were distributed outside of intellectual property law, and often tracks that were not being played on the radio): and this is true of marginal Black New Age artists such as Laraaji or Alice Coltrane as much as of hip-hop DJs.[36] Indeed, cassette culture has often been explicitly cosmopolitical, as we learn from the two most important studies of cassette cultures, Charles Hirschkind's study of cassette sermons made by Islamic preachers in Cairo, Egypt, in the 1990s, and Peter Manuel's study of cassettes of devotional ghazal songs in India in the same period.[37] Given a new and relatively accessible technology of production and distribution of sound, new sonic forms and practices will flourish—as will, as Hirschkind notes, new "counterpublics," new communities of producers and listeners who are able to express new or hitherto undeveloped forms of life. Screw was not beholden to the technical and temporal limits of vinyl, or to the demands of a record label, or to the costs and delays of vinyl record pressing plants, and he could make tapes for friends, duplicate them, or not—and thus something like the 35-minute collective freestyle track made by assorted Screwed Up Click MCs celebrating Demo Sherman's birthday could be made on June 27, 1997—a recording that was disseminated on tape and CD, booming from car stereos around the city of Houston and points beyond, becoming his most-loved recording.

It's worth emphasizing that Screw apparently perceived the ontological dimensions of what he was doing. In a 1997 interview, he observed that "people been listening to my shit so long they're all Screwed Up. When they listen to the radio at regular speed it sounds like the Chipmunks to them. Muthafuckas live and die for my shit."[38] Elsewhere in the interview, he claimed that "I wanna Screw the whole world."[39] He repeatedly asserted that the point of what he was doing was to slow time down—and various parties have contended that Screw's music functioned as a peacemaker in the Houston gang wars of the 1990s.[40] The answers vary as to why. Kelefa Sanneh speculates that "perhaps Screw's innovation fit the city's slow, rambling speech patterns. Perhaps it even matched the region's thick, muggy climate. Or perhaps Screw tapes were simply the perfect entertainment for a highway-happy city where you might spend more time driving to the club than being there."[41] The "perhaps" is telling: as if the act of slowing a record down might be too simple or basic to even have a meaning. As person after person attests, there is something uncanny about what Screw does. One person remarks that he's tried slowing down tracks and it doesn't sound the way Screw made it sound. If I listen to much of the post-Screw slowed music, I feel the same way. In particular, digitally slowed tracks lack the colossal lurching swing that Screw was able to produce on turntables and tape decks; you can feel how active his hands and mind are in modulating the feeling of the sound. A 2017 *Guardian* article reviewing the recent resurgence of chopping and screwing in the popular music, as well as on soundtracks such as *Moonlight*, noted that "it makes moments feel eternal."[42]

The practice of DJing is about constructing a continuity out of discontinuities—even my friend DJ/Rupture, whose name indicates his opposition to crass segues, overly smooth fake sonic homogeneity, and cheap bpm matching bliss, still does this. Playing with rupture and whatever the opposite of rupture is, is essential to this—these are the "shattered soundscapes" that Michael Veal observed in Jamaican dub reggae, where what is subtracted is just as important as what is there.[43] But what is there, "between the notes," as Pandit Pran Nath put it? Listen. Or move to it. Feel it. Note how much easier it is to celebrate and become aware of the ruptures than whatever the opposite is—the opposite being not the crass universality that Baraka and DJ Sprinkles denounced at the beginning of this chapter, but . . . what? We have a very weak language for it. Or do we? Philosophically yes. In DJ culture we speak of flow (the psychology of optimal experience). In Buddhism consciousness is frequently described in terms of "the continuity of discontinuities." Often what's emphasized is the fact that this continuity has been constructed to appear as such, whereas in fact it is just a heap of fragments—a stitched-together discontinuity. Considered mathematically, though, as we have set out in previous chapters of this book, the continuum can be affirmed in a positive sense as that out of which discontinuous points are emergent. This is true in DJing culture, too, where continuity exists not just as the illusion by which a series of tracks are segued together via similar beats per minute or other strategies . . . but because a continuum deeper than that of beats per minute is evoked and leaned into in the sound system session: the real continuum, if you will, of the now in which sound, vibration, and musical experience happen. This is Henriques's basic point in *Sonic Bodies* when he describes the know-how involved in making a successful sound system session. We speak of a politics of vibration in relation to the care with which this leaning-in happens and what the DJ's skills point to: good vibrations, "everybody loves the sunshine," "one nation under a groove"—collective consensual entanglement in vibrational space.

One of the most obvious but still easily overlooked or overheard effects of Screw's slowing things down is the way that it produces a strong and immediate sense of double consciousness—you hear the track you know and retain in memory the sense of the original tempo, while experiencing the new sloweddown tempo. The idea of double consciousness has had a powerful explanatory force in Black studies and thought since W. E. B. Du Bois used the phrase as a figure for the split or ruptured consciousness produced by the legacy of the Middle Passage and slavery in African Americans, who experience life in the New World as a double-displacement.[44] In Gilroy's formulation of "double consciousness," music and the Black Atlantic stand for the possibility of an integrated rhizomatic state of continuity between past and present. With DJ Screw, the sonic evocation of double consciousness—most notable in those places where Screw chops between two copies of a track, one turntable lagging a beat or line behind the other—carries with it all the valences of Du Bois's and Gilroy's thinking, as well as that double consciousness that is produced by certain drugs, themselves redoubled in the state of removal or alienation or ekstasis that comes from slowing down a track. But, going deeper, such a double consciousness could also relate to an experience of vibratory ekstasis that is already immanent to music and song as they are emergent from the continuum, submerged by a dominant time regime until shaken free via the uncanny doubling of a track.

3

Lutz Koepnick argues in his 2014 book, *On Slowness*, that the prevalent understanding of modernity as associated with speed and acceleration needs to be revised in the light of an underrecognized cultural practice of slowness that forms part of the contemporary era. In arguing the case for taking slowness seriously, Koepnick brackets contemporary discourses of slowness, such as those of the slow food movement, that see in a reaffirmed slowness, a possible exit from the traumas of modernity into a preindustrial pastoral world. He argues that slowness should not be thought of as mere opposition to modernity, but as an intervention into dominant notions of time and space that opens us up to the possibility of multiple temporalities: "The aim of these projects, in other words, is neither to provide redemptive meanings nor cling to nostalgic images of the past. Rather, they embrace slowness as a medium to ponder the meaning of temporality and of being present today in general, of living under conditions of accelerated temporal passage, mediation, and spatial shrinkage."[45]

Thus, slowness and the technologies and practice that allow for its elaboration create new cultural and political possibilities: quoting the film theorist Rudolf Arnheim for example, Koepnick argues that through practices of slowness, "effects would be attainable which the spectator would not take for slowed-down versions of actually faster movements but accept as 'originals' in their own right."[46] Koepnick thus echoes Walter Benjamin's famous claim that practices of mechanical reproduction (such as chopping and screwing) may damage or evacuate aura, but they allow the masses to examine reality at a much more intimate and detailed scale—through the photograph for sure but also through the Screwed cassette tape.

Koepnick argues for a critical practice of slowness: "Modernist slowness instead defined a peculiar mode of engaging with the various temporalities and trajectories that energized the spaces of modern life, and, in so doing, it emphasized the coeval, imbricated, and indeterminate relationship of the temporal and spatial. Slowness is what allowed modernists to register, represent and reflect on how modern culture not only accelerated the rhythms of pre-industrial life but in this way also reconfigured material relationships and immaterial interactions across different geographies."[47]

In other words, slowness offers a critical stance against a prevailing politics of speed, such as the one that Paul Virilio has described in such detail. And implicit in this is the subjectivity of those whom speed and its various apparatuses of capture (the military and police, the global financial markets) has literally passed by: those who experience "slowness" as suspended access, as containment outside of neoliberal biopolitics, as "the wretched of the screen" condemned to beat-up old PCs in internet cafes on the outskirts of megacities.

Slowness, then, is untimely, "unheimlich" in Freud's phrase, an uncanny rediscovery of "what a body can do" that perhaps finds no place today other than that of sonic revelation: "Slowness here is the medium by which the present prepares itself for its discontinuous reinscription in some unknown future. It is the medium by which an accelerated present removes itself from its own closure, its vortex of vectorial movement, and exposes itself to the open vagaries of time, a heterogeneous temporality in which the future's task is to reclaim the promises and transformative energies of past generations."[48]

In Koepnick's claims, we might find the beginnings of a critique of Afrofuturist discourses of Afrodiasporic temporalities, such as those found in Kodwo Eshun's jungle- and speed-inspired text, *More Brilliant Than the Sun*.[49] The accelerated temporalities of jungle and to some degree techno are arguably an anomaly within the history of Afrodiasporic dance musics. I argue, however, that Screw's slowness is less concerned with the kind of aleatory or heterogeneous qualities of futures that Koepnick sees in modernist slowness. Echoing some of Alexander Weheliye's comments, Screw's music could be understood as a refusal of accelerationist narratives of futurity and the posthumanism that often accompanies them, one that opens up a different kind of futurity, predicated on the ahuman and the amodern, understood as undervalued potentialities.[50] To slow down was to become aware of such potentialities: both Screw and other members of his Screwed Up Click observed that slowing down hip-hop MCs and repeating particular lines allowed listeners to really hear what was being said for the first time. In an interview in *Rap Pages* in 1995, Screw explained: "The Screw sound is when I mix tapes with songs that people can relax to. Slower tempos, to feel the music and so you can hear what the rapper is saying. When I am mixing, I might run across something a rapper's saying which is important. I may run it back two or three times to let you hear what he is saying—so you can wake up and listen because they are telling you something. I make my tapes so everyone can feel them."[51]

There is a critical aspect to what DJ Screw did, especially in the way in which he would repeat and edit particular lyrical flows that spoke to the situation of his audience: I am thinking in particular of his epic 14:35 version of Spice 1's "Welcome to the Ghetto," with its brutally astute rundown of what it means to be poor and Black in America.[52] To slow down could mean a lot of things: it could mean taking a break from the heated cycles of action and reaction that characterize "beefs" on the streets of southside Houston; it could allow for the kind of endurance needed to wait for a friend "on lock" to be released again from jail, those absent friends that Screw shouts out to repeatedly on various tapes; it could allow for mourning to take place, for surrender to grief at the untimely death of friends which is such a disturbingly inexorable fact of Black life in the Americas.

There are interesting precedents for what Screw was doing in the history of African American music. For example, a young Charlie Parker retired to a cabin in the Ozarks in the summer of 1937 to study recordings of Lester Young on his portable phonograph: "The records were Charlie's most important subject for study. His portable phonograph had a set screw that could be tightened to lower the speed of the turntable. This adjustment made it easier for him to analyze the solos and study the nuances of tone that made Lester sound as if he were singing, shouting, and talking through the saxophone. Charlie learned each solo by heart, replaying the powdery grooves, listening for the notes through the increasing hiss of surface noise. Charlie broke down Lester's method. The bag of tricks."[53]

So "screwing" records has a history that goes back at least to Parker. Apparently, Bela Bartok was doing something similar at the same moment, listening to the recordings he'd made of Hungarian folk music. Bernard Stiegler argues that this was part of a new relationship to music and sound—a new way of listening, mediated by modern technologies, a possibility of hearing something that otherwise happened too fast—and then integrating it into a new sound.[54] In his famous essay on mechanical reproduction, Walter Benjamin argued that, through the technologies of the camera and cinema, the masses of the early twentieth century were able to see reality up close, and in the case of cinema, slowed down, revealing an "optical unconscious" otherwise beyond the reach of perception and consciousness.[55] For Benjamin, this opened up a new political field along with new modes of propaganda and emancipatory possibility. By slowing down recordings via tapes or a turntable, Black musicians were likewise able to explore a "sonic unconscious"—slowing down and repeatedly listening to Lester Young's recordings allowed Charlie Parker to find the breath or fingering techniques that produced a particular, hitherto impossible sound—and for Screw too, slowing things down offered the possibility of hearing what an MC was really saying, perhaps hearing them breathe too. And what might be heard in that sonic unconscious of Screw's beloved Tupac tracks, or, for that matter, Parker's Lester Young 78s?—the possibility of new life, of Black life?

But the politics of Screw's sound involves more than critique or analysis; a great Screw track has a feeling for a fundamental vibratory intensity of being of the kind that Ishmael Reed describes in *Mumbo Jumbo* through the entity known as Jes Grew: an "anti-plague" or "psychic epidemic" that "knows no class no race no consciousness. It is self-propagating and you can never tell when it will hit . . . Jes Grew is electric as life and is characterized by ebullience and ecstasy."[56]

How do we understand Screw in relation to the history of slow and fast musics? Clearly, one could relate Screw's mixes of UGK's "One Day" to the genre of the dirge: a slow, solemn lament for the departed, in which the slowing of tempo conveys a removal from the speed of everyday life, and exposure to the non of death in itself as the end or horizon of lived time. New Orleans marching band music would be an example. But this clearly doesn't cover the range of Screw's interest, although there's no lack of songs about death and listings of those who have died in Screw's music. There is clearly a history of slowness in Afrodiasporic musical traditions. The most obvious example would be the shift from ska to rocksteady and reggae in Jamaican music of the late 1960s and early 1970s—which is often connected to both the use of marijuana and the increasingly explicit politics and sexuality of the music during this period—a slowing of speed connoting the rhythms of sex and sensuality but also the seriousness of political militancy and the altered temporalities of the Rastafari culture, the nyabinghi drums and the history of marronage, as exodus from colonial structures. Another example would be the shift from the frenzied speed of bebop to the Miles Davis sounds of *Kind of Blue* and later. The latter are also connected to the use of heroin by Davis and his band, and the sense of altered temporality that comes with that drug (see section 4). Another example would be the blues sound of Houston-based musicians such as Lightnin' Sam Hopkins, often indexed in an uncritical way to ideas of the rural South but still worthy of exploration, especially given that some of Screw's earliest turntable experiments were made with his mother's blues records.[57] And thinking about that War track "City Country City" that I discussed in chapter 3, where the movement from country to city and back again is sonically presented via shifts between slow and melodic, lyrical passages versus faster, rhythmically dense, jazzy angular passages makes me wonder whether, for Screw, slowing things down evoked Smithville and his childhood with his mom—a trace of the maternal watching over the brotherhood of the Click.[58] Looking beyond the Afrodiasporic tradition, there are many powerful kinds of slow music, often made in places that are hot: for example, the remarkable rudra vina sound of the great Dhrupad performer Zia Moinuddin Dagar with its deep vibrational bass notes and glissandos, and the Javanese gamelan sound of the royal court orchestras of Yogyakarta and Solo, underpinned by bass notes coming from large hand-struck gongs. All of these diverse sounds are structured, albeit via radically different methodologies, by the way in which deep, vibrating bass sounds saturate space and, through their lower frequencies, are experienced as slowing-down tempo and, with it, that most rapidly moving of things, the mind.

There's obviously a difference, though, between playing music slowly and playing recordings of music slowly, in that Screw's music indexes the "correct" tempos that the tracks he plays are normally played at. He's playing with the materiality of the recordings made at the correct tempo, and, in that sense, he's part of the world that opened up with Pierre Schaeffer's musique concrète and the tape manipulations of the minimalists in the 1960s. Bernard Stiegler argues that technics (technological systems or structures) generate our sense of time. I have already discussed the challenges involved in thinking about music as a form of technics—that, on the one hand, musical instruments and musical techniques such as the use of pitch or rhythm structures are clearly technical, but music, emerging from the unconscious, from nature, from the vibrational mathematico-physical-spiritual structuring of the world would also seem to be something other than technical—perhaps something "cosmotechnical" in the sense given by Yuk Hui when he describes an alternative history of technology in China, where technics emerges as alignment with numinous or ontologically foundational forces. In his work, Stiegler pays considerable attention to what he calls the industrialization of memory in the modern world—the photograph, the cinematic film, the phonographic record, the digital file also allow for the recording of the real on an industrial scale. Where Pandit Pran Nath clearly thought recording was a bad idea that would lead one astray from music's cosmopolitical power of revelation of true self and world, DJ Screw inhabited this world of industrialized memory via vinyl records and cassette tapes. But while those technologies presupposed a normative and no doubt racialized organization of time and speed, Screw's music opened up something different—he made discoveries about time itself. By slowing the tracks down, Screw accentuates the bass. Everything pitches lower. Voices become deeper. The resonance of a snare drum expands. The spreading out of the sound moves it in the direction of continuity or the continuum: it is as though you can hear not only the lyrics more clearly but the sound itself, and specifically the way the sound spreads, occupies, and manifests time itself. It is as though you can hear and feel flow itself, but it is more than that too, since the loops and repetitions and rhythms go beyond that Aristotelian model of time as flow, in the direction of eternal recurrence, and finally to that same NOW that I have explored in previous chapters.

4

When I first started working on this book, around 2011, I was interested in the work of the Los Angeles–based crew Odd Future, aka Odd Future Wolf Gang Kill Them All. They were in the process of blowing up: Tyler, the Creator, Earl Sweatshirt, Syd the Kid, Frank Ocean. An illustrious crew. I wrote a long piece about them titled "Abject Future," in which I explored the way in which tropes of abjection appeared in their work and the relation of abjection to the politics of vibration and a vibrational ontology. It felt to me that songs/music videos like Earl Sweatshirt's "Earl" and Tyler's "Yonkers" ritualized abjection through performative grossness, homophobic ambivalence, and spectacular violence as a way of both protecting and resisting the vibrational core of their work. Using Michael Taussig's work on shamanism, I tried to think through this ritual grossness as a form of healing, a mediation of the same space of death that he located in the colonial space of the Colombian Amazon, the violence of the rubber barons against Indigenous people, against the forest and the land, and against the enslaved and others transported to the Amazon from Africa to work in the rubber trade.[59] Taussig called this violent, brutal space "the space of death," a place where souls are captured and destroyed, tortured, terrorized. Yet, it was/is also the space in which a shaman does their work, and where the descendants of this terror, and of "terror as usual" in colonial space, go for healing. This healing, of course, involved psychotropic substances but also strong vibrational elements, in the chanting and humming of the shaman, the swishing of fans, the sound of the jungle at night. My thought was that the musicians and the thinkers of the Black radical tradition were/are also working in this space of death, and that the sounds and texts and visuals (this applies to a filmmaker such as Arthur Jafa as much as Frank Ocean) also served a purpose that was similar to healing. And that Kristeva's theories of abjection provided another way of thinking about what that strange space was/is. Thus, one possibility or element of the topos of music is that the sonic rendering of space opens up the space of death as a place where healing can happen.

The space of death as a place of terror and healing. It's there in DJ Screw's work. There in the work of Earl Sweatshirt. There in Solange's recent tribute to Houston hip-hop, *When I Get Home*. But what is it really? The space of death is the space in which life and death oscillate—human space then, among other things, but human space in awareness of its own precarity, fragility, discontinuous extrusion. The Tibetan Buddhist teacher Chögyam Trungpa, writing of the mandala principle as the principle of "orderly chaos" by which we come to experience a sense of space and something (including "us") "in" "it," speaks of a razor's edge that "we" are "on": "That total energy—totally creative, totally destructive—is what one might call nowness. Nowness is the sense that we are attuned to what is happening. The past is fiction and the future is a dream, and we are just living on the edge of a razor blade. It is extraordinarily sharp, extraordinarily tentative and quivering. We try to establish ground but the ground is not solid enough, because it is too sharp. We are quivering between that and this."[60]

Music happens on this razor's edge—it is in fact the same razor's edge as Brouwer's moment of the "twoity," as understood by Hennix, this nowness in which the mathematician/musician generates her choice sequences, those sonic choice sequences that allow us to inhabit the razor's edge with dignity, joy even. Sometimes.

Trungpa goes on to connect this razor's edge to the first noble truth of Buddhism: that of the pervasiveness of suffering.[61] He also uses the words *depression* and *excitement* to indicate the kinds of gestalt that appear in this exposure to the razor's edge. If this space of death is pervasive for mortal beings, its drama is amplified by the violence of coloniality, whether in the Tibet of the 1950s that Trungpa escaped from; the Colombian Amazon circa 1900 and 1975 that Taussig writes about; the warped postslavery, sublimated settler colonial America of the 1970s that Trungpa escaped to; or the post–oil boom, racialized spaces of Houston in the 1990s in which Screw made his mixes. Orderly chaos. Living on the razor's edge. The unbearability of that and the transition to samsaric (illusory) form—or various kinds of painkillers.

One of the key explanations of the power of Screw's slowed-down sounds relates to the psychoactive substances that were part of the scene that Screw was in, and which ultimately killed him. Michael Hall writes: "When I had asked the rappers Mike D, Hawk, Lil-O, 3-2, and Clay-Doe how important syrup and weed are to Screw music, there had been a pause. 'You want the truth?' asked Mike D. 'Yes,' I replied, knowing what was coming. 'It's everything,' he answered, and the room erupted in laughter. 'With syrup it sounds so right,' said one of the others. 'You right on time,' said Mike D, to more laughter."[62]

"Right on time": this does not just mean punctuality or promptness; it refers to a state of immanence, of "being there," "fully there" in the sense that to be "fully" there is to experience the Now in its Parmenidean completeness. Hall then notes: "Screw was of two minds on the subject. In the liner notes of *3 'N the Mornin'*, he wrote instructions for listening: 'Get with your click and go to that other level by sippin' syrup, gin, etc., smoke chronic indo, cess, bud, or whatever gets you to that other level.' But in that late October interview he said, 'People think just to listen to my tapes you gotta be high or dranked out.... That ain't true. There's kids getting my tapes, moms and dads getting my tapes, don't smoke or drink or nothing.'"[63]

Syrup, purple drank, lean, sizzurp, the preferred intoxicant of the Screwed Up Click is a cocktail of codeine cough syrup (i.e., an opiate) with promethazine, which potentiates the codeine, mixed into a soft drink such as Grape Fanta or Sprite, and usually served up in a big styrofoam cup with ice. Syrup's association with slowed beats recalls the slowing down of time that is a pervasive element in literary descriptions of opiate use. Ann Marlowe named her 2002 heroin memoir *How to Stop Time: Heroin from A to Z*. Jean Cocteau has a lovely anecdote in his *Opium: Journal of a Disintoxication* in which he says that "Everything one does in life, even love, occurs in an express train racing toward death. To smoke opium is to get out of the train while it is still moving. It is to concern oneself with something other than life or death."[64] Cocteau is all too aware of the danger that comes with such a form of slowness—as well as the highly ambiguous relationship to technology and the technical that it manifests. A space of death emerges at the ecstatic horizon of the slowing down of time—a pharmacological space containing the potential both for death from overdose and for healing as the removal of pain.

The temporality of marijuana is slightly different, facilitating a more intense or expanded sense of lived time that could become "slow" as in reggae or drone music, but could equally become fast as in jungle. Asked about why he slowed his music down, Screw noted that "when you smoke weed, you really don't be doing a whole lot of ripping and running. I started messing with the pitch adjusters on the turntables and slowed it all the way down. I thought the music sounded better like that. It stuck with me, because when you smoking weed listening to music, you can't bob your head to nothing fast."[65] La Monte Young claimed that "tuning is a function of time" after extolling the musical virtues of getting high. It is in this sense that we might speak of slowness as ontological, or as a practice that opens up a sense that something ontological is at stake. The vibratory quality of being, emerging at the limits of the senses, of intelligible words and audible pitches, as something felt in the body and/or mind. Michael

Hall articulates this quality succinctly: "Listening to Screw music is like being in a fever dream. At first it sounds like something is wrong—like the tape will be spitting out of the deck at any second or maybe the batteries are so low the machine is about to die. Everything seems to be dying—voice, beat, scratches, melodies. It's like a retreat into a whole new world."[66]

Drugs as sociotechnical artifacts are always actors in a cosmopolitical dispute—first, because they are often illegal and, as such, what they reveal is subject to cosmopolitical prohibition and control in a blunt and brutal, not to mention racialized, way. They are also cosmopolitical because, as effective vectors of cosmopolitical gnosis and psychotropism, they are able to force a change of mind, consciousness, and a "retreat into a whole new world." This effectiveness is, of course, double-edged since it implies the difficulty of entering that other world without the drug—such that one might come to rely on the substance, become addicted to it. In that sense, purple drank's cosmopolitical promise of a new world (a "city of syrup" to quote a Big Moe title) is sutured to some of the harshest structural aspects of the current one.

Screw's music could be heard as an example of what we might call postcolonial slowness, a cousin to Paul Gilroy's postcolonial melancholia perhaps. Gilroy defined *postcolonial melancholia* as a description of the mental state of the imperial or colonizing subject at the point of the unraveling of the modern national empire.[67] It is also the mental state of a postcolonial subject dealing with the dystopian consequences of empire, where the promise of liberation or freedom has mutated into new forms of unfreedom and bondage. In terms of Screw's music, there was a shift in the temporality of suffering in places like Houston's southside in the 1980s, a time when the oil boom in Houston was coming to an end and jobs, including jobs for Black people, were disappearing; when Reaganomics was leading to declines in social spending in a "privatized" city where public programs of support for the poor had never been that well developed; and where the end of formal racial segregation in the 1960s did not result in the end of racism or the marginalization of Black people.[68] It was also the time of the endocolonization of poor, mostly Black neighborhoods by the sale of crack cocaine and the war on drugs. The shift in temporality would include the speed at which money could suddenly be made selling drugs (UGK's "High Life"); the speed of gang violence (the remarkable descriptions of this in *Houston Rap Tapes*, where a culture of brute physical force and fistfights results in situations of uncertain victory, where the winner of a fistfight lingers to savor the existential glory of his dominance, not understanding fully that he could suddenly be shot at any moment in a revenge killing); the speed of police busts; the slowness of detention, trial, and imprisonment; the lightning speed of a death that always comes as a surprise even when you know its inevitability. Poverty, racism, colonization are loops, the prisons of the dominant time regime. By eroticizing their speed and playing with them, are they made bearable? By slowing them down, can one view these loops critically? One enters the space of death—but Houston is different from the Putumayo, just as purple drank is different from ayahuasca. The difference may be significant, as African American activists working on the intractable problem of opiate addiction know, some becoming advocates for the West African hallucinogen ibogaine—which is said to be capable of breaking addiction to opiates through a more complete and intense immersion in the space of death.[69] Music takes on an extraordinary value in this situation—and, in fact, any situation since all human situations seem to involve a time war. And music is a path that leads us temporarily out of the domination of a particular time regime. Sizzurp is activated by the sound. For some, the sound is enough.

Following Kendrick Lamar's penetrating analysis of the relation between depression and the gangsta ethos on his 2015 record *To Pimp a Butterfly*, should we see Screw's slowed tracks as a music of depression, of submerged vitality, the kind of weirdly numb pleasures of having sex through the fog of depression as in his 1995 mixtape *Chapter 16: Late Night Fuckin' Yo Bitch* (a collection of slowed-down slow jams), the high of it still something to be sought out, despite everything? The key lines come from the poem that Lamar recites in between nearly every song on the record—the repetition of it serving as a kind of working through of trauma, in which more consciousness is brought to the drama and the depression with every iteration of the lines:

> I remember you was conflicted
> Misusing your influence
> Sometimes I did the same
> Abusing my power, full of resentment
> Resentment that turned into a deep depression
> Found myself screaming in the hotel room
> I didn't wanna self destruct
> The evils of Lucy was all around me
> So I went running for answers
> Until I came home
> But that didn't stop survivor's guilt . . .[70]

This working through then leads into the possibility of new collective projects of resistance and liberation—which can only become collective when the historically and structurally damaged and/or imperfect nature of those acting together is recognized as Lamar sings in "Mortal Man": "As I lead this army make room for mistakes and depression."[71]

But in order to work it through, depression has to be acknowledged as such. This, for me, is what is so moving about Earl Sweatshirt's trajectory—especially in relation to the heroic, revolutionary virility of his dad, Keorapetse Kgositsile's work. Sweatshirt begins in adolescent defiance, with a kind of celebratory grossness on early tracks like "Earl"; he then goes through a brutal period of depression, documented on *I Don't Like Shit, I Don't Go Outside* (2015), and the extraordinary track collage "Solace" (also 2015), where both his voice and the beats seem to stumble toward an unbearable and absolute stasis (for which hip-hop, vibrations, beats constitute solace), and whose politics he is well aware of. And then, on *Some Rap Songs* (2018), he emerges again, somehow having found a way of working with this impossible situation: "Fingers on my soul, this is 23 / Blood in the water, I was walkin' in my sleep / Blood on my father, I forgot another dream / I was playin' with the magic, hide blessings in my sleeve."[72]

I am not arguing that Screw's music is only concerned with depression. As a friend of mine said, musing on this topic—"It's party music!" Repeatedly in *Houston Rap Tapes*, people associated with Screw refer to the music as "magic." Slowed down, the West Coast gangsta rap that Screw loved to play loses some of its violent edge. No, it doesn't lose it, but the violence is transformed into vibrational force. In an essay from 2003, Fred Moten explores what he calls "Black Mo'nin.'"[73] Responding to the work of Nathaniel Mackey, he situates the wordless moan of singers like Al Green as existing somewhere in between Freud's mourning and melancholia. Mackey, reflecting on Green's voice, describes it initially as "alchemizing a legacy of lynchings," but then, in a moment where he, a Black man in America, finds himself being beaten by a cop, he is forced to recognize that this alchemy has never (yet) been commensurate with the historical conditions that produced it. In other words, while the music aspires to make this alchemization happen, sonically transforming the trauma of the history of lynchings and the broader violence done to African Americans, the persistence of institutional and structural racial violence in America forecloses the possibility of such alchemization actually happening. Mo'nin' is mourning trapped in the loop of melancholia and the structural conditions that produce it. Contrary to Screw's claim that slowing down hip-hop MCs allows one to hear their words more clearly, it is equally possible that slowing them down brings out the wordless moan, the affective timbral qualities of the voices—what Ashon Crawley has identified as their vibrational quality.[74] I don't want this to be an essay about death, but after #BlackLivesMatter, what I hear are the structural conditions that produce the loops of melancholia, which so define Screw's sound. The literal haunting that happens when you listen to a Screw tape on which nearly every MC, not to mention Screw himself, is now—and prematurely—dead. Screw didn't merely mechanically repeat those conditions. He too aspired to alchemize melancholia's static loop into mourning, with its own paths into vibratory exuberance and interbeing.[75] He didn't want this to be about death either. But in his music, that alchemy is suspended, literally returned to loops of traumatic repetition and the enjoyment that comes with them. And slowness is therefore a mode of suspension, the evocation of that space of death which bears within it the possibility of trauma being brought to consciousness.

5

In the summer of 2004, I went through a bad breakup. In the middle of it (July 28, to be precise), I went on my own to see the doom/drone metal band Sunn O))) play at a club in Brooklyn on a hot summer night. I was in a state of agony. When things are falling apart and you're losing someone you love, time can expand to an excruciating degree. Time hurts. There is time because you want there to be that time that consists in love's projection of a future (the poet Charles Olson said that happiness consists in a state of confidence of being alive), but there is no guarantee of such time anymore, or such futurity, only loss.[76] And you know this and maybe at some level you even want this, want to be free of that projection, but still you can't stand it, it is too much for you. Or for me at least—the pronoun itself wavers at the limit of what "I" can handle. It is like being wrenched out of the illusion of continuity back into the illusion of discontinuity. Insofar as love is a profound relationship to continuity, even (or especially) in the contingency and specificity of its object. Feeling close. Being close. It is like breaking an addiction. Or breaking an addiction is like trying to fall out of love. I remember the music that night as one long riff coiling and uncoiling over a period of ninety minutes, while dry ice machines turned the room into a steamy cold sweat blur, behind which three hooded figures with guitars stood. Apparently, the show was recorded as *Live White* and actually had a number of songs. I don't recall any formal break between them. The evening was a series of long shudders, each the length of the riff, long and slow enough to be barely perceptible as vibratory structure, but inexorable too—something that will not end, that you do not want to end, but which also causes you to suffer.

In her reflections on doom, death, and drone in Sunn O)))'s metal music, Aliza Shvarts argues that, the affect of metal that so many people find off-putting—the sentiment of suffering, the emotional investment in the painful and the heavy—is in fact an affect of an aesthetic and political tradition, circulating in the various reproductive labors that structure its operation. These reproductive labors sound like, feel like, doom. For what is drone but the unending echo of generational potential? And what is doom but the repetitive cycle of reproduction that both taunts yet sustains the artist? The heaviness of metal resonates with the weight of aesthetic lineage, and the mimetic technique of a band like SunnO))) allows us to feel this weight. Metal mimetically touches the dark animal bodies—the witches, demons, and heretics—that populate its broader imagery in a historically profound sense. Metal makes audible an enduring material condition of reproductive labor extracted through the brutal disciplining of the sexual division of labor and its concomitant racialization. By lingering in sustained drones, SunnO)))'s music arrests the body in an unresolved reverberation between corporeality and subjectivization—an arrest that is the material history of gendered and raced subjugation, an arrest enacted as a dark and feminine excess that escapes.[77]

Doom/death/drone metal is another music of suspension, where catharsis is replaced by repetition and an uneasy state of homeostatic tension that pushes toward a limit and then falls back. Perhaps drones are always, as Shvarts suggests, the sound of labor, as Phill Niblock's audiovisual drone piece "The Movement of People Working" might suggest. But not all drone metal is about doom: the titles of the tracks on Earth's second record (Earth being the main inspiration for Sunn O)))'s sound)—"Like Gold and Faceted," "Teeth of Lions Rule the Divine," and "Seven Angels"—suggest glory, gloriousness, impossible splendor—the sublime. In fact, Earth's music, which is often much more static than Sunn O)))'s, has a surging dynamism to it that is closer to the ecstatic sound of Young, Hennix, or Charlemagne Palestine. It's Sunn's repetition of the riff, "brutally disciplining" vibration, that conveys the feeling of doom.

The "bad breakup" is one of those moments where some of the violence of reproductive labor is revealed, as the fantasy of romantic or erotic futurity falls apart, leaving this "unresolved reverberation between corporeality and subjectivation," the vibrating body revealed in the abrupt loss of the object through which it seeks to subjectivate. It can be a moment of real illumination; it can be a moment where you feel (and in my experience, appear) pathetic and ugly and weak to others in your inability to disguise your state of need. Or maybe it just feels that way in a moment of narcissistic deflation. And maybe that's a way of thinking about the kitsch Lord of the Rings robes that Sunn wore when they performed—that the aesthetic of doom, especially when performed by white men, is a luxury guaranteed to a degree not granted to other people. Which does not mean that white men are not (also) doomed. But in the end, the aesthetic of doom is always on the edge of folding into self-parody, as doom resolves itself either in actual death or other, different forms of life. Or the same one (again/"encore!"). The breakup too. Which is perhaps a way of saying that the terrain of doom is one of irony, black humor, or (in Shvarts's terms) performativity.[78]

Can one apply a word like *doom* to DJ Screw's mixtapes? If "metal makes audible an enduring material condition of reproductive labor extracted through the brutal disciplining of the sexual division of labor and its concomitant racialization," chopped and screwed sounds can be heard as a reflection of the racialization of labor—the continuing legacy of the slave trade, morphed into post-Reagan imperatives of the drug trade, which are the topic of so many of the lyrics of the tracks that Screw plays. I think in particular about Screw's mix of Spice 1's "Welcome to the Ghetto" from *Chapter 30: G Love* with its "makes me wanna holler" sample from Marvin Gaye's "Inner City Blues." The original is 4:46 and the remix runs to 14:34—one of the most radically extended Screw mixes with an equally radically slowed-down, swanging and banging groove. The first five minutes are instrumental with Screw scratching and playing with the Gaye sample and mumbling shoutouts and wisdom in the background. When the rap comes in, there's a lot of looping of sentences, sometimes smoothly, sometimes with scratching, sometimes with a doubled-up percussive echoing, in which one copy of the track audibly follows the other a beat or half a beat behind. The repetition of lines (which is different from the collage-like use of phrases from classic rap tracks in building certain kinds of hip-hop choruses) is one of the ways that an aesthetic and politics of doom is generated in a Screw mix—what is expression the first time, becomes traumatic repetition, or haunting, or mantra, the second or third time.

Consider, for example, the heaviness of the lyrics of "Welcome to the Ghetto":

> I think about genocide
> And have thoughts of my homies who died
> Everybody backstabbin
> But I ain't the one to talk I'm into gafflin
> Death
> Gives a shit about your color

But yet I see mo dead young brothas
I'm goin crazy out here
Seein 24 brothas die by the end of the year.[79]

When Screw repeats and loops the lines, they get heavier still. In particular, he lingers over the third verse, repeating sequences of lines as follows, without scratching or any obscurations of the words:

(Ain't no justice it's just us
And any nigga with the guts loves to bust
At the police niggas can't get peace
Sendin' troops to the ghetto like the middle east) × 2
(My homie on the block got beat down
And he never sold an ounce, a key, a pound) × 2
(Suicide was a notion, sometimes I wanna run and dive in the ocean) × 2
(But killin' myself ain't the answer cause the problems of the world need a cure like cancer) × 2
(And everybody see the problem but the president) × 4 (and he ain't livin' in the ghetto so that's evident) × 2 [here, Screw's voice can be heard saying "mmhmmm"]
(I quit pullin' over, fuck the police
Cause they beat Rodney King like a savage beast) × 4
Now motherfuckers on my block think its Glock time
Open up season on cop time
So welcome to the ghetto[80]

The repetitions underline the truth contained in the lyrics but also the apparent impossibility of changing the situation. If we use Jared Sexton's definition of *Afro-pessimism* as "a meditation on a poetics and politics of abjection wherein racial Blackness operates as an asymptotic approximation of that which disturbs every claim or formation of identity and difference as such," then the term could be applied to many of the tracks that Screw plays.[81] Screw's work is Afro-pessimistic in that sense.

In thinking about Screw, we might add an idea of "sonic abjection" via Shvarts's work on doom—slowness, repetition, the heaviness of an expanded lower register that is the consequence of slowed-down pitch shifting. Realism is pessimism in these circumstances, yet Moten's position in "Blackness and Nothingness" comes closer—there's a capacity for "desiring otherwise" in relation to a historically and racially imposed nothingness that appears via the groove—and via the politicization of repetition itself, which, like Reed's sonic virus Jes Grew, is seeking something out. Screw is not just playing the Spice 1 track, which itself is a complex meditation on the trope of "ghetto" as the site of a pessimism and realism that is imposed in a militaristic way on Black people who are forced to inhabit its abject space.[82] By politicizing this abjection and the pessimism that is the result of the resolute indifference of those political structures that make the ghetto, Spice 1 (and Screw) also breaks with that pessimism. To slow a track down is to effect a topological transformation of the space—to find a parameter of alterity, of "desiring otherwise" in what would seem to be unchangeable—the recorded track and its tempo but also the entire edifice of space-time in which Black lives have historically and literally been imprisoned.

In his essay "Black Topological Existence," Fred Moten writes:

> There's an internal volition of space with regard to its own deformation and reformation, deconstruction and reconstruction. This preservation-in-differentiation doesn't just come from outside; it works, in the endlessness of the end, to cut the outside and what the outside is supposed to oppose. This is the topological imperative, where topology is how we graph us into the scene we set, the camera neither subject nor object but the difference that is given in seeing and hearing inseparably. Black social life is the continual preparation of a table under conditions of bending, stretching and crumpling. Ours is a mechanics of distress. This is black topological existence. It's what it is to see and hear and feel and touch and smell and taste from within the mass, that celebration of mass that implies the mass and enacts its differentiation. We are anarchic and uncertain. We hesitate. We don't want to wait in vain. The way we be hearing and seeing one another disappear into the way we make a space that is also a way, in and out of no way, ain't no thing. This recessive working, this ruminative message and massage, this rubbing down into and out of depression, this inveterate shaping, is felt in the sound, savoured in the sight, of words, too.[83]

The history of Black life in the space known today as Houston is one of such pressure and distress. From the plantation/slave-based economies via which people of African descent first came to Texas in the 1820s, to the attempts to drive free black citizens from the Republic of Texas in the 1830s, to the growth of segregated spaces and neighborhoods in the Jim-Crow era, to the new forms of privatized space and policing that characterize the Houston Screw lived and worked in—Black life in Houston has been lived in a racialized, pressurized space. DJ Screw's slowing-down of tracks and mixes, and the distribution of the music—not via live performance or commercial recordings but via the informal selling of mixtapes to be played in cars or elsewhere—is topological in exactly the same way that Moten has defined it: as the creation of an impossible possibility via a topological deformation of "the space of music." Impossible, and yet, that is where life, actual living life, including sonic life, is to be found— "just before music," in Lonnie Holley's formulation.[84]

In Screw's version, the slowing down and looping of the track amplify this sense of abjection and containment of racialized space, but slowing down also discovers "a way out" in that space of abjection where "that which disturbs every claim or formation of identity and difference as such" is discovered as a site of pleasure and power: Jes Grew if you will. The funk. What is indicated in the word abjection once the disgust by which the word is normatively positioned is allowed to morph back into desire, pleasure, mere being even. The choreosonic, of which, Crawley writes: "The choreosonic way of life—at once considered discardable and excessive, though also, on the underside of such rhetorical dismissal, were considered moving—is the enunciation of an otherwise world, a world that vibrates against inequities of the one in which labor exploitation [is] foundational. What if joyful noise bespeaks a sociality, a togetherness, that moves oneself and others toward that other world?"[85]

Although the importance of the church in the Houston hip-hop scene is unquestionable, whether we're talking about UGK's musicianship, or Big Moe's incredible vocable freestyling on "The Streets Ain't Right," understanding the choreosonic in relation to Screw's DJing has other levels. Is it in the shift of the tempo of the track, or the colossal lurching swing that Screw could introduce into a track, a playful emphatic perversion of law's supposedly iron-clad principle of repetition? Is it in the tender, respectful "shout-outs" Screw made at the beginnings and ends of the slowed-down mix, paying respect to those who are in the house, or those who will be listening in their cars, on tape, at some point in the future? Or the dead, those who have died, like Screw's friend Fat Pat, MC extraordinaire on various Screw tapes, murdered the same week that Screw opened his store in 1998—about whom Screw says "I been hurtin' in my heart since they took that Fat Pat . . ." on *Chapter 010: Southside Still Holdin'*? The gathering of the dead, the departed, in that thick cloud of unexpiated injustice and undying love—still present as sound, as music, as vibration. In the mix.

The neoliberal figure of the DJ is a solitary one—yet Screw's work emerged out of Black practices of sociality—more specifically the Screwed Up Click whose varying and various members rapped on Screw's mixtapes, and for whom Screw made specific mixtapes—the gathered and shifting voices of those freestyling on tracks like "The Streets Ain't Right"—Big Moe, D-Mo, Haircut Joe, Key-C, Big Pokey, Yungstar, Mike D, Clay Doe, Pooh. Freestyling is often associated with battling, ostensibly pitting individual against individual. But freestyling's history, going back to the South Bronx and the groups that rapped over Grandwizard Theodore or Bambaataa's beats, is a powerful example of the choreosonic as collective assemblage of enunciation, the improvised, shifting but vortex-producing collectivity of it, which is nonetheless interrelated to the breakdancing battles happening on the dance floor or, in Houston, the high school playground and street battles that, according to MCs like K-Rino, birthed rapping in the city.[86] Though soft-spoken, Screw encouraged this—both in the shoutouts and acknowledgments that are an essential part of nearly every mixtape he made—recognition of who was in the house on the night that the tape was made, and who was missing or being missed "in lock"—but also in his inclusiveness, his encouragement of individual voices and MCs to step up and throw down at his house. Person after person recalls that Screw was a good friend. Demo Sherman, for whom the famous *June 27th* tape was made, recalled his first meeting with Screw, after being instructed by his sister Tashia to go pick up a mixtape she'd ordered from Screw's house:

> He say, "So what do you do, you a DJ, you rap or whatever?" I said, "Man, I been rappin' since the Sugarhill Gang. When I heard that, I knew that was me." And I say, "Nobody ever wanted to help me, so I had to become my own DJ and learn how to make beats, and when I started improvin', they really wasn't helpin' me, so I was just always on my own." He like, "Well, man, I DJ, I get down." And man, we talked for hours, just right in his driveway. And that day was the same day I met Fat Pat, I met Hawk, I met a bunch of more other people, but I can remember him tellin' me how much he had love for Fat Pat and Hawk, that's what made it stick with me.

In terms of the choreosonic—and of cosmopolitics—it is "Screw house," and "The Wood Room" in that house on Greenstone in the Golfcrest neighborhood that is significant. It's within that room that Screw made most of his mixtapes—a complex technosocial assemblage, put together from lists of tracks that people would ask him to mix onto a tape, made for particular people, but then distributed through informal networks too. It was in that room that local MCs and friends would gather and freestyle over the beats and sounds that Screw would lay down—while apparently Screw's girlfriend Nikki Williams was trying to sleep. Reading the reminiscences of that room which Lance Scott Walker has collected, one slowly becomes aware that it was a kind of temporary autonomous zone—a place where rival gang members would drop their beefs with each other, where time would slow down as evening shifted to "3 'N the Mornin'" which became 9 or 10 a.m. and the session still continuing.

"A session at Screw house consisted of this: drankin', smokin', and rankin'," said Mike-D, aka Bosshog Corleone, a rapper from Third Ward whose brother Bamino runs South Park mainstay Bam's Auto & Detailing. "What we call rankin' is just us talkin' about each other, playin' The Dozens. We used to go on all day. And the thing about Hawk, Pat, and Screw, is that they may be talkin' about each other, but the minute you laugh at one of them too hard, you in the game now. As soon as you say somethin', they gon' be like, 'Oh what you talkin' bout?' They gonna get you in there, man. Real characters. Never a dull moment."[87]

Screw put up the gate on the house so that he could control who was actually able to enter and leave it. And those who did get inside might find themselves locked in overnight or longer, as a session might roll on, in the absence of outside time, with Screw falling asleep at the turntables and then waking up again. Screw would make his voiceovers, recognizing and acknowledging everyone in the room. The mic would be passed around. A journalist who visited described the atmosphere as follows: "A quiet reverence seems to fill the room as people watch him work. After five hours of recording, two of the rappers fall asleep on their milk crates, while the others drift off with their drinks. Screw's girlfriend, Nikki, comes home with a box of takeout for him, stopping in the kitchen to scold him for not doing the dishes."[88]

Screw was certainly making money from the tapes, but he repeatedly emphasized that "the Rap game is for real, it ain't no play game. This is our life, this is gonna pay our bills. I try to help everybody I can to get some exposure"—no doubt that "way out" of which he spoke earlier in this chapter.[89]

The cosmopolitics of the situation might appear hidden if you believe that hip-hop exists only within the framework of "the industry" and that what happened in the house on Greenstone was just practice, or preparation for fame, and recording contracts and the like. Not to disrespect those things, and the need to make a living—but Screw clearly saw things otherwise. One of his friends dryly observed that Screw was not a capitalist—that he was more about sustaining everyone in the Click—he wanted everyone to come up together.[90] The vibrational space of the wood room and the assembled crew there—getting high, cracking jokes, exploding into lyrical flow, slowed-down bass-heavy beats with the ghosts of Black musical tradition saturating everything—was that space of freedom, the topos of music, flourishing under impossible conditions. Screw understood that, given the situation of Blackness in America, such freedom might require locks and gates in order to protect it, give it a chance. Nonetheless, on at least one occasion, the police tore down the gates of Screw's house, kicked down the door, and busted into the house, searching for drugs that were not there, destroying tapes, asserting domination of that space that fractally and vibrationally eluded their control.[91] Those of us who have DJed in illegal spaces that get busted by the cops know that strange moment after the cops leave, when the play button is pressed again, the turntable starts to spin, the guitar is plugged in again, and the volume is slowly turned up until that vibrational space reappears out of hiding, out of its dormancy, whether it happens later that night (if enjoying the white privilege of "getting away with a warning"), or a different night entirely.

But this was Screw's own home (well, he was renting it). There were problems before, and after, when Screw moved to a house in suburban Missouri City, where the neighbors complained and called the cops on him. The figure of the neighbor is an important one for cosmopolitics, because it's not just the rule of law that sets limits on what music can be but also the neighbor who complains about the noise, or who watches the people pulling up outside or hanging out and complains about it. In fact, the cosmopolitics of the neighbor, understood in a Freudian way as how we get along or don't with the people that we live with, the difficulty of that, is really important in the history of music. And music can allow reconciliation with the irritating or irritated neighbor. Sometimes. You can hear the other side of the story on John Holt's reggae classic "Man Next Door" where the noise of the neighbor makes the singer want to "get away . . . and find a better place."

6

When something traumatic occurs, most sound becomes painful to listen to, it impinges on us too much. Impinging has a particular quality, it is a hostile exteriority, or rather a projection thereof, that presses itself on us in the form of too dense or too rapid a series of sonic events which press abrasively on the emotional surface of our psyches—a surface that manifests as the capacity to feel pain in relation to the outside. Much music from the Black radical tradition assumes the painful impingement of exteriority in much the same way that Fanon does in *Black Skin, White Masks* when he talks about there being no ontology for Black people: that exteriority, phenomenology, is an always already racialized and racist space that impinges on the consciousness of Black people to the point of making it impossible to think, or to be—or to breathe.[92] Conversely, certain kinds of Black music do, in their warmth and sleekness, seek to invert this process, to create zones of vibrational supportiveness, of phenomenological reparation, of pleasurable localized exteriority that does not impinge.

What is the opposite of impingement? A caress; a welcoming or beckoning; gentleness (which then can be instrumentalized as the possibility of seduction or being seduced). Or is it something more distant than that? Something that makes no demands at all yet is present, supportive? That vibrates at the same speed that we do, slightly slower even, recognizing the way that the death drive is operative at such moments, and our desire to return to a state of zero tension, or perhaps just a lower tension via a certain kind of slowness and softness. Again, a kind of vibratory suspension in which the pleasure principle and that which is "beyond the pleasure principle" (i.e., the death drive) are held in equilibrium.

Such thoughts bring to mind two Miles Davis tracks that have been important to me in my own life and struggles: "Lonely Fire" and "He Loved Him Madly." The former originally appeared on *Big Fun*, but is now included in *The Complete Bitches Brew Sessions*. Miles slows it all down. He bides his time (the South Asian tantric master Vimalananda said "There's nothing harder in life than biding one's time").[93] He doesn't say anything that doesn't need to be said. He allows for rhythm. He is grateful for the distraction (of the electronics), but possibly also hates himself for indulging in it, and is contemptuous of it, even as he recognizes its efficacy or his need for it (or his audience's need for it). When I say "he," do I mean me or Miles? And then there's the even slower "He Loved Him Madly" (note: "he," not "I," although apparently the title came from Duke's salutation to the audience after a performance, "I love you—madly!"), Miles's tribute to Duke Ellington on his death on May 24, 1974, which appears on one side of *Get Up With It* (Eno was influenced by it early on, and it is therefore a source of what we call ambient music today). It's 32:05 minutes long. Miles doesn't play on the first half of the track, which consists of a slow droney organ with beautiful minimal guitar work from Pete Cosey. When Miles does play, he plays mostly extraordinary extended notes whose pitch wavers in microtonal slurs in the saddest, most wraith-like way, like reaching out as far as you can to something that is always slightly beyond reach, that is slowly but inexorably disappearing (back) into the sonic nexus, slipping between the fingers and lips that shape and unshape the sound.

Miles had his own relationship to depression: his famous five-year-plus retirement from music, from 1976 to 1981, during which he sat in his townhouse in Manhattan getting high and "doing nothing."[94] Are these the sounds of repressive desublimation? Herbert Marcuse coined the term in his book *One Dimensional Man* to describe the ways in which contemporary capitalism refused the sublimation of desire into poetic forms in favor of an increasing explicitness or realness or directness in culture. While, on the one hand, this seemed to offer the rejection of illusions and ideology manifesting as culture, on the other hand, this directness itself offered a kind of pseudosatisfaction since it happened through the marketplace, which remained structurally unchanged (therefore it is called "repressive"). This insight, taken up by Žižek and others, describes the ways in which capitalism adapted to the various liberation movements of the 1960s, offering new forms of pleasure and experience, no longer repressed (or sublimated)—so long as they could be integrated into a capitalist mode of production. The insight, of course, raises the question of whether there is such a thing as a nonrepressive desublimation—indeed queer, feminist, Black, Indigenous, and other practices affirm that this is so. Or maybe just that sublimation and desublimation are relative. Nonetheless, insofar as Marcuse's term illuminates the commodification of Black male sexuality in the 1970s and otherwise, one might expect that depression would be a symptom of the repressive desublimation of Blackness found in the situation of Black music within the late capitalist marketplace. Reading books of interviews with Miles conducted by white jazz critics whom Miles variably endured or swatted away—one is struck again by the racial and artistic reification he had to put up with. The impasse of Miles's music in the 1970s—the attempt to connect to, or even construct "the whole people" (Baraka), globally, and be able to achieve a new kind of fusion of experimentalism with Afrodiasporic popular musics. Only for these experiments to be increasingly consumed by a white rock audience. The more he tries to make a music of the whole people, the more the people disappear, leaving him strangely separated from "ensemble." For the time being.

This also makes me think of the more recent work of the R&B singer/musician D'Angelo, who in the fourteen-year gap between the recordings *Voodoo* and *Black Messiah*, apparently also struggled with depression, after having been packaged by the music industry as (yet another) Black sex symbol, with all the ambivalent desire and hatred that phrase is made to contain.[95] There are at least three remarkable Screw remixes of D'Angelo tracks: the 13-minute version of "Brown Sugar," on *Chapter 13: Leanin' On a Switch*; "Nothing Even Really Matters," from *Chapter 98: Four Corners of the World*; and "Lady," from *Chapter 105: Everday All Day*. One of the most striking effects of slowing tracks down is the transformation of gendered voice. With D'Angelo's "Lady" and "Brown Sugar," the sexy syncopation of D'Angelo's voice slows down to that bassy, vibrating hypermasculinity, which is there in many of Screw's tracks. But it does not end up sounding hypermasculine. Instead, the performative sensuousness and syncopation of the originals is thrown slightly askew, and the "mo'nin" that I described in section 4 comes to the surface. It is a sound of work, of labor, of having to be a Black man. Pitching lower, slowing down moves in the direction of the state of "zero excitation" that Freud believed was the aim of the pleasure principle. Conversely, by sustaining a state of lower excitation, the sound takes on a tantric quality insofar as tantric eroticism eschews cathartic peaks of excitation and the resulting zero state in favor of a more steady, diffuse (expanding across the whole body and beyond it) state of vibratory pleasure and arousal. In this sense, Screw goes beyond the sound of repressive desublimation that D'Angelo is working through in the direction of a different politics of vibration, a different kind of pleasure (by 2014, with *Black Messiah*, much of this had been achieved. It's 2020 as I write this . . . we eagerly await whatever the next stage brings for D'Angelo!). This pleasure is an untimely one—one of the reasons why Screw mixes still have such a passionate following fifteen plus years after his death.

The last tracks Screw played on various tapes are among his most powerful—shimmeringly slow ballads that are reduced to a kind of vibrating silence very similar to the slowest of Miles's seventies tracks. Particularly remarkable is his version of Erykah Badu's "Other Side of the Game" ("gotta put that question on your mind," Screw says in the intro, in response to the song's opening lyric: "What you gonna do when they come for you?"), an already mournful track about a lady addressing the conflict between her love for her lover and his getting sucked into the Game and the Hustle—in other words, a song about the conflict between love and racialized reproductive labor—and the packaging of that conflict as yet more of the same.[96] The mesmerizingly slow bass introduction makes me think of the other side of the break, not a radical leap between two rhythms, but a slowing down of the gap itself until the gap swells and becomes momentarily everything, "pure now-time" (jetzt-zeit) before voluptuously and slowly lurching back into rhythm—a strange manifestation of sonic continuity.

And then, the striking shift from a feminine to a masculine voice caused by the slowing and throwing of the tempo as though sexual difference itself begins to melt as you enter the zone of vibratory slowness (something Hennix pointed to in chapter 2 of this book). This resonates with the chopped and screwed sounds that Barry Jenkins used in his movie *Moonlight* where the slowed-down sound articulates the rhythms of the unconscious and a queer coming of age in its tensions with heteronormative ideas of masculinity.[97] Moonlight: a little vibrating negativity that you might carry with you for a long time without really knowing it, unconsciously waiting for something or someone to shine a light on it, slow things down, and bring it out.

7

I just listened again to Drake's "November 18," his tribute to Screw's *June 27th* mixtape and in particular the 37-minute freestyle sometimes known as "The Streets Ain't Right," with its beat from Kris Kross's track of the same name (which in turn samples Notorious B.I.G.'s "Warning"). As I did, I had flashbacks to many moments over the last ten years, listening to "June 27th" through a cloud of depression that made most sound and most light unbearable. But somehow that state of mind also makes those slowed-down tempos and warped sweet melodies of a Screw tape feel right when little else does. Depression and sizzurp have a mood or rasa in common. It's as though DJ Screw does the work of traumatic repetition for you, including the phenomenological slowdown that often accompanies depression, so that you can "enjoy your symptom" without even having to reach for, or act out a symptom—beyond putting the tape on.

In *The Undercommons*, Fred Moten argues that white people need to recognize that things are fucked up for them too, rather than engaging in virtue signaling and performative gestures of benevolence:

> The ones who happily claim and embrace their own sense of themselves as privileged ain't my primary concern. I don't worry about them first. But, I would love it if they got to the point where they had the capacity to worry about themselves. Because then maybe we could talk. That's like that Fred Hampton shit: he'd be like, 'white power to white people. Black power to black people.' What I think he meant is, 'look: the problematic of coalition is that coalition isn't something that emerges so that you can come help me, a manoeuvre that always gets traced back to your own interests. The coalition emerges out of your recognition that it's fucked up for you, in the same way that we've already recognized that it's fucked up for us. I don't need your help. I just need you to recognize that this shit is killing you, too, however much more softly, you stupid motherfucker, you know?[98]

This is where the contemporary progressive discourse of allyship finds its limit. Yes, to recognize a shared situation, while not conflating the different positionalities within the situation; to be able to identify, emotionally and otherwise, with a piece of music, without identification becoming appropriation: that for sure is one of the projects of a politics of vibration. And in the/this moment, it is very hard to do this—fucked-up people, especially those who don't know how fucked up they are, tend to be needy people, and if desperate enough they tend to grab at anything that might help in a situation where so little does help—even the discourse of allyship. They/we/I. But that is not Moten's point. If I recognize that yes, this shit is killing me too, what do I do with my sonic entanglement in the work of DJ Screw and others, one of the few resources that has allowed me to reflect on this fucked-up nature/history of things, and to reach out, or be reached? To start off, I recognize my entanglement—and my separation.

In terms of entanglement, one of the things that kept me afloat during this time was reading the YouTube comments on tracks like the "June 27th" freestyle (9,743,863 views, 9,103 comments) as I listened, and realizing that Screw really did "Screw up the world." Reading the comments from others going through their own struggles, whether doing time, or having lost someone, or caught in some kind of pharmaceutical dependency, or some painful love situation, and also "bumping Screw," made me feel more human, like there were other people out there. It made me cry sometimes. وبأ ليللا writes "Im from saudi arabia i smoke big blunt to this shyt mayne RIP Dj Screw" and 158 people reply, some from Houston, others from Tunisia, Brazil, Mexico.[99] Over and over, people who grew up in Houston listening to Screw tapes express their amazement and respect that twenty years on, people across the planet are listening to Screw, and feeling him. Screw's mixes encompass generations of musical recording technology, beginning with turntables and vinyl and cassette mixtapes, to the CDs that Screw started selling toward the end of his life, to the MP3s and YouTube videos (but not Spotify, given the intellectual property issues!) that have globalized and accelerated exposure to previously local and regional musics such as Screw's. Music is a key part of what Marx called the "general intellect" and a key part of the way that, globally, people might recognize each other, beyond language, in their shared destitution and potentiality. Via a series of appropriations of technical possibilities of musical production and distribution, most of which exist in a gray market that ignores intellectual property rights while paying respect to the MCs and producers—Screw tapes now reach the whole world.

Sometimes, Drake's and The Weeknd's music seems like the most depressed music in the world—and it's coming out of Toronto, where I live, and which I find a very depressing or depressed place to live, a postmodern monument/ruin to British attempts to rationalize settler colonialism via the simulacrum of Victorian Englishness, which itself was originally the simulacrum of self-made wealth created out of the spoils of empire. To use the language of the land acknowledgment, Toronto is "the traditional territory of many nations including the Mississaugas of the Credit, the Anishnabeg, the Chippewa, the Haudenosaunee, and the Wendat peoples and is now home to many diverse First

Nations, Inuit, and Métis peoples.... Toronto is covered by Treaty 13 with the Mississaugas of the Credit."[100]

This city can be staggering in the strange way that an imposed pacification of the land manifests as a broken social scene in which connection seems to elude everyone, no matter how much people talk about it. I do believe that the suicides of my young white male musician friends, with which I began this book, has something to do with this environment, this landscape, this history—just as I know that the landscape bears witness to the slow genocide of Indigenous people who were guardians of the land and who still inhabit it, in varying degrees of dispossession. It still hurts. "So I walk around with my mind blown in my own fuckin zone"—UGK, "One Day." And I wonder whether my own attraction to DJ Screw's mournful party music is coming from a similar place as Drake's—that somehow we both find this music coming out of 1990s Houston compelling as a way of negotiating our own, no doubt different, but interrelated geographies of depression and suspension. In fact, although there have been trading posts in the area now known as Toronto as far back as the early eighteenth century, the beginnings of the modern city date to 1793, only forty years before the city of Houston was established—both on lands previously occupied by Indigenous peoples. So maybe the vibration of (un)settlement is similar. Toronto and Houston both sprawl out across the settler colonial landscape, and both are complex, multiracial places emerging from Anglo domination.

There are big differences between Drake and Screw though: "The Streets Ain't Right" runs for 37 minutes, while "November 18" is about 4 minutes long, returning the Kris Kross loop to the pop tune that it originally was, and changing the ontological insistence of Screw's slowness back into a kind of novelty. More importantly, "The Streets Ain't Right" is truly a production of a freestyle ensemble, celebrating Screw Click member DeMo Sherman's birthday and including the MCs Big Moe, Key-C, Yungstar, Big Pokey, Haircut Joe, and Kay-Luv. The Drake track is just Drake, with the sense of community reduced to a statement of privatized desire, loneliness, and solitude, which might easily be read as depression. There's also the singing style—Big Moe clearly comes out of the church and there's no autotuning of his voice, and he's freestyling—Drake sounds autotuned and the connection to the church is faint, distant. Which is not nothing. Drake is fantasizing about Houston, perhaps the way that I am too. I am not attacking Drake—I am saying that I feel him, and his attraction to DJ Screw, and the ever-present desire to leave the 6ix and its confusing emptiness. When Lil Wayne famously advised Drake to just be himself, what if he meant that Drake had to find his own relationship to depression—a different one from the Houston MCs or from Wayne himself?[101] And that, given the pervasiveness of depression in contemporary life, this turned out to be a very attractive and successful move for Drake, albeit one that some have called "emo whining." It's, of course, not the only possible response to that slowed-down Houston sound: there is an amazing recording of the British Grime MC Dizzee Rascal freestyling at a Houston radio station with the local MCs The Grip Boys, with Dizzee's hyperspeed post-jungle MCing style crashing into the ultra-slow drawl of the local MCs—a superpositioning of rhythms and tempos that is both jarring and seamless.[102]

Do I mean depressing or depressed? I write this in the shadow of Mark Fisher's recent self-inflicted death—Fisher, who taught us so much about contemporary topologies of depression—and Drake.[103] There's music that's depressing, and then there's music made by people who are depressed, and also music consumed by people who are depressed, sometimes cathartically or therapeutically. If the blues is fundamentally concerned with depression, how different is it to consume that depression from different subjective points of view? Is it the "alchemization of the lynchings" that can't or doesn't happen? Or: the alchemization that seems to happen to me when I consume Black popular music, but does not happen to others who, as Mackey himself realizes, are not allowed the alchemization of their historical circumstances. So that, in a real sense, the alchemization is also then impossible for me, since the alchemization cannot (like a drug) be a purely internal transformation. To what degree is it our consumption of this music that makes the actual transformation of historical conditions of inequality impossible? And which, therefore, results in that murky stasis in which I maintain a certain privileged agency but whose concurrent symptom is my own depression? This too would be a mode of suspension. It is a familiar situation, if we consider the ways that music or video games or medications are marketed today to youth cultures which are dealing with the "depression" (the word is in quotes to indicate the complex psychopolitical dynamic that it indicates) that comes from exposure to the realities of adult life and resistance to them. In each case, repetition offers the promise of escape, which then feeds structurally back into the marketplace as addiction—or enjoyment. Lacan called this the "discourse of the capitalist."[104]

8

But, immersed in the now (and always) planetary flow of hip-hop's transmission, my understanding of Screw and the sonic decolonization of time shifted again recently after writing about the work of the Indigenous Canadian hip-hop crew A Tribe Called Red (now known as The Halluci Nation). I'd first encountered them when DJing as part of the MAMA crew around 2011–12—in fact, the highlight of our time as DJs was playing a support set for them at the ImagiNative festival in Toronto circa 2013. A Tribe Called Red formed in Ottawa in 2008, where Bear Witness (Cayuga First Nation), Jon "Dee Jay Frame" Limoges (Mohawk Nation), and Ian "DJ NDN" Campeau (Nipissing First Nation), started throwing the now-famous Electric Pow Wow parties on the second Saturday of every month at the Club Babylon (they were soon joined by Dan "DJ Shub" General [Cayuga First Nation], but Shub, Frame, and NDN subsequently left the group, and ATCR is now a duo of Bear and Tim "2oolman" Hill [Mohawk, of the Six Nations of the Grand River]). The parties were intended as a safe space for urban Indigenous people, right in the middle of the settler colonial capital, only a mile or two away from the Parliament buildings.

Early on, the group started making their famous powwow remixes, which are the basis for the various records they've since put out. Powwows are a combination of ceremony, festival, social gathering, and political assembly for North American Indigenous communities. The music for powwows involves drum groups, who are central to the proceedings, who produce a subtle but pounding heartbeat tempo rhythm around which various kinds of singing, dancing, stepping forth, and chanting happen.[105] The sound, heard on the land and in the context of an Indigenous gathering, is powerfully moving. The amplified recordings that A Tribe Called Red work with do the same thing but also extend the range of the vibration through the practices of sound system culture, through bass and volume but also through connections made to other sonic struggles and scenes, which appear in the mix.

"Ninety percent of that is coming from the drumming," Bear told me, when I spoke with him in the fall of 2018. "That's what it feels like when you're at a powwow. That's not changing, we're not doing anything to that groove.... We're really riding that. Maybe we're making it more accessible to an audience outside of the community. Inside the community we know that feeling in your chest that you get when you listen to powwow music, you stand up a little straighter."[106]

When I asked whether A Tribe Called Red emerged out of hip-hop, Bear pointed out that, in fact, many of their earlier tracks are in the somewhat obscure musical genre of moombahton—a briefly popular club style circa 2010 that consists in slowing-down house, reggaeton, and dembow beats, originally at 120+ bpm, to around 108 bpm.[107] Briefly, club nights with names like "Slowed" and "108" proliferated, and the sound was adopted on tracks by the likes of Major Lazer and Justin Bieber. But A Tribe Called Red sutured this slowed-down house beat to heartbeat-paced powwow drum rhythms revealing a different politics and practice of slowness, one still carrying the vibrational trace of DJ Screw—and very much committed to a decolonizing of time.[108]

The amplified polyphony of the voices of the Cree northern choir and that pounding heartbeat rhythm break through the structural depression which is endemic to this place—Toronto, Houston, North America but also "the world is a ghetto" (War). A Tribe Called Red's music resonates with the land. In this sense, it reminds me of the world of contemporary Indigenous Australian art and music in which paintings are often vibrational maps of particular locations—which in turn are the articulation of particular vibrational entities, whether associated with a particular clan or totem or spirit. As my friend Andrew Belletty explained to me: if you want to understand vibration from an Indigenous perspective, you have to come and sit on the land, and let the vibration of the land pass and speak through you. There is a continuity of land, energy, human psyche that is dynamic, situational, and it has its own temporality, in which particular forms emerge from a pervasive "dreamtime" ("Jukurrpa" in Warlpiri) that is immanent to space itself. But how is such a practice possible in urban spaces such as Toronto or Ottawa and for the urban Indigenous people that A Tribe Called Red create music and a scene for? In order to feel the vibration of the land, in order to break the spell of the settler colonial spectacle in its awesome, many-tentacled structural occupation of space and time, one method is to slow down—to heartbeat speed, to relaxed breath speed. If A Tribe Called Red's versioning of chopped and screwed contains within it a message for the Houston scene, it is that it is possible to slow down too much, via too much purple drank and other substances, until the heart stops beating, as it did for Screw, Pimp C, Big Mo, and a number of other Houston musicians. Slowing down (or speeding up—since A Tribe Called Red has its share of 130 bpm bangers) is an alignment with local and/or global rhythmic forces in the project of creating (or re-creating) life-sustaining worlds.

How does what Robinson calls the *spatial subjectivity* that is a part of music, especially from an Indigenous perspective, manifest in a place where the land has been abused, stolen, and neglected? A Tribe Called Red's work involves Indigenous methodologies of working with the local and global as vibrational spaces. It is a music of alliance constellating reggae, Indigenous electronic musics from across the Americas, hip-hop, and soul. Listening to their work and to Bear speak has illuminated what has often felt to me like a deep existential depression with the truth of what the land I am currently living on is, and the way in which alienation from the land itself via its settler colonial veneer is a suppression of vibrational ontology and possibility.

In a talk at the X Avant festival in Toronto that he curated in 2018, Bear said to the small crowd assembled in the basement of the church that is now the Music Gallery's home:

> I'm someone who was fortunate enough that, when I was about fifteen I did a manhood fast and I had a really clear coming of age, going from one thing to the next. Not long after that was when I started going to raves and got into that whole scene and really saw a group of people who were searching for something.
>
> You're going and having these massive group experiences but there was no real goal to it, there wasn't any kind of control to it, it was just this wild almost dangerous energy, and a lot people who get lost because there isn't any rules or any intention or any directive point to it. But what I saw were people looking for that kind of transition, that kind of transformative thing in their lives. So, when I was going to parties and stuff I remember having the realization that there's so much energy here, there's so much power that people are just playing with and throwing around here that if it had a point, if it had a destination, that's the thing these people are looking for. And that was always in the back of my mind, DJing, was that how can we add something real to the party?
>
> And, I saw it in little bits and pieces, like two of my favorite groups were Asian Dub Foundation and Congo Natty: there were people that were really putting out a lot of culture and making political songs at raves, and that's where the sparks started going off in my brain saying, there's something here, there's something to be followed. And then with Tribe I realized one day that we were doing that, that we were having these parties, but that there was more to it. I mean you can just come and dance and interact on that surface level, but if you want to dig deeper and want to be a part of something greater that... being there makes you part of it.
>
> Here in Canada, here in the Americas, it's so difficult to start the conversation that needs to be had between Indigenous people and settlers that even to mention the conversation starts a fight. And when you even talk about Indigenous rights, which are really human rights at this point, you know, we all need to drink water, we all need to breath air, we all need to live on this earth, but to even talk about those Indigenous rights attacks the basis of colonial structure, of colonial lies. So when we start talking about reconciliation, we're three steps ahead of where we are. Like, that conversation is on the table, but we haven't even built the solid

ground to have that conversation on and then we can't build it because we just get into fights every time we try to talk about it.

When I look out at one of our shows, and I see the incredible mix of backgrounds, of ages, of everything that come to our parties, having a common experience. They are all listening to these powwow remixes. I see the same reactions with faces regardless of age, regardless of background. That's a common experience. That is the beginning of having a level piece of ground to build that table on so we can get those conversations.

I remember in Edmonton where we were playing on like a Tuesday night, to a packed crowd going nuts, and I looked up at one point and somebody was crying, somebody was praying, and someone was flashing their breasts. That was one moment in the show. So, I think you have people connecting on so many different levels to what's going on, so some people are just there for the party. So people are just—there was this phenomenon where people started crying at our shows for a long time. I've seen less of it now, but there was a time, about a year ago, where people would just weep through whole chunks of our show. And then again, to see someone pray, you know it's like, all over the place.[109]

"How can we add something real to the party?" Throughout this book, I have tried to present the work of musicians, composers, and artists who believed that there is a power in music that goes far beyond the available models of entertainment and consumer culture with their repetitions of a certain hedonistic impulse, or the notions of art and aesthetics that still prop up thought about music from the conservatory to music journals—popular, experimental, and classical. When Bear says that he seeks something more, it is by connecting to the earth and connecting to the broader sense of a political struggle. In very different but also related ways, Pandit Pran Nath, DJ Screw, and Catherine Christer Hennix also see music as a powerfully directional force and practice, part of a cosmology, a cosmopolitics. A cosmopolitical practice that involves "ways of knowing" (Henriques). Such ways of knowing are always pragmatic, always built on local conditions, but in activating the topos of music, they also reach deep into the actual historical, geographical, and therefore political space in which they occur, which is their cosmopolitical dimension. Conversely, one could say that if there is a topos of music, it is because music really is an emergent property of space and the profound relationships to space that form the basis of Indigenous worldviews and practices.

Hearing Bear speak, and hearing A Tribe Called Red play, has illuminated the abject space in which I live—if illuminated is a visual metaphor, what would the vibrational version be? Maybe to "lively up yourself" in Bob Marley's phrase?[110] It is not done for me, yet I am affected by it, in my depression, the confused, confusing sense of not knowing why things are like this. Feeling only the sadness of the land, the people, the sadness of the vibration, or for that matter the fake imposed happiness and prosperity as much as the poverty and inequality—and not seeing or feeling that there is something other than that—that there is a reality here and we have simply not faced up to it or realized it, but have ignored it. The land speaks, but I didn't hear it. The earth too. My own heartbeat. Every atom. Those who have been listening I have ignored. Idle No More. I am back to my friend Adam's death, with which I began this book. Using the practices of hip-hop, A Tribe Called Red has opened up—I don't want to call it a space of death . . . it's more like a space of death/space of life. Maybe it's always like that. Crying. Laughter. A certain kind of chaos, lack of order, different people's situations, bodies, psyches inhabiting the same space, constructing a field, a complex wave-space. Freedom to enter or leave as you wish—Hennix's "choice sequences." The wave function does not always collapse. We + Not-we = the field, the funk(tion). Oscillation, zig zag, superconductivity. Space of life, space of death. Space of life, space of death. Space of life, space of death.

Coda
July 2, 2020

The time regime most of us on the planet inhabit has been decisively shaken in the last few months. The global pandemic of COVID-19 has slowed many things down, and in that slowdown, other vectors of transformation, good and bad, have accelerated. Millions of people sick or at risk, five hundred thousand dead and the number still going up, all forms of sociality from the workplace to mass transportation to collective gathering spaces impacted and most people forced for a period of time to rest in place, meaning home, if they have one. *The great pause*: the phrase concerns temporality, and in the slowing-down of lived time, therefore also a shift in our relation to sound and vibration. *The time is out of joint*: it always has been, but now it's impossible not to notice. Living in a big city, Toronto, the soundscape has shifted: there are a lot fewer planes overhead, fewer cars on the expressway that's about half a mile from where I live, fewer cars on the street in front of my house. The bird song is brighter and louder. At night, skunks, raccoons, and other critters move mostly silently but with greater confidence through the back alleys, yards, and streets of the city—and "silence, silence is a rhythm too!"[1] Human voices sound muffled beneath their masks but, in the slowly gentrifying neighborhood I live in, the sound of poverty and altercation but also humor, shouting, sonic warfare, and street dominance, persist. Kids cycle through the local parks at night on illuminated bikes with boom boxes attached, blessing the darkness with bass. If this is not the decolonization of time, it is at least a moment of pause in which "otherwise possibilities" become audible.

All the performance spaces that I know of in Toronto and elsewhere have shut down, though some of them seem to be reopening in a provisional way. Most of the musicians and DJs I know, including Hennix, have had all of their live performances, installations, and other kinds of public shows canceled, with an accompanying loss of nearly all of their income. It's a tough moment. As the UK jazz musician Shabaka Hutchings noted on his radio show in May, this is a time for practice, and the question is "WHAT do you practice?" Hutchings said that he is picking up instruments that he has had lying around that he's never played before. In this pause, perhaps there is time to discover what is "at hand" around us that we did not notice. I find myself listening to Worldwide FM a lot, and although club spaces and sweaty collective dancing is now mostly impossible, my Facebook and Instagram feeds are full of DJs and musicians broadcasting sounds out into the world. As Fred Moten noted, we may be apart but we are not alone.

Hennix moved to Istanbul in November 2019, to be closer to the Sufi scene that she is devoted to. For her, the pause has provided another opportunity to change our relationship to music, refocusing again away from music as an artifact of consumer culture and entertainment and in the direction of practice, research, and devotion, the cultivation of the inner or unstruck sound, and the building of sonic shrines, where such a sound might be cultivated and shared. The problem, as she sees it, is that the temporary silencing of consumer culture cannot be taken advantage of by most people because of the anxiety caused by economic precarity, and by fear of the virus, very real for older musicians and artists too. But still, there is that possibility of turning around and, like Shabaka Hutchings, discovering what is sitting there right beside you.

I finally resumed my own practice of sonic meditation with a tambura borrowed from a musician friend. The instrument—which, as Hennix noted is the only one treated as a deity in India—is a powerful presence in my living room, and an object of wonder to me and the kids, who pluck at it with a mixture of curiosity and sonic mischief. It is a deceptively simple instrument, given that there are four strings and no frets. Practice consists mostly of tuning, and even though I can tune the strings by hertz after Hennix gave me the correct ratio (60/120/120/90 Hz, i.e., 2/4/4/3), the tuning does not end with the correct numbers coming up on my iPad screen. You have to tune by ear, beyond the limits of the measurement device, and when you get it right, something magical happens, a strange unfolding of the sound in its living vibrancy, overtones swaying around you, a lovely entity. And then you lean into the presence of that entity, again learning to master the correct plucking/strumming technique, a sequence of fingers, so that the sound is sustained in its recursiveness, and in that recursiveness, a particular rhythm emerges by which one feeds the sound, not overwhelming it but not starving it either. And hopefully not going out of tune again. When you are in that zone, something happens to time, that bubble appears which I have used the word *continuum* to describe. But it is not the bubble: we are!

    The name and sound of DJ Screw surfaced once more this year in the middle of this global COVID-19 pandemic and the worldwide protests against anti-Black racism that followed the death of Houston-born George Floyd at the hands of the Minnesota police. Floyd, born and raised in Houston's third ward, was an affiliate of Screw's Screwed Up Click in the late 1990s and appeared as an MC on a number of Screw mixtapes under the name of Big Floyd—he also had the honor of having his own birthday mixtape (*Chapter 7: Ballin in Da Mall*). He was not a major figure in Screw's corpus; there are maybe twelve minutes of his solid MC flow spread out over several mixtapes, more like someone who associated with the scene, a mentor and friend, who ended up spending some time in jail, like many of the Black men in that scene, and who moved to Minneapolis in search of a new life, which maybe he found for a while, before his new death came, at the hands and knee of a Minneapolis police officer. His life and death matter a lot more than a smooth conclusion to an academic book. But at the same time, who would be crass or smug enough today to say that Floyd's death was completely unrelated to the scene around Screw in the 1990s? And that the slowed-down, chopped-up world that Screw built does not resonate with the slowed-down, chopped-up world that emerged with the coronavirus, a slowing-down in which finally perhaps the relentless pursuit, physical and pharmaco-incarceration, death, and murder of young Black men, including many of those around Screw, as well as Screw himself, is acknowledged and responded to by the world at large. Slowing down has a politics, and in that slowdown—which we are still experiencing such that we are getting to take a look around us in a different, sometimes silent way—the waves coming from Screw's mixes, and the bodies and minds entangled in them, including Floyd's, rolled across the land and people could feel it as waves of bodies took to the streets. UGK's remaining living MC, Bun B (RIP Pimp C, once more) has been one of the most forceful and eloquent participants in the protests both in Minneapolis and Houston, and while it is important to tarry with depression where depression manifests itself (an apocryphal piece of advice that one of my yoga teachers Joan Suval once gave us, "Depression is like a movie: don't leave until the movie is over!"), the transformation of depression into political action and change is alchemy, healing, truth, and survival.

The politics of vibration, then, is this challenge of the conjunction of inner and outer in constellating the field—the bodies on the street, the bodies on the dance floor, quiet attendance to the most ordinary or fundamental of mysteries, the rising up of a wave, its transmission, diffusion, diffraction, fall, and rise again, the repetition of that and how periodicity's patterns condense or dissolve, how we and the world are the product of that, how we might immerse ourselves more deeply in the truth of that, why it is so difficult to do that, and yet the fact of our persistence, in love, in the propagation of it, which is itself an aspect of the whole thing, the whole, in its wholeness.

Acknowledgments

Thanks first of all to my love and partner, Christie Pearson, and my teacher and friend Catherine Christer Hennix, my two extraordinary and constant interlocutors in writing this book, and my guides and instructors in all matters vibrational. Thank you both for your patience, discipline, generosity, and fearlessness in showing the path to that Love Supreme.

Thanks to all those who spoke with me for the Pandit Pran Nath chapter; in particular to La Monte Young and Marian Zazeela for their encouragement and generosity in sharing their thoughts and archives and address books; to Joan Suval, for her love of Guruji, and for sharing her archives and thought. And to the many people who shared their memories of Pran Nath, and information concerning Hindustani vocal music, including Henry Flynt, Simone Forti, Michael Harrison, Jon Hassell, Sri Karunamayee, Mashkor Ali Khan, Shabda Khan, Shashi Maini, Ian Nagoski, Rose Okada, Charlemagne Palestine, Terry Riley, Shanta Serbjeet Singh, Yoshi Wada, and Peter Lamborn Wilson. Thanks also to the many friends, associates, and collaborators of Catherine Christer Hennix who shared their thoughts and archives with me over the years, including Amelia Cuni, Werner Durand, Amir ElSaffar, Henry Flynt, Hilary Jeffery, Lawrence Kumpf, Louise Landes Levi, Susan and George Quasha, Amadeo Schwaller, and Charles Stein. Thanks to Julie Grob, Mike Hall, and Lance Scott Walker for their help in my research concerning DJ Screw.

Thanks to the many musicians, composers, and DJs who have been my friends, respondents over the years, including Vicki Bennett, Alan Bishop, Maga Bo, DJ/Rupture/Jace Clayton, Philip Corner, Omar Dewachi, Dewa Putu Berata and Emiko Saraswati Susilo of Gamelan Çudamani, Marina Gioti, Tim Hecker, Mazen Kerbaj, Alan Licht, Raz Mesinai, Aki Onda, Marina Rosenfeld, Sharif Sehnaoui, Sam Shalabi, Akio Suzuki, David Sylvian, Venus X, and

Wok the Rock. Thanks also to my friends and comrades in the Toronto music scene: to the MAMA crew—Merike Andre-Barrett, Alex Livingston, and Drew Wedman—and those nights and early mornings in the Market; to Daniel Vila and everyone at DoubleDoubleLand, with love and solidarity; and thanks also to Martin Arnold, Jennifer Castle, Eric Chenaux, Tyler Crick, David Dacks, Guillaume Decoufflet, Ryan Driver, Sergio Elmir, Colin Fisher, Brandon Hocura, Sook-yin Lee, Gabriel Levine, Tad Michalak, Sarah Peebles, Sandro Perri, Aimee Dawn Robinson, and Bear Witness. Rest in Peace: Ron Gaskin, Justin Haynes, and Adam Litovitz.

Thanks also to all at the *Wire* for publishing and supporting my work: Chris Bohn, Tony Herrington, Anne Hilde Neset, Derek Walmsley, and Rob Young. And thanks to the many writers and scholars of music, sound, and vibration who have been my friends and interlocutors over the years, including Mitchell Akiyama, Spiros Antonopoulos, Ian Balfour, Eric Cazdyn, Lily Cho, Norma Coates, Roger Conover, Christoph Cox, Julian Dibbell, Raymond Foye, Kenneth Goldsmith, Julian Henriques, Bethany Ides, Brandon Labelle, Christof Migone, Timothy Morton, Ben Piekut, Nina Power, Ben Ratliff, Art Redding, Rasha Salti, Matthew Seidman, Aliza Shvarts, Sparrow, Will Straw, Michael Taussig, Yuval Taylor, Tobias van der Ween, and Lindsay Waters. Particular thanks to Erik Davis for reading and commenting on an early version of the manuscript. Thank you to my editor Ken Wissoker, Josh Tranen, Ihsan Taylor, and the anonymous peer reviewers at Duke University Press for their trust, perseverance, and encouragement in the development of this manuscript.

Work from this book was presented and discussed at various conferences and festivals: thanks to Jan Rohlf at Transmediale; Lars Eckstein, Anja Schwartz, and Nicole Waller of the Minor Cosmopolitanisms research group at the University of Potsdam; David Cecchetto, Marc Couroux, and Eldritch Priest at Tuning Speculations in Toronto; David Levi-Strauss and the Art Writing Program at the School of Visual Arts in New York; Vivian Caccuri, Ronaldo Lemos and Hermano Vianna and the Institute for Technology and Society in Rio de Janeiro; Andrew Belletty, Margie Borschke, Frances Dyson, Douglas Kahn, and Meg Walch in Australia. Some of the ideas in chapter 1, 2, and 3 were first published in the *Wire* and *Sounding Out!* blog.

Thanks to my students at York and Cornell Universities who have taken my classes on music and vibration—and to my colleagues at York for their support of my work. Thanks in particular to my research assistants Matthew Godfrey, Gabriel Levine, Yasmina Jaksic, and Monica de Sousa for their work. And to Lisa Sloniowski for bibliographic assistance. This project came together when I was an A. D. White Fellow at Cornell's Society for the Humanities, 2011–12.

Thanks to all my colleagues that year, including Eliot Bates, Duane Corpis, Sarah Ensor, Ziad Fahmy, Brian Hanrahan, Michael Jonik, Damien Keane, Adriana Knouf, Yongwoo Lee, Eric Lott, Roger Moseley, Timothy Murray, James Nisbet, Trevor Pinch, Jonathan Skinner, and Jennifer Stoever. Particular thanks to Nina Sun Eidsheim for introducing me to the idea of music as a vibrational practice.

Finally, thanks to my old friends and family—our lives and our growth have been thoroughly entangled in music scenes since I was a child. Thank you to my father, Bernard John Boon, who introduced me to jazz and Black music early on; to my mother, Helga Boon, who created a space for the sound to happen; and to my brother and sister, Derek and Annette Boon, both long-standing Fall fans, like myself. Thanks also to those I came up with: Cary Berger, Ben Chant, Michael Dulchin, Kate France, Richard Grant, Nicholas Noyes, Charles Parrack, Allan Sutherland, David Wondrich, and my DJ partner and keeper of the faith, Nick Triggs. Thanks to my sons William and Jesse, for their love of the music and amazing iPhone DJing skills.

I gratefully acknowledge the receipt of a Social Sciences and Humanities Research Council of Canada (SSHRC) Standard Research Grant for work on this project from 2011 to 2014. Thanks also to the Faculty of Liberal Arts and Professional Studies, York University, Toronto, Canada, for the financial support it provided to this work. And finally, thanks again to Yasmina Jaksic for compiling the stellar index for this book.

Notes

INTRODUCTION

1. Lispector, *Agua Viva*, 5.
2. Lispector, *Agua Viva*, 5.
3. Stengers, *Cosmopolitics*; see also Stengers, "Cosmopolitical Proposal." A contemporary example of the use of "cosmopolitics" in articulating and debating a Kantian cosmopolitanism can be found in Cheah and Robbins, *Cosmopolitics*—but the horizon of the cosmopolitical in this text remains a humanist one. Yuk Hui has argued that Kantian cosmopolitanism does in fact concern a particular relationship between the political and nature, but of course a particular, secularized version of nature ("Cosmotechnics as Cosmopolitics").
4. Kant, *Towards Perpetual Peace*, 73. In "Cosmopolitical Proposal," Stengers notes that she was not aware of Kant's usage and that her concerns are different from Kant's. The German "kosmopolitische" is usually translated as "cosmopolitan," to complicate matters.
5. De la Cadena, *Earth Beings*.
6. Parker, quoted in Bradley, *Universal Tonality*, 134.
7. Badiou, *Being and Event*.
8. Mazzola, *Topos of Music*; Hennix, *Poësy Matters*.
9. Moten, "Black Topological Existence."
10. Henriques, *Sonic Bodies*; Moten, *In the Break*.
11. *Encyclopedia Britannica*, online edition, s.v. "vibration," accessed July 15, 2019, https://www.britannica.com/science/vibration.
12. Henriques, *Sonic Bodies*.
13. For a useful history of the relationship of physics to music, see Johnston, *Measured Tones*, and Alexander, *Jazz of Physics*. For a usable popular account of quantum mechanics' explorations of waves and particles, see Greene, *Elegant Universe*, 85–116; and Ford, *Quantum World*.
14. Kahn, *Energies in the Arts*.
15. Within the history of psychoanalysis, the question of what the materiality of libido consists in is a challenging one. It receives its first (undeveloped?) examination in Freud's

early text "Project for a Scientific Psychology" (aka the "Entwurf") via a vocabulary of "excitation," "conduction," "quantitation," and so on. See the entry for "Libido" in Laplanche and Pontalis, *Vocabulaire de la psychanalyse*, 224–26. It is taken up most literally by Wilhelm Reich throughout his career, via concepts such as "bioelectricity" through which libido can ostensibly be measured, but also by Jung as "psychic energy." Arguably, thereafter, there is a split in psychology between somatic-based therapies such as gestalt that directly address energetic or vibrational levels of bodily/psychic organization, and therapies that emphasize language. The early Lacan of Seminar II still explicitly discusses energetic processes, and Jean Laplanche's *Life and Death in Psychoanalysis* focuses on the tension between "the vital order" and the psyche (for example, the assertion that "every function, and finally, every human activity, can be erotogenic" [21]).

16. Jankélévitch, *Music and the Ineffable*. For a recent exploration of music's ineffability, see Gallope, *Deep Refrains*.

17. See Stein, *Being = Space × Action*, *Io* 41: 298 ("Being defines a space together with an action").

18. Hui, *Question Concerning Technology in China*.

19. Stiegler, *Technics and Time*.

20. Moten, "Black Topological Existence."

21. Maddalena, *Philosophy of Gesture*.

22. McPhee, *Music in Bali*; Hood, *Triguna*; Regnault, *Voguing*.

23. Attali, *Noise*.

24. Kgositsile, "For Art Blakey and the Jazz Messengers," in *Homesoil in My Blood*, 224.

25. Barry Shank has usefully summarized some of this literature in his *Political Force of Musical Beauty*. Shank distinguishes between music that is directly involved in a particular political action or message, where music is merely a vehicle for conveying this message, and a Rancièrian model where music participates in a distribution of the sensible and a shared sense of musical beauty that is political in convening a community around it. I value this model, but there is a way in which the political meaning Shank finds in musical beauty is still separated from the topos of music, and its choreosonic decision—and this remains a problem for musical philosophies that assert the importance of ontological difference and listening without considering praxis, and the way that praxis goes beyond phenomenological (i.e., "sensible") models.

26. See Gallope, *Deep Refrains*, for a nuanced reading of this problem.

27. Stoever, *Sonic Color Line*; Crawley, *Blackpentecostal Breath*.

28. Varèse and Chou, "Liberation of Sound," 18.

29. Deleuze and Guattari, "Of the Refrain," 310–50. A whole book could be devoted to tracking the sources of Deleuze and Guattari's vibratory materialism, whether in Guattari's reassertion, within a Lacanian context, of an energetic dynamics of the unconscious (see, for example, Guattari, *Schizoanalytic Cartographies*, 49–50), or in Deleuze's reframing of the problem of vitalism in Spinoza, Nietzsche, and Bergson (consider, for example, the entire discussion of repetition, i.e., periodicity, in Deleuze, *Difference and Repetition*, as a discussion of vibration!).

30. Grosz, *Chaos, Territory, Art*, 62.

31. Grosz, *Chaos, Territory, Art*, 55.

32. Crawley, *Blackpentecostal Breath*, 145.
33. See Latour, *We Have Never Been Modern*, 32–35.
34. Eidsheim, *Sensing Sound*, 180.
35. University of Bern, Institute of Philosophy, "Ontology of Musical Works and Analysis of Musical Practice," accessed November 4, 2021, https://www.philosophie.unibe.ch/research/projects/ontology_of_music/index_eng.html.
36. Kania, "Philosophy of Music."
37. Scruton, *Aesthetics of Music*, 117.
38. Stevens, "Of Mere Being," in *Palm at the End of the Mind*, 398.
39. Heidegger, "The Question Concerning Technology," 311.
40. Jankélévitch, *Music and the Ineffable*; Zuckerkandl, *Sense of Music*.
41. Wilmer, *As Serious as Your Life*.
42. Marcus, preface to *Psychotic Reactions*, x.
43. I first encountered Glissant's idea in Manthia Diawara's brilliant essay on the French-Algerian artist Kader Attia. See Diawara, "All the Difference in the World." The essay can also be found in Glissant's later writings, including his *Une nouvelle région du monde*.
44. I draw here on Étienne Balibar's analysis in Balibar and Jordan, *On Universals*.
45. John Coltrane, liner notes to *A Love Supreme*, 1964.

CHAPTER ONE: LORD'S HOUSE, NOBODY'S HOUSE

1. I make no particular judgment in using the phrase *Indian classical music*; I am aware of the problematic nature of the phrase and its complicity in South Asian colonial history, such that it allows for a valorization of particular kinds of musical tradition within a framework that has been imported from the West as a supposedly universal marker of value or quality.
2. See Lavezzoli, *Dawn of Indian Music*.
3. Zia Inayat Khan, ed., *Pearl in Wine*.
4. Suhani ("Shashi") Maini, Pran Nath's daughter, interview by author, September 12, 2020.
5. Pran Nath, quoted in Pace, "Pandit Pran Nath," 10.
6. Shanta Serbjeet Singh, "Detractors of Punjabi," *Tribune* (India), December 17, 1978.
7. See, for example, Sengupta, *Foundations of Indian Musicology*.
8. Suhani ("Shashi") Maini, interview by author, September 12, 2020.
9. On Kirana, see the chapter on the gharana in Wade, *Khyāl*, 184–226; see also Kinnear, *Sangeet Ratna*, 3–9.
10. My primary source on Abdul Karim Khan are the sleeve notes to *Khansahib Abdul Karim Khan* (Mississippi Records, 2011) written by Ian Nagoski. Nagoski's sources include Kinnear, *Sangeet Ratna*, and Bakhle's chapter on Khan in *Two Men and Music*, 215–55.
11. On Abdul Wahid Khan, see Kinnear, *Sangeet Ratna*, 231–34.
12. See the biography of Abdul Wahid Khan at http://www.kiranawest.com/abmianpage.htm. The source of the quote is unclear.

13. See the biography of Abdul Wahid Khan at http://www.kiranawest.com/abmianpage.htm. The source of the quote is unclear.
14. Dhar, *The Kirana Legacy*, 13.
15. Wade, *Khyāl*, 196.
16. Nath, *In Between the Notes*.
17. Sri Karunamayee, interview by author, May 10, 2001.
18. Daniélou, *Introduction to the Study of Musical Scales*, 10.
19. Latour, *We Have Never Been Modern*.
20. Crawley, *Blackpentecostal Breath*.
21. James, *Varieties of Religious Experience*.
22. Marian Zazeela, interview by author, July 3, 2001.
23. Pran Nath, quoted in Pace, "Pandit Pran Nath," 10.
24. Pran Nath, quoted in Marian Zazeela, "Sayings of Guruji."
25. See Fanon, *Wretched of the Earth*, 174.
26. Transcript of unpublished interview with La Monte Young, Marian Zazeela, and Pran Nath, by Shanta Serbjeet Singh, March 16, 1972, 41.
27. Shanta Serbjeet Singh, interview by author, May 2001.
28. Dhar, *Here's Someone I'd Like You to Meet*, 70.
29. Pran Nath, interview by Sri Karunamayee, in *Raga Notes: The Newsletter of Sur-Laya-Sangam* 2 (1), 1998. The extent of Pran Nath's broadcasts and recordings for All India Radio remains to be researched, but we know via the *India Listener* newspaper that he performed Rags Anand Bhajron and Malgunji on April 22, 1947, at the Lahore studio; Multani and Bhopali on April 27, 1947, and Rag Todi and Rag Eman on Sunday, March 26, 1961, at the Delhi studio.
30. Pran Nath, quoted in Neil Strauss, "Evening Song," *New York Press* 4, no. 42 (October 16–22, 1991): 20.
31. La Monte Young, interview by author, June 2001, but see also Wade's account in *Khyāl*.
32. Dhar, *Here's Someone I'd Like You to Meet*, 66–67.
33. Terry Riley, interview by author, July 2001.
34. Dhar, *Here's Someone I'd Like You to Meet*, 73.
35. See the booklet accompanying *The Tamburas of Pandit Pran Nath* for details. Pandit Pran Nath–style tamburas are still available from Rikhi Ram in Delhi.
36. See Sachs, *History of Musical Instruments*, 391–98.
37. Mathieu, *Harmonic Experience*, 26.
38. Pace, "Pandit Pran Nath," 10.
39. Bhatnagar's work and ideas are contained in his book *Microchakras*, cowritten with David Isaacs.
40. See *Tamburas of Pandit Pran Nath* booklet, 14.
41. La Monte Young, interview by author, June 2001.
42. La Monte Young, interview by author, June 2001.
43. La Monte Young, "Singing of Pran Nath: The Sound Is God," *Village Voice*, April 30, 1970.
44. Daniélou, *Introduction to the Study of Musical Scales*.

45. Young, "Singing of Pran Nath."
46. "To USA with Sound of Music," *Statesman*, January 8, 1970.
47. Pran Nath, quoted in Neil Strauss, "Evening Song," *New York Press* 4, no. 42 (October 16–22, 1991): 20.
48. La Monte Young, interview by author, June 2001.
49. Terry Riley, "Remembering Guruji," *Faqir Pran Nath aka Pandit Pran Nath* (blog), WordPress, November 2009, https://prannath.wordpress.com/.
50. Jon Hassell, interview by author, July 2001.
51. La Monte Young, interview by author, June 2001.
52. Robert Palmer, "The World's Greatest Musician?" *Real Paper*, January 14, 1976, 24.
53. La Monte Young, "For this release . . . ," written statement, n.d., part of La Monte Young and Marian Zazeela's archive, MELA Foundation, New York.
54. Henry Flynt, interview by author, July 2001.
55. Henry Flynt, "On Pandit Pran Nath."
56. Jon Hassell, interview by author, July 2001.
57. Jon Hassell, interview by author, July 2001.
58. Jon Hassell, interview by author, July 2001.
59. See Spicer, review of *Vernal Equinox/Flash of the Spirit*, 72.
60. Jon Hassell, quoted in Gross, "Travelogue of Jon Hassell's 'Fourth World' Journey into the Mystical."
61. Terry Riley, email message to author, December 1, 2021.
62. Catherine Christer Hennix, interview by author, November 2021.
63. Cherry and Knox, "Report to ABF," 151.
64. Bengt Berger, email to the author, Nov. 27, 2021.
65. Charlemagne Palestine, email message to author, October 9, 2020.
66. Charlemagne Palestine, interview by author, July 2001.
67. Charlemagne Palestine, interview by author, July 2001.
68. Charlemagne Palestine, interview by author, July 2001.
69. Forti, *Handbook in Motion*, 129.
70. Forti, *Handbook in Motion*, 131.
71. Yoshi Wada, interview by author, January 2, 2019.
72. Catherine Christer Hennix, interview by author, July 2001.
73. Jon Hassell, interview by author, July 2001.
74. Keefe, "Lord of the Drone."
75. Pran Nath performed at the Dream House on June 17, 28, and September 16, 1979; May 18, and June 1, 15, 29, 1980; May 17, 31, and June 14, 27, 1981; May 9, 23, and June 6, 19, 1982; May 8, 22, and June 5, 18, 1983; May 6, 20, and June 3, 16, 1984. Pran Nath CV, n.d., part of La Monte Young and Marian Zazeela's archive, MELA Foundation, New York.
76. Pran Nath performed at the Rothko Chapel in Houston, Texas, on November 15, 1981, and April 17, 1983.
77. Henry Flynt, personal communication.
78. Mohlajee, "Ascetic Musician Makes Home in California."
79. Grimshaw, *Draw a Straight Line*, 84–113.
80. Terry Riley, interview by author, July 2001.

81. Charlemagne Palestine, interview by author, July 2001.

82. Catherine Christer Hennix, interview by author, July 2001.

83. Sue Fox, "How We Met: Yehudi Menuhin and Ravi Shankar," *Independent*, accessed November 4, 2021, https://www.independent.co.uk/arts-entertainment/how-we-met-yehudi-menuhin-and-ravi-shankar-1575503.html.

84. Performance notes written by La Monte Young, 1986.

85. For discussion of the complex histories of Islamic and specifically Sufi cosmopolitanism, see Gedacht and Feener, *Challenging Cosmopolitanism*.

86. In fact, Xenakis also presented at the festival in 1968 and 1969. See Gluck, "Shiraz Arts Festival," 23.

87. Mahasti Afshar, "Festival of Arts: Shiraz-Persepolis," 11–12. https://asiasociety.org/files/uploads/126files/Festival%20of%20Arts%2C%20Shiraz-Persepolis%201967-77.pdf.

88. Peter L. Wilson, personal communication, September 2020. In two reviews written for the *Daily Bulletin* of the festival at the time, Wilson noted that, on the first evening, Pran Nath performed Ragas Jaijaivanti, Bageshwari, and Mishra Kafi, and on the second, Dulia Tilang and Anant Bhairavi.

89. Peter L. Wilson, "Pran Nath Again," in *Daily Bulletin of the 8th Iran Festival of Arts*, n.p., 1974.

90. See P. L. Wilson, *Sacred Drift*. There is a significant literature on Islamic cosmopolitanism. See, for example, Alavi, *Muslim Cosmopolitanism*.

91. Terry Riley, "Reminiscences of Pandit Pran Nath," from *20th Century Music* 3, no. 9 (September 1996), cited in *Raga Notes: The Newsletter of Sur-Laya-Sangam* 1 (1), 1997.

92. Paul Hertelendy, "'Music . . . It Is a Holy Thing' Says Nath," *Oakland (CA) Tribune*, January 3, 1977.

93. Nath, *In Between the Notes*.

94. Terry Riley, interview by author, July 2001.

95. Shabda Kahn, interview by author, March 2001.

96. Young and Zazeela, *Faquir Pran Nath*, 5.

97. Peter L. Wilson, *Midnight Ragas*, booklet for 8th Iran Festival of the Arts, n.p., 1974.

98. Riley, "Remembering Guruji."

99. Marian Zazeela, interview by author, June 2001.

100. Shabda Kahn, interview by author, July 2001.

101. Shanta Serbjeet Singh, "Return of the Maestro," *Economic Times of India*, June 17, 1973.

102. Nataraj, *Travels with Pran Nath*, 30.

103. Riley, "Remembering Guruji."

104. Nath, *In Between the Notes*, 8140.

105. Shabda Kahn, interview by author, March 2001.

106. Sri Karunamayee, quoted in Marcus Boon, "Ocean of Sound (Ocean of Silence)," 22.

107. Shabda Khan, interview by author, March 2001.

108. Terry Riley, interview by author, July 2001.

109. Žižek, *Sublime Object of Ideology*, 227–63.

110. Colacello, "Remains of the Dia."

111. Riley, "Remembering Guruji."

CHAPTER TWO: THE DRONE OF THE REAL

1. Catherine Christer Hennix, quoted in Boon, "Shaking the Foundations," 29.
2. Flynt, "Altered States."
3. Foucault, *Care of the Self*; Foucault, "Ethics of the Concern of the Self."
4. Reich, *Sex-Pol*.
5. See Boon, "Eternal Drone."
6. Key sources on Young's work include Duckworth and Fleming, *Sound and Light*; Potter, *Four Musical Minimalists*; and Grimshaw, *Draw a Straight Line*.
7. Young, "Notes on the Continuous Periodic Composite Sound Waveform," 7.
8. Helmholtz, *On the Sensations of Tone*.
9. Daniélou, *Tableau comparatif des intervalles musicaux*.
10. Daniélou, "Influence of Sound Phenomena," 23.
11. Grimshaw, "Ideology of the Drone."
12. Conrad's critique of Young can be found in a series of essays written in the 1990s, including "Slapping Pythagoras," in *Writings*, 320–37.
13. See Branden Joseph's discussion in *Beyond the Dream Syndicate*. Also recent surveys of Conrad's work such as *Tony Conrad: Writings* and Cathleen Chaffee's edited volume, *Introducing Tony Conrad: A Retrospective*.
14. Daniélou, *Introduction to the Study of Musical Scales*, 16.
15. Hennix, interview by author, August 22, 2010.
16. Hennix, interview by author, August 22, 2010.
17. Hennix, interview by author, August 17, 2019.
18. Flynt, "Meta-Technology."
19. Bataille, *Accursed Share*, vol. 1.
20. The drone is in fact the one used in Young's work, *Map of 49's Dream the Two Systems of Eleven Sets of Galactic Intervals Ornamental Lightyears Tracery*.
21. Hennix, interview by author, August 22, 2010.
22. This work has never been published, and for a long time I wondered if it was apocryphal or nothing more than a title. However, Hennix showed me her manuscript copy, much of which consists of proofs written in the language of set theory, as favored by Hennix in the early 1970s. The manuscript consists of a set of categories, each of which consists of conditions relating to the presence or absence of ratios of concurrent frequencies involved in a particular composition. Algorithms tell you which frequency ratios will be absent . . . and *category* and *algorithm* are used more or less interchangeably in the text. Hennix argues that Xenakis only spoke about specifying everything present in a composition or a score—and the same with Cage or Tenney in making computer music. The use of algorithms allows a formalism for denoting an absence—one of Hennix's innovations. It should be noted that *category* in this piece is used in the Aristotelean sense, although Dennis Johnson, a key collaborator of Young's, was a mathematician and specialist in category theory and wrote his doctoral thesis under Edwin Spanier, an algebraic topologist, at Berkeley.
23. Hennix, interview by author, August 22, 2010.
24. Gagaku recordings were available in America and Europe in the 1960s, but UCLA, where Young studied, also had a Gagaku group. Hennix says she read Eta Harich-

Schneider's books on Gagaku (*The Rhythmical Patterns in Gagaku and Bugaku* [Leiden: Brill, 1954] and *A History of Japanese Music* [New York: Oxford University Press, 1973]) and listened to documentation of Gagaku at the Asian Museum in Stockholm with Hans Isgren.

25. Hennix, interview by author, August 22, 2010.
26. Hennix, interview by author, August 22, 2010.
27. Hennix, interview by author, August 22, 2010.
28. Bataille, *Unfinished System of Nonknowledge*
29. Young, interview by author, summer 2001.
30. See Hennix, "Hilbert Space Shruti Box," 283n1.
31. On Yessenin-Volpin, see Nathans, *Alexander Volpin*; on Grothendieck, see Scharlau, *Wer ist Alexander Grothendieck?*; on Brouwer, see van Dalen, *Mystic, Geometer, and Intuitionist*. On Lawvere, the interviews found on Lawvere's website offer some biographical insight: http://www.acsu.buffalo.edu/~wlawvere/index.html (accessed December 29, 2020).
32. I have benefited greatly from the following texts regarding Hennix and mathematics: Spencer Gerhardt's essay "Domains of Variation." Also Henry Flynt's various parsings of Hennix's work, including "Modalities and Language for Algorithms by Christer Hennix"; Hennix and Flynt, "Intensions, Illuminations, and Toposes"; Flynt, "Philosophy of C. C. Hennix"; and Flynt, "Encyclopedic Glossary." Charles Stein's introductory essay to *Being = Space × Action* remains an extremely helpful introduction to Hennix's philosophical and mathematical ideas.
33. Hennix, "Proposal" to Mills College (unpublished manuscript, summer 1973).
34. Hennix, "Abstracts for Infinitary Compositions," 13.
35. For nontechnical and historical introductions to Brouwer and intuitionism, see van Dalen, *Mystic, Geometer, and Intuitionist*; and Hesseling, *Gnomes in the Fog*.
36. Brouwer, *Cambridge Lectures on Intuitionism*.
37. Hennix, "Notes on Intuitionistic Modal Music," 39.
38. Knox, "Brief Presentation of Brouwer's Lattice and the Deontic Miracle," 52.
39. See Hennix, *Nadam Brahman*.
40. The composite waveform consisted of a tetrachord in just intonation.
41. The program of the Dream Music Festival is contained in the booklet accompanying *Brouwer's Lattice*. According to Hennix, some of the early performances in the program were cancelled because of technical problems related to creating feedback, but the rest occurred, including the presentation of works by La Monte Young, Charles Ives, and Terry Jennings, because the group "wanted to emphasize that even 3 people can be very versatile" (Hennix, interview by author August 14, 2019) and to present musics that had not been heard in Sweden at that time. Of the Ives piece, "Blank Page Music," Hennix notes that it can be found in Cage's *Notations* book, and that the performance consisted of the group throwing multiple copies of the notation page into the audience.
42. Hennix, interview by author, August 14, 2019.
43. Hennix, *Electric Harpsichord*; Hennix, "Well-Tuned Marimba."
44. Flynt, "Christer Hennix," liner notes to Hennix, *Electric Harpsichord*, CD; reprinted in Hennix, *Poësy Matters and Other Matters*, 2:164.

45. Yessenin-Volpin, "On the Logic of the Moral Sciences."
46. Hennix, "Notes on Toposes and Adjoints," 84–85.
47. Hennix quoted in Knox, "Brief Presentation of Brouwer's Lattice and the Deontic Miracle," 53.
48. Hennix, "Modalities and Languages for Algorithms," 141.
49. Hennix, "Modalities and Languages for Algorithms," 148.
50. This piece was first conceived in 1970 as "Solo for Tambura" but then reconceived as a piece for two tamburas as a duet in Amsterdam in the early 1990s, which then became a solo piece since no one wanted to play with her. The recording of the piece we listened to was made in Berlin in 2014.
51. See Melchiori, "Psychoanalysis in Early Italian Feminism."
52. Lacan, *Four Fundamental Concepts*, 6.
53. For example, in Lacan, *Seminar XX: Encore! On Feminine Sexuality*.
54. Lacan, *Four Fundamental Concepts*, 268.
55. Hennix, interview by author, August 22, 2010.
56. Hennix and Flynt, "Philosophy of Concept Art."
57. Flynt's work also remains shockingly understudied. Flynt has documented his own writing and thought on his website http://www.henryflynt.org. Important accounts of parts of Flynt's work can be found in Piekut, "Demolish Serious Culture!"; and Grubbs, "Henry Flynt on the Air."
58. Catherine Christer Hennix and Henry Flynt, "Press Release for Feb. 7, 1979, show at the Kitchen Center for Video and Music," 1979.
59. Hennix and Flynt, "Press Release for Feb. 7, 1979, show."
60. Ken Emerson, "Music: Kitchen Trancing," *New York Times*, February 9, 1979, C 27.
61. Hennix and Flynt, "Press Release for Feb. 7, 1979 show."
62. See Henry Flynt's unpublished "HESE Logic" and the various texts on metatechnology found on Flynt's website (http://www.henryflynt.org), notably, in terms of the history of the concept, "Preface to Collected Writings on Meta-Technology."
63. Flynt, "Christer Hennix," 164.
64. Hui, *Question Concerning Technology in China*.
65. Stiegler, *Technics and Time*.
66. See Flynt's important essay "The Collectivity after the Abolition of the Universe and Time."
67. Young and Zazeela, "Dream House," 16.
68. Flynt and Hennix, "Illuminatory Sound Environment," 269.
69. Lawvere, "Comments on the Development of Topos Theory," 716.
70. Grothendieck's discussion of the topos can be found in "Topos" in the *Théorie des topos et cohomologie étale des schemas, Séminaire de Géométrie Algébrique du Bois Marie*, 4, 1963–4, 1: 299–518. For Lawvere, see Lawvere, "Comments on the Development of Topos Theory."
71. Badiou, *Mathematics of the Transcendental*, 253–54.
72. The best introduction to category and topos theory remains Robert Goldblatt's *Topoi: The Categoric Analysis of Logic* (1984). A more recent introductory text is David Spivak's *Category Theory for Scientists* (2013). The philosophically engaged reader may

find Alain Badiou's *Mathematics of the Transcendental* and *Logics of Worlds* to be helpful, as well as Fernando Zalamea's *Synthetic Philosophy of Mathematics*.

73. Montague, *Formal Philosophy*; Lambek, "Mathematics of Sentence Structure."

74. This paper has yet to be published.

75. Freud's first topographical model, comprising unconscious, preconscious, and conscious cognitive systems and their interplay, was set out in *The Interpretation of Dreams* (1900). His second model, consisting of superego, ego, and id was set out in *The Ego and the Id* (1922). Lacan's interest in topological models of the psyche was extensive but is best known via the Borromean Knot of symbolic, imaginary, and real set out first in *Seminar XX: Encore! On Feminine Sexuality* (1972–73).

76. See Hennix, "La Séminaire," 207–21, and also the important note on "Topos One" and "L'étourdi," in *Sonoilluminescences*, 11.

77. The idea of an intension can be traced back at least to Frege and the idea of a gap between meaning and designation. For Hennix, Montague's use of the term *intensional logic* in his set theoretical work on grammar was significant, yet Hennix's own use of the term is more complex since it is applied to perception and the logic (linguistic, mathematical) by which a perception is given meaning—with the idea that it is possible to propose alternative intensional logics to those normatively obtained by humans participating in society.

78. Hennix, "17 Points on Intensional Logics" (unpublished manuscript), 2.

79. Hennix, "Excerpt from Notes on the Composite Sine Wave Drone," 26.

80. Hennix, "Excerpt from Notes on the Composite Sine Wave Drone," 20–21.

81. Hennix, "Excerpt from Notes on the Composite Sine Wave Drone," 27, corrected for typos using 2010 text accompanying CD.

82. See van Dalen, "Return of the Flowing Continuum." Note in particular this quote from Brouwer: "Ur-intuition of two-ness (twoity): The intuitions of the continous and the discrete join here, as the second is thought not by itself, but under preservation of the recollection of the first. The first and the second are thus kept together and the intuition of the continuous consists in this keeping together (continere = keeping together)" (138).

83. There is an important untranslated 100-page text by Hennix regarding Lacan and perspectivism, which was prepared for a 1995 Stockholm show.

84. Wen, *Quantum Field Theory of Many-Body Systems*. For a summary of Wen's work accessible to nonspecialists, see Wen, "Choreographed Entanglement Dances."

85. Hennix, "Hilbert Space Shruti Box," 277–91.

86. Hennix, "Bismillāhi-r-Raḥmāni-r-Raḥīm," in *Sonoilluminescences*, 47.

87. Kristeva, *Revolution in Poetic Language*, 25.

88. The psychoanalytic description of the body/psyche as an energy matrix begins with Freud's early writings. It is there in Lacan's early work, notably "The Mirror Stage as Formative of the Function of the *I* as Revealed in Psychoanalytic Experience," and *Seminar II: The Ego in Freud's Theory and in the Technique of Psychoanalysis*. Jean Laplanche's *Life and Death in Psychoanalysis* has an important discussion of energy. Julia Kristeva's work on the chora can be found in *Revolution in Poetic Language*, 25–30. For a broader consideration of energy as artistic medium, see Douglas Kahn, *Earth Sound, Earth Signal*, and his edited collection, *Energy and the Arts*.

89. The question as to how feasible this is is an interesting one: Hennix's friend and interlocutor Bill Dietz examined this in his essay "More Repression," which he begins by audaciously dismissing both music and sex as normatively trapped in relation to the pleasure principle and "reproductive mimesis."

Back to music and sex: the failure of both to radically transform normal life is tied to their pathological and ideological tendency toward 'formlessness,' an effect of the 'exceptional' positions (temporal, spatial) of each vis-à-vis the everyday. Composition is also made up of forms and materials, but moves to dynamize instead of annihilate its body. Here, it becomes critical not only to insist on but also to affirm repression: not to be nonstructured, but to be changeably structured; not to be singularly or normatively repressed, and also not to be nonrepressed, but to be changeably repressed; to compose and recompose, (as) a species, a community, (our) repression; our bodies, bounds, relations.

90. Freud, "Uncanny."
91. See also Hennix, "Excerpts from Parmenides and Intensional Logics."
92. Hennix, "OM," 305.
93. Heidegger wrote about and taught Parmenides on several occasions: the 1932 lecture course on Parmenides (and Anaximander) published as vol. 35 of Heidegger's *Collected Works* in German and as *The Beginning of Western Philosophy: Interpretation of Anaximander and Parmenides* (Bloomington: Indiana University Press, 2015); and the 1942–43 lecture course on Parmenides (and Heraclitus), published as vol. 54 of the *Collected Works*, and as *Parmenides* (Bloomington: Indiana University Press, 1998).
94. Parmenides in Stein, "Notes Towards a Translation of Parmenides," 426–27.
95. Hennix, *Blues Alif Lam Mim*, 6.
96. Hennix, *Blues Alif Lam Mim*, 7.
97. It should be noted that Brouwer himself seems to have worked philosophically in a more or less Kantian framework of space and time—and that he himself was not necessarily aware of the implications of his own mathematical thought for such a philosophy, despite his own evidently spiritual disposition. The same thing could be said for Grothendieck, who, despite his own obsession with spirituality, especially in his later written works such as *Récoltes et semailles*, apparently never made a direct connection between his own spiritual interests and the concept of the topos.

CHAPTER THREE: MUSIC AND THE CONTINUUM

Epigraphs: Baraka, "Changing Same," 216; Hennix, "Excerpts from Notes on the Composite Sound Form," 32.

1. Catherine Christer Hennix, interview by author, May 2016.
2. Many of the great mathematicians of the twentieth century, including Brouwer, Weyl, Gödel, and Cohen responded to the problem of the continuum. There is no single book that surveys this history. See, however, Buckley, *Continuity Debate*.
3. Van Dalen, "Return of the Flowing Continuum."
4. Weyl, *Continuum*. See also Giuseppe Longo's discussion of different mathematical and philosophical models of continuity in "Mathematical Continuum," 401–27.
5. Toussaint, *The Geometry of Musical Rhythm*.

6. Christoph Cox has emphasized the importance of the idea of the continuum in his work on the ontology of sound. In Cox's work, the continuum consists of an infinite sonic multiplicity or flux, one that is virtual in relation to music and speech which consist of local "contractions" of this continuum. Cox draws on Leibniz and Deleuze in his work—I believe that the model Hennix proposes (and which I draw on) has some affinities with this work, but Cox, and indeed most Deleuzian vibrational theorists, miss the connections between the continuum of sound and the problem of the mathematical continuum, not to mention the real continuum, if there is one. This is why Badiou's dispute with Deleuze regarding mathematics matters. See Cox, *Sonic Flux*.

7. Zalamea, *Peirce's Logic of Continuity*.
8. See Peirce, "On Multitudes," 198.
9. Zalamea, *Peirce's Logic of Continuity*, 17.
10. Hennix, "Notes on Intuitionistic Modal Music," 39.
11. Hennix, "Notes on Intuitionistic Modal Music," 39.
12. Rouget, *Music and Trance*.
13. Latour, *Inquiry into Modes of Existence*; Badiou, *Logics of Worlds*; Agamben, *Use of Bodies*, 195–262. But note also Souriau's *Different Modes of Existence*—an important influence on Stengers and Latour even if Souriau in fact takes a (Parmenidean) position that asserts the very ontological ground that Stengers and Latour seek to avoid.
14. Maceda, *Gongs and Bamboo*.
15. Zalamea, *Synthetic Philosophy of Contemporary Mathematics*.
16. Caramello, *Theories, Sites, Toposes*.
17. Mazzola, *Topos of Music*.
18. Mazzola, *Topos of Music*, 437.
19. Note that Mazzola, who is also a practicing jazz musician, does address these topics in some of his other publications, including works on free jazz/improvisation and Hindustani classical music. See Mazzola and Cherlin, *Flow, Gesture and Spaces in Free Jazz*; and Chakraborty, Mazzola, Tewari, and Patra, *Computational Musicology in Hindustani Music*.
20. Lomax, *Alan Lomax: Selected Writings 1934–1997*, 238. Lomax's major statement on this project, "Song Structure and Social Structure," is contained in this volume.
21. Henriques, *Sonic Bodies*.
22. Henriques, *Sonic Bodies*, 20–24.
23. Mazzola, *Topos of Music*, 2nd ed., 1:21.
24. See chap. 2, note 74 for references.
25. Nishida, "Logic of 'Topos.'"
26. Negarestani, *Intelligence and Spirit*.
27. Hennix, "Bismillāhi-r-Raḥmāni-r-Raḥīm," in *Sonoilluminescences*, 45.
28. Boon, "Catherine Christer Hennix with Marcus Boon, Part 2."
29. The topic remains remarkably neglected. See Cornel West, "In Memory of Marvin Gaye," 473.
30. Xenakis, *Formalized Music*, 193–94.
31. Cott and Stockhausen, *Stockhausen*, 151.
32. Bebey, *African Music*, 8.

33. Daniélou, *Sémantique musicale*.
34. Philip Corner, interview by author, 2003.
35. Stobart, *Music and the Poetics of Production*, 244.
36. Philip Corner, interview by author, 2003.
37. Phill Niblock, interview by author (unpublished), April 21, 2014.
38. Stockhausen, "How Time Passes," 10.

39. Stiegler's work contains an equally obvious set of aporias, notably those relating to non-Western philosophical traditions, as Hui points out, but also those related to feminist philosophy, as in the work of Luce Irigaray, which addresses these problems in a different and significant way.

40. Stiegler, *Technics and Time*.
41. Stiegler, *Symbolic Misery*, 2:11.

42. Husserl's initial discussion of melody can be found in *On the Phenomenology of the Consciousness of Internal Time*, 11–14; Stiegler's in *Technics and Time, 1*, 245–46. Stiegler's most extensive discussion can be found in *Technics and Time, 2*, 190–227.

43. Stiegler, *Technics and Time*, 3:187–223.
44. Zuckerkandl, *Sound and Symbol*.
45. Zuckerkandl, *Sound and Symbol*, 339.
46. Deleuze, *Bergsonism*.

47. Santos's *Ritmanálise* was evidently only circulated in mimeographed form, which is how Bachelard read it—unfortunately, no copies of the manuscript have been preserved. However, three articles published in the Brazilian press by Santos have been summarized in the remarkable biographical article by Geraldo Dias, "Nietzsche, precursor da *Ritmanálise*?" Evidently, Santos developed a phenomenology of rhythm that could address the question stimulated by quantum physics as to how vibration could condense as different forms of matter. Santos saw Nietzsche as the precursor of "rhythmanalysis."

48. Bachelard, *Dialectic of Duration*.
49. Bachelard, *Dialectic of Duration*, 131–32.
50. Miles Davis, quoted in Carr, *Miles Davis*, 247.

51. There are references to "ma" and "ma ontologies" going back at least as far as "The Yellow Book," Hennix's contribution to Being = Space × Action. The most recent and stunning version is to be found in the 2021 text "MA-ONTOLOGIES: From the MA-Notebooks...," which remains unpublished.

52. Moten, "Manic Depression."
53. Stein, "Notes towards a Translation of Parmenides."

54. For a brilliant rethinking of gesture emerging out of Peirce and Zalamea's work, see Maddalena, *Philosophy of Gesture*.

55. Serres and Latour, *Conversations on Science, Culture, and Time*, 59.
56. Sri Karunamayee, interview by author, 2001.
57. Brouwer, *Cambridge Lectures on Intuitionism*, 4–5..
58. Haino, interview by Alan Cummings.
59. Morton, *Hyperobjects*.

60. Although Bruce Chatwin's *The Songlines* has been criticized for inaccuracy, more recent texts, such as Barbara Glowczewski's support the notion of a geomantic vibrational

continuum as a component of Indigenous Australian thought. Glowczewski, *Desert Dreamers*.

61. Rouget, *Music and Trance*.
62. Robinson, *Hungry Listening*, 96.
63. Viveiros de Castro, "Cosmological Perspectivism."
64. Kopenawa, *Falling Sky*, 58–59.
65. Baraka, *Digging*, 250.
66. Baraka, *Digging*, 250.
67. Quoted in Shabda Khan's contribution to "Guruji in Memory," accessed December 9, 2021, https://srikarunamayee.com/guruji-in-memory/.
68. Bachelard, *Dialectic of Duration*, 122.
69. Lacan, "Instance of the Letter in the Unconscious," 430.
70. Haino, interview by Alan Cummings.
71. Sloterdijk, *You Must Change Your Life*.
72. Of Charlie Patton's recordings, Moten says: "What I would mean to say is that it's a tremble which produces the narrow and specific, fleeting and utterly and necessarily incomplete notion of the self among a bunch of other things that it does. There's this phenomenon we like to call the self and one of the effects of the music comes under that name, or gives us a sense of what comes under that name, but at the very moment it gives us a sense of that it gives us a sense of the absolute limitations and smallness of that, and maybe even what I would call the unreality of that." Fitzgerald, "Interview with Fred Moten, Part 2."
73. Eidsheim, *Sensing Sound*.
74. My friend Eric Chenaux taught me this. See Boon, "Global Ear."
75. Robert Palmer, quoted in P. N. Wilson, *Ornette Coleman*, 57.
76. Schuyler, "Joujouka/Jajouka/Zahjoukah."
77. Lacan, *Seminar XX: Encore! On Feminine Sexuality*, 5. The translation is mine, and is precisely the translation that Fink says one should not make. Lacan is evidently being ironic when he makes this statement, but, following Hennix, I take an ironic position on this irony, such that the barred O̶n̶e̶ remains at least mappable.
78. Here, I draw on Étienne Balibar's analysis in *On Universals*.
79. Fink, *Lacanian Subject*, 24.
80. Leikert, "Object of Jouissance in Music."
81. Knox and Knox, "Pandit Pran Nath: The Sayings of Gurgi," 452.
82. Scruton, *Aesthetics of Music*, 117.
83. Frankie Knuckles, email to Global House discussion group, May 18, 1997.
84. Bataille, *Erotism*, 13, 15.
85. Bataille, *Erotism*, 15.
86. Grosz, *Chaos, Territory, Art*.
87. My reading of Bataille here is inflected by Jacques Derrida's famous essay on Bataille, "From Restricted to General Economy." It also opens up onto the territory explored by Jean-Luc Nancy in his book *Listening*.
88. See Kapchan, *Traveling Spirit Masters*; and Becker, *Blackness in Morocco*.
89. Bataille, *Erotism*, 15.

90. Bataille, *Erotism*, 15.
91. Sister Sledge, "Lost in Music," on *All American Girls* LP.
92. Karma-gliṅ-pa, *Tibetan Book of the Dead*, loc. 998–1001, Kindle.
93. Karma-gliṅ-pa, *Tibetan Book of the Dead*, loc. 1104–1108, Kindle.
94. Karma-gliṅ-pa, *Tibetan Book of the Dead*, loc. 3715–3720, Kindle.
95. "Continuum" would be "samtāna" in Sanskrit, and "rgyud" in Tibetan, "a term used to designate an uninterrupted sequence of cause and effect, especially a sequence of mental moments" (Lopez Jr. and Buswell Jr., *The Princeton Dictionary of Buddhism*, loc. 57322, Kindle). But it is also "tantra" (in Tibetan, another meaning of "rgyud"). "In Sanskrit, lit. 'continuum'; a term derived from the Sanskrit root tan ('to stretch out,' 'to weave'), having the sense of an arrangement or a pattern" (Lopez Jr. and Buswell Jr., *The Princeton Dictionary of Buddhism*, loc. 67450, Kindle).

CHAPTER FOUR: SLOWED AND THROWED

Epigraph: Shabazz Palaces, *Black Up*, CD, 2011.

1. I take the idea of a "time regime" from Heidegger's historicization of the concept of time in his 1925 lecture course, published as *History of the Concept of Time*, and his critique of the "vulgar [i.e., chronological] concept of time" in *Being and Time*, 371–75. See also Paul Virilio's analysis of "chronopolitics" in "Colonization of Time," 67–76.
2. Lamar, "Mortal Man," on *To Pimp a Butterfly* CD.
3. Veal, *Fela*.
4. On Sun Ra, see Szwed, *Space Is the Place*; on Perry's Black Ark, see Katz, *People Funny Boy*. The term *Afrofuturism* has gone through a number of iterations: I have learned from the "Afrofuturism" special issue of *Social Text* (20, no. 2 [2002]), edited by Alondra Nelson; and Mark Dery's "Black to the Future."
5. Shortly before completing the final draft of this book, I read Jayna Brown's *Black Utopias*, with its brilliant chapter on Alice Coltrane's ashram music and spirituality, finally setting out some of what was at stake in Coltrane's radical practice—and her lucid reading of Sun Ra's life and work. What she calls "utopian" and what I call "cosmopolitical" resonate in powerful ways.
6. I draw here on Greg Tate's important essay "Hip Hop Turns 30," in which he argues that hip-hop in America could never have been simply an autonomous folk culture emerging in the Bronx in the 1970s, and that what hip-hop is cannot be separated from the ways in which it has adapted to the (racist, capitalist, global) marketplace. Yet hip-hop also cannot be separated from a certain cosmopolitical insistence on the "otherwise" that continues to emerge in powerful and surprising ways.
7. Lefebvre, *Production of Space*.
8. Lipsitz, "Racialization of Space"; Robinson, *Hungry Listening*.
9. Reed, *Mumbo Jumbo*, 211.
10. Reed, *Mumbo Jumbo*, 5.
11. Reed, *Mumbo Jumbo*, 211.
12. Tutuola, *My Life in the Bush of Ghosts*.
13. Kgositsile, *Homesoil in My Blood*, 222.

14. Kgositsile, *Homesoil in My Blood*, 223.
15. Keorapetse Kgositsile, quoted in Jaji, "Sound Effects," 293.
16. The idea of decolonizing time can be found in a variety of disciplines, for example the anthropologist Kathleen Pickering's "Decolonizing Time Regimes"; see also political scientist Nichole Shippen's *Decolonizing Time*.
17. Baraka, "Changing Same," 206.
18. Baraka, "Changing Same," 206.
19. Morrison, *Beloved*.
20. Stoever, *Sonic Color Line*, 7.
21. Baraka, "Changing Same," 213.
22. Baraka, "Changing Same," 226.
23. DJ Sprinkles, "Midtown 120 Blues Intro," on *Midtown 120 Blues* CD.
24. My preference is the appearance of this vocal on the 1988 remix of Mr. Fingers's "Can You Feel It."
25. Hegel, *Phenomenology of Spirit*, 9.
26. Gilroy, *Postcolonial Melancholia*.
27. See Beverly, *Sweet Jones*, 128–31.
28. "One Day" appears on the mixtapes *Chapter 70: Endonesia*, *Chapter 71: The Final Chapter*, and on *Chapter 208: Austin to Houston Part 2*.
29. Walker, *Houston Rap Tapes*, 228.
30. As of this writing, Lance Scott Walker's long-awaited biography of DJ Screw is due to be published in 2022. Walker's oral history books, *Houston Rap* and *Houston Rap Tapes: An Oral History of Bayou City Hip-Hop*, remain the best sources for historical and biographical information about Screw and his Click. I have also drawn in this chapter on the following articles: Hall, "Slow Life and Fast Death of DJ Screw"; Walker, "Fast Life in Slow Motion"; Jesse Washington, "Life in the Slow Lane," *Houston Press*, January 18, 2001, https://www.houstonpress.com/news/life-in-the-slow-lane-6562149; Matt Sonzala's interview with Screw's mother, Ida Davis, "DJ Screw," in *Murder Dog* 9, no. 3 (2002): 100–101; the interview with Screw's long-term girlfriend Nikki Williams in the documentary film *DJ Screw: The Untold Story*; and the biography of Screw on the official DJ Screw website, https://www.djscrew.com/dj-screw.
31. On the history of Houston, see McComb, *Houston*.
32. On the history of people of African descent in Houston, see Beeth and Wintz, *Black Dixie*; and Steptoe, *Houston Bound*.
33. On the history of Black music in Houston, see Steptoe, *Houston Bound*; Hartman, *History of Texas Music*, 56–99; and Walker, *Houston Rap Tapes*.
34. Screw released *All Screwed Up*, vol. 2, and *3 'N the Mornin'*, parts 1 and 2, all in 1995 on Bigtyme Recordz; in 1999 he released *All Work No Play* on Jam Down Records.
35. LaBelle, *Acoustic Territories*.
36. Alice Coltrane issued recordings made at Sai Anantam Ashram such as "Turiya Sings" and "Divine Songs" under the name Turiyasangitananda as cassettes and CDs on her Avatar Book Institute label; Laraaji issued cassettes of his vibrational/therapeutic music such as "Om Namah Shivaya" on his Celestial Vibration label in the 1980s.
37. Hirschkind, *Ethical Soundscape*; Manuel, *Cassette Culture*.

38. "Interview with DJ Screw from *Murder Dog*," October 1997, accessed December 1, 2021, http://web.archive.org/web/20020602153227/www.murderdog.com/archives/djscrew/djscrew.html.

39. Paul Wall, quoted in Rys, "Houston Rappers Remember DJ Screw."

40. Walker, *Houston Rap Tapes*.

41. Kelefa Sanneh, "The Strangest Sound in Hip Hop Goes National," *New York Times*, April 17, 2005, http://www.nytimes.com/2005/04/17/arts/music/the-strangest-sound-in-hiphop-goes-national.html.

42. Sheldon Pearce, "From DJ Screw to Moonlight: The Unlikely Return of Chopped and Screwed," *Guardian*, January 24, 2017, https://www.theguardian.com/music/2017/jan/24/chopped-screwed-hip-hop-dj-screw-moonlight.

43. Veal, *Dub*.

44. See Du Bois, *Souls of Black Folk*, 9.

45. Koepnick, *On Slowness*, 10, Kindle.

46. Koepnick, *On Slowness*, 20, Kindle.

47. Koepnick, *On Slowness*, 27–28, Kindle.

48. Koepnick, *On Slowness*, 45, Kindle.

49. Eshun, *More Brilliant Than the Sun*.

50. Weheliye, "'Feenin.'"

51. DJ Screw, quoted in Allah, "DJ Screw: Givin' It to Ya Slow," 84.

52. DJ Screw, *Chapter 30: G Love*, n.d.

53. Russell, *Bird Lives!*, 91.

54. Stiegler, *Symbolic Misery*, 2:15.

55. Benjamin, "Work of Art in the Age of Its Reproducibility," 117. There are other references within Benjamin's work, and also a considerable secondary literature on the optical unconscious—usefully summarized in Shawn Michelle Smith and Sharon Sliwinski's introduction to their edited collection *Photography and the Optical Unconscious*.

56. Reed, *Mumbo Jumbo*, 4–6.

57. On the history of the blues in Houston, see Faniel, *Hip-Hop in Houston*.

58. "City Country City" appears on War's 1972 album *The World Is a Ghetto*.

59. Taussig, *Shamanism, Colonialism, and the Wild Man*.

60. Trungpa, *Orderly Chaos*, 18.

61. It's also the title of one of the key avant-funk tracks emerging out of New York in the early 1980s, Defunkt's "The Razor's Edge."

62. Hall, "Slow Life and Fast Death of DJ Screw."

63. Hall, "Slow Life and Fast Death of DJ Screw."

64. Cocteau, *Opium*, 36.

65. Screw, quoted in Allah, "DJ Screw: Givin' It to Ya Slow."

66. Hall, "Slow Life and Fast Death of DJ Screw."

67. Gilroy, *Postcolonial Melancholia*.

68. See Fisher, "Organizing in the Private City."

69. De Rienzo, Dana Beal, and Members of the Staten Island Project, *Report on the Staten Island Project*.

70. Lamar, "Mortal Man," on *To Pimp a Butterfly* CD.

71. Lamar, "Mortal Man," on *To Pimp a Butterfly* CD.

72. Earl Sweatshirt, "Red Water," *Some Rap Songs*, https://genius.com/Earl-sweatshirt-red-water-lyrics.

73. Moten, "Black Mo'nin,'" 60.

74. Crawley, *Blackpentecostal Breath*.

75. I take the word *interbeing* from the Vietnamese Buddhist monk Thich Nhat Hanh's work—but I relate it to the description of social or collective embodied spirituality found in Crawley's descriptions of the Black church.

76. Olson, *Muthologos*, 1:62.

77. Shvarts, "Troubled Air," 14–15.

78. Passages open up here in the direction of Eric Lott's work on the cultural history of blackface in *Love and Theft* and *Black Mirror*; and Jennifer Stoever's work on the sonic color line in *Sonic Color Line*.

79. Spice 1, "Welcome to the Ghetto," on *Spice 1* CD. Transcription of lyrics taken from Rap Genius website, July 1, 2018, https://genius.com/Spice-1-welcome-to-the-ghetto-lyrics.

80. DJ Screw mix, "Welcome to the Ghetto."

81. Sexton, "Afro-Pessimism."

82. Moten, "Blackness and Nothingness."

83. Moten, "Black Topological Existence," 7.

84. Lonnie Holley, *Just before Music* (Dust to Digital CD, 2012).

85. Crawley, *Blackpentecostal Breath*, 176.

86. See K-Rino's interview in Walker, *Houston Rap Tapes*, 102–14.

87. Walker, "Fast Life in Slow Motion."

88. Megan Halverson, "Swangin' and Bangin' . . . and Getting to That Other Level with the Disciples of Screw," *Houston Press*, February 27, 1997, https://www.houstonpress.com/news/swangin-and-bangin-and-getting-to-that-other-level-with-the-disciples-of-screw-6574814.

89. DJ Screw, quote from "Interview with DJ Screw from *Murder Dog*," October 1997.

90. See interviews with Screw's friends in the documentary *DJ Screw: The Untold Story*.

91. See Shorty Mac's recollections in *Houston Rap Tapes*, 2nd ed., 226–27.

92. Fanon, *Black Skin, White Masks*, 110.

93. Svoboda, *Aghora III*.

94. Davis, *Miles*.

95. Wallace, "Amen! (D'Angelo's Back)."

96. DJ Screw, *Chapter 47: Pussy Weed and Alcohol* (1998).

97. Michael Cooper, "Hear How 'Moonlight' Got Its Sound: Violins, Chopped and Screwed," *New York Times*, February 21, 2017, https://www.nytimes.com/2017/02/21/arts/music/moonlight-movie-score-music-oscars.html.

98. Harney and Moten, *Undercommons*, 140–41.

99. Comments to DJ Screw, "June 27th," track uploaded December 21, 2010, comment made "4 years ago," YouTube, accessed November 10, 2021, https://www.youtube.com/watch?v=DZeu29nOwjw.

100. Taken from the city of Toronto's Land Acknowledgment webpage, December 2, 2021, https://www.toronto.ca/city-government/accessibility-human-rights/indigenous-affairs-office/land-acknowledgement/.

101. "Lil Wayne's Advice to Drake: 'Be Yourself,'" CBS interview, YouTube, October 5, 2010. https://www.youtube.com/watch?v=IQKSc-bv7I0.

102. Dizzee appeared on KPFT's *Damage Control* show on April 15, 2005. Dizzee's track "H Town," with Bun B.

103. Fisher, "Man Who Has Everything"; see also Fisher, *Ghosts of My Life*.

104. Lacan's main statement on the topic is found in Lacan, "Du discours psychanalytique"; see also Vanheule, "Capitalist Discourse, Subjectivity and Lacanian Psychoanalysis."

105. For a useful discussion of powwow music, see Hoefnagels, "Northern Style Powwow Music."

106. Bear Witness, interview by author, October 2018.

107. Chris Kelly, "How Moombahton Went from the Hot Sound to Passe to Influencing Today's Biggest Pop Hits," *Washington Post*, August 23, 2017, accessed July 15, 2019, https://www.washingtonpost.com/lifestyle/moombahton-ran-its-course-but-now-it-can-be-heard-in-pop-musics-biggest-hits/2017/08/23/c2e282e0-867d-11e7-a94f-3139abce39f5_story.html?noredirect=on&utm_term=.8d4eebd5973e.

108. In fact, the tempo of powwow rhythms, like that of heartbeats, is variable, with a speeding up of tempo occurring in certain songs—although (tellingly) ethnomusicological studies of powwow rhythms say very little about actual tempos or bpms.

109. Bear Witness, comments made at X-Avant Panel, Music Gallery, Toronto, October 2018, transcribed by the author.

110. Bob Marley and the Wailers, "Lively Up Yourself."

CODA

1. The Slits, "In the Beginning There Was Rhythm."

Bibliography

Agamben, Giorgio. *The Use of Bodies*. Translated by Adam Kotsko. Stanford, CA: Stanford University Press, 2016.

Alavi, Seema. *Muslim Cosmopolitanism in the Age of Empire*. Cambridge, MA: Harvard University Press, 2015.

Alexander, Stephon. *The Jazz of Physics*: The Secret Link between Music and the Structure of the Universe. New York: Basic Books, 2016.

Allah, Bilal. "DJ Screw: Givin' It to Ya Slow." *Rap Pages*, November 1995.

Attali, Jacques. *Noise: The Political Economy of Music*. Translated by Brian Massumi. Minneapolis: University of Minnesota Press, 2014.

Bachelard, Gaston. *The Dialectic of Duration*. Translated by Mary McAllester Jones. London: Rowman and Littlefield International, 2016.

Badiou, Alain. *Being and Event*. Translated by Oliver Feltham. London: Continuum, 2006.

Badiou, Alain. *Logics of Worlds: Being and Event II*. Translated by Alberto Toscano. London: Bloomsbury, 2009.

Badiou, Alain. *Mathematics of the Transcendental*. Translated by A. J. Bartlett and Alex Ling. London: Bloomsbury, 2014.

Bakhle, Janaki. *Two Men and Music: Nationalism in the Making of an Indian Classical Tradition*. Oxford: Oxford University Press, 2005.

Balibar, Étienne. *On Universals: Constructing and Deconstructing Community*. Translated by Joshua David Jordan. New York: Fordham University Press, 2020.

Baraka, Amiri. "The Changing Same: R&B and New Black Music." In *Black Music: Essays*, 205–41. New York: Akashic, 2009.

Baraka, Amiri. *Digging: The Afro-American Soul of American Classical Music*. Berkeley: University of California Press, 2010.

Bataille, Georges. *The Accursed Share*. Vol. 1. Translated by Robert Hurley. New York: Zone Books, 1988.

Bataille, Georges. *Erotism: Death and Sensuality*. Translated by Mary Dalwood. San Francisco, CA: City Lights Books, 1962.

Bataille, Georges. *The Unfinished System of Nonknowledge.* Translated by Michelle Kendall and Stuart Kendall. Minneapolis: University of Minnesota Press, 2004.

Bebey, Francis. *African Music: A People's Art.* Westport, CT: Lawrence Hill Books, 1980.

Becker, Cynthia. *Blackness in Morocco: Gnawa Identity through Music and Visual Cultures.* Minneapolis: University of Minnesota Press, 2020.

Beeth, Howard, and Cary D. Wintz, eds. *Black Dixie: Afro-Texan History and Culture in Houston.* College Station: Texas A&M University Press, 1992.

Benjamin, Walter. "The Work of Art in the Age of Its Reproducibility, Second Version." In *Selected Writings*, 3:101–33. Cambridge, MA: Harvard University Press, 2002.

Beverly, Julia. *Sweet Jones: Pimp C's Trill Life Story.* Atlanta: Shreveport Ave Inc., 2015.

Bhatnagar, Shyamji, and David Isaacs. *Microchakras: InnerTuning for Psychological Well-Being.* Rochester, VT: Inner Traditions, 2009.

Boon, Marcus. "Catherine Christer Hennix with Marcus Boon, Part 2." *Brooklyn Rail* (October 2020). https://brooklynrail.org/2020/10/music/CATHERINE-CHRISTER-HENNIX.

Boon, Marcus. "The Eternal Drone." In *Undercurrents: The Hidden Wiring of Modern Music*, edited by Rob Young, 59–70. London: Continuum, 2003.

Boon, Marcus. "Global Ear: Toronto." *Wire*, no. 263 (January 2006). http://marcusboon.com/global-ear-toronto/.

Boon, Marcus. "Ocean of Sound (Ocean of Silence)." *Ascent* 14 (Summer 2002). https://marcusboon.com/ocean-of-sound-ocean-of-silence-siri-karunamayee-talks-to-marcus-boon/.

Boon, Marcus. "Shaking the Foundations: An Interview with Catherine Christer Hennix." *Wire*, no. 320 (October 2010): 28–31.

Bradley, Cisco. *Universal Tonality: The Life and Music of William Parker.* Durham, NC: Duke University Press, 2021.

Brouwer, L. E. J. *Cambridge Lectures on Intuitionism.* Cambridge: Cambridge University Press, 1981.

Brown, Jayna. *Black Utopias: Speculative Life and the Music of Other Worlds.* Durham, NC: Duke University Press, 2021.

Buckley, Benjamin Lee. *The Continuity Debate: Dedekind, Cantor, du Bois-Reymond and Peirce on Continuity and Infinitesimals.* Boston, MA: Docent Press, 2012.

Caramello, Olivia. *Theories, Sites, Toposes: Relating and Studying Mathematical Theories through Topos-Theoretic 'Bridges.'* Oxford: Oxford University Press, 2018.

Carr, Ian. *Miles Davis: The Definitive Biography.* New York: Thunder's Mouth Press, 1998.

Chaffee, Cathleen, ed. *Introducing Tony Conrad: A Retrospective.* Buffalo, NY: Albright-Knox Art Gallery, 2018.

Chakraborty, Soubhik, Guerino Mazzola, Swarima Tewari, and Moujhuri Patra. *Computational Musicology in Hindustani Music.* Cham: Springer International, 2014.

Cheah, Pheng, and Bruce Robbins, eds. *Cosmopolitics: Thinking and Feeling beyond the Nation.* Minneapolis: University of Minnesota Press, 1998.

Cherry, Don, and Keith Knox. "Report to ABF." In *Blank Forms 06: Organic Music Societies,* edited by Lawrence Kumpf, 141–55. Brooklyn, NY: Blank Forms Editions, 2021.

Cocteau, Jean. *Opium: The Illustrated Diary of His Cure*. London: Peter Owen, 1990.

Colacello, Bob. "Remains of the Dia." *Vanity Fair*, April 30, 2008. https://www.vanityfair.com/magazine/1996/09/colacello199609.

Conrad, Tony. *Tony Conrad: Writings*. Brooklyn, NY: Primary Information, 2019.

Cott, Jonathan, and Karlheinz Stockhausen. *Stockhausen: Conversations with the Composer*. London: Picador Books, 1974.

Cox, Christoph. *Sonic Flux: Sound, Art, and Metaphysics*. Chicago: University of Chicago Press, 2018.

Crawley, Ashon. *Blackpentecostal Breath: The Aesthetics of Possibility*. New York: Fordham University Press, 2017.

Daniélou, Alain. "The Influence of Sound Phenomena on Human Consciousness." Translated by Paul Huebner and Ralph Metzner. *Psychedelic Review*, no. 7 (1965): 20–26.

Daniélou, Alain. *Introduction to the Study of Musical Scales*. London: India Society, 1943.

Daniélou, Alain. *Sémantique musicale: Essai de psychologie auditive*. Paris: Éditions Hermann, 1967.

Daniélou, Alain. *Tableau comparatif des intervalles musicaux*. Pondicherry: Institut français d'Indologie, 1958.

Davis, Miles. *Miles: The Autobiography*. New York: Simon and Schuster, 1990.

de la Cadena, Marisol. *Earth Beings: Ecologies of Practice across Andean Worlds*. Durham, NC: Duke University Press, 2015.

Deleuze, Gilles. *Bergsonism*. New York: Zone Books, 1991.

Deleuze, Gilles. *Difference and Repetition*. London: Continuum, 2004.

Deleuze, Gilles, and Félix Guattari. *A Thousand Plateaus*. Translated by Brian Massumi. Minneapolis: University of Minnesota Press, 1987.

de Rienzo, Paul, Dana Beal, and members of the Staten Island Project. *Report on the Staten Island Project: The Ibogaine Story*. Brooklyn, NY: Autonomedia, 1997.

Derrida, Jacques. "From Restricted to General Economy." In *Writing and Difference*, translated by Alan Bass, 251–77. London: Routledge and Kegan Paul, 2010.

Dery, Mark. "Black to the Future: Interviews with Samuel R. Delany, Greg Tate, and Tricia Rose." In *Flame Wars: The Discourse of Cyberculture*, edited by Mark Dery, 179–222. Durham, NC: Duke University Press, 1994.

Dhar, Sheila. *Here's Someone I'd Like You to Meet*. Delhi: Oxford University Press, 1996.

Dhar, Sheila. *The Kirana Legacy: Celebrating 70 Years of Ustad Niaz Ahmed Khan*. Mumbai: International Foundation for Fine Arts, 2000.

Dias, Geraldo. "Nietzsche, precursor da *Ritmanálise*? A recepção luso-brasileira do pensamento nietzschiano pelo *Filósofo fantasma* Lúcio Pinheiro dos Santos." *Revista Trágica: Estudos de filosofia da imanência, Rio de Janeiro* 11, no. 3 (2018): 41–58.

Diawara, Manthia. "All the Difference in the World." Kader Attia. Accessed November 11, 2021. http://kaderattia.de/all-the-difference-in-the-world-manthia-diawara-on-the-art-of-kader-attia/.

Dietz, Bill. "More Repression." *Ear | Wave | Event*, no. 3 (2014). http://earwaveevent.org/article/more-repression/.

DJ Screw: The Untold Story (Double Platinum, 2006), DVD.

DJ Sprinkles. *Midtown 120 Blues*. Japan: Mule Musiq, 2009. CD.

Du Bois, W. E. B. *The Souls of Black Folk*. Oxford: Oxford University Press, 2007.

Duckworth, William, and Richard Fleming, eds. *Sound and Light: La Monte Young, Marian Zazeela*. Lewisburg, PA: Bucknell University Press, 1996.

Eidsheim, Nina Sun. *Sensing Sound: Singing and Listening as Vibrational Practice*. Durham, NC: Duke University Press, 2015.

Eshun, Kodwo. *More Brilliant Than the Sun: Adventures in Sonic Fiction*. London: Verso Books, 2018.

Faniel, Maco. *Hip-Hop in Houston: The Origin and the Legacy*. Charleston, SC: History Press, 2013.

Fanon, Frantz. *Black Skin, White Masks*. New York: Grove Press, 1967.

Fanon, Frantz. *The Wretched of the Earth*. Translated by Richard Philcox. New York: Grove, 2005.

Fink, Bruce. *The Lacanian Subject: Between Language and Jouissance*. Princeton, NJ: Princeton University Press, 1995.

Fisher, Mark. *Ghosts of My Life: Writings on Depression, Hauntology and Lost Futures*. London: Zero Books, 2014.

Fisher, Mark. "The Man Who Has Everything: Drake's Nothing Was the Same." *Electronic Beats*. Accessed July 1, 2018. http://www.electronicbeats.net/started-from-the-bottom-mark-fisher-on-drakes-nothing-was-the-same/.

Fisher, Robert. "Organizing in the Private City: The Case of Houston Texas." In Beeth and Wintz, *Black Dixie*, 253–77.

Fitzgerald, Adam. "An Interview with Fred Moten, Part 2." *Literary Hub*. Accessed November 11, 2021. http://lithub.com/an-interview-with-fred-moten-pt-ii/.

Flynt, Henry. "Altered States." *Artforum*, January 2011. https://www.artforum.com/inprint/issue=201101&id=27040&show=activation.

Flynt, Henry. "Christer Hennix: The Electric Harpsichord." In Hennix, *Poësy Matters and Other Matters*, 2: 163–67.

Flynt, Henry. "The Collectivity after the Abolition of the Universe and Time: Escaping from Social Science," 1996. http://www.henryflynt.org/anarchic/collectivafter.html.

Flynt, Henry. "Encyclopedic Glossary." Unpublished manuscript, 1995.

Flynt, Henry. "HESE Logic." Unpublished manuscript, 1979.

Flynt, Henry. "Meta-Technology: An Analytical Sketch." Accessed February 11, 2021. http://www.henryflynt.org/meta_tech/metatech.html.

Flynt, Henry, ed. "Modalities and Language for Algorithms by Christer Hennix." 2nd ed. Unpublished manuscript, 1983.

Flynt, Henry. "On Pandit Pran Nath." Accessed November 11, 2021. http://www.henryflynt.org/aesthetics/on_pandit_pran_nath.htm.

Flynt, Henry. "The Philosophy of C. C. Hennix." Unpublished manuscript, 1996.

Flynt, Henry. "Preface to Collected Writings on Meta-Technology." 2006. http://www.henryflynt.org/meta_tech/metatech_preface.htm.

Flynt, Henry, and Catherine Christer Hennix. "The Illuminatory Sound Environment, ZKM Subraum Version, 21 III 13–12 V 13." In Hennix, *Poësy Matters and Other Matters*, 2:269.

Ford, Kenneth. *The Quantum World: Quantum Physics for Everyone*. Cambridge, MA: Harvard University Press, 2005.

Forti, Simone. *Handbook in Motion*. Halifax: Press of the Nova Scotia College of Art and Design, 1974.

Foucault, Michel. "The Ethics of the Concern of the Self as a Practice of Freedom." In *Ethics: Subjectivity and Truth*, translated by Robert Hurley, 281–301. New York: New Press, 1994.

Foucault, Michel. *The History of Sexuality*. Vol. 3, *The Care of the Self*. New York: Vintage Books, 1988.

Freud, Sigmund. "Project for a Scientific Psychology." In *The Standard Edition of the Complete Psychological Works of Sigmund Freud*, 1:283–99. London: Vintage Books, 2001.

Freud, Sigmund. "The Uncanny." In *The Standard Edition of the Complete Psychological Works of Sigmund Freud*, 17:219–52. London: Vintage Books, 2001.

Gallope, Michael. *Deep Refrains: Music, Philosophy, and the Ineffable*. Chicago: University of Chicago Press, 2017.

Gedacht, Joshua, and R. Michael Feener, eds. *Challenging Cosmopolitanism: Coercion, Mobility and Displacement in Islamic Asia*. Edinburgh: Edinburgh University Press, 2018.

Gerhardt, Spencer. "Domains of Variation: Choice Sequences, Continuously Variable Sets, Remarks on *The Yellow Book*." *Blank Forms*, no. 4 (2019): 95–150.

Gilroy, Paul. *Postcolonial Melancholia*. New York: Columbia University Press, 2006.

Glissant, Édouard. *Une nouvelle région du monde: Ésthétique I*. Paris: Gallimard, 2006.

Glowczewski, Barbara. *Desert Dreamers: With the Warlpiri People of Australia*. Minneapolis, MN: Univocal, 2016.

Gluck, Robert. "The Shiraz Arts Festival: Western Avant-Garde Arts in 1970s Iran." *Leonardo* 40, no. 1 (2007): 21–28.

Goldblatt. *Topoi: The Categoric Analysis of Logic*. 2nd ed. Amsterdam: Elsevier, 1984.

Goodman, Steve. *Sonic Warfare: Sound, Affect, and the Ecology of Fear*. Cambridge, MA: MIT Press, 2012.

Grimshaw, Jeremy. *Draw a Straight Line and Follow It: The Music and Mysticism of La Monte Young*. London: Oxford University Press, 2011.

Grimshaw, Jeremy. "Ideology of the Drone." In *Draw a Straight Line and Follow It*, 84–113.

Greene, Brian. *The Elegant Universe: Superstrings, Hidden Dimensions, and the Quest for the Ultimate Theory*. New York: W. W. Norton, 1999.

Gross, Jason. "A Travelogue of Jon Hassell's 'Fourth World' Journey into the Mystical." *Pop Matters*, January 20, 2015. https://www.popmatters.com/189828-a-travelogue-of-jon-hassells-fourth-world-journey-into-the-mystic-2495568887.html.

Grosz, Elizabeth. *Chaos, Territory, Art: Deleuze and the Framing of the Earth*. New York: Columbia University Press, 2008.

Grothendieck, Alexandre, and J. L Verdier. "Topos." In *Théorie des topos et cohomologie étale des schemas, Séminaire de Géométrie Algébrique du Bois Marie, 4, 1963–64*. Vol. 1, 299–518. Berlin, Springer-Verlag, 1972.

Grubbs, David. "Henry Flynt on the Air." In *Records Ruin the Landscape: John Cage, the Sixties, and Sound Recording*, 19–44. Durham, NC: Duke University Press, 2014.

Guattari, Félix. *Schizoanalytic Cartographies*. New York: Continuum, 2012.

Haino, Keiji. "Keiji Haino: An Interview by Alan Cummings." *Halana*, no. 2, pt. 4. Accessed, November 11, 2021. https://www.halana.com/haino.html.

Hall, Michael. "The Slow Life and Fast Death of DJ Screw." *Texas Monthly*, April 2001. https://www.texasmonthly.com/articles/the-slow-life-and-fast-death-of-dj-screw/.

Harney, Stefano, and Fred Moten. *The Undercommons: Fugitive Planning and Black Study*. Wivenhoe, UK: Minor Compositions, 2013.

Hartman, Gary. *The History of Texas Music*. College Station: Texas A&M University Press, 2008.

Hegel, Georg W. F. *Phenomenology of Spirit*. Translated by A. V. Miller. Oxford: Oxford University Press, 1977.

Heidegger, Martin. "The Question Concerning Technology." In *Basic Writings*, 311–41. New York: HarperCollins, 1997.

Heidegger, Martin. *Being and Time: A Translation of "Sein und Zeit."* Translated by Joan Stambaugh. Albany: SUNY Press, 1996.

Heidegger, Martin. *History of the Concept of Time: Prolegomena*. Bloomington: Indiana University Press, 1992.

Heller-Roazen, Daniel. *The Fifth Hammer: Pythagoras and the Disharmony of the World*. London: Zone Books, 2011.

Helmholtz, Hermann von. *On the Sensations of Tone as a Physiological Basis for the Theory of Music*. New York: Dover Publications, 1954.

Hennix, Catherine Christer. "Abstracts for Infinitary Compositions." In Hennix, *Poësy Matters and Other Matters*, 2:11–15.

Hennix, Catherine Christer. *Blues Alif Lam Mim: Blues in Ba*, April 22, 2014. New York: Issue Project Room, 2014.

Hennix, Catherine Christer. *The Electric Harpsichord*. Milan: Die Schachtel, 2010. CD/book.

Hennix, Catherine Christer. "$\frac{1}{2\pi} \kappa$ (Excerpt from Notes on the Composite Sine Wave Drone over Which The Electric Harpsichord Is Performed)." In Hennix, *Poësy Matters and Other Matters*, 2:19–32.

Hennix, Catherine Christer. "Excerpts from Parmenides and Intensional Logics." Stockholm, October 1979, edited 1995. Unpublished manuscript.

Hennix, Catherine Christer. "Hilbert Space Shruti Box (of the Quantum) Harmonic Oscillator." In Hennix, *Poësy Matters and Other Matters*, 2:277–91.

Hennix, Catherine Christer. "La Séminaire." In Hennix, *Poësy Matters and Other Matters*, 203–24.

Hennix, Catherine Christer. "Modalities and Languages for Algorithms." 2nd ed. Edited by Henry Flynt. In Hennix, *Poësy Matters and Other Matters*, 2:135–60.

Hennix, Catherine Christer. *Nadam Brahman [In Tune w/ the Universe: An Alternative Concept of the Music within, 17 XI 07]*. Privately printed, 2007.

Hennix, Catherine Christer. "Notes on Intuitionistic Modal Music." In Hennix, *Poësy Matters and Other Matters*, 2:39–40.

Hennix, Catherine Christer. "Notes on Toposes and Adjoints." In Hennix, *Poësy Matters and Other Matters*, 2:61–134.

Hennix, Catherine Christer. "OM: When a Divine Name Confers a Radiance of Infinite Blessings." In Hennix, *Poësy Matters and Other Matters*, 1:303–6.

Hennix, Catherine Christer. *Poësy Matters and Other Matters*. 2 vols. Brooklyn, NY: Blank Forms, 2019.

Hennix, Catherine Christer. "17 Points on Intensional Logics for Intransitive Experiences, 1969–1979." Unpublished manuscript, 1979.

Hennix, Catherine Christer. *Sonoilluminescenes*. Included in program notes to Maerzmusik: Festival for Time Issues, Berlin, 2017.

Hennix, Catherine Christer. "The Well-Tuned Marimba." On *Selected Early Keyboard Works*. Brooklyn, NY: Blank Forms, 2018. 2 x LP.

Hennix, Catherine Christer, and Henry Flynt. "Intensions, Illuminations, and Toposes." Draft 3. Unpublished manuscript, August 5, 1981.

Hennix, Catherine Christer, and Henry Flynt. "The Philosophy of Concept Art." In Hennix, *Poësy and Other Matters*, 2:169–94.

Henriques, Julian. *Sonic Bodies: Reggae Sound Systems, Performance Techniques, and Ways of Knowing*. New York: Continuum, 2011.

Hesseling, Dennis. *Gnomes in the Fog: The Reception of Brouwer's Intuitionism in the 1920s*. Boston, MA: Birkhäuser, 2003.

Hirschkind, Charles. *The Ethical Soundscape: Cassette Sermons and Islamic Counterpublics*. New York: Columbia University Press, 2006.

Hofnagels, Anna. "Northern Style Powwow Music: Musical Features and Meanings." *MUSICultures* 31 (2004). https://journals.lib.unb.ca/index.php/MC/article/view/21605.

Hood, Made Mantle. *Triguna: A Hindu Balinese Philosophy for Gamelan Gong Gede Music*. Münster: LIT Verlag, 2010.

Hui, Yuk. "Cosmotechnics as Cosmopolitics." *e-flux* 86 (November 2017).

Hui, Yuk. *The Question Concerning Technology in China: An Essay in Cosmotechnics*. Falmouth, UK: Urbanomic, 2016.

Husserl, Edmund. *Collected Works*. Vol. IV, *On the Phenomenology of the Consciousness of Internal Time (1893–1917)*. Translated by John Barnett Brough. Dordrecht: Springer, 1991.

Irigaray, Luce. *An Ethics of Sexual Difference*. Ithaca, NY: Cornell University Press, 1993.

Jaji, Tsitsi. "Sound Effects: Synaesthesia as Purposeful Distortion in Keorapetse Kgositsile's Poetry." *Comparative Literature Studies* 46, no. 2 (2009): 287–310.

James, William. *The Varieties of Religious Experience: A Study in Human Nature*. London: Penguin Books, 1982.

Jankélévitch, Vladimir. *Music and the Ineffable*. Translated by Carolyn Abbate. Princeton, NJ: Princeton University Press, 2003.

Johnson, Marguerite. *Houston: The Unknown City, 1836–1946*. College Station: Texas A&M University Press, 1991.

Johnston, Ian. *Measured Tones: The Interplay of Physics and Music*. 3rd ed. Hoboken, NJ: CRC Press, 2009.

Joseph, Brandon. *Beyond the Dream Syndicate: Tony Conrad and the Arts after Cage*. Cambridge, MA: Zone Books, 2008.

Kahn, Douglas. *Earth Sound, Earth Signal: Energies and Earth Magnitude in the Arts*. Berkeley: University of California Press, 2013.

Kahn, Douglas, ed. *Energies in the Arts*. Cambridge, MA: MIT Press, 2019.

Kania, Andrew. "The Philosophy of Music." *Stanford Encyclopedia of Philosophy*. Accessed October 7, 2020. https://plato.stanford.edu/entries/music/.

Kant, Immanuel. *Towards Perpetual Peace and Other Writings on Politics, Peace, and History*. New Haven, CT: Yale University Press, 2006.

Kapchan, Deborah, *Traveling Spirit Masters: Moroccan Gnawa Trance and Music in the Global Marketplace*. Middletown, CT: Wesleyan University Press, 2007.

Karma-gliṅ-pa. *The Tibetan Book of the Dead: The Great Liberation by Hearing in the Intermediate States*. Translated by Gyurme Dorje. New York: Penguin Books, 2010. Kindle.

Katz, David. *People Funny Boy: The Genius of Lee "Scratch" Perry*. Edinburgh: Payback Press, 2000.

Keefe, Alexander. "Lord of the Drone: Pandit Pran Nath and the American Underground." *Bidoun*, Spring 2010. https://bidoun.org/articles/lord-of-the-drone.

Kgositsile, Keorapetse. *Homesoil in My Blood*. Midrand, South Africa: Xarra Books, 2017.

Khan, Hazrat Inayat. *The Mysticism of Sound and Music*. Boston, MA: Shambhala, 1996.

Khan, Pir Zia Inayat, ed. *A Pearl in Wine: Essays on the Life, Music and Sufism of Hazrat Inayat Khan*. New Lebanon, NY: Omega Publications, 2001.

Kinnear, Michael. *Sangeet Ratna: The Jewel of Music; A Bio-Discography of Khan Sahib Abdul Karim Khan*. Victoria, Australia: self-published, 2003.

Knox, Keith, and Rita Knox. "Pandit Pran Nath: The Sayings of Gurgi." In Kumpf et al., *Blank Forms 06: Organic Music Societies*, 450–54.

Knox, Rita. "A Brief Presentation of Brouwer's Lattice and the Deontic Miracle." In Hennix, *Poësy Matters and Other Matters*, 2:51–54.

Koepnick, Lutz P. *On Slowness: Toward an Aesthetic of the Contemporary*. New York: Columbia University Press, 2014. Kindle.

Kopenawa, Davi. *The Falling Sky: Words of a Yanomami Shaman*. Translated by Bruce Albert. Cambridge, MA: Belknap Press of Harvard University Press, 2013.

Kristeva, Julia. *Revolution in Poetic Language*. Translated by Leon Samuel Roudiez and Margaret Waller. New York: Columbia University Press, 2006.

Kumpf, Lawrence, Naima Karlsson, and Magnus Nygren, eds. *Blank Forms 06: Organic Music Societies*. Brooklyn, NY: Blank Forms, 2021.

LaBelle, Brandon. *Acoustic Territories: Sound Culture and Everyday Life*. New York: Bloomsbury, 2016.

Lacan, Jacques. "Du discours psychanalytique." In *Lacan in Italia, 1953–1978: En Italie Lacan*, edited by G. B. Contri, 32–55. Milan: La Salamandra, 2011.

Lacan, Jacques. *Écrits: The First Complete Edition in English*. Translated by Bruce Fink. London: W. W. Norton, 2006.

Lacan, Jacques. "The Instance of the Letter in the Unconscious, or Reason since Freud." In Lacan, *Écrits*, 412–41.

Lacan, Jacques. "The Mirror Stage as Formative of the Function of the *I* as Revealed in Psychoanalytic Experience." In Lacan, *Écrits*, 75–81.

Lacan, Jacques. *The Seminar of Jacques Lacan, Book XI: The Four Fundamental Concepts of Psychoanalysis*. Translated by Alan Sheridan. New York: W. W. Norton, 1981.

Lacan, Jacques. *Seminar II: The Ego in Freud's Theory and in the Technique of Psychoanalysis*. London: W. W. Norton, 1988.

Lacan, Jacques. *Seminar XX: Encore! On Feminine Sexuality; The Limits of Love and Knowledge, 1972–1973*. Translated by Bruce Fink. Edited by Jacques-Alain Miller. New York: W. W. Norton, 1999.

Lamar, Kendrick. *To Pimp a Butterfly*. Top Dawg Entertainment, 2015. CD.

Lambek, Joachim. "The Mathematics of Sentence Structure." *American Mathematical Monthly* 65, no. 3 (1958): 154–70.

Laplanche, Jean. *Life and Death in Psychoanalysis*. Baltimore, MD: Johns Hopkins University Press, 2013.

Laplanche, Jean, and J. B. Pontalis. *Vocabulaire de la psychanalyse*. Paris: Presses Universitaires de France, 1967.

Latour, Bruno. *An Inquiry into Modes of Existence: An Anthropology of the Moderns*. Translated by Catherine Porter. Cambridge, MA: Harvard University Press, 2013.

Latour, Bruno. *We Have Never Been Modern*. Translated by Catherine Porter. Cambridge, MA: Harvard University Press, 1993.

Lavezzoli, Peter. *The Dawn of Indian Music in the West: Bhairavi*. London: A and C Black, 2006.

Lawvere, F. William. "Comments on the Development of Topos Theory." In *Development of Mathematics, 1950–2000*, edited by J-P Pier, 715–34. Basel: Birkhäuser, 2000.

Lefebvre, Henri. *The Production of Space*. Translated by Donald Nicholson-Smith. Oxford: Blackwell, 1991.

Leikert, Sebastian. "The Object of Jouissance in Music." In *Lacan in the German-Speaking World*, edited by Elizabeth Stewart, Maire Jaanus, and Richard Feldstein, 1–10. Albany: SUNY Press, 2004.

Lipsitz, George. "The Racialization of Space and the Spatialization of Race: Theorizing the Hidden Architecture of Landscape." *Landscape* 26, no. 1 (2007): 10–23.

Lispector, Clarice. *Agua Viva*. Translated by Stefan Tobler. New York: New Directions, 2012.

Lomax, Alan. *Alan Lomax: Selected Writings, 1934–1997*. Edited by Ronald D. Cohen. London: Routledge, 2003.

Lomax, Alan. "Song Structure and Social Structure." In Cohen, *Alan Lomax*, 248–74.

Longo, Giuseppe. "The Mathematical Continuum: From Intuition to Logic." In *Naturalizing Phenomenology*, edited by Jean Petitot, 401–27. Stanford, CA: Stanford University Press, 1999.

Lopez, Donald, Jr., and Robert E. Buswell Jr., eds. *The Princeton Dictionary of Buddhism*. Princeton, NJ: Princeton University Press, 2014. Kindle.

Lott, Eric. *Black Mirror: The Cultural Contradictions of American Racism*. Cambridge, MA: Harvard University Press, 2017.

Lott, Eric. *Love and Theft: Blackface Minstrelsy and the American Working Class*. Oxford: Oxford University Press, 1993.

Maceda, José. *Gongs and Bamboo: A Panorama of Philippine Music Instruments*. Quezon City: University of the Philippines Press, 1998.

Maddalena, Giovanni. *The Philosophy of Gesture: Completing Pragmatists' Incomplete Revolution*. Montreal: McGill–Queen's University Press, 2015.

Manuel, Peter. *Cassette Culture: Popular Music and Technology in North India*. Chicago: University of Chicago Press, 1993.

Marcus, Greil. Preface to *Psychotic Reactions and Carburetor Dung*, by Lester Bangs, ix–xviii. New York: Vintage Books, 1987.

Marcuse, Herbert. *One-Dimensional Man: Studies in the Ideology of Advanced Industrial Society*. London: Routledge, 2008.

Marley, Bob, and the Wailers. "Lively Up Yourself." *African Herbsman*. Trojan Records, 1973.

Mathieu, W. A. *Harmonic Experience: Tonal Harmony from Its Natural Origins to Its Modern Expression*. Rochester, VT: Inner Traditions, 1997.

Mazzola, Guerino. *The Topos of Music: Geometric Logic of Concepts, Theory, and Performance*. Basel: Birkhäuser Verlag, 2002.

Mazzola, Guerino. *The Topos of Music*. Vol. 1. 2nd ed. Cham, Switzerland: Springer, 2017.

Mazzola, Guerino, and Paul B. Cherlin. *Flow, Gesture, and Spaces in Free Jazz: Towards a Theory of Collaboration*. Berlin: Springer, 2009.

McComb, David G. *Houston: The Bayou City*. Austin: University of Texas Press, 1969.

McPhee, Colin. *Music in Bali: A Study in Form and Instrumental Organization in Balinese Orchestral Music*. New Haven, CT: Yale University Press, 1966.

Melchiori, Paola. "Psychoanalysis in Early Italian Feminism: The Contributions of the Practice of the Unconscious." In *Contemporary Italian Political Philosophy*, edited by Antonio Calcagno. Binghamton: SUNY Press, 2016.

Mohlajee, Prem M. "Ascetic Musician Makes Home in California." *Spotlight*, April 29, 1989.

Montague, Richard. *Formal Philosophy*. New Haven, CT: Yale University Press, 1974.

Morrison, Toni. *Beloved*. New York: Vintage International, 2004.

Morton, Timothy. *Hyperobjects: Philosophy and Ecology after the End of the World*. Minneapolis: University of Minnesota Press, 2014.

Moten, Fred. "Black Mo'nin' in the Sound of the Photograph." In Moten, *In the Break*, 192–210.

Moten, Fred. "Black Topological Existence." In *A Series of Utterly Improbable Yet Extraordinary Renditions*. Booklet for Arthur Jafa exhibition at the Serpentine Gallery, Kensington Gardens, London, September 2017.

Moten, Fred. "Blackness and Nothingness." *South Atlantic Quarterly* 112, no. 4 (2013): 737–80.

Moten, Fred. *In the Break: The Aesthetics of the Black Radical Tradition*. Minneapolis: University of Minnesota Press, 2003.

Moten, Fred. "Manic Depression: A Poetics of Hesitant Sociology." Talk given at the University of Toronto, April 4, 2017.

Nancy, Jean-Luc. *Listening*. New York: Fordham University Press, 2007.

Nataraj [Todd Nataraj Lapidus]. *Travels with Pran Nath*. N.p., 2018.

Nath, Pran. *In Between the Notes: A Portrait of Pandit Pran Nath, Master Indian Musician*. California College of the Performing Arts, San Rafael, 1986. Videotape.

Nathans, Benjamin. *Alexander Volpin and the Origins of the Soviet Human Rights Movement*. Washington, DC: National Council for Eurasian and East European Research, 2006.

Negarestani, Reza. *Intelligence and Spirit*. Falmouth, UK: Urbanomic, 2018.
Nelson, Alondra, ed. "Afrofuturism." Special issue, *Social Text* 20, no. 2 (2002).
Nishida, Kitaro. "The Logic of 'Topos' and the Religious Worldview." Translated by Yusa Michiko. *Eastern Buddhist* 19, no. 2 (1986): 1–29.
Olson, Charles. *Muthologos*. Vol. 1. Bolinas, CA: Four Seasons Foundation, 1978.
Pace, Robert. "Pandit Pran Nath." *EAR Magazine*, December 1987.
Peirce, Charles Sanders. "On Multitudes." In *Philosophy of Mathematics: Selected Writings*, edited by Matthew E. Moore, 189–200. Bloomington: Indiana University Press, 2010.
Pickering, Kathleen. "Decolonizing Time Regimes: Lakota Conceptions of Work, Economy, and Society." *American Anthropologist* 106, no. 1 (March 2004): 85–97.
Potter, Keith. *Four Musical Minimalists: La Monte Young, Terry Riley, Steve Reich, Philip Glass*. Cambridge: Cambridge University Press, 2000.
Piekut, Benjamin. "Demolish Serious Culture! Henry Flynt Meets the New York Avant Garde." In *Experimentalism Otherwise: The New York Avant Garde and Its Limits*, 65–101. Berkeley: University of California Press, 2011.
Reed, Ishmael. *Mumbo Jumbo*. New York: Scribner, 1996. First published in 1972.
Regnault, Chantal. *Voguing and the House Ballroom Scene of New York City, 1989–92*. Edited by Stuart Baker. London: Soul Jazz Books, 2011.
Reich, Wilhelm. *Sex-Pol: Essays, 1929–1934*. New York: Verso Books, 2013.
Robinson, Dylan. *Hungry Listening: Resonant Theory for Indigenous Sound Studies*. Minneapolis: University of Minnesota Press, 2020.
Rouget, Gilbert. *Music and Trance: A Theory of the Relations between Music and Possession*. Translated by Brunhilde Biebuyck. Chicago: University of Chicago Press, 1985.
Russell, Ross. *Bird Lives! The High Life and Hard Times of Charlie (Yardbird) Parker*. New York: Charterhouse, 1973.
Rys, Dan. "Houston Rappers Remember DJ Screw, 15 Years after His Death." *Billboard*, November 16, 2015. https://www.billboard.com/articles/columns/the-juice/6762500/dj-screw-houston-rappers-remember.
Sachs, Curt. *The History of Musical Instruments*. Mineola, NY: Dover Publications, 2006.
Scharlau, Winfried. *Wer ist Alexander Grothendieck? Anarchie, Mathematik, Spiritualität*. 3 vols. Norderstedt: self-published, 2010–11.
Schuyler, Philip. "Joujouka/Jajouka/Zahjoukah: Moroccan Music and Euro-American Imagination. In *Mass Mediations: New Approaches to Popular Culture in the Middle East and Beyond*, edited by Walter Armbrust, 146–60. Berkeley: University of California Press, 2000.
Scruton, Roger. *The Aesthetics of Music*. Oxford: Oxford University Press, 2007.
Sengupta, Pradip Kumar. *Foundations of Indian Musicology*. New Delhi: Abhinav, 1991.
Serres, Michel, and Bruno Latour. *Conversations on Science, Culture, and Time*. Translated by Roxanne Lapidus. Ann Arbor: University of Michigan Press, 1995.
Sexton, Jared. "Afro-Pessimism: The Unclear Word." *Rhizomes*, no. 29 (2016). http://www.rhizomes.net/issue29/sexton.html.
Shabazz Palaces. *Black Up*. Sub Pop Records, 2011. CD.
Shank, Barry. *The Political Force of Musical Beauty*. Durham, NC: Duke University Press, 2014.

Shippen, Nichole. *Decolonizing Time: Work, Leisure, and Freedom*. New York: Palgrave Macmillan, 2014.
Shvarts, Aliza. "Troubled Air: The Drone and Doom of Reproduction in SunnO)))'s metal Maieutic." *Women and Performance: A Journal of Feminist Theory* 24, nos. 2–3 (2014): 203–19. https://doi.org/10.1080/0740770X.2014.978112.
Sister Sledge. *All American Girls*. Cotillion, 1981. LP.
Sloterdijk, Peter. *You Must Change Your Life: On Anthropotechnics*. Cambridge: Polity, 2013.
Smith, Shawn Michelle, and Sharon Sliwinski, eds. Introduction to *Photography and the Optical Unconscious*. Durham, NC: Duke University Press, 2017.
Sonzala, Matt. "DJ Screw." *Murder Dog* 9, no. 3 (2002): 101–2.
Souriau, Étienne. *Different Modes of Existence*. Minneapolis, MN: Univocal, 2015.
Spice 1. *Spice 1*. Jive, 1992. CD.
Spicer, Daniel. Review of *Vernal Equinox/Flash of the Spirit*. *Wire*, no. 434 (April 2020): 72.
Spillers, Hortense. "Mama's Baby, Papa's Maybe: An American Grammar." *Diacritics* 17, no. 2 (1987): 64–81.
Spivak, David. *Category Theory for Scientists*. 2013. Accessed November 11, 2021. https://math.mit.edu/~dspivak/CT4S.pdf.
Stein, Charles, ed. *Being = Space × Action: Searches for Freedom of Mind through Mathematics, Art, and Mysticism*. Berkeley, CA: North Atlantic Books, 1988.
Stein, Charles. "Introduction." In Stein, *Being = Space × Action*, 1–47.
Stein, Charles. "Notes towards a Translation of Parmenides." In Stein, *Being = Space × Action*, 423–33.
Stengers, Isabelle. "The Cosmopolitical Proposal." In *Making Things Public*, edited by Bruno Latour and Peter Weibel, 994–1003. Cambridge, MA: MIT Press, 2005.
Stengers, Isabelle. *Cosmopolitics*. 2 vols. Translated by Robert Bononno. Minneapolis: University of Minnesota Press, 2010.
Steptoe, Tyina. *Houston Bound: Culture and Colour in a Jim Crow Society*. Oakland: University of California Press, 2016.
Stevens, Wallace. *The Palm at the End of the Mind: Selected Poems and a Play by Wallace Stevens*. Edited by Holly Stevens. New York: Alfred A. Knopf, 1971.
Stiegler, Bernard. *Symbolic Misery*. Vol. 2, *The Katastrophe of the Sensible*. Translated by Barnaby Norman. Cambridge, UK: Polity, 2015.
Stiegler, Bernard. *Technics and Time*. Vol. 1, *The Fault of Epimetheus*. Translated by Richard Beardsworth and George Collins. Stanford, CA: Stanford University Press 1998.
Stiegler, Bernard. *Technics and Time*. Vol. 2, *Disorientation*. Translated by Stephen Barker. Stanford, CA: Stanford University Press, 2008.
Stiegler, Bernard. *Technics and Time*. Vol. 3, *Cinematic Time and the Question of Malaise*. Translated by Stephen Barker. Stanford, CA: Stanford University Press, 2010.
Stobart, Henry. *Music and the Poetics of Production in the Bolivian Andes*. Aldershot: Ashgate, 2006.
Stockhausen, Karlheinz. "..... How Time Passes. . . . ." *Die Reihe* [English version], no. 3 (1959): 10–40.
Stoever, Jennifer. *The Sonic Color Line: Race and the Cultural Politics of Listening*. New York: New York University Press, 2016.

Svoboda, Robert. *Aghora III: The Law of Karma*. Albuquerque, NM: Brotherhood of Life, 1998.

Szwed, John. *Space Is the Place: The Lives and Times of Sun Ra*. New York: Da Capo, 1998.

Tate, Greg. "Hip Hop Turns 30." In *Flyboy 2: The Greg Tate Reader*, 246–51. Durham, NC: Duke University Press, 2016.

Taussig, Michael. *Shamanism, Colonialism, and the Wild Man: A Study in Terror and Healing*. Chicago: University of Chicago Press, 1987.

Toussaint, Godfried T. *The Geometry of Musical Rhythm: What Makes a "Good" Rhythm Good?* London: CRC Press, 2013.

Trungpa, Chögyam. *Orderly Chaos: The Mandala Principle*. Boulder, CO: Shambhala Publications, 1991.

Tutuola, Amos. *My Life in the Bush of Ghosts*. London: Faber and Faber, 2014.

van Dalen, Dirk. *Mystic, Geometer, and Intuitionist: The Life of L. E. J. Brouwer*. New York: Oxford University Press, 1999.

van Dalen, Dirk. "The Return of the Flowing Continuum." *Intellectica* 51 (2009/1): 135–44.

Vanheule, Stijn. "Capitalist Discourse, Subjectivity and Lacanian Psychoanalysis." *Frontiers in Psychology*, December 9, 2016. https://www.frontiersin.org/articles/10.3389/fpsyg.2016.01948/full.

Varèse, Edgard, and Chou Wen-Chung. "The Liberation of Sound." *Perspectives of New Music* 5, no. 1 (1966): 11–19.

Veal, Michael. *Dub: Soundscapes and Shattered Songs in Jamaican Reggae*. Middletown, CT: Wesleyan University Press, 2007.

Veal, Michael. *Fela: The Life of an African Musical Icon*. Philadelphia, PA: Temple University Press, 1997.

Virilio, Paul. "The Colonization of Time." In *Pure War*, by Paul Virilio and Sylvère Lotringer, 67–76. New York: Semiotext(e), 1983.

Viveiros de Castro, Eduardo. "Cosmological Perspectivism in Amazonia and Elsewhere." In *The Relative Native Essays on Indigenous Conceptual Worlds*, 191–294. Chicago: HAU Books, 2015.

Yessenin-Volpin, A. S. "On the Logic of the Moral Sciences." In Stein, *Being = Space × Action*, 107–54.

Wade, Bonnie. *Khyāl: Creativity within North India's Classical Music Tradition*. Cambridge: Cambridge University Press, 1984.

Walker, Lance Scott. "A Fast Life in Slow Motion." Red Bull Music Academy, May 20, 2015. https://daily.redbullmusicacademy.com/2015/05/dj-screw-feature.

Walker, Lance Scott. *Houston Rap*. Los Angeles: Sinecure, 2013.

Walker, Lance Scott. *Houston Rap Tapes: An Oral History of Bayou City Hip-Hop*. Los Angeles: Sinecure Books, 2013.

Walker, Lance Scott. *Houston Rap Tapes: An Oral History of Bayou City Hip-Hop*. 2nd ed. Austin: University of Texas Press, 2018.

Wallace, Amy. "Amen! (D'Angelo's Back)." *GQ*, December 14, 2014. https://www.gq.com/story/dangelo-gq-june-2012-interview?currentPage=1.

Weheliye, Alexander. "'Feenin': Posthuman Voices in Contemporary Black Popular Music." *Social Text* 20, no. 2 (2002): 21–47.

Wen, Xiao-Gang. "Choreographed Entanglement Dances: Topological States of Quantum Matter." *Science* 363, no. 6429 (February 22, 2019): eaal3099.

Wen, Xiao-Gang. *Quantum Field Theory of Many-Body Systems: From the Origin of Sound to an Origin of Light and Electrons*. Oxford: Oxford University Press, 2010.

Weyl, Hermann. *The Continuum: A Critical Examination of the Foundation of Analysis*. New York: Dover Publications, 1987.

West, Cornel. "In Memory of Marvin Gaye." In *The Cornel West Reader*, 471–73. New York, NY, Basic Civitas, 1999.

Wilmer, Valerie. *As Serious as Your Life: The Story of the New Jazz*. London: Serpent's Tail, 2000.

Wilson, Peter Lamborn. *Sacred Drift: Essays on the Margins of Islam*. San Francisco: City Lights, 1993.

Wilson, Peter Niklas. *Ornette Coleman: His Life and Music*. Berkeley, CA: Berkeley Hills, 2000.

Xenakis, Iannis. *Formalized Music: Thought and Mathematics in Composition*. Stuyvesant, NY: Pendragon Press, 1990.

Young, La Monte. "Notes on the Continuous Periodic Composite Sound Waveform Environment Realizations of 'Map of 49's Dream the Two Systems of Eleven Sets of Galactic Intervals Ornamental Lightyears Tracery.'" In Young and Zazeela, *Selected Writings*, 5–9.

Young, La Monte, and Marian Zazeela. "Dream House." In Young and Zazeela, *Selected Writings*, 10–16.

Young, La Monte, and Marian Zazeela. *Faquir Pran Nath: Day of Remembrance Raga Cycle*. New York: MELA Foundation, 1999. Program notes.

Young, La Monte, and Marian Zazeela. *Selected Writings*. Munich: Heiner Friedrich, 1969.

Zalamea, Fernando. *Peirce's Logic of Continuity: A Conceptual and Mathematical Approach*. Boston, MA: Docent Press, 2012.

Zalamea, Fernando. *Synthetic Philosophy of Contemporary Mathematics*. Falmouth, UK: Urbanomic, 2012.

Zazeela, Marian. "The Sayings of Guruji." Unpublished manuscript, 2000.

Žižek, Slavoj. *The Parallax View*. Cambridge, MA: MIT Press, 2009.

Žižek, Slavoj. *The Sublime Object of Ideology*. New York: Verso Books, 1989.

Zuckerkandl, Victor. *The Sense of Music*. Princeton, NJ: Princeton University Press, 1971.

Zuckerkandl, Victor. *Sound and Symbol*. New York: Pantheon Books, 1956.

Index

A Tribe Called Red, 16, 186, 220–25
abjection, 114–15, 199, 209, 210, 224–25
acoustics, 5, 6, 9, 135; acoustic space, 102–3, 113, 149, 176
aesthetics, 53, 95
affect, 53, 79–80
Afrofuturism, 180, 195
Afro-pessimism, 183, 208
Agamben, Giorgio, 130; *The Use of Bodies*, 130
Akhtar, Begum, 34
Al-Farabi, 83
algebra, 103–5; algebraic aesthetics, 89–90
algorithms, 89, 95–97, 106–7
Allekotte, Joan, 49
Amacher, Maryanne, 87
animals, 5, 36, 41, 57, 63, 159, 227
anthropology, 4, 36, 134, 167
Apollo 11 launch, 84–85
April Snow, 175–77
Arnheim, Rudolph, 194
Artaud, Antonin, 53
Asian Dub Foundation, 223
assemblage, 9, 37; vibrational, 19, 20; collective assemblage of enunciation, 211
astrology, 156–57
Atre, Prabha, 174
Attali, Jacques, 11, 73, 166, 173
Aulia, Nizamuddin, 67
AUM, 32, 88
avant-garde, 71, 84
awareness, 91–92
Ayler, Albert, 82, 159–60, 161

Baba, Shirdi Sai, 68
Bachelard, Gaston, 151–52, 160; *Dialectic of Duration*, 151–52
Badiou, Alain, 5, 88, 104, 128, 130, 135, 173–74; *Being and Event II: Logics of Worlds*, 130
Badu, Erykah, 216
Bakhle, Janaki, 36, 40–41, 71
Balibar, Étienne, 237n44
Bambaataa, Afrika, 191, 211
Bangs, Lester, 26
Baraka, Amiri, 125, 145, 159–60, 183–84, 193, 215
Barodekar, Hirabai, 34, 39, 62
Bartok, Bela, 196
Bataille, Georges, 77, 85, 88, 168–70
Bear Witness, 221–25
Bebey, Francis, 142
beginnings and endings in music, 86, 88, 91, 122, 171, 174, 210, 216
behaviorism, 79–80
Being = Space × Action, 94, 110
Benjamin, Walter, 194, 196
Berger, Bengt, 56
Bergson, Henri, 150–53, 160; *Creative Evolution*, 150; *Time and Free Will*, 150; *Matter and Memory*, 150
Bharata, *Natyashastra*, 32
Bhatkhande, Pandit Vishnu Narayan, 33
Bhatnagar, Shyam, 45
Bieber, Justin, 162
Big Moe, 210, 219
biology, 77

biopolitics, 140, 195
birdsong, 35, 158
Blackness, 208–10, 213–16
Black Radical Tradition, 16, 17, 25, 26, 52, 64, 115, 139, 157, 162, 173–74, 180, 184, 199, 213
Blakey, Art, 182
blues, the, 46–47, 53, 54, 77, 113, 118, 129, 160, 190, 220
Bollywood, 146
Bose-Einstein condensation, 8, 122
bossa nova, 171–72
breathing, 155–56, 213–14
Brouwer, L. E. J., 88, 89, 90–92, 97, 107, 114, 122, 123, 126, 129, 131, 138, 154–55, 245n97
Brown, James, 184
Brown, Trisha, 57
Buddhism, 77, 105, 126, 193; Tibetan, 2, 174–75, 200; Zen, 68
Bun B, 188, 229

Cage, John, 64, 65, 77, 78, 79, 83, 84, 102, 141, 152, 167; *4′ 33″*, 78, 152
Cale, John, 30, 45, 61, 78, 80
Cantor, Georg, 126, 128
capitalism, 134, 140, 173, 178, 214–15
Caramello, Olivia, 132
cars, 191
Carter, Betty, 178
category theory, 104–6, 132, 139; definition of, 104–5
Chambers Street Loft Series (ca. 1960), 57
chaos, 19, 128, 153, 200
Chatham, Rhys, 30, 86
Chenaux, Eric, 248n74
Chenier, Clifton, 190
Cherry, Don, 31, 55–56
Cherry, Moki, 56
children, 19, 162, 189
Choi, Jung Hee, 52
choice sequences, 90–91, 116, 123, 131–32, 200
chora, 114–15, 170
Chora(s)san Time-Court Mirage, The, 111, 113–15, 117–20
chronopolitics, 40, 188
Clay-Doe, 200
Cocteau, Jean, 201; *Opium Journal of a Disintoxication*, 201
Coleman, Ornette, 163–64

collectivity, models of: the choreosonic, 153, 210–12; and COVID-19, 227–28; ensemble, 164; Flynt's, 100–101; in hip-hop, 211–12; soundsystem as 7, 9, 166, 193. *See also* Henriques, Julian
colonialism, 39–40, 183, 199–200, 218–25
Coltrane, Alice, 180, 191, 249n5, 251n36
Coltrane, John, 26, 27, 28, 52, 54, 60, 82, 112, 120, 138, 178, 181; *A Love Supreme*, 27–28, 120; *Selflessness Featuring My Favourite Things*, 26
computers, 83, 87, 89, 106, 133–34, 137, 141
condensed matter theory, 8, 32, 113, 122, 136, 150, 152
Congo Natty, 223
Conrad, Tony, 30, 45, 78, 79, 80, 82, 86, 97, 111
contagion, 145, 181–82, 184
continuity, 149–50
continuum, 15–16, 105–6, 121–23, 144–45, 154–56, 161, 169–70, 193, 198–99, 246n6; definition of, 109–10; and music, 109–10, 125–32, 171–78; Afrodiasporic conceptions of, 182–87; and Buddhism, 249n95
Corner, Philip, 143–44
correlationism, 88
Cosey, Pete, 214
cosmology, 44–45, 81–82
cosmopolitanism, 4, 65
cosmopolitics, 4–5, 24, 32, 35, 37, 48, 44–45, 71, 77, 95, 99, 100–102, 129–30, 136, 139, 140, 166, 180, 202, 224; definition of, 235n3; and global standardization, 146; and the neighbor, 213
cosmotechnics, 10–11, 100, 146, 147, 149, 198
counterpoint, 143
COVID-19, 226–30
Cowell, Henry, 64
Crawley, Ashon, 20–22, 37, 40, 153, 184, 204, 210; *Blackpentecostal Breath*, 153
crying, 225
cultural appropriation, 25, 55, 217
Cuni, Amelia, 111, 118
Cunningham, Merce, 65, 84

D'Angelo, 215–16; *Black Messiah*, 215, 216; *Voodoo*, 215
Dagar Brothers, 31, 39, 56, 72, 198
dance, 11, 57–59, 152–53; breakdancing, 211

270   INDEX

dancehall, 16–18, 166
Daniélou, Alain, 36, 47, 79, 81–82, 125, 142–43, 145, 146, 181; *Introduction to the Study of Musical Scales*, 81; *Semantique Musicale*, 8; *Tableau Comparatif des Intervalles Musicaux*, 79, 125
David-Ménard, Monique, 111
Davis, Miles, 54–55, 145, 152, 197, 214–16; *Bitches Brew*, 54–55, 214; *Get Up With It*, 214; *Kind of Blue*, 197
death, 174–78, 188; death drive, 17–18, 168–70, 214; George Floyd, 229–30; the space of death, 199–200, 203, 205, 225
de Broglie, Louis, 8
Debussy, Claude, 64
decolonization, 39–40, 72, 182–83, 221–25, 228; and time, 250n16
de la Cadena, Marisol, 4
Deleuze, Gilles, 11, 150, 153, 236n29; *Difference and Repetition*, 153
Deleuze, Gilles, and Félix Guattari, "Of the Refrain," 19, 236n29
de Maria, Walter, 61
democracy, 39–40, 82
Deontic Miracle, the, 86, 92–93, 97, 109, 110, 111, 137–38
depression, 25–26, 186–87, 200–205, 209, 213–20, 222, 224–25, 229–230
Derrida, Jacques, 146, 147, 249n87
Dhar, Sheila, 41, 42, 43
dhrupad, 31, 43–44, 72
Dia Art Foundation, 48, 61, 72
Diawara, Manthia, 237n43
Dietz, Bill, 245n89
dignity, 99, 103, 105
disappearance, 167
discipline, 41, 53, 96, 161–64
disco, 17
Dizzee Rascal, 220
DJ Darryl Scott, 187, 190
DJ Frankie Knuckles, 168
DJing, 168, 177, 187, 192–93, 210–12, 223
DJ Michael Watts, 187
DJ OG Ron C, 187
DJ Screw, 16, 146, 152, 186–225, 229–30; *Chapter 010: Southside Still Holdin'*, 210; *Chapter 12: June 27th*, 188, 192, 211–12, 217–19; *Chapter 16: Late Night Fuckin' Yo Bitch*, 203; *Chapter 30: G Love*, 207; *Chapter 070: Endonesia*, 187
DJ Sprinkles, 184–86, 193; *Midtown 120 Blues*, 184–86
DJ/Rupture, 192
DNA, 75
Dolphy, Eric, 82
doom, 206–9
Doors, The, 161, 174
double consciousness, 188, 193–94
Drake, 188, 217–20
Dream House, 29–30, 38, 59, 61, 72, 101–3, 111, 119–20, 123
dreams, 96, 101–2, 122–23
Dreyblatt, Arnold, 30
Driver, Ryan, 1–2, 176–77
drone, 46, 51–52, 61, 77–78, 83, 85, 91–92, 93–94, 109–10, 111, 114, 121, 144–45, 201, 206
drugs, 50, 61, 86, 194, 197, 220, 229; syrup, etc., 200–203
drums, 82, 139, 197, 198, 221
Du Bois, W. E. B., 193–94
duration, 95, 150, 160, 191
Dzogchen, 126

Earl Sweatshirt, 182, 199, 204; *I Don't Like Shit, I Don't Go Outside*, 204; *Some Rap Songs*, 204
Earth, 206
ecstasis, 103, 105, 120, 157, 172
Edwards, Greg, 176
Eidsheim, Nina Sun, 21–22, 44, 162; *Sensing Sound*, 162
8th Iran Festival of the Arts (Shiraz, 1974), 65–66
Eilenberg, Samuel, 104
Einstein, Albert, 152
Electric Pow Wow, 221
Electronic Music Studio, Stockholm, 83
electrons; electron diffraction experiments, 7–8; and hydrogen, 113–14
Eliade, Mircea, 81
Ellington, Duke, 214
ElSaffar, Amir, 111, 117
energy, 9, 75, 76, 152; physics of, 114–15
Eno, Brian, 54, 214; *Fourth World Music Volume 1: Possible Musics*, 60

INDEX 271

environment, 156–57, 165
epistemology, 95–97
equal temperament, 46
Eranos conferences, 81
eros, 17, 165–66, 168–70, 177, 206–7, 214
Eshun, Kodwo, 195
ethics, 94–95, 191
ethnomusicology, 12, 130–31, 157–60
Euclidean space, 150
evolution, 19
excess, and aesthetics, 85

Fagunwa, 182
Fahlström, Öyvind, 84
Fanon, Frantz, 39–40, 184, 213; *Black Skins, White Masks*, 184, 213; *The Wretched of the Earth*, 39–40
Fat Pat, 210, 211, 212
fear of music, 164
Feynman, Richard, 8
field, 7, 23, 78, 167–68; field models of music, 136–37, 149, 225
Fink, Bruce, 165
Fisher, Mark, 220
flamenco, 172–73
flow, 193
Floyd, George, 229–30
Fluxus, 78, 102
Flynt, Henry, 14, 30–31, 38, 52–54, 61, 71, 76, 77, 85, 94, 97–101, 110, 111; *Celestial Power*, 98; "The Collectivity after the Abolition of the Universe and Time," 100–101; *C-Tune*, 98; "Graduation," 52; "On Pandit Pran Nath," 52–53
folk music, 46–47, 52–53, 134, 172
food, 50
footwork, 162
forms of life, 27, 81, 146, 192
Forti, Simone, 31, 57–59; *Handbook in Motion*, 57–59
Foucault, Michel, 76
Fourier, Jean-Baptiste, 83
Fourier analysis, 83
Fourth World music, 31, 45, 54–55
Frege, Gottlob, 244n77
Freud, Sigmund, 136, 169–70, 181–82, 213, 216, 235–36n15, 244–45n88, 244n75; *Civilization and Its Discontents*, 17–18

fugitivity, 11, 25, 73
Funkadelic, 14
fusion, 145

Gagaku, 86, 242n24
Gallope, Michel, 236n16, 236n26
gamelan, 64; Balinese, 11, 20; Javanese, 198
Gandhi, Mohandas Karamchand, 39
GarageBand, 162
Gaye, Marvin, 207
geometry, 103–4, 149, 164
gesture, 11, 133, 153, 155
gharana, definition, 32
Gilberto, João, 171
Gilroy, Paul, 183, 186, 193–94, 202; *The Black Atlantic*, 183
Giriji, Swami Narayan, 34, 50
Glass, Philip, 64, 176
Glissant, Edouard, 26–27
Glowczewski, Barbara, 248n60
Gnawa, 138, 169–70
Godard, Jean-Luc, 171; *Contempt*, 171
Gödel, Kurt, 90, 113, 123
gongs, 130–31, 133, 143, 198
Goodman, Steve, 16–19, 76, 81, 173
Gordon, Dexter, 82
gqom, 162
Grand Wizard Theodore, 211
Graves, Milford, 7
Green, Al, 204
grime, 220
Grimshaw, Jeremy, 62
Grip Boys, The, 220
Grosz, Elizabeth, *Chaos, Territory, Art*, 19, 169
Grothendieck, Alexander, 89, 97, 103–5, 107, 131, 132, 133, 135, 139, 174, 245n97
Grubbs, David, 243n57
Guenon, René, 81
guitar, 7, 54, 171 73, 205, 214

Hafez, 65–66
Haino, Keiji, 155–56, 157, 161
Hall, Michael, 200, 201–2
Halprin, Anna, 57
Hampton, Fred, 217
Hạnh, Thich Nhat, 252n75
happiness, 205
harmolodics, 163–64

harmonics, 75, 81–82, 113–14, 136, 143–44
Harrison, Michael, 13
Hassell, Jon, 30, 31, 45, 50, 54–55, 60, 86; *Aka/Darbari/Java: Magic Realism*, 54; *Fourth World Music, Vol. 1: Possible Musics*, 54; *Fourth World Music, Vol 2: Dream Theory in Malaya*, 54; *Vernal Equinox*, 54, 55
Hawk, 200, 211, 212
healing, 199–200
heartbeat, 7, 149, 221–22
Hegel, G. W. F., 137, 186
Heidegger, Martin, 23, 40, 120–21, 122, 131, 147, 249n1; on Parmenides, 245n93; *Being and Time*, 23, 40, 147
Helmholtz, Hermann, 78–79; *On the Sensations of Tone*, 78
Hendrix, Jimi, 161
Hennix, Catherine Christer, 6, 8, 13–15, 25, 44, 48, 52, 60, 62–63, 71, 75–123, 125–28, 131, 132, 146, 152–53, 164–66, 173–74, 191, 206, 224, 228–29; "17 Points on Intensional Logics for Intransitive Experiences," 98, 108; *Blues Alif Lam Mim*, 117–18, 122–23; *Brouwer's Lattice*, 91–92, 93; Dream Music Festival, 242n41; *The Electric Harpsichord*, 76, 80, 91–92, 93–94, 98, 109–10, 111, 112, 118–19; "The Hilbert Space Shruti Box," 113; "La Seminaire," 106–7, 109, 111; "Modalities and Languages for Algorithms," 95–96; "Notes on Toposes and Adjoints," 108–9; *Solo for Two Tamburas and One Player*, 96, 117; and toposes, 136–40; *Toposes and Adjoints*, 92, 95–96; and visual artworks, 106–7, 111. *See also* Chora(s)san Time-Court Mirage, The
Hennix, Peter, 86
Henriques, Julian, 6, 7–8, 19–20, 37, 134–35, 140, 176, 186, 193, 224
Heraclitus, 141
HESE (hallucinatory/ecstatic sound environment), 98–99
Higgins, Dick, 84
Hilbert, David, 88, 90, 126, 128
Hill, Tim "2oolman," 221
hip-hop, 146, 186–225
Hirschkind, Charles, 191–92
Hoffman, E. T. A., 26
Holley, Lonnie, 210

Holt, John, 213
homelessness, 63
Hopkins, Lightnin' Sam, 190, 197
Hopper, Jessica, 26
house music, 184–86
Houston, musical history of, 190
Hubble frequency, 88
Hui, Yuk, 10–11, 27, 100, 146, 149, 198, 235n3
Hurston, Zora Neale, 26
Husserl, Edmund, 106, 147; *On the Phenomenology of the Consciousness of Internal Time*, 148
Hutchings, Shabaka, 228
Huxley, Aldous, 81

ideology, 62, 71, 72, 73, 80
illuminations, 57
immersion, 85, 156, 170
improvisation, 11, 26, 57–59, 93–94, 97; freestyling, 211
Indian classical music, 9–10, 31–45, 72–73, 79, 82, 156; definition of, 237n1
Indigeneity: Australian, 156, 222, 248n60; Canadian, 157–58, 218–25; Colombian Amazon, 199; Quechua, 4, 143; Yanomami, 158–59
Indigenous concepts of space, 181
informality, 162–64, 173, 177
information ontology, 136, 150
inner sound, 138, 154–55
intellectual property, 80, 82, 191–92
intervals, 90, 152
intuitionism, 105, 121–22; and the continuum, 126; intuitionism and music, 90–92, 93–94, 129, 154–55
Irigaray, Luce, 170, 247n39
Isgren, Hans, 56, 86
Isley Brothers, 188
iteration, 149, 167
Ives, Charles, 64

Jacquet, Illinois, 190
Jafa, Arthur, 199
James, William, 38
Jankélévitch, Vladimir, 9, 10, 12
jazz, 76, 77, 82–83, 87, 97, 110, 120, 133, 139–40, 162, 163–64, 181–82, 190, 196
Jefferson Airplane, 84
Jeffery, Hilary, 111

Jenkins, Barry, 216
Jennings, Terry, 86
Jewish music, 56–57
Johns, Jasper, 84
Johnson, Dennis, 85
Johnson, Marc, 110
Johnson, Robert, 54
Joshi, Bhimsen, 41
jouissance, 85, 105, 109, 116, 140, 164–70
journalism, 26
Judd, Donald, 61
Jung, Carl, 81, 235–36n15
Junger, Ernst, 81
jungle, 195
just intonation, 46–48, 51–52, 78, 79–82, 90, 99, 102–3, 119, 125, 127

Kahn, Douglas, 9, 244–45n88
Kant, Immanuel, 4, 135, 139, 141, 147, 154
Karunamayee, 41, 154
Kgositsile, Keorapetse, 12, 182, 183, 204
Khan, Abdul Wahid, 32, 33–34, 38, 41, 50, 57, 62, 71, 72
Khan, Abdul Karim, 33, 34, 36, 39, 40, 62, 68
Khan, Ali Akbar, 31, 34, 45, 64
Khan, Bade Ghulam Ali, 32, 39
Khan, Bismillah, 45, 65, 178
Khan, Hafizullah, 38
Khan, Hazrat Inayat, 31, 63, 67, 68
Khan, Mashkor Ali, 50, 177
Khan, Nusrat Fateh Ali, 67, 68
Khan, Pir Vilayat, 65, 67
Khan, Salamat and Nazkat Ali, 34, 41, 72
Khan, Shabda, 49, 50, 67, 68–69, 70, 71
Khusrau, Amir, 33, 68
King, B.B., 189
Kirana gharana, 40–41, 45–46, 63, 117
Koepnick, Lutz, 194–95
Kool Herc, 180
Kopenawa, Davi, 158–59
K-Rino, 211
Kris Kross, 217, 219, 246n6
Kristeva, Julia, 114–15, 199, 244–45n88
Kronos Quartet, 63; *Short Stories*, 63
Kuti, Fela, 180

Labelle, Brandon, 191
labor, 207, 216

Lacan, Jacques, 97, 107, 110–11, 112, 114, 115–17, 131, 136, 160, 164–66, 169–70, 220, 235–36n15, 244–45n88, 244n75; *Seminar XX: Encore!*, 116
Lamar, Kendrick, 26, 162, 180, 203–4; *To Pimp a Butterfly*, 180, 203–4
Lance, Scott Walker, 250n30
land (*terroir*), 71–72, 218–25
language, and vibration, 5, 9, 23; and the body, 114–15; general intellect and, 218; mathematical logic and, 95–96, 104–7; music as universal, 186; music in relation to, 68–69; the Real and, 165–66, 169–70; speculative philosophy and, 87–88
Laplanche, Jean, 235–36n15, 244–45n88
Laraaji, 191
Latour, Bruno, 27, 36, 37, 71, 130, 153; *Inquiry into Modes of Existence*, 130
law of the excluded middle, 91, 105
Lawrence, Timothy, 17; *Love Saves the Day*, 17
Lawvere, William, 88–89, 97, 103–4, 132, 174
Lazer, Major, 221
Lefebvre, Henri, 181
Leikert, Sebastian, 166
Leoninus, 118
Levan, Larry, 168
Lewis, Samuel, 68
Lil-O, 200
Lil Wayne, 219–20
Lispector, Clarice, 3–5; *Agua Viva*, 3–4
listening, 22
Loft, the, 168
logic, 91, 103, 123
Lomax, Alan, 134
loss, 173–74, 177–78; breakups, 205–7
Lott, Eric, 252n78
love, 162, 230

Maceda, Jose, 130–31, 133, 147; *Gongs and Bamboo*, 130–31, 133
Mackey, Nathaniel, 26, 152, 204, 220
Mac Lane, Saunders, 104
MacLise, Angus, 30, 78
Maddalena, Giovanni, 11
magic, 36–37, 168
Mallarmé, Stéphane, 114
Mane, Suresh Babu, 34

maqam, 113–14, 117–18, 127, 138
Marcus, Greil, 26
Marcuse, Herbert, 214–15
Marley, Bob, 224–25
Marlowe, Ann, 201; *How to Stop Time*, 201
maroons, 180
Marshall, Ingram, 64
Marx, Karl, 64, 218
Master Musicians of Jajouka, the, 163–64
maternity, 169–70
mathematics, 6, 47–48, 78; of feeling 79–80; foundations of, 77, 88–92, 104–5; and Islam 83; mathematical ontology, 88; and music 83, 87, 132–40; of scales, 80
Mathieu, W. A., 44; *Harmonic Experience*, 44
Mazzola, Guerino, 6, 132–40, 142, 153, 155, 246n19; *The Topos of Music*, 132–35
MC5, 84
McLuhan, Marshall, 146
McQueen, Steve, 166; *Lovers Rock*, 166
melody, 149–50, 159; and Husserl, 148–49
Menuhin, Yehudi, 64
metatechnology, 85, 99, 100
midnight, 49
Mike D, 200, 212
militarization, 16, 202–3
Miller, Jacques-Alain, 110–11
minimalism, 64
Minsky, Marvin, 106, 110
miracle, 96
mixtapes, 190–92, 211–12, 218
modal music, 91–92, 96, 107, 148–49, 167; ontology and, 129–32, 135, 153
monism, 120–23
Montague, Richard, 106, 244n77
moombahton, 221–22
Moonlight, 192, 216
Morrison, Jim, 161
Morrison, Toni, 183; *Beloved*, 183
Morton, Timothy, 156
Moten, Fred, 6, 11, 73, 152–53, 162, 177, 204–5, 208–10, 217–18, 228; *The Undercommons*, 217–18
music, 4–12; definition of, 18; festivals, 64–66; as gift; 159–60; and healing, 75; and logic, 105–6; musicology, 88; as property, 160; and space, 210, 222–25; and spirituality, 66–69; and trance, 157–58

musical instruments, construction of: and technics, 147–48, 198; Yoshi Wada, 60
musique concrète, 142–43, 198

Nada Brahma, 31, 36, 43, 69, 122
Nancy, Jean Luc, 249n87
Narayan, Pandit Ram, 56, 65
Nascimento, Milton, 128
Nataraj, 69
Nath, Pandit Pran, 9–10, 13–15, 23–24, 29–73, 76, 77, 82, 86–87, 95, 100, 111, 117, 154, 156, 160, 163, 167, 193, 198, 224; *Earthgroove*, 48; *The Raga Cycle*, 49; *Ragas of Morning and Night*, 48; *Ragas Yaman Kalyan Punjabi Berva*, 48
nationalism, 71
Nayak, Gopal, 33, 67
Negarestani, Reza, 136–37
neuroscience, 47, 92, 102–3, 136
New Orleans marching bands, 197
Niblock, Phill, 110, 144, 206
night, 211–12
Nishida, Kitaro, 136
Nizami, Feroz, 34
noise, 21
nonhumans, 4–5, 9, 35, 37, 81, 139, 140, 143–44, 153, 156, 158–59, 165, 181
nonknowledge, 88
notation, 80, 133, 160, 163
Notorious B.I.G., 217

Occidentalism, 65
Ocean, Frank, 188, 199
Odd Future, 170, 182, 199
Olson, Charles, 205
One, the, 105–6, 109, 112–13, 127, 131, 139, 164–66
Ono, Yoko, 57
ontology, 37, 78; and music, 22–28, 37, 69, 70–71, 76–77, 88, 135, 151–53, 157, 192–94; ontology of sound, 103; philosophy, 27; and slowness, 201–2
opera, 166
Orientalism, 61–62

Palestine, Charlemagne, 30, 31, 56–58, 63, 64, 206; *Hommage a Faquir Pandit Pran Nath*, 57; *Karenina*, 57; *Schlingen Blangen*, 57

INDEX 275

Palmer, Robert, 163
Paradise Garage, 15
Parker, Charlie, 181, 196–97
Parker, William, 5
Parlan, Horace, 133
Parmenides, 77, 105, 107, 120–22, 127, 131, 141, 144, 153, 164, 166, 201, 245n93
Partch, Harry, 64, 127
parties, 177–78
Patton, Charlie, 248n72
Peirce, Charles Sanders, 128–29, 132, 152, 161
periodicity, 7
Perri, Sandro, 1–2
Perry, Lee, 180
perspectivism, 158–60
P-Funk, 176
phenomenology, 77, 78, 87–88, 91, 111
phonograph, 196
physics, 6–9, 47, 77, 235n13
piano, 51
Piekut, Ben, 243n57
Pimp C, 188, 229
Pinheiro dos Santos, Lúcio Alberto, 151, 247n47
Plato, 146
Platonism, 90
pluralism, 135, 177–78
police, 202–3, 204, 208, 212–13, 229–30
political economy, 73, 236n25
politics, 12; of vibration, 80–82
Pop Group, the, 14–15
powwow, 221–23, 253n108
practice, 19–20, 21–22, 35, 37, 49–50, 53, 71–72, 87, 100, 172–74, 228
pragmatism, 129–32, 142, 162; and technics, 147–48
Price, Michael, Jr. (DJ), 190
Prince, 175–78; "I Wanna Be Your Lover," 176–77; *Purple Rain*, 176–77
Principe Discos, 162
prophecy, 173–74
psychoanalysis, 9, 76–77, 97, 107–8, 110–11, 122, 123, 164–70, 204, 244–45n88; and energy, 235–36n15
punk, 14–15
psychotropism, 122–23, 136
Pythagoras, 81, 88, 141

Qawwali, 31, 67

quadrivium, 12, 83
quantum physics, 76, 113–14; quantum cosmology, 106; quantum ether, 112; quantum field theory, 8–9, 152
queerness, 216

racialization, and space, 181, 184
racism, 152–53, 182, 202–5, 209–10, 217–20
radiation, 76
Radigue, Eliane, 175; *Trilogie de le Mort*, 175
radio, 176
raga, 2, 36, 38, 46–48, 57, 59, 70–72, 79, 96, 113, 118, 127, 139, 156, 160; specific ragas: Bhairavi, 174; Bhimpalasi, 33; Darbari, 34; Dipak, 36; Malkauns, 30, 49; Miyan ki Malhar, 36; Multani, 80, 93; Tilang, 52, 60; Todi, 34; Yaman Kalyan, 69
rain, 1–2, 36, 38, 156
Rakha, Alla, 64
Rane, Saraswati, 34
rasa, 38
raves, 223–25
Ray, Satyajit, 72; *The Music Room*, 72
R&B, 190
real, the, 165–67
real estate, 213. *See also* Dream House
reconciliation, 223–25
recording, 48–49, 147, 159, 160, 177–78, 189–99
Redding, Otis, 181
Reed, Ishmael, 7, 14, 181–82, 197; *Mumbo Jumbo*, 7, 181–82, 197
reggae, 193, 197, 201; reggae sound system, 7, 19–20
rehearsal, 172
Reich, Steve, 64, 176
Reich, Wilhelm, 76–77, 235–36n15
religion, 21, 66–69
repetition, 35, 58–59, 78, 109–10, 153, 167, 205–10, 220, 236n29
repression, 245n89
Rhames, Arthur, 110
rhythm, 7, 127, 139, 148–49, 149–50, 151–52, 171
Rhythm Controll, 185–86
Riley, Terry, 13, 30, 31, 42, 43, 45, 48, 49–52, 54, 56, 57, 60, 63, 64, 66, 68, 71–72, 73, 78, 86, 111; *Descending Moonshine Dervishes*, 31,

51; *In C*, 54; *Shri Camel*, 51, 54; *Songs for the Ten Voices of the Two Prophets*, 52
Roberts, Chuck, 185–86
Robinson, Dylan, 157–58, 222
Rouget, Gilbert, 129, 157
Roy, Badal, 55
Russell, Arthur, 110

Sa, 57
Sabiri, Hazrat Allaudin, 67
Said, Edward, 62
sameness, 78
Sanders, Pharaoh, 138
Sanneh, Kelefa, 192
Sarangadeva, *Sangita'ratnakara*, 32
Saraswati, 44–45
saudade, 173
scales, 79, 154; politics of, 81–82
Schaeffer, Pierre, 145, 198
Schelling, Friedrich Wilhelm Joseph, 186
Schrodinger, Erwin, 8, 113
Schuyler, Philip, 163
Scorsese, Martin, 30; *Taxi Driver*, 30
Screwed Up Click, 201, 210–13, 229
Scruton, Roger, 23
semantics, 106
semiotics, 95, 133
Senghor, Léopold Sédar, 142
serialism, 145
Serres, Michel, 153
Sexton, Jared, 208
sexual difference, 109, 115–17, 118, 215–16
sexuality, 19, 165–70, 197, 215–16. *See also* eros
Shabazz Palaces, 179
Shakur, Tupac, 180, 197
Shalabi, Sam, 146, 173
shamanism, 159, 199
Shank, Barry, 236n25
Shankar, Ravi, 31, 64, 65
Shankar, Uday, 31
Sharma, Shiv Kumar, 65
Sherman, Demo, 192, 211
Shorty Mac, 189
Shrine, the (Lagos), 180
Shvarts, Aliza, 205–7
sickness, and health, 69–70; brain damage, 143–44
silence, 78, 152, 154, 228

Simondon, Gilbert, 148
Simone, Nina, 162
sinewaves, 83, 85
Singh, Shanta Serbjeet, 41
singing, 21–22, 57, 71, 100
Sister Sledge, 173
Sloterdijk, Peter, 161; *You Must Change Your Life*, 161
slowness, Pandit Pran Nath, and, 71; DJ Screw, 189, 194–99; history of, 197–99; slowness, postcolonial, 202–5
Snow, Michael, 171; *Wavelength*, 171
Solange, 188, 200; *When I Get Home*, 188, 200
sonic warfare, 76, 81
sound environment, 103
sound studies, 36, 88
sound system, 7, 8, 20, 37, 93, 129, 131, 134, 166–67, 180, 193, 221
space, 7, 10, 105–10, 130, 131, 157–60, 149–53, 167–68, 176, 181, 209–13, 211–13; Hennix's conception of, 138–39; sonic, 103, 193; and subjectivity, 137, 158, 222
Spice 1, 196, 207–9
spirits, 5, 41, 70, 143, 157–60
spirituality, 66–69, 94, 99–100
Spotify, 146, 218
Stein, Charles, 94
Stengers, Isabelle, 4, 12, 27, 37, 235n3, 235n4
Steptoe, Tyina, *Houston Bound*, 190
Stiegler, Bernard, 10–11, 100, 146–49, 196, 198, 247n39; *Technics and Time*, 147–48
Stobart, Henry, 143
Stockhausen, Karlheinz, 54, 55, 64, 65, 77, 83, 111, 141–42, 145, 153; *Hymnen*, 55
Stoever, Jenny, 184
subjectivity, 9–10, 20–21, 103, 107–8, 115–17, 136, 157–60, 164–70
Sufism, 33–34, 38, 65–66, 73, 83, 105, 117–18, 122–23, 138, 228
Sugar Hill Gang, 211
Sulieman, Idrees, 25, 82, 118
Summer, Donna, 13
Sun City Girls, 146
Sunn O))), 205–7; *Live White*, 205
Sun Ra, 180
Suval, Joan, 230
Suzuki, Akio, 156–57
swara (pitch), 69

Syd the Kid, 199
symmetry, and asymmetry, 58–59
synesthesia, 108
synthesis, 145
synthesizers, 146

taboo, 156, 169
tactics of attention, 24, 103
tambura, 34, 43–44, 51–52, 54, 59, 60, 86–87, 98, 112, 167, 228–29
tantra, 32, 216
Tarabai, 33
target states, 138–40, 149
Tarski, Alfred, 87
Tate, Greg, 26, 249n6
Taussig, Michael, 199–200
Taylor, Johnny, 189
technics, 10–11, 100–103, 146–49, 198
techno, 195
teleology, 71
temperature, 84–85
Tenney, James, 84
Tenniscoats, 27
Theater of Eternal Music, 30, 45–46, 54, 62, 78, 80–82, 102, 111
Tibetan Book of the Dead, 174–75
Tiedje, Stefan, 111, 119
time, 10, 78, 86, 91, 110, 123, 188; and historiality, 147; and memory, 147; and music, 141–42, 146–53
time regime, 179–80, 203, 227; definition of, 249n1
topology, 9, 11, 44, 104, 158; and music, 209–10; of the subject, 137, 152–53
topos, 23, 89, 103–10, 115, 130, 167, 180–81, 224; definition of, 103–5; and music, 176, 199; theory, 132–40, 141
Toussaint, Godfried, 127
tradition, 71, 81–82
trains, 201
transfeminism, 116
trauma, 213–20
trembling, 26
Tropicalia, 146
Trungpa, Chögyam, 200
Tudor, David, 83
tuning, 44–45, 46–48, 78
Turrell, James, 61

Tutuola, Amos, 182; *My Life in the Bush of Ghosts*, 182
Tüzer, Imam Ahmet Muhsin, 117
Tyler, the Creator, 199

UGK, 187–88, 197, 202, 210, 219, 229; "One Day," 187–89; *Ridin' Dirty*, 188
ultraintutionism, 87, 94
uncanny, the, 116–17, 195
unconscious, the, 96–97, 100, 107–8, 113, 114, 117, 158, 165–67; sonic, 196–97
universalism, 27, 53, 55, 162, 164, 185–87
Upadhyay, Chintan, 43

Varèse, Edgard, 18
Veal, Michael, 193
Velvet Underground, 45
Via Cherubini Collective, 97
vibration, 58–59; definition, 2–3; physics of, 75; Yoruba conception of, 182
vibrational ontology, 3–12, 16–22, 32, 37, 72, 76–77, 88, 149, 180–86; practice and, 44–45, 68, 69, 77, 93–94, 162, 186, 210, 212
Vimalananda, 214
Virilio, Paul, 195, 249n1
Viveiros de Castro, Eduardo, 4, 158
voguing, 11
volume, 84–85, 93, 155–56
vuvuzelas, 144–45

Wada, Yoshi, 31, 59–60, 86; *Lament for the Rise and Fall of the Elephantine Crocodile*, 59
Wade, Bonnie, 34
Wagner, Richard, 78, 140; *Das Rheingold*, 78
Walker, Lance Scott, 211–12; *Houston Rap Tapes*, 202, 204
Walker, Peter, 172–73, 178
War, 168, 197, *City, Country, City*, 168, 197
waterfalls, 143–44
wave particle duality, 8
waves, 5–6, 7, 151–52, 171
Weeknd, The, 218
Weheliye, Alexander, 195
Weil, Simone, 122
Wen, Xiao-Gang, 112–13, 119, 122, 136, 150
West, Cornel, 26, 139
West, Kanye, 128

278 INDEX

West African music, 142
Weston, Randy, 138
Weyl, Hermann, 126
whiteness, 25–26, 184, 207, 217–20
Williams, Nikki, 211
Wilson, Peter Lamborn, 65–66
Wilson, Robert, 65
Wittgenstein, Ludwig, 132
World Cup 2010 (South Africa), 144–45
world music, 55

X Avant festival, 223–25
Xenakis, Iannis, 65, 111, 141–42; *Formalized Music*, 141–42; *Polytope De Persépolis*, 65

yearning, 160
Yessenin-Volpin, Alexander, 87, 89, 94, 111, 113
Young, La Monte, 13, 29–30, 41, 45–48, 49–52, 57, 59, 60, 61–63, 64, 65, 67, 73, 76, 78, 79, 80, 85–86, 88, 89, 94, 97, 101–3, 107, 111, 114, 117, 125, 201, 206; *The Black Record*, 46, 85; *Drift Study 15 × 70*, 85; *Map of 49's Dream*, 46, 85; *The Tamburas of Pandit Pran Nath*, 51–52; *The Two Systems of Eleven Categories*, 85, 241n22; *The Well-Tuned Piano*, 31, 51, 60, 78
Young, Lester, 196–97. *See also* Dream House
YouTube, 218
yoga, 47, 59, 77

Zalamea, Fernando, 47, 128–29, 132, 139, 145, 186; *Peirce's Logic of Continuity*, 128–29; *Synthetic Philosophy of Contemporary Mathematics*, 47, 132
Zazeela, Marian, 13, 29–30, 38, 46, 48, 49–50, 61, 65, 67, 78, 85, 101–3. *See also* Dream House
Zeno, 110
Žižek, Slavoj, 72, 73, 140, 215
Zuckerkandl, Viktor, 149–50; *Sound and Symbol*, 149
zydeco, 190